The Man Who
HATED
WOMEN

The Man Who
HATED
WOMEN

SEX, CENSORSHIP, AND CIVIL LIBERTIES IN THE GILDED AGE

AMY SOHN

FARRAR, STRAUS AND GIROUX

New York

Farrar, Straus and Giroux
120 Broadway, New York 10271

Printed in the United States of America
First edition, 2021

Library of Congress Cataloging-in-Publication Data
Names: Sohn, Amy, 1973– author.
Title: The man who hated women : sex, censorship, and civil liberties
    in the gilded age / Amy Sohn.
Description: First. | New York : Farrar, Straus and Giroux, 2021. |
    Includes bibliographical references and index.
Identifiers: LCCN 2021002669 | ISBN 9781250174819 (hardcover)
Subjects: LCSH: Comstock, Anthony, 1844–1915. | Postal inspectors—
    United States—Biography. | Women—Sexual behavior—United States—
    History. | Pornography—United States—History. | United States—Moral
    conditions.
Classification: LCC HE6499 .S54 2021 | DDC 363.28 [B]—dc23
LC record available at https://lccn.loc.gov/2021002669

Our books may be purchased in bulk for promotional, educational, or business
use. Please contact your local bookseller or the Macmillan Corporate and
Premium Sales Department at 1-800-221-7945, extension 5442, or by email at
MacmillanSpecialMarkets@macmillan.com.

www.fsgbooks.com
www.twitter.com/fsgbooks • www.facebook.com/fsgbooks

1   3   5   7   9   10   8   6   4   2

For my grandmother Bess Rosenfeld Katz

Comstock is dead, but there are women dying everywhere.
Ida, tell me again how much we cannot speak of.
Oh, these Gods and Masters!

—from JULIANNA BAGGOTT,
"Margaret Sanger Addresses the Ghost of Ida Craddock"

Contents

List of Illustrations

The Man Who
HATED
WOMEN

Dancer from Cairo Street

1

THE DANSE DU VENTRE

It was the summer of 1893, and Ida C. Craddock was in the Cairo Street Theatre at the Chicago World's Fair, watching the belly dancers. There were about twelve of them, all in their late teens to early twenties, and as each one performed, the others sat behind her on divans to watch. Musicians played drums, woodwinds, and strings. The Algerian and Egyptian dancers wore ornamented headdresses, tiny cymbals on their fingers, knee-length peasant skirts, fringed epaulets, hip belts with vertical fabric flaps, and long beaded necklaces. Black stockings covered their legs. They had white muslin drawers to the knees, and high-heeled slippers. Their skirts' waistbands, shaped like coiled snakes, rose only to their hips, and their netted silk undervests were semitransparent. Spectators could see their navels—as shocking as a camel ride, another attraction at the World's Fair. American women were never seen in public without corsets, much less with their abdomens exposed. Victorian-era dances were led by dancing masters, who directed steps and patterns—no improvisation or gyrations.

The dancers moved their bellies coyly, clicking cymbals and swaying the upper part of their bodies. Some held bottles of water on their heads. Their gyrations grew more agitated and spasmodic as they rang their cymbals faster. Very few made direct eye contact with male audience members. When the performances reached a climax, the women would stand stock still, as if seized by something violent, and then visibly grow exhausted.

Viewers took in the belly dance with bemusement, horror, and titillation. Some cried out "Disgusting!" and fled the theater. Some men who stayed had looks on their faces that, as Craddock put it, "they would have been ashamed to have their mothers or their girl sisters see." To her, those people were philistines.

She was a thirty-six-year-old teacher with brilliant blue eyes; her complexion was clear, her features cameo-cut, and her fingers delicate and tapering. She was living in her domineering mother's Philadelphia living room behind a partition she called "the cubicle."

After having tried and failed to be the first woman admitted to the University of Pennsylvania's liberal arts program, she had become a lay scholar of comparative religion, reading voraciously at Philadelphia's Ridgway Library. She was at work on two manuscripts, one on the origin of the devil, and one on "sex worship," or sexual symbols in ancient world religions. She taught stenography at Girard College, a school for orphaned boys. By the time of her World's Fair visit, she had taught herself, and written a book on, a form of shorthand, which she believed could help ambitious men and women work their way up in business.

In the danse du ventre, Craddock saw a visual fusion of her two passions: sex and symbolism. While a teenager at Philadelphia's prestigious Friends' Central School, founded by Quakers, a lesson on botany ignited her curiosity about sex. As she recalled in a short memoir titled "Story of My Life: In Regard to Sex and Occult Teaching," the instructor, Annie Shoemaker, told the class, "Girls, whenever I take up this subject, I feel as though I were entering a holy temple." As Craddock learned how plants were fertilized, she felt "all on fire with the delight of my discovery, intellectually keen and eager . . . From that hour, dates the birth of my idealizing of sex."

In Chicago, twenty years after that lesson, she understood that the belly dancers' thrusts were simulating a woman's movements during intercourse. The bottle of water was an erect penis on the verge of ejaculation. And the extreme self-control was a reference to male continence, or *coitus reservatus*, a better-sex and contraceptive technique in which a man orgasms without ejaculating. When three women behind her at the show made sarcastic comments, she turned and said, "If you knew what that dance signifies, you would not make yourselves conspicuous by laughing at it." She believed it was a religious memorial of purity descending from ancient days. To serve God was not to choose asceticism but to experience self-controlled pleasure. After a gentleman overheard Craddock's rebuke, he was so impressed he vowed to return with his wife. This was the highest compliment she could be paid: he had been listening, he had taken her words seriously, and he was coming back.

The World's Fair, or Columbian Exposition, had opened three months earlier, on May 1, 1893. The economy was uncertain; beginning with the collapse of a major railroad that spring, the Panic of 1893 was in full swing. The U.S. Treasury was bankrupted; Americans had rushed to withdraw money from their bank accounts. By the end of the year, more than fifteen thousand banking institutions would declare bankruptcy and hundreds of thousands of Americans would be out of work.

The fair drew half the nation's population—28 million people— and introduced such marvels as ragtime music, Cream of Wheat, Pabst Blue Ribbon, the dishwasher, and the Ferris wheel, which took 2,160 people 264 feet above Lake Michigan and the city. A visitor could see a fluorescent lightbulb and eat an omelet made from the eggs of ostriches that lived at the fair.

The Woman's Building, a showcase of women's achievements, was installed in an Italian Renaissance–style villa. It was an optimistic moment for women, despite the fact that the suffrage fight was still raging, forty-five years after the Woman's Rights Convention in Seneca Falls, New York, had launched the movement. The Woman's

Building was managed by a Board of Lady Managers, who also hosted important dignitaries and addressed the concerns of women visitors and performers.

Radicalism was flourishing in the nation, and the International Anarchist Convention, which coincided with the fair, was banned by the police but held secretly at the offices of *The Chicago Times*. Several years earlier, at a rally for an eight-hour workday in Chicago's Haymarket Square, a bomb had detonated in the middle of a group of policemen. Eight anarchists were arrested and eventually convicted; four of them were executed, igniting fury among radicals. During the fair, on June 25, about eight thousand people attended a dedication of a monument to the Haymarket Square anarchists in the city's Waldheim Cemetery. A day later, the governor of Illinois unconditionally pardoned the remaining Haymarket anarchists on the grounds that they did not have a fair trial. Later that summer, in New York, a rising anarchist activist named Emma Goldman would give speeches advocating for labor rights and rights of the unemployed. She would be arrested and charged with incitement to riot.

The centerpiece of the fair was the Midway Plaisance, a mile-long stretch from Jackson Park to Washington Park conceived as a living outdoor museum of the world. Curated by a Harvard ethnologist, its highlights included an Algerian village, a Samoan settlement, an Eskimo camp, a Lapland village, and an Austrian village—but the hottest attraction was A Street in Cairo, which featured camel rides, donkeys, bazaars, snake charmers, fakirs, and child acrobats. Up to four hundred performers of Egyptian, Nubian, and Sudanese descent, and their dogs, donkeys, camels, and snakes, lived on Cairo Street for the six-month duration of the exposition.

The belly dance, or danse du ventre, was the Cairo Street Theatre's most controversial show, performed for forty minutes every hour on the hour. The Midway Plaisance general manager Sol Bloom called it "a masterpiece of rhythm and beauty." He had discovered the dancers at the 1889 Exposition Universelle in Paris and bought the rights to bring them to the Americas. He claimed to have composed the song associated with belly dancing, which would be called the "Hoochy-Koochy," "Koochy-Koochy," "Huta-Kuta Dance," and "Muscle Dance," performed at burlesque shows and dance halls around the country, and which may even have inspired the hokey pokey. The term *hoochy-koochy* derived from the French word *hochequeue*—to shake the tail—from a bird that flutters its tail feathers while standing. At a press preview of the dance, only a pianist was provided, and to give him an idea of the rhythm, Bloom hummed a tune and then sat down at the piano and picked it out with one finger himself. A score was arranged from that improvisation, and the melody became better known than the dance. Children still sing it today, with the lyrics "There's a place in France / Where the naked ladies dance." In his 1948 memoir, Bloom lamented that his failure to copyright the song cost him at least a few hundred thousand dollars in lost royalties.

When the public learned that *danse du ventre* meant "belly dance," Bloom recalled in the memoir, "they delightedly concluded that it must be salacious and immoral. The crowds poured in. I had a gold mine." *The Princeton Union* (a weekly newspaper published in Princeton, Minnesota) and *The New York World* called it an "abomination" and "veiled wickedness." The *Chicago Tribune* pronounced it "a depraved and immoral exhibition." As one reporter described it, "The dusky beauties, with a clatter of cymbals, execute the dances, more peculiar than poetic—somewhat more gross than graceful, til one feels a touch of sympathy with the chap near us who, after wondering observation, turned to his mother with the query: 'What ails the lady, is she sick?'"

It was only a matter of time before word of the belly dance reached the nation's chief vice hunter, Anthony Comstock, who served as a post office inspector (a federal position with law enforcement power) and secretary of the New York Society for the Suppression of Vice (NYSSV). Forty-nine years old during the fair and rounding out his second decade in power, he had red muttonchops covering a scar inflicted by an irate smut dealer who stabbed him in the face. He had

Anthony Comstock

enormous shoulders, a big chest, short tree-trunk legs, a dome-like forehead, light blue-gray eyes, a broad brow, and the build of a fighter. Walking on the balls of his feet, he was short and stout, resembling "a New Englander who eats pie for breakfast, dinner and supper." He favored starched shirts with bow ties. Beneath his clothes, no matter the weather, he wore red flannel underwear. His shoes, which he bought from a police and fireman supply store, were size thirteen heavy-soled boots. While crossing the street in New York one day, he was nearly run over by a mail wagon. He shook his badge at the horse and cried, "Don't you know who I am? I'm Anthony Comstock!" A reporter once called his office and asked an assistant whether Comstock had been punched in the face that morning. The answer was concise: "Probably."

Comstock learned about the belly dance while in Wisconsin for the Monona Lake Assembly, a religious revival. On July 27, Comstock delivered a talk called "The Foes of Society." Three activities, he said, were crime-breeders: intemperance, gambling, and evil reading. Each degraded people, wrecked homes, impoverished women and children, and created and fostered crimes. A foul story or tainted picture was a stain on children, at first imperceptible but soon filling their imaginations with corrupt influences as dreaded as smallpox or scarlet fever. He concluded by telling of his good work at the NYSSV.

After a lawyer at the revival told Comstock that he and his family had visited the fair's Cairo Street Theatre, only to discover the obscene show, Comstock took action, deciding to make a detour to Chicago on his way back to his summer home in New Jersey. He was a moral scold wherever he went; in the sleeping car, a man accused a

Black porter of stealing his wife's watch after he made the bunk bed, but Comstock intervened, finding it in the pillowcase lining. "That's one of the cases where I'm sorry I got the property back," Comstock said later, "for the man hadn't the decency to apologize to the porter." Comstock arrived at the fair on August 1, but did not announce his plans; as he wrote in the NYSSV *Annual Report* for that year, "It was thought by the agent best not to be known until the blow was struck." Insofar as a nationally famous, two-hundred-pound man with red muttonchops could be incognito, Comstock was going to try.

Anthony Comstock was one of the most important men in the lives of nineteenth-century women, a product of his upbringing, religion, and time. Growing up before the Civil War on a farm in New Canaan, Connecticut, he was raised to believe in the Victorian ideal of womanhood—a saintly, pure wife and mother whose domain was the home. When he arrived in New York as a young veteran in search of a dry goods job, he was shocked by the sounds, smells, and mores of the new American city, with its streetwalking, gambling, saloons, and brothels, and pornography peddled openly on the street. He became convinced that obscenity, which he called a "hydra-headed monster," led to prostitution, illness, death, abortions, and venereal disease.

After he joined the Young Men's Christian Association (YMCA), then a nascent group in the United States, he befriended the Anglo-Saxon scions of New York. They had last names such as Morgan (finance) and Colgate (soap), and with their support he went to Washington and passed the 1873 Comstock Act, which made the distribution, sale, possession, and mailing of obscene material and contraception punishable with extreme fines and prison sentences. It was the first federal obscenity law to link obscenity and contraception, the latter of which was defined as "any drug or medicine, or any article whatever for the prevention of conception or for causing unlawful abortion." After the law's passage, state legislatures enacted "little Comstock laws" modeled on the federal legislation. Connecticut's was more restrictive than the federal law: it criminalized the act of trying to prevent pregnancy, which could even include withdrawal (*coitus interruptus*).

In the twenty years between the 1873 passage of the Comstock law and the World's Fair, nearly two thousand people had been arrested under the law, more than half of whom had been convicted, and a hundred thousand dollars in fines had been imposed. Eight hundred thousand obscene pictures and photos had been seized, as had one hundred thousand "articles for immoral use," meaning sex toys and contraceptives, plus more than four thousand boxes of abortifacients—pills and powders purporting to induce miscarriage.

Comstock altered American reproductive rights for nearly a hundred years, until long after his death. Though today his name is not widely known, in his tenure he was feared and reviled. *Comstockery* and *Comstockism* came to connote prudishness, control, censoriousness, and repression of thought. The NYSSV was nicknamed "Mr. Comstock's Society." Even those who agreed with him questioned his nefarious methods. Though he was an extremely pious Congregationalist, he frequently brandished his revolver in his work. Many of his victims were impoverished, uneducated, or old. And though he pursued far more men than women, he delighted in punishing those radical, intellectual women whose views on contraception stemmed from liberal ideas about women's rights.

For someone as powerful and well-connected as he was, Comstock was extremely sensitive to criticism. Radical newspapers filled their pages with anti-Comstock screeds, and he attended atheist and freethinker meetings to shout at these detractors. He was a zealot who drew no distinction between sex workers and sex radicals, between dealers of lewd postcards and gynecologists. His interest in women's health and well-being stopped at contraception and abortion, which he often conflated. The man who did more to curtail women's rights than anyone else in American history had nearly no understanding of reproduction; he believed a fetus could form seconds after unprotected sex. Though he revered his mother, and all Christian mothers, he despised the midwives and abortionists who helped women in trouble and who saved them from destitution and death. To his mind these practitioners were evil, manipulative, and in it for the money. He did not believe he was a man who hated women. He believed his work was to save the young and innocent from those out to get them.

Sitting in the Cairo Street Theatre watching the dancers, he was as transformed as Craddock had been. He felt that he was seeing "the most shameless exhibition of depravity" he had witnessed in his work. Calling on the Board of Lady Managers, he insisted that they visit the "pestilential places." Three managers toured the Middle Eastern theaters. The board issued a report to the fair's director-general, George R. Davis, requesting that he shut down all the belly dances. One manager, Mrs. Barker, wrote, "I would sooner lay my two boys in their graves than that they should look upon the sights I saw yes'erday." An investigative committee was formed, with Comstock at the head.

In an interview with Joseph Pulitzer's popular and salacious *New York World*, Comstock said the dancers defiled "the magnificence of that Columbian Exposition" with their "nastiness." He rose from his chair and began to demonstrate, waving his arms above his head. As the journalist described it, "He is a pretty stout man and the performance was very interesting, but not at all libidinous. He writhed his shirt-sleeved arms over his head and made his ginger-colored side-whiskers shiver in the air." As Comstock bent back to demonstrate further, he nearly fell over. An attendant in the room shook his head and clucked.

On August 5, Davis ordered the shuttering of all of the Oriental dances, which were performed at a few other theaters in addition to Cairo Street, until new regulations could be established. The manager of the Persian Palace demanded an order in writing, and informed the press that he would ignore such an order even if he received it. The dance could be stopped only by force, he said, and then he would get an injunction and sue for damages.

Despite national controversy and Comstock's intervention, ultimately the only alteration made to the fair's belly dancing was costuming: the dancers swapped their gauze blouses for thin woolen undershirts. The vice hunter had lost in Chicago. But he would not forget the dancers, and would have four of them arrested and fined when they came to New York that winter. New York, after all, was Comstockland.

Ida C. Craddock

By the time Ida Craddock traveled to the World's Fair, there was plenty of sex information for progressive, curious young people. The German psychiatrist Richard von Krafft-Ebing's *Psychopathia Sexualis*, which coined the terms *sadism* and *masochism*, had been translated into English a year earlier. In 1894, Havelock Ellis, an English psychologist and doctor, would publish a volume on human sexuality titled *Man and Woman: A Study of Human Secondary Sexual Characters*. And the Illinois physician Dr. Alice B. Stockham's popular *Tokology: A Book for Every Woman* (1883) provided anatomical details about male and female bodies, and promoted strategies for coping with labor pains. Physicians and free lovers wrote manuals on hygiene, child-rearing, pregnancy, and better sex—many advertised in radical journals such as New York's *Truth Seeker*, edited by D. M. Bennett, and the Kansas-based freethinker and free love journal *Lucifer, the Light-Bearer*, edited by Moses Harman.

Beginning before the Civil War, utopian communities for Separatists, Shakers, and Transcendentalists had thrived in the United States.

Oneida, in upstate New York, was one of the most visible free love communities, featuring a system of polyamorous "complex marriage." Couples could choose to have "propagative" or "amative" sex. During the latter, men practiced male continence, or *coitus reservatus*, which the Oneida founder John Humphrey Noyes considered more pleasurable, contraceptive, and generally healthy for men, as semen loss was thought to provoke anxiety. Of male continence, in which men abstained from ejaculation through self-control, Noyes wrote that it protected women "from the curses of involuntary and undesirable procreation" and stopped "the drain of life on the part of man."

Most free lovers, however, did not believe in complex marriage as practiced by the Oneidans. Instead, they advocated for looser divorce laws and self-generated marriage contracts. Less concerned with free sex than with equal rights, free lovers supported egalitarian marriage, with fair division of work, and consensual, sometimes non-procreative sex. The free love movement, which had taken off in the 1840s, grew out of abolitionist principles: women were not to be enslaved by men, the church, or the government. From its inception, free love was closely linked with Spiritualism—the idea that living people could commune with the dead. As for sexuality, Spiritualists believed that a man and a woman could have a spiritual affinity for each other, an attraction based on complementary auras. To free lovers, this bond was superior to the marital bond.

Opposite the free lovers and Spiritualists were the Baptists, Congregationalists, and Protestants active in the YMCA. As they had in their rural communities, they wanted to protect young men from temptation in the city, guiding them to lead pious lives among pious women. These "Comstockians" opposed prostitution, into which many young women were driven by poverty and alcohol. Social purists—a strange alliance of women's rights advocates, conservative women, and temperance organizations such as the Women's Christian Temperance Union—similarly believed that marriage and the home were the backbones of society, that the family was more important than the individual, and that intercourse was only for reproduction. Interestingly, social purists (*social* being a euphemism for *sexual*) aligned with free lovers on certain issues. Both opposed the sexual double standard, which held that women were expected to be faithful but men were not, though the one side proposed male fidelity and the other polyandry as the solution.

Once Craddock returned to Philadelphia after seeing the belly dance, she felt inspired to write an essay in its defense. She sent it to *The New York World*, where it was published as part of a roundup of commentary on the dance. Other contributors included the American modern dance pioneer Loie Fuller, who called it a "graceful pantomime." Even the third archbishop of New York, who admitted he had not seen it, seemed supportive: "Perhaps Mr. Comstock was too sensitive in the matter, he and the good old ladies who were so shocked. They might have seen worse dances on a Saturday night in New York, dances where real evil is meant."

Craddock's essay stood out from the others. She was writing as a representative not of dance or Catholicism, but of phallic worship. Popular with European religious scholars, this area of scholarship examined the use of priapic symbols in world religions. Craddock defended the dance as the continuation of phallic worship, which taught "self-control and purity of life," meaning male and female continence. Sex, she said, was "the chief educator of the human race in things material and things spiritual." Far from shutting their eyes to the belly dance, young couples ought to learn from it. If husband and wife moved their hips like belly dancers during sex, and orgasmed spiritually, they would have heightened pleasure and fewer unwanted babies. As though that notion was not incendiary enough, she also took aim at Comstock: "Let the real significance of this dance as a religious memorial of purity and self-control be spread broadcast, so that Anthony Comstock and his helpers may be enlightened on the subject and may refrain from their attacks." It was a declaration of war on Comstock, and an advertisement for herself as a "sex-ologist."

The Cairo Street Theatre was the first place where the marriage reformer and the post office inspector would cross paths, but not the last. Their confrontations would span another nine years. The Quaker-educated, Philadelphia-born Craddock and the Congregationalist, Connecticut-born Comstock, only thirteen years apart in age, represented two poles of the rapidly changing American identity: woman and man, modernist and traditionalist, urban and rural, feminist and guardian of the family. That summer in the White City—the nickname given to the fairgrounds for the color of its buildings—they may have sat in the Cairo Street Theatre for the same performance and not known it. He would go on to circle her in three other states. Their dance would end in bloodshed, and only one would survive.

Craddock was one of many women who challenged the Comstock laws in the last decades of the nineteenth century and the early decades of the twentieth. New ideas about money, class, gender, and sex were circulating after the Civil War. Women, who were disproportionately harmed by poverty, unwanted parenthood, lack of employment, and low wages, could only stand to gain by challenging the status quo. Could, and should, motherhood be chosen? Was a wife obligated to have sex whenever her husband wanted? Were women to accept serial infidelity on the part of their men, including infidelity with prostitutes? Could they decide when to make love, and when not to? Could they work outside of the home? And if they did, should they be paid the same as men?

The women who fought the Comstock laws could be categorized as sex reformers, though this book will use the term *sex radicals* to avoid confusion with more Puritan-minded reformers. The sex radicals understood that women's liberation was possible only if sex was wholly reimagined. Alongside Craddock, they included the suffragist, stockbroker, publisher, and presidential candidate Victoria C. Woodhull; her sister, and partner in brokerage and publishing, Tennessee Claflin; the free lover and editor Angela Tilton Heywood; the Fifth Avenue abortionist Ann "Madame Restell" Lohman; the homeopathic physician Dr. Sara B. Chase; the anarchist and labor organizer Emma Goldman; and the birth control activist Margaret Sanger, whose friend Otto Bobsein coined the phrase *birth control* in her Manhattan apartment in 1914.

With the exception of Sanger, the women were eccentrics even within the women's rights and progressive movements. Their more mainstream male peers did not always support them, distancing themselves from their frank speech and bold writing, while conservative suffragists were afraid of their edgy ideas about sex. Some sex radicals focused on the terrors of unwanted pregnancy, some on the inverse relationship between fear and delight. What could enlightened, free-loving men do to help women enjoy sex? Was it possible that contraceptive practices such as male continence could increase joy for women by extending the act?

The sex radicals believed it was not fair for men to have orgasms when women did not, or for men to rape their wives or any other women. They thought sex should be loving, bonded, and sensual. Mutuality would lead to respect, equality, and reasonably sized families. The idea of contraception, then as now, was not only about the body. It was about pleasure: How could a woman enjoy sex when she lived in terror of life-threatening childbirth? It was women who took responsibility for the raising of children; additional babies were harder on the mothers than on the fathers.

What makes the Comstock women all the more remarkable is that they did their agitating, writing, and speaking out against him at a time when women did not have the right to vote (though Comstock was appointed and could not be voted out of his position). In court, their fates were decided by men; women were not appointed to judgeships until 1921 and could not serve on federal juries until 1957. With one exception, the Comstock women retained male lawyers who encouraged them to plead guilty and were ineffective advocates, in part because the men did not understand their clients' thinking.

The sex radicals informed and were informed by other radical movements—abolition, suffrage, Spiritualism, free love, free thought—as there was no "birth control" movement until around 1910. Angela and Ezra Heywood were abolitionists before they came to their free love ideas. Woodhull's 1872 nomination for president of the United States brought increased attention to the suffrage cause. Woodhull, Heywood, and Craddock identified as Spiritualists, claiming they could communicate with the dead. The Heywoods agitated for fair wages and civil, nonreligious marriages in their widely read journal, *The Word*, and at conventions of the New England Free Love League. Free thought, a broad term that encompassed secularism, freedom of religion, and freedom of speech, caught on in the 1830s, boosted by independent papers such as the *Boston Investigator* and New York's *Free Enquirer*, and by the end of the nineteenth century included groups such as the American Secular Union, of which Craddock became secretary.

At the time of their arrests for Comstock law violations, the women were as young as twenty-seven and as old as sixty-six. They were married, single, mothers, child-free, virgins, widows, and divorcées. None took reproduction lightly; one had an intellectually disabled son. Woodhull lived with present and former husbands and children; Craddock, alone; Lohman, with her adult grandchildren. Chase's husband filed for divorce on grounds of abandonment. Sanger's marriage was open, despite the wishes of her husband. Goldman, who inspired tens of thousands with her rousing speeches, was in a decade-long dysfunctional relationship with her philandering manager. Facing down Comstock, postal inspectors, and Vice Society agents, the women were unafraid and willing to be imprisoned for their cause. Nearly all were impoverished and could not afford their legal fees. The fact that several were past middle age when Comstock pursued them—and *still* they fought—shows their resilience.

It is no coincidence that nearly all were writers. They were products of a rich period of radical publishing, when the nationally read journals where their names appeared enjoyed wide circulation. These publications, sent by mail, included *The Word*; the *Boston Investigator*; *Dr. Foote's Health Monthly*; *Lucifer, the Light-Bearer*; *Woodhull & Claflin's*

Weekly; The Physiologist and Family Physician; and *The Truth Seeker*. In papers, pamphlets, and books, the sex radicals used their pens to excoriate Comstock, the NYSSV, and the law. Nothing Comstock tried—arresting them multiple times, illegally baiting them with so-called test letters that tricked them into breaking the law, harassing them, searching their homes, menacing them in the courtroom—could deter them.

Their primary years of activism took place between the first women's rights convention in 1848 and the passage of woman suffrage in 1920, which granted white women the right to vote; many women of other races were not able to vote until the passage of the Voting Rights Act in 1965. Yet the sex radicals are not as well-known as the suffragists Susan B. Anthony, Elizabeth Cady Stanton, and Alice Paul. Many were outcasts because they were outspoken about sex. They believed in plain speech, using terms such as *vagina, penis, semen*, and *clitoris*. They arrived at their views through direct experience with rape, child marriage, alcoholic partners, and poverty, and they used autobiography to advance their political views. They made the personal political.

Though four of them were nurses or health practitioners, they lacked the medical clout of the twentieth-century sex pioneers Dr. Alfred Kinsey and Dr. William Masters. Many were self-taught or educated outside of the traditional medical colleges and societies that were founded by, and for, men. Their writing was explicit and detailed, in an era when men found libidinous women alternately terrifying or titillating, but rarely enlightening.

They laid the groundwork for the eventual legalization of birth control and protection of American women's abortion rights. Goldman located the necessity for birth control in the context of economic oppression, while Sanger moved away from such a class-based justification in order to broaden its appeal. Sanger believed in, and popularized, the idea that women were different from men, and could coalesce to fight for what they deserved as a group, as a gender.

The radicals' attitudes arose from romantic, not hedonistic, ideals.

If anything, they could be accused of being *too* idealistic about sex—they elevated it, believing in its power to unite man and woman. If marriage were reconceptualized as a romantic institution, entered into on the basis of love instead of money, it could yield greater liberty for women. Though most were not scientists, they had an earnest, scientific view of sex. Energy was exchanged. Currents went back and forth. (Many free lovers viewed sex as an exchange of electric or magnetic forces—dubbed *magnetation*.) Nudity could increase intimacy. If only women could be in charge of sex! If men listened to women, families would be stronger; if reasonable people married reasonably, there would be fewer unintended pregnancies.

This last concept stemmed from a romanticized view of the heterosexual bond. If women could experience sex as exalted and hallowed, and if they could play some role in selecting a partner, then they could have and control their own orgasms, bear fewer babies, and enjoy sex more. They would learn to recognize the difference between amative and procreative sex. When they did, they would see that amative sex had its own valid aims.

Despite their extraordinary contributions to civil liberties, most of the sex radicals have been written out of feminist history (they were too sexual), sex history (they were not doctors), and progressive history (they were women). Nonetheless, they were the connective tissue between nineteenth-century abolitionism and twentieth-century free speech. The free speech historian David M. Rabban calls nineteenth-century freethinkers "libertarian radicals." They opposed laissez-faire capitalism and the idea that progressive thought required social harmony. Both free thought and free love, Rabban writes, "interposed personal sovereignty and rationality in social, religious, and sexual spheres against the power of church and state." Libertarian radicals such as Woodhull, Angela Heywood, and Craddock laid the foundation for the modern civil liberties movement and the formation of the American Civil Liberties Union (ACLU). The Free Speech League (1902–1917), which counted Goldman as an early supporter, was a predecessor of the ACLU, itself founded in 1920. Sex radicals, who based their ideas on individual autonomy, made free speech possible.

In their willingness to take on a monomaniac whose mission was to keep contraception and abortion from women, they paved the way for early twentieth-century "birth controllers" and 1970s feminists alike. Risking destitution, imprisonment, and death, they defined reproductive liberty as an American right, one as vital as those enshrined in the Constitution. They brought women's reproductive rights to the public dialogue. Without them, there would be no Pill, no Planned Parenthood, no *Roe v. Wade*. And yet, more than fifty years after Sanger's death, reproductive rights are still a battleground. Without understanding the sex radicals, we cannot fight the assault on women's bodies and souls that continues even today.

2

VICELAND

Anthony Comstock was born in New Canaan, Connecticut, on March 7, 1844, the fourth of ten children and the third to survive past early childhood. His parents were Thomas Anthony Comstock and Polly Comstock, née Lockwood, a direct descendant of the first Puritans in New England. Anthony grew up in a farmhouse set on 160 acres, from which the family could see the Long Island Sound. Thomas made his living operating a sawmill and a gristmill and supervised about thirty employees.

The most important influence in Comstock's life, the person who would forever shape his view of women, family, and marriage, was Polly. The epitome of the New England Christian mother, she read the children Bible stories and emphasized the value of self-sacrifice and moral courage. "She looked upon every one of her children as character builders," Comstock reflected late in life to his biographer Charles Trumbull. "I cannot but feel that the teachings of my mother are vastly superior to anything that my opponents can offer or recommend."

On Sundays the Comstock family traveled two and a half miles in a wagon to worship at the Congregational church, where Comstock would squirm in a pew opposite the center column. After the morning service came Sunday school in the gallery of the church, lunch in the shed, and afternoon preaching. The family then went home before returning for evening services, and they ended their nights in the farmhouse, eating pie and drinking milk.

According to Trumbull, Comstock was a dutiful Sunday school student and devoted son, but at school he was frequently whipped for misbehaving. His teacher would make him fetch his own switch, but Comstock would put nicks in it on his way back from the woods, so if it hit him too hard it would break. On some occasions his punishment was to sit with the girls, wearing a sunbonnet. (Whether this turned him against women, or made him insecure about his masculinity, we will never know. None of his private letters—only excerpts of his Civil War and early marriage diaries—remain.) A formative youthful interaction with alcohol crystallized his belief in its evil: One night, returning home from the pasture with the cows, he dropped in to see a friend, a boy his parents didn't like and whom they had forbidden him from visiting. His chum brought out homemade wine, and Comstock returned home drunk and sleepy, waking with a terrible hangover that made working in the cowshed miserable. He claimed that that was the last time he consumed alcohol as a beverage.

When he was ten years and ten days old, he arrived from school to the farmhouse and found "the loveliest mother that ever lived, dead." None of his speeches or writings, nor biographers, mentions the cause, but town records show that Polly died of a hemorrhage, or "flooding," the day she gave birth to Comstock's baby sister Harriet. Though childbirth had killed his mother, Comstock would spend his life defending motherhood as woman's highest purpose. Women like his mother, he would believe until his last day, committed a noble sacrifice, fulfilling the commandment to be fruitful and multiply.

At sixteen, he left school to work as a clerk at a country store in Winnipauk, present-day Norwalk, near the Connecticut coast. One day, he heard that a rabid mastiff was running through the streets. Determined to save the town, he went to his room, prayed for courage, grabbed several guns, locked the store, and went after the dog. After climbing a wall, he heard a howl. The dog was twenty feet away. Its mouth was open and foaming. Comstock scrambled down, and, as the dog approached, he raised his pistol, fired, and hit it in the chest. The dog rolled over. Comstock shot it again, this time in the brain.

With the outbreak of the Civil War, Comstock's older brother Samuel enlisted in the Union Army; injured at Gettysburg, Samuel ailed for nearly three months before perishing. To honor Samuel's memory, Comstock enlisted at age nineteen. He joined Samuel's regiment, the Seventeenth, on Folly Island, South Carolina.

Finding no chaplain and no religious services, he started a worship group with a few other soldiers. After his regiment was sent to St. Augustine, Florida, his experience of the service was largely peaceful. He worked for the United States Christian Commission, aiding the sick and destitute and distributing religious reading material to citizens and soldiers. The commission, which had branches in eight cities, had been founded before the war by members of the New York branch of a new group known as the Young Men's Christian Association.

During the war, railway mail service had led to faster, cheaper sorting and delivery, meaning that young men could easily order "rich and spicy" or "sporting" books and photographs—all coming from New York. The YMCA became concerned about the effects of this obscene literature, and the Christian Commission's Committee on Publications inserted an anti-obscenity clause into an 1865 omnibus postal bill that made the mailing of any "obscene book, pamphlet, picture, print, or other publication of a vulgar and indecent character" a misdemeanor. Penalties ran up to five hundred dollars and a year in prison. The bill would be a major influence on Comstock's eponymous legislation.

By November 1864, less than a year into his service, Comstock was made clerk in the office of the provost marshal, in a division of the military police. The position seems to have set off his lifelong passion for administrative record keeping. For decades, he would keep a meticulous logbook—in cursive—of everyone arrested under the auspices of the NYSSV.

His war records are peppered with medical problems: diarrhea, headaches, sore eyes, and boils. There were social problems, too. Due to his religiosity, he was deeply disliked. When he received his whiskey ration, he would dump it out so no other soldiers could drink it. This led to fistfights. "Seems to be a feeling of hatred by some of the boys," read one of his diary entries, "constantly falsifying, persecuting and trying to do me harm. Can I sacrifice Principle and conscience for Praise of Man. *Never.*" A year into his service, he returned to his quarters to find the windows closed tight, the room filled with smoke, and his bunk full of trash. "Boys were initiating me," he wrote. "Had good laugh."

If he came off as a scold, he was not immune to fleshly delights— probably masturbation—himself: "O I deplore my sinful weak nature so much. If I could but live without sin, I should be the happiest soul living." Another day: "Satan has sorely tried me; yet by God's grace did not yeild [*sic*]." (Comstock was an atrocious speller.) "This morning were severely tempted by Satan, and after some time in my own weakness I failed."

After mustering out on July 19, 1865, he moved to New Haven and took a job as a grocery store clerk. The family farm had been foreclosed, and his father had remarried and moved to London. Comstock briefly worked as an outdoor superintendent at a Christian school in Chattanooga, Tennessee, but became sick and returned to the Northeast. Staying with his brother Chester in New Canaan, he held a string of dead-end jobs, dreaming of opening his own grocery store.

But he had no savings. In Norwalk, one day in 1867, he ran into a relative of his mother, a banker named M. LeGrand Lockwood. Lockwood told him to go to New York. Comstock replied that he had no money and no friends.

Lockwood gave him five dollars and said, "Go to New York and find something to do!"

Comstock arrived at New York's City Hall a few days later with $3.45 in his pocket.

As he roamed the streets of lower Manhattan in search of a place to sleep, he was surely deafened by the sounds: railroad whistles, steamboat bells, carts hauling goods, horses galloping, urchins begging for money. When Comstock arrived, about a million and a half people lived in New York. It was exciting and terrifying; in 1857, George Francis Train, a temperance activist and eccentric, called New York the "locomotive of these United States." Between 1865 and 1898, it would be the center of both extraordinary poverty and the greatest concentration of wealth in history.

While Comstock walked in search of a boardinghouse, he thought about his mother and prayed to God to give him a job. High above the other buildings, he probably spotted the spire of Trinity Church, nearly three hundred feet high and the tallest building in New York. On Lower Broadway, the tourist industry was booming, offering cigar shops, bookshops, jewelers, watchmakers, tailors, and hatters. In Alexander Stewart's dry goods emporium on Broadway between Chambers and Reade, customers could examine wares on mahogany counters—an early iteration of what would come to be called a "department store."

If New York was bustling and thrilling, it was also bleak and fraught with crime. "It is said that New York is the wickedest city in the country," wrote James McCabe in *New York by Sunlight and Gaslight* (1881). Exploring the area near City Hall, Comstock might have stepped onto Nassau Street. It was the artery of the city's trade in erotica, a stone's throw from Printing-House Square, where *The New York Times*, *The Sun*, and the *New-York Tribune* were headquartered. Littered with bookshops, stationery stores, and watch and jewelry dealers, it was so narrow that vehicles could scarcely get through. As McCabe described it, "Half the passers through the street are obliged to take to the roadway . . . It has been said that Nassau street is a good place to hide in."

Peddlers hawked "rubber goods" (sex toys and contraceptives), dirty *cartes de visite*, or calling cards, at a quarter each, dirty playing cards, watches, and brothel guides. Smut was not just ubiquitous; it was public. It was also affordable to young clerks with low salaries. The erotic pamphlet *The Love Feast, or a Bride's Experience* (1865) was three inches by four inches and could be hidden in a pocket or under a pillow. It was said to be printed by "the Associated Female Press, Blind Alley, Coneyhatch, Maidenhead." "Fancy books," costing two dollars or more, were clothbound, with engravings. They described orgies, masturbation, and group and public sex, with explicit illustrations. Many were narrated by fictitious women overcome by sexual desire, called "starved" women. Popular titles included *The Lustful Turk*, *Peep Behind the Curtains of a Female Seminary*, *Lord K's Rapes and Seductions*, *Peeps into the Boraglio*, *The Gay Girls of New York*, and *The Writings of Paul de Kock*.

Erotic images benefited from recent advances in photography. Small-format pictures showed everything from arty-looking nudes to intercourse, and could be hidden. The stereoscopic view, invented in 1857, allowed viewers to look at a print through a special box, creating a seemingly multidimensional image. Two weekly newspapers, *The National Police Gazette* and *Days' Doings*, were the leading publications in what was known as the "sporting press." These were Zagat guides for the libido, catering to young men, filled with tales of crime, sport, and scandal, and ads for brothels and condoms. Comstock would call them "stanch, well-constructed traps of the devil, capable of catching and securely holding the mind and heart of the young." But given a popular press hungry for ad revenue, notices for contraception and abortions also proliferated in daily newspapers such as *The New York Herald* and the *New-York Tribune*.

Not far from the obscene book trade on Nassau Street, Comstock took a room in a cheap boardinghouse on Pearl Street. His experience was typical for young men from New England in postbellum New York. By 1860, 46 percent of the male population of New York was between the ages of fifteen and thirty. In another era, these young men would have lived with their employers, but in the 1860s they saved money by staying in boardinghouses. They could not afford to keep fires in their rooms at night, so they went out for the plentiful entertainment offered to "sporting," meaning single and adventurous, young men.

An anonymous clerk at a mercantile house described what it felt like to be a young newcomer:

> Inexperienced young men flock here in thousands from all parts of the country; leave friends and relatives behind. Their first acquaintance is a boarding-house of dissipated young men and "diseased furniture" [rotted wood] . . . After tea the question goes around amongst the young men: "Well, Harry, what are you going to do with yourself tonight?" "I'll play you billiards for drinks." "Where are you going, Jack?" "I'm for the opera." "Well, come, take a drink before you go." One is going to see his little milliner in Houston Street, another to play [the table game] bagatelle for lager, others to play [the card game] faro (particularly if it is pay day), some to have a show at cards, some down to Madame Vonderbush's, to see if she has any fresh emigrant girls.

The city was filled with prurient and violent delights: barrooms, saloons, bawdy houses (brothels), boxing, gambling, and pool halls. At "pretty waiter girl" saloons such as the Flowing Sea Inn and the Jolly Tar, waiter girls persuaded customers to drink and received a cut of the bottles in return. If they hooked a man, they took him to a nearby rented room. At Harry Hill's, on Houston and Mulberry, men were admitted for a quarter, women for free. The famed defense attorney William Howe, who would frequently clash with Comstock in court, wrote in *In Danger; or, Life in New York* (1888), "It is a safe conclusion, that no waiter girl in a concert saloon is virtuous, nor was there ever a really good girl engaged in any such saloon. They are there to be bought by any one fancying them, and therein lies the charm."

Of course, prostitutes were not only available in saloons. Walt Whitman, the poet and a future Comstock target, wrote in 1857: "After dark, any man passing along Broadway, between Houston and Fulton Streets, finds the western sidewalk full of prostitutes, jaunting up and down there, by ones, twos or threes—on the look-out for customers." Prostitution was exploding due to population growth, immigration, and changes in real estate. In 1866, two separate estimates put the number of prostitutes in New York at twenty thousand and the number of brothels at around five hundred. Even seemingly benign businesses were often fronts for brothels. Cigar, or "segar," shops featured attractive female shopkeepers who would advise male customers about a room upstairs or in the back. The busiest time was lunch.

Clinton Place, located in present-day Greenwich Village, was home to "bawdy houses" with names such as "the Black Crook" and "the Gem." Brothels' names were advertised with gas lamps that blazed through red glass: Flora, Lizzie, the Seven Sisters. Some prostitutes were famous enough to open their own brothels or barrooms. The former prostitute and saloonkeeper Gallus Mag, "the Queen of Cherry Street," was known to bite off the ears of rough patrons and store them in a bottle of alcohol above the bar. Most prostitutes were under twenty-three years old and new arrivals to New York from elsewhere in the Northeast or Ireland. Between 5 and 10 percent of all nineteenth-century women ages fifteen to thirty in New York prostituted themselves at one point. They did it for the money: while a factory worker earned six to twelve dollars a week, a prostitute could make thirty dollars a night. But the industry was dangerous, even

life-threatening; according to one study, at least 40 percent of prostitutes reported having contracted syphilis or gonorrhea.

To avoid these, women and men could purchase condoms (also
known as "French male safes," "badruches," "cundrums," "capotes,"
"caps," "skins," "rubber goods for men," "gentlemen's protectors," and
"rubbers"), which were marketed as preventives to pregnancy and
disease. In the early part of the century, they had been made of animal skins, but vulcanized rubber, invented by Charles Goodyear in
the 1850s, enabled the manufacture of "gonorrhea bags," which Goodyear called "well adapted to the purpose for which they are made."
Other new inventions included rubber vaginal syringes and pessaries
(plugs or blocks to the cervix). There were "French caps" or "womb
veils" (cervical caps), sponges, diaphragms, intrauterine pessaries
(also called "uterine elevators," "ladies' shields," "womb supporters,"
and "copper molds"), vaginal and intracervical pessaries, and semen-
absorbing tampons.

Since the 1820s, women had utilized syringes, which were inex-
pensive and easy to purchase, for both hygienic and contraceptive
purposes. They could be employed to flush out semen after sex and
were available through druggists, retailers, doctors, and mail-order
companies. Women douched with water, astringents, and spermicides, including tannin, powdered opium, iodine, vinegar, bicarbon-
ate of soda, and salts. An adjustable 1885 model could also be used
for watering plants. By nineteenth-century standards, douching was
at least somewhat effective; according to several studies, women who
douched shortly after sex and used no other contraception bore children at intervals twice as far apart as those who did not.

For women who failed to prevent pregnancy, there was a robust
market in abortifacients. These were called "Female Regulators,"
"Portuguese Female Pills," "Female Pills," "Lunar Pills," "French Renovating Pills," "Female Renovating Pills," "Female Remedy," "Female
Antidote," or "French Periodical Pills." Some ads openly proclaimed
the pills' ability to produce miscarriages. While some powders were

placebos, others contained ergot, oil of tansy, oil of savin, or turpentine and may have caused some miscarriages. Beginning in 1840, some southern physicians claimed that cottonroot, used by slave women, was an effective, mild abortifacient. By the late 1850s, druggists around the country had begun to stock it, and it would remain popular until the 1880s.

When abortifacients failed, women sought surgical abortions. In Boston or New York, an abortion cost about ten dollars. It involved dilation of the cervix, piercing the amniotic sac, and scraping the uterus—with no anesthesia. The procedure had been legal in most states until "quickening," or detectible fetal movement, and even after quickening it was a high misdemeanor, not a felony, if the woman died. State abortion law grew more stringent beginning in the 1840s: abortionists could face charges of second-degree homicide or manslaughter (regarding the fetus), and women who sought abortions could face criminal prosecution. An 1845 New York state law stiffened the offense to manslaughter in the second degree if an abortionist provided the procedure at any stage of pregnancy, except to save the woman's life. The minimum sentence was three years. A woman who took abortifacients was guilty of a misdemeanor, with a minimum punishment of three months.

The population of abortion seekers was shifting when Comstock arrived in New York. White, Protestant, American-born, middle- and upper-class women, many of them married, increasingly sought abortions after 1840, wanting to delay childbearing or avoid having more children. Physicians complained that bourgeois women often aborted pregnancies that occurred in the first years of marriage, which these women considered déclassé. They were the type Comstock would have known in New Canaan.

The rise in abortions was partly due to increased visibility, as practitioners reached patients through advertisements in the popular press. The abortion historian James Mohr has called abortion "one of the first specialties in American medical history." Abortionists were mostly European-born women, some of them trained as midwives and some self-taught. The most notorious in New York was Madame Restell, who lived in a mansion at Fifty-Second Street and Fifth Avenue, a block from St. Patrick's Cathedral. About a decade after his arrival in New York, Comstock would have her prosecuted.

But on his first night in New York, while his boardinghouse mates were out cavorting with pretty waiter girls, his only thought was of dinner. He ate at a cheap restaurant, unable to afford anything better. When he returned to his room, he read his Bible. The next morning, he went out in search of a dry goods position. After one week without luck, he secured a job as a third porter, lifting large cases for a wholesale house on Warren Street called Ammidon, Lane and Company.

Comstock had a place to live and a job. He had not yet made it in the big city, but he hoped one day he would.

Right around the time Comstock moved to New York, the YMCA was working to help new arrivals such as him. In an 1865 pamphlet called *The Work of the Young Men's Christian Association*, the author, Dr. Verranus Morse, reflected on the shock experienced by rural men like Comstock as they transitioned to urban life:

> Multitudes of young men come from the country to our city, every year, to find employment . . . In their country homes they have been taught to honor and cultivate virtue and manliness. There, female society uses its power to cheer, refine and elevate; seldom to debase and ruin. There, vice, when it does exist, is seen in its natural loathsomeness, making it easy to be recognized and avoided. There, those who indulge in one immoral practice, or cherish a single immoral habit, are sure to lose the respect and confidence of their associates.

In the country it was difficult to be private. In the city, it was easy.

In fact, one of the key instigators of Comstock's ire was the movement of private behavior into public space. If the soldiers in the Civil War chuckled to themselves over photos and books, that was bad enough. But it was an outrage to Comstock and the YMCA alike that men could walk down the street and have sex peddled to them in the form of streetwalkers or smut.

The American YMCA, founded in 1852, was modeled on the YMCA in England and aimed to improve the "spiritual, mental and social condition of young men." Its first New York home was the Stuyvesant Institute, a lecture hall, library, and museum in today's SoHo. Members were required to be under the age of forty and belong to a local evangelical church.

In 1866, the New York Y was incorporated by the state, and five men had become visible leaders of the organization: Morris K. Jesup, William E. Dodge, Cephas Brainerd, Robert R. McBurney, and J. Pierpont Morgan. Jesup had made a fortune in railroads and banking. A Connecticut Congregationalist like Comstock, he had helped to form the Christian Commission. Dodge, a Presbyterian, was a partner in Phelps Dodge, the nation's largest copper mining company. Brainerd was an influential lawyer, and McBurney was an Irish immigrant who began as an organization member and worked his way up. Dodge, McBurney, and Morgan were officers for 1866–1867, while Brainerd and Jesup were on the board of directors.

With the number of young male arrivals skyrocketing, the YMCA's executive committee undertook a study of their lives and housing conditions. Written by Brainerd and McBurney, it was titled "A Memorandum Respecting New-York as a Field for Moral and Christian Effort Among Young Men; Its Present Neglected Condition; and the Fitness of the New-York Young Men's Christian Association as a Principal Agency for Its Due Circulation." Its primary concern was the obscene book trade on Nassau Street. The federal obscenity law initiated by the Christian Commission turned out to be poorly enforced. This was a problem; in the minds of the YMCA leaders, dirty books were "feeders for brothels." In the report, the board proposed a permanent home for the YMCA, one that would provide young men with rented rooms, as an alternative to boarding-houses. There would be a library, a lecture room for religious meetings, and conversation rooms, so that men need not go to theaters or concert saloons "to waste their time and money, and peril their health and character."

On the heels of their 1866 memorandum, the board formed the Committee on Obscene Literature to try to pass an anti-obscenity law in New York. In April 1868, the committee achieved its goal, with the establishment of the Obscene Literature Act. It prohibited the sale, advertisement, or manufacture of "any obscene and indecent book," which included papers, pamphlets, stereoscopic pictures, and more, and any "article of indecent or immoral use, or article or medicine for the prevention of conception or procuring of abortion," as well as advertisements or circulars (advertising brochures) for dirty books, contraception, or abortion. Those convicted could be imprisoned for up to one year or fined up to a thousand dollars for each offense. A third of the fine would be paid to the informer, a third to the school fund, and a third to the treasurer of the Female Guardian Society, a home for women and children in Manhattan. The law allowed magistrates to issue orders that permitted police officers to seize obscenity and contraceptives and turn them over to the district attorney to be destroyed.

State obscenity laws had existed for about twenty years, but the new batch—Michigan and New Jersey passed similar laws in 1869—included contraception. Most important, the New York Obscene Literature Act took aim at the mail system itself, recognizing that its low cost and discreet nature facilitated the purchase of smut, condoms, and other contraceptives. Anyone who *mailed* the "obscene and indecent articles and things," or ads or information for them, was subject to the same fines and penalties as the manufacturers. Comstock called the U.S. mail *"the great thoroughfare of communication leading up into all our homes, schools and colleges. It is the most powerful agent, to assist this nefarious business, because it goes everywhere and is secret."* If he could control the mail, he could control everything.

Legally speaking, the definition of obscenity, crucial in many of Comstock's cases, was based on an English case called *The Queen v. Hicklin* (1868). The *Hicklin* test was whether "the tendency of the matter charged as obscenity is to deprave and corrupt those whose minds are open to immoral influences, and into whose hands a publication of this sort may fall." In other words, a work did not need to urge its readers to have sex, only to arouse sexual thoughts, specifically in the young, inexperienced minds most susceptible to outside influences. Juries had to imagine that anything available to the general public could fall into the hands of such youths. Equally crucial to Comstock's cases was the finding in *Hicklin* that only the intent to corrupt, in an isolated passage—not the *overall* intent of the author—was to be considered. If a jury found obscenity in any part of the work, whatever its general nature, the jury had an obligation to judge the work obscene.

The year the Obscene Literature Act was passed, Comstock joined the Varick Street branch of the YMCA. He had a new dry goods job on Warren Street and described his coworkers, other young men, as "falling like autumn leaves about me from the terrible scourges of vile books and pictures." One day, a coworker confessed to Comstock that he had bought obscene pictures and, in the words of Comstock's biographer Charles Trumbull, "been led astray and corrupted and diseased." It is unclear whether the colleague had visited a prostitute and caught venereal disease, masturbated, or both, but to Comstock it would have made no difference. Common belief held that masturbation led to insanity, illness, and death—one reason he had been so anxious about his masturbation during the war. Whatever happened to his workmate, Comstock blamed it on obscene books. Determined to exact revenge, he went after the dealer who had sold his coworker the pictures.

Charles Conroy was a heavy man. One of his hands was missing all but two fingers, due to amputation. He worked out of a basement on Warren Street, a block from Comstock's firm. Comstock went to his store and bought a dirty book, watching closely as Conroy went to the rear of the space to retrieve it. Comstock darted over to the local precinct with the book and returned with the police captain, who arrested Conroy and seized his entire stock. It was Comstock's first time assisting in an obscenity arrest.

The same year that New York passed the Obscene Literature Act, two beautiful young women arrived in the city. Hucksters since childhood, they had been born into poverty and knew how to manipulate men. They were determined, brash, and ripe with sexual power. They had moved to New York to change the world and get rich—not necessarily in that order—and their outspoken beliefs, writings, and lifestyles would soon draw Comstock's wrath. They were the embodiment of the pulsing, prurient, new New York, and would make an indelible mark. They were Victoria C. Woodhull and Tennessee Claflin, and they were sisters.

Victoria C. Woodhull

Tennie C. Claflin

3

THE BEWITCHING BROKERS

It was while living in Pittsburgh with her second husband, James Blood, the story goes, that Victoria Woodhull had a vision. It was 1868, the year after Comstock had arrived in New York. Woodhull was seated at a marble table when her spirit guide, a Greek orator, materialized in a tunic and named himself for the first time, writing on the table "Demosthenes." The writing became so lustrous that brightness filled the room. Demosthenes told her to go to New York, where she would find a fully furnished house at 17 Great Jones Street.

She and her sister Tennessee Claflin arrived in the city on the New York and Harlem line, owned by Cornelius Vanderbilt, the richest man in the country. He had earned millions in the shipping and railway wars, and one of the New York Central locomotives was named the *Commodore Vanderbilt*. The house on Great Jones Street was a few doors from his office on Washington Place. Woodhull would say that Demosthenes had guided them to the commodore.

At Forty-Second Street, the sisters' train stopped, the locomotive was removed, and the cars were hitched to teams of horses, which took the passengers to the Twenty-Seventh Street terminus. The horse-drawn railroad car carried them down Park Avenue, through Murray Hill, and then the Bowery, home to the Cooper Institute, where Woodhull would one day give a speech that decried Comstock and all he represented. The sisters arrived before the door of 17 Great Jones as the sun was setting. Woodhull's trembling hand moved the knocker. The front door opened and a woman said, "Oh, you've come about the rooms." In the entrance hall, Woodhull noticed a library, the room she had seen in her vision. She entered it and selected a book from one of the shelves. The title was *The Orations of Demosthenes*. Whether any of it was true, the Claflin sisters had their origin story, a requirement for anyone wanting to make it big in New York.

On September 23, 1838, about five and a half years before Comstock came into the world, Victoria Claflin was born in Homer, Ohio. The sixth of ten children, daughter to Buckman (Buck) and Roxana (Anna) Claflin, she was named after Queen Victoria, who was crowned that year. According to her future lover and biographer Theodore Tilton, she had high cheekbones and a stormy face, and liked to stand on a mount and tell tales to other children, her hair flowing thick and uncombed. Her father beat her and the other children, and she said he never kissed her. Anna saw visions, and at night she would go to an orchard, pray for her neighbors' sins, and curse until she foamed at the mouth.

Spiritualists such as Anna believed that communing with the dead could lead to divine truth. In 1848, two girls in Hydesville, New York, reported that they were hearing strange sounds in the night. Their house was rumored to be haunted by a man who had been murdered there. The girls, Kate and Margaret Fox, had conversations with him in which he tapped out his answers. By June 1850, they were giving demonstrations for a dollar a head at Barnum's American Museum in New York, owned by the showman P. T. Barnum. Though the Fox sisters were later revealed to be frauds, Spiritualism continued to swell in popularity following the mass casualties of the Civil War. Late nineteenth-century estimates put the number of American Spiritualists somewhere between a few hundred thousand and eleven million.

Ordinary Americans held séances, joined psychic societies, read books about clairvoyance, and practiced techniques such as automatic writing, which summoned spirits in the form of strange handwriting and unexpected words. By the time Victoria was a little girl, Spiritualism was emerging as a progressive force, supporting separation of church and state, freedom of religion, and free love. Many prominent leaders in the Spiritualist movement were women; it was inherently woman-positive. Spiritualism evolved alongside technological innovations such as the telegraph and the phonograph, as Americans reckoned with their meaning. As the free love historian Hal D. Sears has recounted, Spiritualism "promised that the same forces that caused upheaval in their lives (symbolized, for instance, by electricity), allowed them benefits, two in particular—victory over the ultimate alienation called death, and liberation from sexual and familiar constrictions."

Victoria herself claimed to have seen her first spirit—the ghost of a dead nurse who had cared for her, who took her into the spirit world above—at the age of three. Demosthenes, her primary spirit guide, told her she would live in a stately house, rise to distinction, win great wealth in a crowded city, publish a journal, and become ruler of her people.

Victoria's younger sister Utica was born in 1843, and Tennessee— named for the home state of President James Polk, whom Buck admired—on October 26, 1845. Tennie was pretty and fair-haired, with blue eyes. Like Victoria, she had supernatural powers; while living with relatives in Williamsport, Pennsylvania, she told a man where his lost calf was, and how it was tied. She also predicted a fire in the cupola of a seminary with such detail that at first she was accused of starting it (an investigation determined that she had not).

In Homer, after Buck set a fire in his own gristmill to pocket the insurance money, residents bought the family a wagon and supplies and told them to leave town. They moved to Mount Gilead, Ohio, where the eldest daughter, Maggie, was living. Buck hung a shingle in front of their boardinghouse advertising Victoria, fourteen, and Tennessee, seven, as mediums. Soon the money was flowing.

That year, a Rochester-born doctor named Canning Woodhull opened a medical practice in Mount Gilead. He claimed to be a relative of New York's mayor, Jacob Westervelt. When Victoria developed rheumatism, Dr. Woodhull was brought in to care for her. Smitten, he invited her to a Fourth of July picnic. When he took her home, he said she should tell her parents he wanted her for a wife. She was furious, but her parents were delighted. On November 20, 1853, at age fifteen, Victoria was married.

It turned out that Canning had no steady income and no regular patients. He spent his nights at whorehouses, quaffing champagne. Once, she followed him, watching at the window. Everything she had believed of marriage and society, she would later write of that moment, was "a cloak made by their devotees to hide the realities and to entice the innocent into their snares. I found everything was reeking with rottenness."

The couple moved to Chicago, where Victoria gave birth to a son, Byron, in the dead of winter, alone, with icicles clinging to the bedpost. Byron was intellectually and developmentally disabled, which, following a common misconception, Victoria attributed to Canning's alcoholism. She would later refer to Byron's disability in her speeches, calling forced maternity an "impacted mass of hypocrisy and corruption."

With Canning unable to hold a steady job, she took him and Byron to California for a new start. The gold rush had drawn more than forty thousand people to San Francisco by the time they arrived. Victoria, then sixteen, took on work as a seamstress and an actress, but Canning drank most of the money. When a spirit voice told her, "Victoria, come home," she took Canning and Byron on a steamer to Columbus, where Tennie was living with Anna and working as a medium. Victoria went into business with them. They toured the country, and in one year, she claimed, she made a hundred thousand dollars, more than $1 million today.

She was desperate for a second child, and in 1861, in a rented room on Bond Street in New York, she gave birth to a girl she named Zula

Maud. Canning cut the cord, left Zula in Victoria's arms, and staggered outside. Victoria awakened in a pool of blood that had oozed from the baby's bowels. Using a broken chair rung, she pounded against a wall for help. A neighbor finally found her and entered through the basement. The baby survived. Three days later, Victoria looked out the window and spotted Canning, drunk, ascending the steps of the house across the street, believing it was his own. That was when she considered the idea that she could leave him.

During the Civil War the Claflin family offered clairvoyant and healing services to veterans wounded in the war and families seeking to commune with the departed. Wherever they went, gossip followed. Tennie was named in adultery and blackmail suits; prominent residents asked the family to relocate again. In Chicago, Tennie married a man named John Bartels, who accompanied the family on a fortune-telling and séance tour of the Midwest, but after she and John began to quarrel, Tennie and Victoria gave him a twenty-thousand-dollar payment for his promise to leave her alone. From then on, she referred to herself as "Mrs. Tennie C. Claflin" and claimed to be married. One rumor in Cincinnati had the Claflins running a brothel. Whether or not Woodhull herself ever tricked, she was vocally supportive of prostitutes, writing in a speech, "There may be prostitution in marriage and proper commerce in the bawdy house. It depends upon the specific conditions attending the act itself and not where or how it is obtained."

By the spring of 1864, as General William T. Sherman was marching south from Tennessee toward Georgia, the Claflin family had settled in St. Louis. One client there who sought Victoria's aid as a clairvoyant was Colonel James Harvey Blood, twenty-nine, a married veteran and president of the St. Louis Railroad. They fell in love instantly and she went into a trance, whispering that his destiny was to be linked with hers in marriage. Per Theodore Tilton's account, they were married on the spot by "the powers of the air," meaning, perhaps, that they made love then and there.

Leaving their families behind, Blood and Woodhull took to the road in a covered van with a fringed top. She told fortunes as "Madam Harvey," and James Harvey Blood became "James Harvey, Esquire." On July 14, 1866, in Dayton, after both were divorced from their spouses, they signed a document stating their intention to marry.

Despite having a new husband, she remained Victoria Woodhull, probably because the name had publicity value. Blood believed in anarchism, free love, mysticism, and Greenbacking (an anti-banking, anti-monopolist movement). A supporter of woman suffrage and free love, he taught Woodhull about abolition and the burgeoning women's rights movement. She began to believe that she was destined to help other women.

Once Woodhull and Claflin had settled on Great Jones Street in 1868, they summoned family, including Blood, Buck, Anna, and two of their other sisters' families. The sisters were well suited to New York. The city was a playground for financiers, builders, and merchants. Boss Tweed's Democratic machine controlled city politics. The sporting men who so angered Comstock had created a city of lax moral standards, new money, and women in search of rich husbands. The most visible symbol of this era was Cornelius Vanderbilt.

In the spring of 1868, Buck Claflin arranged a meeting between his daughters and Vanderbilt, then a recent widower who had lost $7 million in his war with the robber barons James Fisk and Jay Gould to control the Erie Railway Company. In his early seventies, Vanderbilt wore a frock coat, a flowing white cravat, and a top hat. His diet consisted of foie gras, venison, Burgundy, and beer. He often consulted magnetic healers for his ailments, which included kidney stones and an enlarged prostate.

The sisters presented their business cards, identifying them as clairvoyants. When Vanderbilt set eyes on twenty-two-year-old Tennie Claflin, he was smitten. As their relationship deepened, she insisted he not eat rich foods, administered enemas, manipulated his prostate, and laid on her hands. Servants reported that they found her in his bed in the mornings. He called her "Ample" and "little sparrow." She pulled on his whiskers, calling him "old boy" and "the old goat."

A family friend recalled that Claflin asked him how many lovers he had had. "A thousand," he said.

"Then I am only half as bad as you are," Claflin reportedly replied, "for I have had five hundred."

That spring, the sisters were frequent guests at his dinner table. He visited them on Great Jones Street, and Woodhull led private séances. By the end of the year, Vanderbilt was giving the sisters some of the profits from stock trades, as Victoria offered him financial advice while in a trance state. Once asked how to make financial decisions, he replied, "Do as I do. Consult the spirits." That fall, he asked Claflin to become his wife. But the Vanderbilt family was scandalized by the Claflin sisters; instead he married a respectable woman from Alabama. For years the rumor circulated that Tennie was his lover.

Innately aware of their power, unable to see why the rules should be different for them, the sisters wanted the privileges accorded to men. One evening, they went to Delmonico's, on Fourteenth Street and Fifth Avenue, where Woodhull ordered tomato soup for two. The waiter said, "I beg your pardon, Madam, but it is after six o'clock and there is no gentleman with you." Charlie Delmonico, who knew and admired them, came to the table and told them to pretend to talk to him as he walked them to the door, seeking to avoid embarrassing them. They had a different plan in mind. Claflin went outside and found a cabbie who was sitting on his box. "Come down off your box and come in here," she told him. She ushered him into the restaurant and down the center aisle.

"Now, waiter," Claflin declared. "Bring tomato soup for three."

In January 1869, Woodhull went to the National Women's Rights Convention, the first of its kind to be held in the nation's capital, in Caroll Hall. Leading representatives of the movement were there, including Elizabeth Cady Stanton, Susan B. Anthony, and Lucretia Mott. In a high point of the convention, Stanton said the movement needed "a new evangel of womanhood" who would "lift man up into the high realms of thought and action."

At the time, Congress was debating the Fifteenth Amendment,

which would guarantee voting rights to freed male slaves. One convention speaker, Virginia Minor, professed that women did not need an amendment in order to vote because the Fourteenth Amendment, which guaranteed the rights of citizenship, already gave it to them: if women were citizens, they could vote. Minor would later sue for the right to vote; her case would make it to the U.S. Supreme Court. Woodhull, inspired by this talk, would continue to mull over this rationale for suffrage as her own opinions evolved.

The reformer, abolitionist, and orator Frederick Douglass, the only African American to have attended the Seneca Falls convention in 1848, stood up and told Stanton that woman suffrage (which, as he understood it, meant "white woman" suffrage) was less urgent than Negro suffrage. Stanton's patronizing, elitist response triggered Woodhull's sympathy for Douglass and her skepticism about the conservative wing of the women's movement. It was becoming clear to her that suffrage activism was dominated by self-congratulatory snobs, among whom she would never quite fit in.

After the convention, the movement would split into two competing groups: Anthony and Stanton's radical, New York–based National Woman Suffrage Association (NWSA) and Lucy Stone's more genteel, Boston-based American Woman Suffrage Association (AWSA). The NWSA favored less strict divorce laws and empowerment through sexual knowledge, and allied itself with labor. Its leaders wanted to pass suffrage as a constitutional amendment. The more moderate AWSA leaders thought that suffrage should be accomplished on the state level.

Though Stanton and Anthony gave Woodhull very few pages in their *History of Woman Suffrage* (published in multiple volumes between 1881 and 1922), she made a mark at the convention. An article called "The Coming Woman" in Washington's *Evening Star* noted that "Mrs. W." possessed "a commanding intellect, refinement, and remarkable executive ability, and will undoubtedly play a conspicuous part in such changes should they come . . . She will certainly form a prominent character in coming years." She was also interviewed by a *New York World* reporter, who wrote that "Mrs. Woodhull takes the most lively interest in all the genuine reforms of the day and entertains her own distinctive views." He noted that she "only partially" agreed with the stances of the convention. She was marking herself as distinct from the established suffrage movement, a newcomer, an outsider, and an instigator.

She next emerged as a prominent player in what became known as the Gold Panic. In September 1869, the speculator Gould and his partner Fisk tried to corner the gold market on the New York Gold Exchange. They began buying gold and raising its price. As prices rose, stocks plummeted. When President Ulysses S. Grant discovered their plot, he ordered the federal government to sell $4 million in gold. September 24, 1869, later known as Black Friday, saw large volumes of stock sell-offs as Wall Street descended into the Gold Panic. Woodhull told *The New York Herald* that she sat in her carriage for four days, from morning to evening, playing the markets, and came out a winner, later helping friends get back on their feet after they were plunged into poverty. After the crash, she bought cheap stocks, and by early 1870 she claimed that she and Claflin had made seven hundred thousand dollars. Whatever the figure, the sisters were rich.

They moved into a mansion at 15 East Thirty-Eighth Street, between Madison and Fifth. They brought the entire family with them, including Canning, Woodhull's first husband, who turned up one day, drunk and shaking. Known as "A Modern Palace Beautiful," the four-story brownstone featured gold chandeliers, purple velvet curtains, and a dome of gilt and frescoes that blinded visitors with a flood of light and depicted the loves of Venus. Woodhull claimed that their living expenses were $2,500 a month.

One frequent visitor to the house was the free lover, Spiritualist, writer, and orator Stephen Pearl Andrews. He was an individualist anarchist, concerned with personal autonomy as a universal right, believing that rights around one's body, time, and property superseded the rights of the government. A decade and a half before he met Woodhull, he had founded Modern Times, a free love commune on Long

Island. After the commune declined, he opened a free love league in today's SoHo, called "the Club," with five to six hundred members. The meetings were refined and social—not sexual—but after Horace Greeley's *Tribune* published a piece calling it a "secret society" for practicing free love in "sexual relations," the police raided the club. Four people were arrested, though Andrews was not in attendance.

Andrews was a proponent of a philosophy he called the Pantarchy, a vision of wholeness in human affairs, and he wrote frequently for the radical press. Woodhull encouraged him to have intellectual meetings in her parlors. According to Andrews, the household "resembled the salon of Mme. Roland during the First French Revolution—a rendezvous for men of genius, and women of genius, and the men interested in radical progress, and the women of similar interest."

A few months after the Gold Panic, in January 1870, Woodhull and Claflin opened Woodhull, Claflin & Company, the country's first woman-owned brokerage house, in the Hoffman House hotel in Madison Square. The *Herald* dubbed the sisters the "Queens of Finance." A half mile from Delmonico's, Hoffman House featured modern conveniences and Parisian cuisine. The brokerage office was decorated to resemble a woman's drawing room, with a sofa, a piano, and a small framed motto: "Simply to Thy cross I cling." The *Herald* reporter called Tennie "to all appearance, the photograph of a business woman—even, shrewd, whole-souled, masculine in manner and apparently a firm foe of the 'girl of the period' creation." When he asked if she found it "awkward" to be a woman stock operator, she replied, "Were I to notice what is said by what they call society, I could not leave my apartment except in fantastic walking-dress and ball-room costume." She declared, "I think a woman is just as capable of making a living as a man," and added that she and her sister had "the counsel of those who have more experience than we have." Their clients, she meant, would receive Vanderbilt's advice. Orders themselves were fulfilled by a Vanderbilt protégé named Randall Foote, as women were not allowed to trade. The first woman to buy a seat on the exchange would do so in 1967.

The sisters told the *Herald* they were ready for "the censure or approval of individuals who assume the right to adjudge us as treading upon forbidden ground." To them, the founding of Woodhull, Claflin & Company was revolutionary: "We are not of those who affect to believe our sex is despoiled of most of their rights by the domineering will of man, but, on the contrary, think we assert many we are illy prepared to make the best use of."

In February, with the help of a seven-thousand-dollar gift from Vanderbilt, they moved to larger offices at 44 Broad Street, down the street from the exchange. Their desks were carved with a Greek design, in honor of Demosthenes. A telegraphic stock indicator, which Blood's seat faced, occupied the front. Their official opening was announced on the stock and gold exchanges. On the first day, every financial house sent a representative. Boss Tweed and James Fisk came to pay their respects. By noon, the street was so crowded that more than a hundred policemen arrived to keep order. The sisters became known as the "bewitching brokers."

Woodhull would sit at a walnut desk in her office, eating strawberries and pasting news clippings about herself and Claflin into a scrapbook. The sisters adopted a uniform of dark blue walking suits, short hair, and jockey hats. A private entrance in the rear led to a room for women clients only. After Susan B. Anthony came to visit, she wrote an article in praise of the sisters for the NWSA newspaper, *The Revolution*. In better times, she wrote, women would vote into law the right to put "money in their pockets, without asking men's leave."

In April 1870, Woodhull published a letter in the *Herald* announcing herself as a candidate for president of the United States—even though the election was more than two years away. (Andrews was likely the real author; he would write her printed articles and speeches for many years.) Calling herself "the most prominent representative of the only unrepresented class in the republic, and perhaps the most practical exponent of the principles of equality," Woodhull claimed "the right to speak for the unenfranchised women of the country."

Advocates of women's political equality, the letter continued, had "a great undercurrent of unexpressed power which is only awaiting a fit opportunity to show itself." Among Woodhull's positions were prison reform, better care for the poor, and improved conditions for the working class. The *Herald* declared that her candidacy possessed "the merits of novelty, enterprise, courage and determination" and urged passage of a Sixteenth Amendment, giving women the right to vote.

One day, Woodhull invited Andrews to the brokerage offices. He climbed the three flights of crooked stairs, and there, as Blood stroked his side-whiskers nearby, Woodhull told him of her plans to launch a newspaper. Andrews needed a mouthpiece for his ideas. The sisters needed material. A deal was struck: he would be their editor.

On May 14, 1870, the Claflins released the first issue of *Woodhull & Claflin's Weekly*, a platform for Woodhull's campaign and one of the most important leftist publications of its time. The slogan of the four-column, sixteen-page *Weekly* was "Progress! Free Thought! Untrammeled Lives!" Similar freethinker publications advocated "mental liberty," separation of church and state, social and economic justice, individual autonomy, freedom of speech, and women's rights.

The *Weekly*'s inaugural issue contained columns on literature, theater, and finance, but its primary focus was women. In an article called "Woman's Position," the sisters forecast that women would "enter an enlarged sphere of action and use . . . Let [Woman] learn to be independent; self reliant; self supporting; then she will never be thrown upon the mercy of the world nor driven to conditions against which her soul revolts." According to the managing editor, Blood, Woodhull's articles were written in trances late at night. He would take notes and publish the contents "without correction or amendment."

From the outset, the *Weekly* was a mishmash of high and low culture. It covered prostitution, labor rights, vegetarianism, and the perils of marital sex but also published the writing of the French novelist George Sand, along with ads for clairvoyants and quack medicine. It was the first American paper to print the English translation of Karl

Marx and Friedrich Engels's *Communist Manifesto*. It was, in short, an outlet for all of the ideas Comstock despised.

In the second issue, an article about a man who had murdered his ex-wife's lover took aim at critics of free love. The term *free love*, the piece stated, "has no terror for us. All love to be holy, to be true, must be free. Who can love by compulsion?" Lack of honest sexual information, read another piece, "consigned many a youth to a lifelong death and many a wife to an early grave." This alluded to the transmission of venereal disease from prostitutes to husbands to wives.

Like most free lovers of the time, the sisters opposed abortion. By 1868, the state of New York classified it as manslaughter in the second degree—at any stage of pregnancy, even before quickening. And yet the sisters knew that the procedure was sometimes necessary, and that it was unfair for a woman to be vilified for seeking an abortion when a man had impregnated her. In an early essay called "My Word on Abortion, and Other Things," with a nod to New York's notorious abortionist Madame Restell, Claflin wrote:

> Who proposes to disturb Madam[e] Restel[l]? Who really wants that there should be no opportunity to secure an abortion *under particularly trying circumstances?* A thousand gentlemen within the purlieus of Wall street and Broad street, have occasion within the year, to invoke the aid of the *professionals* in behalf of their female friends who have got *into difficulty.* A thousand women and girls, the friends of these gentlemen, and among them their own daughters, who are the friends of their friends, are saved to *respectability* by the same means.

Still, Claflin called abortion "a symptom of a more deep-seated disorder of the social state." The remedy? Social freedom, which would allow women to be freely educated in "Physiology," meaning anatomy, and contraceptive techniques, such as rhythm or male continence.

For her part, Woodhull contended that the state should help

parents of young children. The government, she proclaimed, should render care "for all child-bearing and nursing women who may need its services." Though this idea was remarkably progressive for its time, her views on wanted and unwanted children were more complex. To her mind, when a loving couple procreated, only children who were meant to be born would result, and contraception and abortion were unnecessary. One of her theories was that happy mothers bore healthier children; she believed that Byron's disability had been caused in part by her own misery. "The mother who produces an inferior child," read an early article, "will be dishonored and unhappy in consequence, and she who produces superior children will feel proportionately pleased. When a woman attains this position, she will consider superior offspring a necessity and be apt to procreate only with superior men."

This latter belief, that superior people bred superior children, was commonly held by free lovers. The Oneida founder, John Humphrey Noyes, named it *stirpiculture* (derived from the Latin *stirps*, meaning "stock" or "stem") and advocated the inbreeding of "enlightened" people at Oneida as an example for the rest of society. It was thought that the method would lead to a harmonious world order. Advocates of stirpiculture believed that only *unwanted* children were morally or physically defective, though the concept was scientific bunk. In the 1920s and 1930s, eugenics, the idea that hereditary qualities could be improved by the social control of human reproduction, would be advocated by many doctors, political leaders, and educators in the United States—not to mention Nazis, whose belief came from fascist ideology.

But both American and Nazi eugenics were perversions of what has been labeled nineteenth-century "feminist eugenics." As the birth control historian Linda Gordon has written, "Hereditarian thought in the nineteenth century . . . was employed primarily in an optimistic, perfectionist vein, to demonstrate the possibilities of improvement of the human condition; environmental and reproductive control were not distinct." Feminist eugenicists wanted to fix social ills such as sexism, rape, crime, and alcoholism, by decreasing the number of accidental children.

Like many free lovers, Woodhull and Claflin held an exalted view of women, viewing them as inherently moral and calling motherhood "the special and distinctive feature of women." But unlike conservative women's rights advocates who believed a woman's only place was in the home, the Claflin sisters argued that there were "spheres of usefulness" outside of motherhood. Women could do other things besides bear and raise children. Having just declared herself a candidate for president, Woodhull was a living, breathing example of women's potential.

As the NWSA was preparing to open its third annual convention in early 1871, Woodhull testified before the House Judiciary Committee, then chaired by Benjamin Butler, a high-ranking Massachusetts congressman and Civil War veteran. During the war, Butler had freed African Americans who entered Union lines as contraband. He was also a supporter of women's rights. He and Woodhull became friends after she told him that Susan B. Anthony had come to visit her at the brokerage house.

The first woman to testify before a congressional committee, Woodhull walked nervously into the room with Butler and Claflin. Anthony and her fellow suffragists Isabella Beecher Hooker and Paulina Wright Davis were also present. Woodhull was dressed in a dark dress and a blue necktie, her hair curled under an Alpine hat. The "little woman with the far-off look," as one observer called her, delivered what became known as "the Woodhull memorial," or petition, telling the committee that the Fourteenth and Fifteenth Amendments already granted women voting rights. Early in her speaking career, she was still tentative. Nonetheless, facing eight men across a rectangular table, she protested local election laws that prevented women from voting, and demanded that the committee draft legislation that granted women suffrage. Though the memorial caused a sensation, the Judiciary Committee rejected it, 6–2.

Isabella Beecher Hooker introduced Woodhull at the simultaneous NWSA convention, where Woodhull read the memorial and reported on her experience delivering it. The NWSA decided to use the Fourteenth Amendment as a rationale to vote, and to sue if they were not able to register. Isabella was supportive of Woodhull, admiring her spirituality and convinced that her wealth would empower the women's rights movement. But Isabella's sisters, Catharine Beecher and the writer Harriet Beecher Stowe, were opponents of suffrage who had come to loathe Woodhull. Catharine believed suffrage destroyed society. Harriet's novel *My Wife and I*, serialized in *The Christian Union*, featured a trampy character based on Woodhull—Audacia Dangyereyes, who forced men to subscribe to her paper. Catharine and Harriet would be thorns in Woodhull's side.

After the memorial in Washington, the Woodhull & Claflin brokerage offices were converted to campaign headquarters and a group of supporters organized the "Victoria League" on behalf of her candidacy. In May 1871, both wings of the suffrage movement held conventions in New York. Though it was called the Woman's Rights Convention, suffrage was so closely associated with Woodhull that it was referred to as the "Woodhull Convention." "We are plotting revolution," she proclaimed during the proceedings in a speech called "The New Rebellion." "We will over[throw] this bogus republic and plant a government of righteousness in its stead."

That month, however, she endured a family drama that would embolden her detractors and harm her political ambitions. Without informing Woodhull of her plans, her mother, Anna, brought a complaint against Woodhull's husband Blood, alleging that he had threatened her physically. On the stand, Blood revealed that Woodhull's first husband, Canning, also lived in the mansion. Asked whether Woodhull and Canning were legally divorced, Blood said he was not sure. If Blood was to be believed, Woodhull was living under one roof with two husbands.

She wrote an impassioned letter to the *Times*, calling Canning "sick, ailing, and incapable of self-support," and saying Blood approved of the cohabitation. This might have been the end of it, but Woodhull was vulnerable, and angry, and decided to plant a salacious detail in her letter, a detail not about her own family. She would not be made a scapegoat, she wrote, a victim to society by those who cover over the foulness of their lives and the feculence of their thoughts with hypocritical mouth of fair professions, and by diverting public attention from their own iniquity and pointing the finger at me . . . My judges preach against "free love" openly, practice it secretly . . . For example, I know of one man, a public teacher of eminence, who lives in concubinage with the wife of another public teacher of almost equal eminence. All three concur in denouncing offenses against morality.

The first "public teacher" was known to be the Reverend Henry Ward Beecher, pastor of Plymouth Church in Brooklyn Heights and a brother of Isabella, Catharine, and Harriet. The second "public teacher" was his friend and protégé Theodore Tilton.

Beecher was one of the most revered religious leaders in the nation and a prominent abolitionist. Every Sunday, "Beecher boats" brought people from Manhattan to Brooklyn to hear his sermons. He had an erect carriage with a youthful, expressive face and was wildly popular on the lecture circuit. He was also enmeshed in a scandal, which Woodhull had first heard about from Stanton in May 1871: he was having an affair with Elizabeth "Libby" Tilton, the wife of Theodore, and had gotten her pregnant. After Theodore learned of the affair, he and Libby had an argument, one so violent that it shocked her into a miscarriage. The story had infidelity, sex, violence, and hypocrisy, and Woodhull knew that if it came out, it would be explosive.

The day the letter was published, Tilton came to see Woodhull at the *Weekly* office. She had spotted him at the suffrage convention earlier that month. He was handsome, with dark eyes and longish red hair. He asked if she had meant Beecher in her article. She said, "I mean you and Beecher," and told him that she had a mission to bring Beecher's hypocrisies "to the knowledge of the world." Tilton told Woodhull the entire tale: the argument, and the miscarriage at six months. He'd torn the wedding ring from Libby's finger, ripped a picture of Beecher from his wall, and buried the fetus, Libby beside him as he did so. A few weeks after Tilton visited Woodhull, the *Weekly* ran an article extolling him. He soon contributed to the paper and rewrote General Butler's report on the Woodhull Memorial as a speech for her. According to Woodhull, she and Tilton entered into an affair. They would swim at Coney Island and talk on the roof of her house. He wrote an adulatory biography of her, for which he was roundly mocked. The author and poet Julia Ward Howe called the book "a tomb from which no author rises."

On a warm Friday evening in 1871, Woodhull met Beecher at Tilton's house. He claimed she rushed out to greet him, extending both hands. Far from having an argument, the preacher and Woodhull discussed what she called the "social problem," or free love. She told a later paramour that she and Beecher made love that night. He was nearing sixty, with graying hair and downturned, thoughtful eyes. She took pleasure in his sexuality and wanted him to know that she thought marriage was a corrupt institution. Did she tell him she wanted him to pay for his hypocrisy, or his adultery? Did he dare her to blackmail him, or express contrition? Only Woodhull and Beecher knew for certain.

That fall, Woodhull toured Cleveland, Chicago, Baltimore, Philadelphia, and Hartford, delivering speeches on suffrage and free love. On November 20, she was booked to deliver a speech called "'The Principles of Social Freedom' Involving the Question of Free Love, Marriage, Divorce and Prostitution" in New York's Steinway Hall, which adjoined the Steinway piano showroom. The stage could accommodate a hundred orchestra members, and the hall itself could hold twenty-five hundred people. Many illustrious speakers had graced the hall, including Charles Dickens and Mark Twain.

Understanding that Beecher's true nature was complex, and believing that she had sexual power over him, Woodhull came to the idea that he should defend her publicly and avow the principles of free love. She requested an interview with him on the day of the speech.

After supplying him with the text, she met him at Tilton's house to try to persuade him to introduce her at Steinway. Beecher replied that if he did so, "I should sink through the floor. I am a moral coward on the subject, and I know it." He told her that the social system was corrupt and marriage "the curse of society," but that he would not say so in public.

That evening, she was dressed all in black, with a watch hanging from her neck and a red rose at her throat. "The Woodhull had an inspired look," a reporter wrote, with "a pair of dark eyes burning with suppressed fire, and a color that cannot be described when seen at night only." She had become her own noun.

Beecher never appeared. She walked onto the stage to a full house and thunderous applause. "A hundred ravenous male bipeds leaned over the platform," reported the *Herald*, "standing up in front of the audience." Half of the attendees were women. Woodhull read a speech, written by Andrews, in favor of marriage based on love: "How can people who enter upon marriage in utter ignorance of that which is to render the union happy or miserable be able to say that they will always 'love and live together'?" Unhappy couples should part ways. Unloving sex was adultery, and loathing-filled sex was prostitution, "whether it be in the gilded palaces of Fifth Avenue or in the lowest purlieus of Greene Street."

Women were to be men's equals, she announced, and "Their entire system of education must be changed. They must be chagrined to be like men, permanent and independent individualities, and not their mere appendages or adjuncts." The state should have no role in love, and women should control childbearing decisions. Any modesty that shut off discussion and knowledge of these subjects was false and perverse.

Someone shouted, "Are you a free lover?"

Departing from her printed words, she cried, "Yes, I am a free lover. I have an inalienable, constitutional and natural right to love whom I may, to love as long or short a period as I can; to change that love every day if I please, and with that right neither you nor

"Get thee behind me, Mrs. Satan," Thomas Nast
illustration in Harper's Weekly

any law you can frame have any right to interfere." Most free lovers
were monogamous; these "exclusivists" believed romantic love could
exist only between two people. Only a minority of free lovers, "varietists," believed that love required variety and multiple partners.
Sex outside of marriage, called fornication or adultery, was illegal in
most states, and, of course, Woodhull was married to Blood. She had

revealed herself not only as a free lover—scandalous enough—but also as a varietist.

Her speech was so explosive that the *Harper's Weekly* caricaturist Thomas Nast drew a cartoon of her as Mrs. Satan holding a sign that said, "Be Saved by Free Love." Within two days of the speech, Mrs. Satan had received thirteen new lecture invitations.

Despite the fact that she now had a national speaking career, Woodhull would never forgive Beecher for failing to introduce her at Steinway Hall. She had power, celebrity, and a newspaper, and she would get revenge. She didn't know that there was another prominent New Yorker as confident and media-conscious as she was. His name was Anthony Comstock.

4

THE SENSATIONAL COMEDY OF FREE LOVE

Date:	Nov. 2, 1872
Name:	Victoria C. Woodhull
Address:	23 Irving Place, N.Y. City
Age:	35
Nationality:	Irish descent, American born
Religion:	Free-love Spiritualist
Education:	Fair
Married or Single:	Married
No. of Children:	1
Occupation:	Broker, Publisher and Lecturer
Offence:	Mailing obscene papers

Name:	Tennie C. Claflin
Address:	23 Irving Place, N.Y. City
Age:	28
Nationality:	Same as above
Religion:	Free-love Spiritualist
Education:	Common
Married or Single:	Single
No. of Children:	0
Occupation:	Same as above
Offence:	Mailing obscene papers

Around the time that Woodhull was delivering her suffrage memorial in Washington, Comstock was falling in love. Her name was Margaret Hamilton; she was one year younger than he, and the daughter of a Presbyterian elder. Extremely quiet, she dressed only in black and weighed eighty-two pounds. A relative called her a "fussy, old fashioned, clinging doll. Very proper and narrow minded, easily horrified at the least misconduct."

Comstock and Maggie were a perfect match, bonding over their shared religiosity. With a new dry goods job, he bought a house on Brooklyn's Grand Avenue for six thousand dollars. The couple married on January 25, 1871, and honeymooned in Philadelphia. In his diary, Comstock wrote that "my darling is at last *free* from her long years of cares. Surely God's hand is in all this." From Philadelphia, they traveled to Washington and visited the Senate and the House; the Post Office; the Patent Office; and, for Sunday services, President Grant's Methodist church. The White House, he wrote, had "beauty and grandeur." Only a few years later, he would meet the president.

In his diary, he referred to Maggie as "dear M," "my precious little wife," and "Wifey." He frequently brought her flowers, and he made her a birdhouse. After teaching Sunday school at Clinton Avenue Congregational Church, he cooked for her and her father. One day, coming home to find a half-finished dress on the sewing machine, he completed it for her. "How she laughed," he wrote.

Disrupting their happiness, however, was the saloon just a block from their house. It stayed open all day on Sundays, and cockfights and dogfights were run inside. He called the police to ask that it be closed. When the officer refused, Comstock brought charges before the police commissioners. The saloonkeeper, a man named Chapman, was arrested for violating the closing law, but once released, he repeatedly menaced Comstock on the street. Comstock bought a revolver. One day, Chapman threatened to break his neck, but when Comstock drew his revolver, the saloonkeeper bolted. Comstock continued to hector him until he shut the business.

He was finding that his true skill lay in vice hunting, not dry goods. "Trade still holds dull," he wrote repeatedly in his diary. But the financial pressure increased after his sister-in-law Jennie moved in with him and Maggie.

Then came the biggest financial headache of all, though a joyous one. On December 4, 1871, Maggie gave birth to a girl. His diary entry read, "A little daughter born this morning about 8:15 A.M. Weighs 9 Lbs."

By the time Comstock became a father, the New York YMCA was thriving. Almost five thousand men used the facilities, enrolling in language classes, Bible study, and gymnastics. The New York headquarters opened in 1869 on Twenty-Third Street and Fourth Avenue. Yet even as it expanded its influence, the association had made little progress on obscene books.

Comstock, too, was frustrated by what seemed to be an anti-smut law that he called "not adequate." Though the Warren Street bookseller Charles Conroy had been convicted, he was soon back at work. When Comstock learned of another well-known smut dealer, William Simpson of Centre Street, he told a patrolman that Simpson sold obscene books, and went inside the shop. As Comstock was looking over a price list, the cop summoned a clerk and tipped Simpson off. Comstock was so furious that he went to the Board of Police Commissioners and had the policeman dismissed. In Comstock's version, the *Sunday Mercury* newspaper wrote disparagingly that if he were the Christian man he professed to be, he could find plenty of other booksellers on Ann and Nassau Streets, and elsewhere. Using the article as a form of reconnaissance, he searched in sporting newspapers for the addresses of stores on Ann and Nassau Streets.

On March 3, 1872, with a *Tribune* reporter in tow, he assisted in seven arrests, seizing such books as *The Confessions of a Voluptuous Young Lady of High Rank*, *La Rose d'Amour*, and *Women's Rights Convention*. "In order to secure the necessary evidence against these parties," the *Times* reported, "ANTHONY COMSTOCK, of No. 464 Broadway, entered the establishments named and there purchased several obscene books and pictures. Capt. WARD subsequently visited the stores mentioned and placed under arrest all the persons found there."

After the March arrests, Comstock discovered that most of the obscene books in New York were issued by only four publishers. By the time he arrived at the Brooklyn home of one of them, William Haynes, Haynes was dead. Comstock believed it was suicide, writing in his arrest logbook that an associate had warned Haynes, "'Comstock is after you. He won't look at money,'" and adding ominously, "That night he died." Comstock was obsessed with the deaths he may have caused; in January 1874, a society report on the obscene book trade—most likely written by him—noted that "three publishers, one manufacturer, one abortionist, one expressman, and one prisoner in jail, or a total of seven have died since April, 1872." At the Haynes home, the widow Mary Haynes cursed at him and said he had killed her husband. Comstock demanded the obscene book plates, but she wanted money. He offered $450—the only problem being that he had no such sum.

He decided to write a letter to the YMCA's corresponding secretary, Robert R. McBurney, to ask for help. "My private resources are exhausted," he explained. "I have borne the expense thus far myself. I have a family to support, and I appeal directly to your Association for whatever may be necessary to complete this work."

Spotting the letter on McBurney's desk, the YMCA's president, Morris K. Jesup, went to visit Comstock at his dry goods firm. "Mr. Comstock impressed me so greatly with his earnestness," Jesup recalled of that visit, "with his fidelity, with his whole heartedness, that I made up my mind that what little I could do to aid in fighting this sin, I would do that." Jesup invited him to his mansion in Murray Hill. The next day, Jesup had McBurney send Comstock a check for $650—$450 for Mary Haynes's plates and the rest for Comstock. At the Haynes house, Comstock seized twenty-four plates and had them destroyed in the lab of Brooklyn's Polytechnic Institute.

A few months later, Jesup invited Comstock to his home again, this time to meet with the Brooklyn district attorney, an assistant district attorney, the YMCA board member William E. Dodge, and other prominent businessmen, lawyers, and clergymen. Comstock told them that the money he gave Mrs. Haynes had yielded thirty to forty thousand dollars' worth of obscene plates.

The YMCA decided to form the Committee for the Suppression of Vice to go after the obscene book trade, hiring Comstock to carry on the work—but "without it being publicly known at the time under whose auspices he was operating." Anti-vice work was unseemly, even unpopular. The committee would raise its money separately from the association, cover Comstock's expenses, and pay him a hundred dollars a month.

That spring, the state's Obscene Literature Act was retooled to grant citizens the ability to initiate prosecutions and receive half of any relevant fines, which allowed Comstock to make money on top of his stipend. In June, federal obscenity law was expanded to include envelopes and postcards "upon which scurrilous epithets may have been written or printed."

The YMCA Committee for the Suppression of Vice moved to 150 Nassau Street, right in the heart of the obscene book trade. The fifth-floor space—which consisted of Comstock's office, the "seizure" room for confiscated items, and the reception area—held a portrait of Abraham Lincoln on the wall and a copy of Lincoln's letter to Mrs. Lydia Bixby consoling her on the loss of her five sons in the Civil War. Comstock installed a large photograph of himself over his rolltop desk. One of the most important moral-policing institutions of the nineteenth century was open for business.

In the spring of 1872, Americans were focused on the upcoming presidential election. The incumbent, Grant, was seeking renomination at his party's national convention, to be held in June. Horace Greeley, the *Tribune* publisher, wanted to take on Grant, campaigning on civil service reform and the end of Reconstruction. Democratic Party leaders believed Greeley could win.

Meanwhile, Woodhull was gaining a national reputation with her presidency bid, but she had made enemies in the suffrage world, which enraged her. She printed proofs of an article, "Tit for Tat," which included the sexual histories of prominent women's rights activists who, she felt, were gossiping about her. Suffragists claimed that she offered them immunity for five hundred dollars. Angela Heywood's husband and copublisher, Ezra Hervey Heywood, contended that Susan B. Anthony had called Woodhull a blackmailer. Woodhull claimed that blackmailing was a crime "which we have never either committed or attempted to commit."

Though "Tit for Tat" was never printed, the incident gave Anthony cause for concern about Woodhull as a public representative of suffrage. The tensions between Woodhull and movement leaders rose to a peak in May 1872, when the NWSA held its annual convention in Steinway Hall. Woodhull took the floor. Anthony objected and tried to adjourn the meeting. The group argued, and finally decided to adjourn and meet the next day in Apollo Hall, after which Woodhull exited, the audience following. The Anthony-Woodhull friendship was over.

At Apollo Hall, the new Equal Rights Party was formed to nominate Woodhull as a candidate for president, the first woman to be nominated by any party. Its first resolution read, "We recognize the equality of all before the law, and hold that it is the duty of government in its dealings with the people to mete out equal and exact justice to all, of whatever nativity, race, color, sex or persuasion, religious or political." Because she would be thirty-four at the time of the election, according to the Constitution she was not old enough to run; she would never be an official candidate or appear on the ballot.

Cartoon depicting Victoria C. Woodhull's nomination
for president at Apollo Hall, May 1872

When Judge Alfred Carter of Cincinnati said, "I propose the name of Victoria C. Woodhull to be nominated president of the United States," men jumped and threw their hats in the air, and women screamed, waving handkerchiefs. As the audience rose to their feet, Woodhull, wearing a high-crowned hat, shook hands with the men and kissed the women. Delegates to the Equal Rights Party convention included the Heywoods, the progressive doctor and editor Edward Bliss (E. B.) Foote, and prominent abolitionists. The reformer Moses Hull nominated Frederick Douglass as Woodhull's running mate, calling him one of the most "distinguished representatives of the race which, with women, is almost equally downtrodden by the persons that are installed in the places of trust and power." He called Woodhull a representative "of all the principles of reform, including even the colored woman." Douglass was never consulted; when the nominations were ratified, he was home in Rochester, New York.

Weeks after Woodhull's nomination alongside Douglass, Claflin broke another cultural barrier when the "Spencer Grays," or the Eighty-Fifth Regiment, composed of six hundred men and the only African American regiment in the state, invited her to be their colonel. She had tried unsuccessfully to become colonel of the Ninth

Regiment of the New York National Guard after its colonel, James Fisk, was shot, having been murdered by a business associate. Though there was some opposition within the Spencer Grays, the troops needed money for uniforms and for an inherited debt related to their armory, and Tennessee Claflin was wealthy.

After the Spencer Grays reached out to her, an article on the matter appeared in the Rochester papers, and a few days later there was an arson attack on the Douglass home. The historian Amanda Frisken has speculated that racist outrage about Claflin's colonelcy, combined with Douglass's and Woodhull's nominations, may have led racists to set the fire. Douglass attributed the attack to the KKK and left Rochester, where he had lived for twenty-five years, for Washington.

As for the vice-presidential nomination, he never acknowledged it, never campaigned with Woodhull, and, in fact, supported Grant and the Republican ticket, favoring its expanded enforcement of civil rights laws. When Greeley was nominated at the Democratic National Convention on the Liberal Republican ticket, Douglass felt that it was merely a token tribute to abolitionism.

At the Equal Rights Party ratification meeting at Cooper Institute on June 6, the room was full. The Spencer Grays were on the platform, and after Woodhull spoke, their captain, Thomas Griffin, said that the party guaranteed "equal rights . . . to every intelligent respectable being in the land, without regard to caste, condition, or sex." Claflin was elected to her own position about a week later. She said that she would rather "accept the colonelcy of a colored regiment than that of one composed of white men," and that she could pick out more white men than Blacks who would run from the field of battle. This was met by long applause. She was elected by a margin of three to one, the first and only white woman to be elected colonel of a Black regiment. Papers mocked her with racist articles, suggesting that she wear blackface and a uniform.

Just a month and a half after the Equal Rights Party convention was held, the Comstocks suffered a personal loss from which they would never fully recover. On Friday, June 28, 1872, Comstock left Maggie and a nurse at home with the baby, Lillie, and went to court to testify against a Nassau Street obscene photo and card dealer named John Meeker. By the time he returned, Lillie was dead of cholera infantum, or summer diarrhea, a common and often fatal disease in infants at that time.

At age ten, he had come home to find his mother dead of uterine hemorrhage, a complication of childbirth, but his infant sister alive. At twenty-eight, he lost his own infant girl.

That night, he wrote in his diary, "The Lord's will be done. Oh, for grace to say it and live it!" Over the weekend, the Comstocks buried Lillie in Brooklyn's Evergreens Cemetery. On Monday he was back in court. A photographer named William Horace Wood said that Comstock had threatened him with state prison if he did not testify against Meeker the dealer.

Though Woodhull's nomination was the most significant victory of her life, by the time it came she was in financial trouble. Vanderbilt had withdrawn his support of the *Weekly* after his contract with the sisters ended. They paused publication, unable to afford the printing costs. With their mansion too expensive to maintain, they were forced to move. Under assumed names, they took rooms at Gilsey House hotel, until they were recognized and kicked out. A carriage arrived bearing four African American lieutenants who were taking Claflin to a drill. The proprietor of Gilsey told Claflin, "If you go off with those men in that carriage you need not come back here!" Woodhull wrote in the *Weekly*, after they had resumed publishing it, that she and her family were expelled because "we hold social theories and have the courage to advocate them." That night, Woodhull, Blood, Claflin, and Zula walked the streets, finally resorting to sleeping on the floor in her office on Broad Street.

In need of well-connected friends, Woodhull turned to Beecher. "Will you lend me your aid in this," she wrote him. If he could vouch for their credibility, she felt, Gilsey House would let them back in.

He refused. She took a smaller office, down Broad Street, and when the family had no place to spend the night they slept there. As far as she was concerned, Beecher had now betrayed her twice, first by not introducing her at Steinway Hall, then by refusing to help her family.

That September, at a meeting of the American Association of Spiritualists, she started to give her stump speech but stopped suddenly and launched into the story of the Beecher-Tilton adultery. A woman in attendance wrote, "Mrs. Woodhull tossed back her hair, in high tragic style, and poured out a torrent of flame. It made our flesh to creep and our blood to run cold." But there was no pickup in the newspapers; editors decided that her words were too obscene to print. She was going to have to publish the tale herself.

A twelve-thousand-word article ran in the November 2, 1872, issue of the *Weekly*, the first to come out since the publication break, and days before the presidential election. The headline on page 9 read: "The Beecher-Tilton Scandal Case: The Detailed Statement of the Whole Matter by Mrs. Woodhull." It opened, "I propose, as the commencement of a series of aggressive moral warfare on the social question, to begin in this article with ventilating one of the most stupendous scandals which has ever occurred in any community." She detailed the adultery and the miscarriage, and reported that Tilton had said, "I stamped the ring with which we had plighted our troth, deep into the soil that covered the fruit of my wife's infidelity."

In the exposé, Woodhull claimed that she stood in opposition not to affairs but to hypocrisy, and the powerful institutions of Christianity and marriage. She praised Beecher's "immense physical potency." His crime was "not infidelity to the old ideas, but unfaithfulness to the new," meaning free love. But the article was hardly a defense of Beecher. His hypocrisy made him "a poltroon, a coward and a sneak." Tilton's shame and hurt were the result of "sickly religious literature" and "Sunday School morality."

In the same issue of the *Weekly* appeared an article titled "The Philosophy of Modern Hypocrisy—Mr. L. C. Challis the Illustration."

Attributed to Claflin, the article stated that it would be the first in a series that outed prominent men for their wrongdoings:

> A man being even the President of the United States, governor of a State, pastor of the most popular church, president of the most reliable bank, or of the grandest railroad corporation, may constantly practice all the debaucheries known to sensualism—many of which are so vicious, brutal and degrading as to be almost beyond belief—and he, by virtue of his sex, stands protected and respected . . . But let a woman even so much as protect herself from starvation by her sexuality, lacking the sanction of the law, and every body in unison cries out, "Down with the vile thing."

Claflin announced that she would take "leading personages" from society and tell the world about their private lives, so it would not appear that their victims were "the only frightful examples of immorality." These men would be "made to stand before the world beside the women with whom they have heretofore reveled behind the screen of manly immunity."

The article chronicled a gang rape connected to the annual French masked ball at the Academy of Music on Fourteenth Street, a four-thousand-seat opera house that was a playground for the city's social elite. The ball was a prominent social affair for women, politicians, and businessmen, all mingling in masks. The women, many of them prostitutes, were beautiful and wore dresses that exposed their ankles, cleavage, and shoulders. The balls were known to turn into public orgies.

According to Claflin, the rape occurred in 1869—three years before publication of the article. She and Woodhull had attended the ball dressed as shepherdesses and wearing white masks, and sat in a red-damask-draped box where they could observe the events unseen. The businessman Luther Challis and a male friend plied two teenage girls with wine, took them to a house of prostitution, and raped them. "And this scoundrel Challis," Claflin wrote, "to prove that he had *seduced a maiden, carried for days on his finger, exhibiting in triumph, the red trophy of her virginity.* After a few days, these Lotharios exchanged beds and companions, and when weary of this they brought their friends, to the number of one hundred and over, to debauch these young girls—mere children." If the women brought Challis to court, Claflin contended, no one would have believed them. Challis later claimed that Claflin had sent him a letter demanding two hundred dollars not to publish the story, but he refused. Later she sent him a proof of the article, which he also ignored. The Claflin sisters were frustrated blackmailers, exposers of male hypocrisy, masters of public relations, or all three.

Initially, the sisters printed thirty-one thousand copies of the Beecher-Tilton issue. Newsboys and news dealers crowded Broad Street and ultimately, with additional print runs, sold 150,000 copies. By the evening of October 28, the day it was first printed, each issue was going for as much as forty dollars. The less fortunate rented it for one dollar a day.

Word of the scandalous issue reached Comstock that day. To nab the sisters, he instructed two clerks at Plymouth Church to order copies of the *Weekly* by mail. After trying and failing to obtain arrest warrants in state court, he used an alias ("M. Hamilton," his wife's maiden name) to request the issue by mail. When it was sent, he was able to secure a federal arrest warrant from Noah Davis, U.S. district attorney for the Southern District, a powerful friend of Beecher and a parishioner of Plymouth Church. The charges were brought under the federal obscenity statute.

On Saturday, November 2, two deputy marshals showed up at the *Weekly* offices, but the sisters were out. At 12:15, just as the marshals were about to leave, a carriage arrived with the women, who were dressed in black with purple bows. Bankers, brokers, and clerks flocked to the offices. The *Times* reported that three thousand copies of the paper were found in the carriage and seized by the police. The sisters invited one of the officers to sit in the carriage. Misunderstanding the offer, he sat in Claflin's lap. Later, Woodhull's husband, Blood, would also be arrested on a libel charge filed by Challis. By the time the sisters arrived at the courthouse, a crowd had gathered.

In his arrest logbook, under "Religion," Comstock would label Woodhull and Claflin "Free-love Spiritualists." There were rumors that Beecher had paid him to have them arrested, but Comstock wrote in his diary, *"I know no Beecher or Challis or any other man, but to vindicate the laws* and protect the young of our land for the leprosy of this vile trash."

At the U.S. District Court arraignment, the sisters were represented by the attorney and suffragist James D. Reymert. The *New York Dispatch* reported, "Tennie was flushed like a rose, and her blue eyes sparkled nervously. As she glanced around the room, a smile of contempt seemed to gather about her ruby lips." Assistant District Attorney General Henry E. Davies called the Beecher article "a most abominable and unjust charge against one of the purest and best citizens of this State, or in the United States." U.S. Commissioner John E. Osborn cried, "An example is needed and we propose to make one of these women!" Commissioners performed judicial functions for the federal government; this one set bail at eight thousand dollars each, even though the charges were misdemeanors.

The sisters were taken to Ludlow Street Jail, where, even after a friend offered to post bail, they decided to spend the weekend; Reymert had told them that if they were freed they would be rearrested on other charges. Inside, they were met by the defense attorney William Howe, who was, with his partner, Abe Hummel, known for a clientele of murderers, madams, chiefs, and gangs.

Ludlow Street held county and federal prisoners and was governed by a caste system—the upper two floors were filthy and bedbug-ridden, with barely edible food, but on the ground floor the conditions were clean, the air fresh. The sisters' cell was lighted by gas and had a door with a cloth-covered window. Their row was known as "Fifth Avenue." Other prisoners were asked not to smoke, on the sisters' behalf. They shared a bathroom with the warden's family and ate the same food: broiled chicken and potatoes, with condiments and tea. They were provided with linen and utensils, a rug, and bedding. During their stay, the warden, Mr. Tracy, read the sisters excerpts from the writings of the English poet Alexander Pope, informing them that Pope's work was dirtier than anything they had published.

At the examination, Howe, dressed in plaid pantaloons, a purple vest, and a blue satin scarf, called the sisters victims of "private malice," implying collusion between Comstock and Beecher. He said that if the *Weekly* was obscene, then the mailing of the Holy Bible, Lord Byron's poems, and Shakespeare's works ought to be stopped because they were open to the same objection.

The next day, Tuesday, November 5, 1872, was Election Day. Anthony and fourteen Rochester women attempted to vote and were able to persuade some of the voting officials to let them inside the polling place. Anthony was arrested three weeks later. Equal Rights Party delegates wrote Woodhull's name on ballots for president. The candidate spent election night in cell 11 in Ludlow Street. Grant swept the election, defeating Greeley.

The indictment called the offending matter "a certain obscene publication which said obscene publication is too indecent to be herein set forth," and initially, the prosecution said that the arrests were made on account of the Challis article. The day the sisters were brought to the court, Challis also filed a libel claim. The *Herald* named the Challis case the "sensational comedy of free-love."

As delays piled up in the obscenity proceedings, with the sisters still in jail, Comstock was attacked in the press. *The Brooklyn Daily Eagle* reported, "Without having generally known it, the people of this country are living under a law more narrow and oppressive than any people with a written constitution ever lived under before." The *Eagle* declared that Comstock had become the sisters' "prosecutor and world wide advertiser. Even then we never referred to him, for the same reason that we do not refer to last year's flies—he is entirely unimportant." The *Sunday Mercury* argued that it was wrong for the machinery of the federal government to be "at the back of a man who has, somehow or other, chosen it for his private business to deprive this woman of her liberty."

The sisters stayed in Ludlow Street Jail for all of November. Free lovers such as the Heywoods said that the sisters' arrest was a "mean and diabolical act" that "every Federal official, from the President down, should be ashamed of. Whatever Mrs. Woodhull's views upon social reform or other questions may be, every friend of impartial liberty should now stand by her; for in her person, the freedom of the press and the freedom of the mails is struck down."

From prison, Woodhull wrote a letter to the *Herald*, stating that the Beecher and Challis articles were political: "I desire that woman shall be emancipated from the sexual slavery maintained over her by man. I declare that woman shall, so far as her support is concerned, be made independent of man, so that all her sexual relations result from other reasons than for maintenance; in a word, shall be wholly and only for love." Those named in the stories, she said, "may succeed in crushing me out, even to the loss of my life; but let me warn them and you that from the ashes of my body a thousand Woodhulls will spring to avenge my death by seizing the work laid down by me and carrying it forward to victory."

On December 5, the sisters decided to obtain bail provided by two male friends—and were freed. There were more arrests on the libel charges, more bonds paid by other friends. On December 23, Woodhull was booked for a speech at the Boston Music Hall called "Moral Cowardice & Modern Hypocrisy; or, Four Weeks in Ludlow-Street Jail." Harriet Beecher Stowe appealed to the Massachusetts governor's wife, and the lecture was stopped. Speaking in Springfield, Massachusetts, instead, Woodhull mocked Comstock. In the *Weekly*, she called him an "illiterate puppy" and "the special, though self-appointed agent of Christ." The YMCA was "the Young Men's Christian (Christ forgive the connection) Association."

On January 9, 1873, she was set to give a speech at the Cooper Institute. The institute's Great Hall was a popular destination for progressive activists. Abraham Lincoln had spoken there as a young candidate for president of the United States, and Frederick Douglass had taken the stage as well. The hall was the largest secular meeting room in New York.

Comstock had heard that bootleg copies of the Beecher/Challis issue were still commanding up to ten dollars each, two months after the initial publication. He decided to have Woodhull arrested before the lecture. He went to Greenwich, Connecticut, and ordered six copies of the issue under the alias "J. Beardsley," deliberately using poor English and enclosing $1.50. He then went by sled to Norwalk to order another six, under a different name. This interstate travel was deliberate: throughout his career he would try to secure federal convictions by traveling to and renting post boxes in different states.

After the issues arrived in Greenwich, he swore out new warrants against Woodhull and Claflin and had Blood arrested at the offices of the *Weekly*. Of the staff he encountered there, he wrote that there "were about six or eight of the hardest kind of free-lovers, judging by their looks, to be found anywhere." When he went to the sisters' house, he could not find them; Blood had sent a warning, and they had moved in with their sister Maggie. Claflin was hiding under a washtub and would not be seen in Woodhull's company that night. After escaping to Jersey City, Woodhull stayed in a hotel until dark, then, dressed in a coat and veil, took the Twenty-Third Street ferry back to Manhattan.

A crowd was gathered in front of the Cooper Institute, while deputy marshals and officers stood by the doors. The audience was "a cross between a Bowery congregation and those who attend scientific lectures." There were about a thousand attendees, mostly women. Woodhull's sister Utica and her daughter, Zula, were among them.

Marshals told the audience that there would be no speech. As eight o'clock drew nearer, the crowd made its way inside. They waited an hour and began to call and shout. A carriage arrived, carrying an old Quaker woman. She wore a gray silk bonnet under a thick veil that covered her face, and a gray dress under a black-and-white shawl. As she entered, she passed a half dozen federal marshals. One assisted her into the hall. She said nothing and appeared to be deaf.

Laura Cuppy Smith, a Spiritualist trance speaker and friend of the sisters, went onstage and told the crowd that neither Woodhull nor Claflin would appear, calling Woodhull a "martyr" who was battling on behalf of a great cause. "Is this a free country?" Smith asked. "Have we free speech? Have we a free press? Are the citizens of New York conscious of their duty?"

As Smith spoke, the old Quaker lady was making her way to the rostrum via the middle aisle, attendees laughing all the while at her bizarre appearance. She disappeared behind a pillar and darted out onto the stage. Then she flung off her bonnet, veil, and shawl—revealing herself as Woodhull. She raised her arms high in the air. Fans clapped and shouted. She gulped for breath, her hair tumbling down around her. As the applause and yelling died down, she said she had come from "a cell in the American Bastille, to which I was consigned by the cowardly servility of the age." She called the obscenity charge "scandalous . . . trumped up by the ignorant or corrupt officers of the law, conspiring with others to deprive me, under the falsest and shallowest pretenses, of my inherited privileges as an American citizen."

An audience member described "an overwhelming inspirational fire scintillating from her eyes and beaming from her face." The Quaker costume at her feet, her breast heaving with emotion, "her head thrown defiantly back like the head of the Apollo Belvedere, she looked the personification of Liberty in Arms. Her voice rose in clear and piercing tones." People put their feet on the railing in front of the stage to block the marshals from arresting her. She apologized for her clunky shoes but said they would be useful at Ludlow Street Jail. In a ninety-minute speech, she argued that the phrase "red trophy of her virginity" from the Challis article was "not half so bad as a hundred isolated passages which might be selected from the Bible."

She charged that the YMCA was a hypocritical organization and said that one day a woman could "be arrested for adultery, for kissing her own boy baby." She claimed that Comstock worked for Beecher, and that the district attorney discriminated against women. But she ended on a triumphant note, announcing that sexual freedom would "burst upon the world, through a short and sharp encounter with the forces of evil. We who are assembled in this very hall to-night, will, many of us, meet in a few months or years, to celebrate the glorious incoming of the age of a rounded-out and completed Human Freedom." When she finished, she kissed Smith, Utica, and Zula goodbye, after which a deputy marshal escorted her to a carriage. She was accompanied by Smith and her attorney Hummel. The crowd dispersed quietly and a few admirers attempted to follow the carriage to the Ludlow Street Jail, until the police told them to go home. That night, Woodhull slept in cell 12 with Blood. Warden Tracy had arranged for it.

5

——

MR. COMSTOCK GOES TO WASHINGTON

On January 1, 1873, about a week before Woodhull's Cooper Institute speech, Comstock wrote in his diary that on every day in the new year, he would to try to do "something for Jesus." The coming March would mark the end of the congressional session, and he wanted to expand federal obscenity law to include newspapers such as the *Weekly*. He had the complete support of the Committee for the Suppression of Vice, which, by the close of 1872, had paid him $1,950 for his part-time obscenity arrest work.

But the Woodhull-Claflin case continued to vex him. In the winter of 1873, McBurney and Charles E. Whitehead, a YMCA board member who had spearheaded the state obscenity law, accompanied Comstock to the nation's capital, where they introduced him to the Republican New York congressman Clinton L. Merriam. Comstock showed Merriam and several other congressmen a sampling of confiscated articles, and arranged to return a few weeks later. On January 18, he sent Merriam a letter arguing that existing postal law was not strong enough: "There are scores of men that are supporting themselves and families to-day by sending out these rubber goods, & c., through the mails, that I cannot touch for want of law."

There were already two obscenity measures pending before Congress. One, which originated with the Washington, DC, YMCA, dealt with obscene materials in the District of Columbia and the federal territories. A separate bill, with an unknown sponsor, strengthened existing penalties for obscenity peddlers. Comstock and the committee wanted to merge the two, creating a new bill that would ban obscene newspapers, plus contraception, contraception advertising, and abortion advertising. Comstock was convinced that abortions would decline if women could not find abortionists in classified ads. He was even more conservative on abortion than President Grant. That coming April, Comstock would have two providers at the Albany Medical Institute arrested, each sentenced to one year of hard labor, and Grant would pardon them, believing that the facts had been misrepresented during their trials. In his diary, Comstock would call the pardons an "infamous outrage . . . O, that I had known of this in time to have got the facts before Grant. It would not have been granted."

It was not the worst time in history to propose a strong anti-obscenity law. Both houses of Congress had been shamed by the scandal surrounding Credit Mobilier, a construction company owned by financiers who also held stock in the Union Pacific Railroad. The financiers had grown wealthy by arranging contracts between Credit Mobilier and the railroad that were unfair to the latter. As fears grew that the conspiracy would be exposed, the financiers bribed members of Congress to avoid a probe. An investigation revealed that a congressman from Massachusetts had distributed bargain-rate Credit Mobilier shares to buy the silence of fellow House members. Other beneficiaries included Vice President Schuyler Colfax, a YMCA supporter who had attended the dedication of the association's Twenty-Third Street building, and Congressman James A. Garfield, a future president of the United States. Thirteen members of Congress were involved, and two were eventually censured. In the face of such corruption, to support an anti-obscenity bill seemed morally upright.

Throughout the winter, Comstock went back and forth between Washington and New York, where the Claflin sisters' case dragged on. Their preliminary examination came up before U.S. Commissioner John Davenport on January 10, 1873. At the examination, Howe said that he would show that the arrests of the sisters were the result of "a conspiracy to put two women in jail." He repeated his assertion that if the *Weekly* was suppressed, the court would also have to suppress Shakespeare and Byron. He asked Comstock to point out a passage in the *Weekly* that he could say was obscene; the prosecutor objected, but the commissioner overruled him. Comstock identified the Challis passage, the line about Challis carrying on his finger the hymen of the girl he had allegedly raped. The fluidity of obscenity charges would prove to be a major obstacle to those tried for obscenity. A body of case law supported the idea that phrases such as "publication is too indecent to be herein set forth," used in the sisters' indictment, were sufficient for an indictment.

In court, the *Herald* reported, Howe opened the Bible to Deuteronomy: "Then shall the father of the damsel, and her mother, take and bring forth the tokens of the damsel's virginity unto the elders of the city in the gate." He asked Comstock if it was obscene; Comstock said no. Howe again cited Byron and Shakespeare and asked if Comstock was "a man of literary turn of mind." After he was asked to define obscenity, Comstock said that it was a picture or sentiment repulsive to human decency. Howe brought up the fact that Comstock used an alias, but this argument went nowhere. When Woodhull spoke, she said Comstock did not care about the morals of the United States, but wanted to suppress her and Claflin. She said they could not kill her, and she had been held up to the public as a "charlatan and prostitute" by people who said they would hound her to death. Bail was fixed at five thousand dollars.

Comstock wrote in his diary that Howe and his co-counsel "were very anxious to break down my testimony, but utterly failed. Truth was too much for them. They do not take stock very largely in that commodity."

On February 3, Commissioner Davenport rendered his decision in the Challis case: the article was obscene. However, Davenport wrote, when Congress had passed the obscenity statute under which Woodhull, Claflin, and Blood were charged, "I am quite clear that a case of this character was never contemplated." Ordinarily, he would release them. But because the questions involved had "subtlety," the prisoners were anxious, and the community sought "definite settlement," he wanted to await the action of the grand jury. For now, though, the sisters were free.

Back in Washington two days later, to garner support for his obscenity act, Comstock organized the most vivid exhibition of sex toys the capital had ever seen. In Vice President Colfax's room in the Capitol Building, Comstock set out a display on a mahogany table beneath a shimmering chandelier. The sampling probably included contraceptives; obscene engravings, plates, woodcuts, photos, books, and playing cards; abortifacients; and "rubber articles" (which could mean contraceptives or sex toys). A group of senators—and Colfax—came in to see what he had to show.

"At first, a few were present," Comstock recalled. But then, "as they became impressed with the facts presented, they went for their colleagues, until the room was well filled. Ignoring the sallies made at me by one of the Senators, I continued to state my case, until he vehemently exclaimed, 'Gentlemen, I say let us make a law to hang devils who use such means as this to corrupt the children.'"

Comstock explained to the politicians that smut dealers used aliases, along with coded phrases such as *stereoscopic view, rich and unique*, or *French*. They shared or sold customer lists, and mailed circulars directly to potential customers, some of whom were minors. According to Comstock's diary, as the senators handled the toys and cards, they declared themselves ready to grant him any law he "might ask for, if it was only within the bounds of the Constitution . . . All said they were ready to pass my bill promptly this session."

The bill introduced the phrase "obscene, lewd or lascivious" to describe illegal matter. Its first section made it a misdemeanor to sell, lend, give away, exhibit, publish, or possess obscenity, articles "of an immoral nature," or contraception. It would also be a misdemeanor to advertise the same, or to give notice of how any of the items could be purchased or obtained, or to manufacture them. Penalties were six months to five years of hard labor in the penitentiary, or fines of one hundred to two thousand dollars, plus court costs. In a revision relevant to the Claflin sisters, the second section expanded the earlier obscenity law to include "papers," meaning newspapers, and strengthened fiscal penalties for mailing them to a maximum of five thousand dollars and hard-labor sentences to a maximum of ten years. The nation's broadest, most punitive obscenity act, and the first to categorize contraception as obscene, was drafted with the specific intent of sending two highly public and highly vocal women to prison.

To gain support from additional legislators, Comstock stayed in Washington for three more weeks, during which Maggie visited him. The Committee on Appropriations set aside $3,425 to be paid to what was then called a "special agent" (a job title that would be changed in 1880 to "post office inspector") with the postmaster general promising that Comstock would be appointed. But Comstock's detractors were waging a war. Week after week, Woodhull and Claflin used their platform against him. "We should no more think of comparing Comstock, alias Beardsley, alias ——, with Torquemada," one *Weekly* article stated, referring to his frequent decoying, "than of contrasting a living skunk with a dead lion." Some felt he was hypocritical not to pursue popular newspapers and their abortionist ads. On February 15, 1873, the sisters reprinted in the *Weekly* a selection from the *Herald*'s "medical" ads, calling it a "bouquet to the Comstockians of Twenty-third Street and Fourth Avenue, as a peace-offering . . . Members of the Y.M.C.A., if you mean business, here is game worthy of your steel. Will you venture to assail it? Or are you only valorous enough to attack women?"

The sisters were not alone in their animosity toward Comstock. Writing anonymously or under pseudonyms, book and picture dealers flooded Congress with letters calling him a disreputable perjurer. Some opponents of the bill resisted the banning of contraception and contraception ads, understanding that these were not obscene. A Vermont senator, George F. Edmunds, suggested an amendment that allowed people to buy contraception "on a prescription, of a physician in good standing, given in good faith."

Frustrated, Comstock wrote of Edmunds, "Has he friends in this business that he desires to shield?" William A. Buckingham from

Norwich, Connecticut, a YMCA supporter, squelched Senator Edmunds's exemption, proposing to alter the bill at a later date. No one noticed the omission, and it was never restored.

But there were tensions brewing between Comstock and the Y. The Committee for the Suppression of Vice passed a resolution stating that if the bill became law, Comstock would not receive a salary from the YMCA. He claimed not to want one. "I do not want any fat office created," he professed in his diary, "whereby the Government is taxed or for some politician to have in a year or two. Give me the Authority that such an office confers, and thus enable me to more effectually do this work, and the Salary and honors may go to the winds."

As Comstock's act was nearing passage, the Claflin sisters were soon arrested again. Howe noted that the sisters were under $60,000 bail for an alleged misdemeanor—more than Boss Tweed, whose bail was set at $51,000 for robbing the city treasury of millions of dollars. Howe wanted decreased bail for Woodhull and Claflin and an immediate trial. The judge lowered bail to $2,000 for Blood and $1,000 each for Woodhull and Claflin, but trial delays persisted.

The case had drawn increased national attention to Woodhull, and the free love movement wanted her as a speaker, recognizing her power to draw crowds. That spring, Ezra Heywood invited her to speak at the fourth convention of the New England Labor Reform League, which aimed to establish a free society and was a platform for labor issues and women's rights. When she was announced as a speaker, the mayor of Boston tried to shut down the convention, saying that the organizers needed a license from the city. The venue, the Baptist church Tremont Temple, canceled the contract. Ezra and Angela Heywood had Woodhull speak in a different location, and she delivered her "Suppressed Speech" five times. In it, she said the defendants in her case claimed freedom for themselves and "frankly accord it to others, holding it is simply nobody's business what anybody eats, drinks, or wears, and just as little who anybody loves or how he loves, if the two parties to it are satisfied." In the end, Tremont Temple paid $250 in damages to the Labor Reform League for breaking the contract.

The speeches in Boston were a turning point in Woodhull's relationship with free love. Several participants formed a new group, the New England Free Love League, the immediate goal of which was to send her throughout New England to lecture. Angela Heywood was one of the vice presidents. The league's long-term goals were to abolish legal and compulsory marriage and create a new social system that would "guarantee to all individuals the power to exercise their right of freedom at their own cost in matters of love."

In Washington, meanwhile, Congress was consumed by Credit Mobilier. "Men assailing one another's character while legislation goes begging," Comstock wrote in his diary. "Malice fills the air. Party bitterness and venom. Loud talk of constitution, law, justice. It seems a burlesque on our Forefathers." Congress stayed in session all weekend, and as Saturday, March 1, approached Sunday, March 2, he remembered his mother's admonition to keep the Sabbath day holy. That evening, he idealized his long-dead mother, seeking to restore his nation to Victorian ideals she embodied.

Shortly before midnight, he left the Capitol Building, walking to Pennsylvania Avenue and up to his lodging house. It was frigid but he was sweating profusely, his biographer wrote, so intense was "the stress." He felt doubting and rebellious, and suddenly distrusted God. According to his biographer, he passed the night "beset by the Devil"— meaning either insomnia or his own desire to masturbate. In the wee hours of the morning, he walked a few blocks to the First Congregational Church on G Street and heard the bells ringing, but he couldn't bring himself to go in. He wanted to be alone. In his room, he read a sermon on Christian life and then dropped to his knees, praying that his bill be passed, "but over and above all, that the will of God be done." When he finally accepted that fate was not in his hands, his heart felt more peaceful than a summer's day.

In the afternoon, he ran into the Senate chaplain, John Philip Newman, at the Y. "Your bill passed the House just about midnight last night," the chaplain announced. There had been no quorum, so the rules were suspended. It passed the House with thirty votes against it. It passed the Senate with no debate and without a recorded vote.

In his speech on the floor, Congressman Merriam said, "The purity and beauty of womanhood has been no protection from the insults of this trade," referring to the smut industry. He read Comstock's letter, which included this ominous line: "There were four publishers on the 2d of last March: to-day three of these are in their graves, and it is charged by their friends that I worried them to death. Be that as it may, I am sure the world is better without them."

President Grant signed the bill into law on Monday, March 3, 1873. Comstock stayed to watch Grant's second inauguration. It was one of the coldest inauguration days on record: six degrees, with driving winds. From his balcony seat, he saw women wrapped in furs, and onlookers crowding the shop windows along Pennsylvania Avenue. That night, he attended the inaugural ball, held in a temporary wooden building at Judiciary Square, decorated with flags, banners, and flowers, and illuminated with gas jets. There were reports that the champagne froze. The canaries in cages dangling from the ceiling were too cold to sing. Comstock helped hang a painting called *Angel of Peace* in President Grant's supper room. A few days after the inauguration, Comstock was officially appointed a special agent, authorized to read and seize mail, issue search warrants, and make arrests. A staff of inspectors would help him, all expected to give him tips.

The train home was so crowded that he had to stand all the way to Philadelphia. He returned to the house in Brooklyn, arriving shortly past one in the morning on Friday. He had just turned twenty-nine. A few days later, he clipped an article about his bill from *The New York Journal of Commerce*. It said, "Something will be forgiven to a Congress which thus powerfully sustains the cause of morality."

As soon as the law was passed, the *Herald* (which had drawn the Claflin sisters' ire) removed ads for abortionists and midwives. The *Times* editorialized that Comstock had done a good job; the ads, it said, "have brought ruin to the souls and bodies of countless human beings." *The Sun* also took out its abortionist ads, and a *Sunday Mercury* reporter asked Comstock to tell the paper what should be stricken. "Who shall say anything is now impossible," Comstock mused in his diary.

Though Comstock had scored a crucial victory for the YMCA, the board was increasingly concerned about its association with the Committee for the Suppression of Vice. The reason for the concern was, in Jesup's biographer's words, "the odium which attached to those who supported Comstock." The solution was an independent group, one separate from the Y but with many board members at its helm.

On May 16, 1873, not three months after the passage of the federal Comstock law, the New York Society for the Suppression of Vice was incorporated as an independent private society by the New York legislature. Seventeen men subscribed to incorporation papers, including Jesup, Dodge, McBurney, Morgan, and William H. S. Wood, a medical publisher and future president of the Bowery Savings Bank. Comstock was not among the incorporators, indicating that the society may have been trying to limit his role. The private NYSSV would be able to enforce state and federal obscenity laws and to rely on the aid of the police.

In June 1873, New York's obscenity law was strengthened so that the possession of obscene matter was punishable with a maximum sentence of two years of hard labor and a maximum fine of five thousand dollars for each offense, as was the sale, advertising, or possession of an article to prevent conception or cause abortion. Separately, in April 1872, the legislature had enacted a law that made abortion a felony punishable by up to twenty years in prison. The new obscenity law used phrases from the national Comstock law and was the model for similar Comstock laws around the nation. In the twelve years following 1873, twenty-four state legislatures passed "little Comstock laws" modeled on the federal or New York statutes. Connecticut outlawed the act of attempting to control reproduction. Fourteen states prohibited the verbal transmission of contraceptive or abortion information.

Eleven made it a criminal offense to possess instructions for the prevention of conception. Colorado prohibited people from bringing contraceptive information into the state. Though some states allowed medical colleges, medical books, and druggists to be exempt, in seventeen states and the District of Columbia, a doctor could not discuss contraception with a patient.

Even though Comstock's federal law quickly led to increased state-level restrictions, the bigwigs at the Y remained wary of their one-time protégé. Six months after its charter was issued, the NYSSV held its first organizational meeting. Jesup chaired it, and Comstock was named chief agent and secretary. Comstock wrote this in his diary about the YMCA's decision to separate itself from the society: "None of them seemed to realize the importance of this Society except to relieve the Committee of its present burden. Only one Man thinks as I do and that is Mr. Je[s]up. He is alive."

While the Comstock law was being passed and the NYSSV incorporated, the Claflin obscenity trial was stumbling along. Facing constant trial delays and the steep cost of printing their paper, the sisters grew distraught. In a letter, Woodhull tried to mend fences with Susan B. Anthony, but no reply came forth. When the suffrage conventions opened in May 1873, Woodhull was not allowed to attend. She said she had lost her friends and believed the state was colluding with the church to vindicate Beecher's reputation.

In late June, one day after jury selection in the Beecher trial began, a Plymouth Church founder, Henry C. Bowen, came to visit Woodhull, accompanied by his sons, an investor, and a stenographer. Claflin attended the meeting, as did other family members, lawyers, and a reporter. The Plymouth group asked Woodhull to turn over documents connected with the Beecher-Tilton story. She said she would not do anything until the trial's conclusion, but if she was not punished, she would not publicize any evidence of the affair. That was that.

Three days later, as jury selection was completed, Comstock grew anxious. "The judge seems to lean toward the defend[a]nts. His ruling in this case is all in their favor," he mused. "I pray for grace to lay aside all my feelings and submit."

Comstock took the stand and had his name corrected for the record; papers such as the *Tribune* had been printing it as "Anthony J. Comstock," and he had no *J.* in his name. As Comstock took questions from the prosecutor Ambrose H. Purdy, the sisters' defense lawyer, Charlie Brooke, began to object—and Judge Samuel Blatchford upheld every objection. Purdy continually rubbed the left side of his head.

Brooke argued that the new statute had added the word *paper* to the list of obscene material, so it could be inferred that the 1872 law, in place at the time of the indictments, did not cover newspapers. Agreeing with Brooke, Blatchford disposed of the case and said that the prosecution could not be maintained. Purdy entered a nolle prosequi, declining to prosecute. Blatchford decided that the sisters were entitled to a verdict. The jury delivered a not-guilty verdict, and after court was adjourned the sisters were surrounded by friends and half smothered by bouquets.

Woodhull later petitioned the Senate and House Committees on Claims for damages, arguing that public courts had been used for private purposes. She was not awarded any money. To the *Eagle*, the prosecution had been "an Inglorious Failure." The radical world also cheered the verdict. The Heywoods' Labor Reform League passed a resolution that the suppression attempt on the *Weekly* had been an effort "to limit freedom of speech and the press, by ecclesiastical and political authorities determined to stifle investigation of industrial and social evils" to be resented by "all true friends of progress."

In his arrest logbook, Comstock called the judge's decision an "outrage." Just a few days after the acquittal, he had Peter Dwyer, a thirty-four-year-old smut dealer, arrested. Dwyer received a sentence of a hundred-dollar fine and three months' hard labor.

The year 1873 was remarkable for Comstock. He no longer needed the money from his dry goods job, and he quit. His NYSSV salary was raised by 50 percent, and, for appearance's sake, he waived his government salary. Anti-vice work was increasingly in sync with other reform movements throughout the country. Poverty and child abuse were new urban concerns. Crime was high, and children, who had no legal rights, were routinely exploited and beaten. The Society for the Prevention of Cruelty to Children, the first child protection agency in the world, was founded in late 1874, inspired in part by the 1866 founding of the American Society for the Prevention of Cruelty to Animals.

But if Comstock had some new allies in his endeavors, he had plentiful antagonists in the bookselling world. In November 1874, he learned that Charles Conroy, the Warren Street book dealer, was again in business, using aliases. Comstock arrested him in New Jersey without a warrant, for receiving letters under an assumed name. As the men approached the Newark jail in a carriage, Conroy grew desperate and attacked Comstock's face with his pocketknife, cutting through his hat. He slashed him from the temple to the chin, severing four facial arteries. Comstock brandished his revolver and threatened to shoot Conroy if he resisted further. Conroy received two years in the state prison in Trenton for this "atrocious attack on an officer." Those who hated Comstock dubbed him "Scar-faced Tony."

After the not-guilty verdict on the obscenity charge, Woodhull went on the road, advocating the sexual emancipation of women. One of her primary concerns was marital rape. To women who felt their religious duty was to submit to their husbands, she proclaimed, "I say damn such Christianity as that." Men had to understand that "the free consent of women is a necessary precedent to sexuality; and if woman will be brave and firm, this can soon be brought about." She vowed to tell the world "of all the infernal misery hidden behind this horrible thing called marriage . . . No more sexual intercourse for men who do not fully consent that all women shall be free." If women were to be liberated from men, marriage laws had to be abolished.

Income from her speeches supported the paper. Over time she developed a speaking style looser than the one she had employed in the speeches penned by Andrews. She talked of female orgasm, sex education for women, and the importance of a good sexual relationship. She delivered one of her most famous lectures, titled "Tried as by Fire, or the True and the False, Socially," one hundred fifty times consecutively, to a quarter of a million people.

The Challis libel trial staggered on until March 1874—a year and a half after the article's publication. It came to a head in the Court of General Sessions, a county court that handled jury trials in felony cases not punishable by death or life imprisonment. On the stand, Woodhull said she had published the story to show that men guilty of immorality should be ostracized. She was subjected to questions about her first and second marriages, intended to make her seem like a poor witness. Challis denied the sisters' account of the gang rape, but witnesses gave contradictory testimony.

According to the *Times*, after the jury found the sisters not guilty, the applause went on so long that it took several minutes for the courtroom to be silenced. When the noise died down, the jury's statement was read to the court. The jury men were concerned about the "character and tendency" of the sisters' teachings, but had found them not guilty to yield to them the "charitable presumption of innocence." Judge Josiah Sutherland said, "It is the most outrageous verdict ever recorded; it is shameful and infamous, and I am ashamed of the jury who rendered such a verdict." Woodhull and Claflin wept, and "the greatest excitement prevailed."

In the *Weekly*, the sisters claimed they had never held ill will toward Challis but "against the practices of a whole class of men." The verdict was "a condemnation of the ignorance in which young maidens are allowed to develop into womanhood."

Theodore Tilton was expelled from Plymouth Church and filed a complaint against Beecher for adultery. The adultery case, which opened in 1875, would last six months, become a national sensation, and end with a hung jury. Meanwhile, as a nationally famous speaker,

Woodhull no longer needed the *Weekly* as a platform. Publication ceased in June 1876.

Due in part to her attention to free love, a movement formed around abolition of marriage laws. In the spring of 1876, the free lovers and unmarried companions Leo Miller and Mattie Strickland were arrested in Waterford, Minnesota, and charged by the grand jury with "lewd and lascivious cohabitation." They wanted to be jailed as the first American couple to be convicted of violating marriage laws. But Strickland grew ill and was not tried, and Miller received only ten days in the Dakota County jail, a shorter sentence than he was hoping for.

Though there was rising support for a redefinition of marriage, Woodhull began to soften her public statements. After she gave an interview saying that she never advocated "promiscuity of sexual intercourse" and calling marriage "a most divine law" and "great responsibility," the Heywoods felt betrayed by her abandonment of the cause. "Why does the wit, so apparent when she was obsessed by 'Demosthenes,' desert her now that she is the 'chosen vessel' of Christ?" they wrote in *The Word*.

In 1877, Woodhull and Claflin moved to England. Woodhull revised her biography to excise her past as a free lover and married a wealthy banker named John Martin. She had filed for divorce from Blood the prior year on the grounds of adultery—the only grounds in New York. Claflin would go on to marry a wealthy businessman and merchant, Sir Francis Cook. Ever since they were young women, the Claflin sisters' names had been synonymous with obscenity, prostitution, and scandal, but they had always known the truth: it's never too late for reinvention.

Angela T. Heywood

6

THE BINDING FORCES OF CONJUGAL LIFE

Date:	Nov. 2, 1877
Name:	Ezra H. Heywood
Address:	Princeton, Mass.
Aliases:	Co-operative Publishing Company, Princeton, Mass.
Religion:	Free love & Spiritualist
Education:	Collegiate
Married or Single:	M
No. of Children:	3
Occupation:	Printer & Free-love agitator, Summer boarding house at Princeton
Offence:	Obscene books through the mails

The year the Claflin sisters absconded to England, Angela and Ezra Heywood received a fan letter from a reader calling himself "E. Edgewell." Edgewell requested a copy of their 1876 free love treatise, *Cupid's Yokes*. "Reason, Knowledge, and Continence," declared *Cupid's Yokes*, were to become a part of a loving bond, and the sexual instinct no longer "a savage, uncontrollable usurper." Edgewell also ordered R. T. Trall's book *Sexual Physiology* (1866), which was in its twenty-third printing and was advertised in radical newspapers such as *The Word*, which the Heywoods had been publishing for more than five years. Like others in the progressive press, the couple received commissions as "agents" for political and medical books they supported. "Press on as you are going and be sure in the end justice will be done you," the Edgewell letter read. "It is a long lane that has no turn. You have labored hard, but many eyes have followed your efforts. Truly Yours, E. Edgewell." It was postmarked "Squan Village, New Jersey," on the coast of the state, near New York.

Before the Comstock laws, many families obtained sex and contraceptive advice from frank medical books by doctors, including not only Trall's *Sexual Physiology* but also the Massachusetts traveling physician Charles Knowlton's *Fruits of Philosophy* (1832), the English-born lecturer Frederick Hollick's *The Marriage Guide* (1850), and the New York publisher E. B. Foote's *Medical Common Sense* (1858). Trall advocated various forms of contraception, including sponges; post-coital vaginal exercises; and "narcotic drugs" such as cayenne pepper, savin, and quinine. *Medical Common Sense*'s portion on contraception focused on what *not* to do—withdrawal, caustic washes, and water douches. Foote was coeditor, with his son, Dr. E. B. "Ned" Foote, Jr., of *Dr. Foote's Health Monthly*. In 1877, Comstock had sent a decoy letter to the elder Foote, who mailed a pamphlet, *Words in Pearl*, that contained two essays with information on contraceptives. He was arrested under the Comstock law and eventually fined $3,500 for a single count of obscenity. His total costs, including legal fees, reached about $5,000, or $120,000 today.

Topics in health journals such as *Dr. Foote's Health Monthly* included hygiene, homeopathy, child-rearing, pregnancy, better sex, and civil liberties. Many doctors were rationalists and believed that Americans needed sound information about human sexuality and physiology. But following the passage of the Comstock law, publishers and contraceptive suppliers (often the same people) grew nervous. Some publishers rejected ads as unfit. Products such as syringes, which could be used to administer spermicidal fluids, were advertised for "married women," and druggists warned customers that small packages would be examined at post offices. Advice literature was hit especially hard. New editions removed explicit contraceptive advice. Postbellum books were inferior and poorly organized. Distribution channels suffered, because book publishers were forced to rely on small entrepreneurs who were becoming less visible.

When Ezra received the letter requesting *Sexual Physiology* and *Cupid's Yokes*, he sent the books. The following month, he and Angela printed Edgewell's adulatory letter in *The Word*. Little did they know that E. Edgewell of Squan Village, New Jersey, was Anthony Comstock, special agent to the Post Office. When Comstock wrote to two of the best-known free lovers in the country that "many eyes have followed your efforts," surely he felt a shiver of sadistic delight.

A few months after Ezra innocently sent off the books, he and Angela presided at a New England Free Love League convention at Boston's Nassau Hall. While they were in the hall, speaking to an audience of two hundred fifty free lovers, Comstock arrived at Mountain Home, their home and inn in the bucolic town of Princeton, Massachusetts, in Worcester County. It was early in the morning on Friday, November 2, 1877, and he had a warrant for their arrest.

Four and a half years had elapsed since the passage of the Comstock law. With the support of the New York Society for the Suppression of Vice, the law's eponym had spent much of the past year focused on gamblers and organizers of illegal lotteries. But he also hated free lovers, whom he viewed as destroyers of marriage and family. He called them "an enervated, lazy, shiftless, corrupt breed of human beings, devoid of common decency, not fit companions, in many cases, to run with swine." As far as he was concerned, Nassau Street postcards and philosophical pamphlets on the meaning of marriage were an equal affront to public morals, not to mention illegal under the Comstock law. To free lovers, marriage was bondage—"love is lust; celibacy is suicide; while fidelity to marriage vows is a relic of barbarism," as Comstock would write in his book

Traps for the Young, an account of his anti-vice work. "Nothing short of turning the whole human family loose to run wild like the beasts of the forest, will satisfy the demands of the leaders and publishers of this literature."

When the young vice hunter arrived at Mountain Home, Angela's sister Flora Tilton (no relation to Theodore Tilton) was home with the two Heywood children, Vesta and Hermes. Though it is not clear whether Comstock identified himself, Flora told him that the Hey-

Ezra Heywood

woods were at a free love convention in Boston. He went from Princeton to Boston by train and took a carriage to the hall. Arriving around 8:30 p.m., he told the carriage driver to wait outside and bought a ticket to the convention.

As he entered, he saw Ezra addressing the crowd. Ezra had a long nose and chiseled jaw, wore his hair slightly below his ears, and had a dreamy, contemplative look. In Comstock's version, he heard Ezra "railing at 'that Comstock.' I took a seat without being recognized. The address was made up of abuse of myself and disgusting arguments for their cause." He examined the audience and

> could see lust in every face. After a little while the wife of the president (the person I was after) took the stand, and delivered the foulest address I ever heard. She seemed lost to all shame. The audience cheered and applauded. It was too vile; I had to go out. I wanted to arrest the leader and

end the base performance. There my man sat on the platform, puffed up with egotism. I looked at him and at the
250 eager faces, anxious to catch every word that fell from
his wife's lips.

Angela had warm eyes, a downturned mouth, and, like her sisters
Flora and Josephine, a strong brow. What were the words that fell from
her lips? In Comstock's recollection, she stood next to Ezra—a shocking
sight in and of itself—and told the audience of young and middle-aged
men, "I am going to talk to you about sexual intercourse. I mean the
fleshly coming together of men and women. Now, steady boys."

A man in the audience riffed, "Steady by jerks."

"It is not all jerks," Angela replied.

"All jerks!" the man shouted.

At that point Angela came to the front of the platform, put her
hands on her hips, and said, "Now boys, it was not all jerks in my case.
If it had been I should not have been here." In Angela's account of
what came next, she said she had used the word *penis* and that her talk
"raised a tumult of revolt among 'nice' reformers."

Angela violated everything Comstock believed about how women
should act. Several years earlier, he had attended an official function
in Washington and was so incensed by the fashionable women he'd
seen there that he called them "caricatures of everything but what
a modest lady ought not [sic] to be . . . brazen—dressed extremely
silly—[enameled] faces and powdered hair—low dresses—hair most
ridiculous and altogether most extremely disgusting to every lover of
pure, noble, modest woman. What are they? Who do they belong to?
How can we respect them? They disgrace our land and yet consider
themselves ladies."

As Comstock listened to Angela, he felt completely alone. He had
to get Ezra arrested, and he needed help. He walked outside and
searched for a policeman, in vain. When he returned, the "chieftain's wife" was continuing "her offensive tirade against common
decency. Occasionally she referred to 'that Comstock.' Her husband

presided with great self-complacency. You would have thought he was the champion of some majestic cause instead of a mob of free-lusters."

Comstock sat down again and Ezra went backstage, leaving Angela to preside. Comstock slipped after him. "Is your name Ezra Heywood?" Comstock claimed he asked.

"Yes," answered Ezra.

"I have a warrant for your arrest for securing obscene matter through the mail. You are my prisoner."

"Who are you?" Ezra asked.

"I am a deputy United States marshal."

Ezra told Comstock he wanted to address the convention, but Comstock said no. Ezra asked if he could fetch his overcoat and hat and see Angela. Comstock told him she had to come backstage, worried that the crowd would to try to interfere. A doorkeeper fetched Angela, who came in, accompanied by a pamphlet seller, and demanded to know where Comstock was taking Ezra. Charles Street Jail, Comstock said—the infamous Boston prison that would one day house the Italian anarchists Sacco and Vanzetti and a crook by the name of Charles Ponzi.

Angela told Comstock that she would adjourn the convention and accompany them to the jail. Comstock recalled that he "felt obliged, out of respect to my wife, sisters, and lady friends, to decline the kind offer of her (select) company. It was about all I wanted to do to have one of that slimy crowd in charge." She went back into the hall, and Comstock told Ezra to come along. Ezra ignored him.

Comstock took him by the shoulder and they headed downstairs. There was a yell. The conventioneers were coming after them. Comstock grabbed Ezra by the nape of the neck and they tumbled down the stairs. He wrangled his prisoner into the carriage, which took them to Charles Street Jail. As Comstock recalled, "The devil's trapper was trapped."

The freethinker and *Truth Seeker* editor D. M. Bennett, after his own arrest under the Comstock law, wrote that only someone who had "experienced the anxiety of mind and the feeling of disgrace attendant upon an arrest by Comstock, upon such charges as he prefers, can realize the utter wretchedness which such an arrest produces. There is nothing in the world like it for making one feel forsaken and booked for a term of prison life."

In Ezra's account of the night's events, Comstock never identified himself or told him where they were going—only the charge. It was not until the following morning that an officer let Ezra read the arrest warrant. That was when he learned that the "rude stranger was 'Anthony Comstock.'"

Mountain Home circa 1872

Angela and Ezra were among the most influential thinkers on and propagandists of free love, and Angela informed much of Ezra's writing. She coedited their journal, *The Word*, for its two-decade run. A friend of the couple, the radical publisher Lucian V. Pinney, wrote that to leave her out of an account of the Heywoods would be "like leaving Joan of Arc out of the history of France." He called her "the light, the life, and I am tempted to say the emotive power of the establishment."

Despite her important role in free love, Angela was overshadowed by Ezra and his very public court battles and given only passing mention in the history of the movement. Though some of Ezra's obscenity arrests and trials, over a thirteen-year period, were due to Angela's writings, Comstock never had her charged with obscenity, perhaps recognizing that as a wife and mother she was too sympathetic. (Ezra did the actual mailing of their newspaper and pamphlets, which made him indictable for the act of *sending* the material.)

Angela Fiducia Tilton was born in Deerfield, New Hampshire, on May 1, 1840. A descendant of the philosopher John Locke, she was the fourth of six children born to Daniel and Lucy Tilton. Her younger sisters, Flora and Josephine, would also become activists in anarchism, free love, and labor reform. Daniel was a farmer, and all three girls worked when they were children. When Angela was ten, she left home to serve as a domestic, later working in a factory and a sweatshop and as a dressmaker, barn cleaner, cook, public library attendant, and milkmaid. Her agrarian and working-class background gave her everlasting sympathy for the poor.

Angela's mother, Lucy, despised formal education but was an avid reader and follower of politics. According to Angela, Lucy taught her "never to defer to doctors, lawyers, clergymen but meet them simply as persons." Angela inherited her mother's disdain for intellectual snobbery. Ezra and Angela's daughter Psyche (who had chosen to go by her middle name, Ceres) wrote as an adult that her mother's "whole soul revolted against the superciliousness and pretension of superiority by the rich and 'cultured' over the skilled workers, who knew more, it might be, in a day, of real useful knowledge, than they would know in a life-time."

According to Angela, Lucy Tilton taught her children to respect and study sex. One day, a stallion was brought to the farm to mate with a mare. Lucy arranged the chairs by the window so the children could watch, explaining the proceedings. Angela's own older children were present at or soon after the births of her younger, so that, as she described, "they might have palpable evidence, and individually sense, at what cost human beings are produced. To the minutest particulars, both before and after, I informed them of what takes place on such occasions and how; of the methods, experiences, processes involved in creating them."

Though Angela's sympathy to free love may have been due to her mother's influence, she became an adherent during abolition. After joining an abolitionist church, she attended anti-slavery lectures by the journalist and reformer William Lloyd Garrison and the poet Ralph Waldo Emerson. She met Ezra through the movement and they married in Boston on June 5, 1865, when she was twenty-five and he was thirty-five. They were skilled writers and debaters, unabashed and unambivalent proponents of free thought. Angela's critique of marriage, which she would articulate dozens of times in *The Word*, likened the institution to slavery. Marriage was "the auction-block of primitive sale and slavery of woman to man, as unreliable and ill binding as such forsaken-fidelity to personal Integrity could permit"; its fruits were "prostitution, abortions, infanticide and thousands of skulking fathers."

Ezra had attended Brown University, receiving a master of arts and then entering the divinity school. Stephen Pearl Andrews described him as "an iconoclast—a hero of ideas, a pronounced, decided and very distinctiv[e] character . . . the John Brown of the social revolution." Ezra had hopes of becoming a Congregational minister but became interested in abolition after hearing Garrison speak. Phebe Jackson, a friend of Garrison's wife, met Ezra when he was living at a boardinghouse near Brown. An early model for Ezra of a strong, opinionated woman, Phebe awakened his social consciousness. He left the university to become a traveling lecturer for the Massachusetts Anti-Slavery Society.

Angela and Ezra settled in Worcester, where their first child, Vesta, was born in 1869. They moved to nearby Princeton in 1871, building a home on the corner of the common with money from Ezra's brother Samuel. The house had a mansard roof and an L-shaped wing at one side. Princeton was an agricultural town, accessible by train, and hosted summer visitors from surrounding cities. Offering stunning views of

Mount Wachusett, it featured hostels with wide porches and rocking chairs.

In May 1872, the month Woodhull was nominated for president and a year before the Comstock law's passage, the Heywoods published the first issue of their journal, *The Word*. The paper was four pages long and devoted to "abolition of speculative income, of woman's slavery and the war government." The Heywoods supported the free use of land; the extinction of interest, rent, dividends, and profit except for work done; the abolition of the railway and other corporations; and the repudiation of debts. Like the Claflin sisters, they believed in labor rights, and their antipathy toward marriage was based in part on concerns that it harmed women financially.

The couple assembled an impressive group of *Word* contributors, including Elizabeth Cady Stanton, John Humphrey Noyes, Stephen Pearl Andrews, and Henry Ward Beecher. The paper soon came to focus on free love, which the Heywoods defined as "the regulation of the affections according to conscience, taste, and judgment of the individual, in place of their control by law." Similar publications followed in the ensuing years; Moses Harman, for example, launched *Lucifer, the Light-Bearer* (originally called *The Valley Falls Liberal*) in Valley Falls, Kansas, in 1880.

The Heywoods named their publishing house the Co-operative Publishing Company. Angela's sisters became agents for the paper, selling it for a commission. Regular ads for "canvassing agents," male and female, appeared in *The Word*: "Girls and Women, Boys and Men can win needed funds, and quicken people to regenerating thought, by aiding us in spreading reformatory ideas. Working Girls tired of housework, shop and factory life, will find this a healthful and remunerative avocation." The idea was that the paper itself could be a tool of economic empowerment. In a series of letters on book canvassing, likely written by Angela, prospective "lady agents" were warned that if a potential male customer became too flirtatious, the agent should "call his idle curiosity and rising heats to order" and "fix his attention by the serious sincerity of your manner."

Angela likely cowrote many of the articles in the early editions of *The Word*, though much of the paper was unbylined. One piece credited to her took issue with the free love advocate Moses Hull, who had argued that it was better for a husband to visit a prostitute than to force unwanted sex on a wife who did not desire him. Angela wrote, "Is Mr. Hull's sister, mother, wife, or daughter the regular prostitute to whom he refers, or is it some other less fortunate woman who he so coolly damns to the lecherous uses of his brother man?"

Like Woodhull, Angela was a Spiritualist. Andrews called her "in a very high degree mediumistic, inspirational and prophetic." While Ezra was methodical and moderate, Angela was intuitive. "She has visions, hears voices, and dreams dreams," wrote their friend Pinney, "and she is at times a whirlwind of words."

To support their publishing ventures, the Heywoods turned their house into Mountain Home, a forty-two-room inn that they rented to agitators and Spiritualists during the summer. A visitor wrote, "The large airy rooms, abundant, wholesome fare, the neatness and quiet, and the attractive hospitality, are such, as not only to promote health, but mental and spiritual recreation, rest and reinvigoration." All of the children—Vesta; Hermes (1874); Psyche Ceres, who was told to give her name as "Psyche Ceres Soul and Body Heywood" (1881); and Angelo (1883)—would eventually work in the inn. (Angela dressed Hermes in girls' clothes and let his hair grow long; a Princeton neighbor was astonished when she learned that the little girl with whom she had been playing was a boy.)

Angela managed Mountain Home, which meant she brought in the money that paid for *The Word* and the pamphlets. She prided herself on being the drudge and housewife. In traditional marriages, she wrote, the wife was a serf and the husband was "king of brutes." In her own marriage, in contrast, "such bondage is foreign to my girl and woman ideas; while SERVING I always felt to be royally worthy."

Though guests at Mountain Home respected and liked her, she was unpopular with some Princeton residents. On Sunday mornings she chose to wash and hang her clothes as Princetonians gathered for church services across the Common. But the Heywoods were well-liked enough that the town's communion wine and bread were kept in Mountain Home. Contrary to Comstock's assumptions about free lovers, the Heywoods appear to have had a happy, monogamous marriage. Unlike Woodhull, who claimed to be a varietist, they were exclusivists. A farmer in Princeton told a reporter, "They're no more lovers in their conduct than I am. I believe they are as true to each other as any married couple in the world ever was."

Still, perhaps because of their monogamy, they supported varietists, writing in *Cupid's Yokes* that "sexual love is not restricted to pairs" and that love was not satisfied by one partner. "The one-love theory, based on jealousy, comes not from loving hearts, but from the greedy claimant. The law of marriage 'worketh wrath'; provokes jealousy; unites unmatched natures and sunders matched ones; and making no provision for sexual appetite, causes disease, masturbation, prostitution, and general licentiousness."

Their treatise on women's rights, *Uncivil Liberty: An Essay to Show the Injustice and Impolicy of Ruling Woman Without her Consent*, was published in 1872. Credited to Ezra but likely cowritten by Angela, *Uncivil Liberty* sold eighty thousand copies. The dedication page read, TO THE WOMAN WITH WHOM THIS AUTHOR HAS THE HONOR TO SHARE A HOME, THIS ESSAY IS RESPECTFULLY INSCRIBED. Calling for political enfranchisement of women, the authors argued that women were morally superior. As many men already believed women to be "purer" than men, wouldn't the woman vote lead to sound political policies? The Heywoods contended that the act of voting required "intellect, conscience, character." Yet a twenty-one-year-old "boy" could vote, but not his mother. If women had the vote, their morality would make the world a better place, delivering more reformers into office.

Angela's first lengthy credited contribution to *The Word* was an 1876 essay called "Woman's Love: Its Relations to Man and Society," in which she contended that wage inequality forced women into prostitution. If women could be spared economic dependency, they could marry for love. Unequal wages were "a devouring usurpation of man over woman" that enabled a man to feel less responsible for sex, when he "should be held to be so." Girls' lives, she contended, were "not matters of choice, but of persuasion and compulsion."

A few months later, she wrote an essay called "Love and Labor," again advocating for women's economic equality:

> When hungry, I have passed a baker's shop, and made half a dinner on the sweet scent of bread below. Did it cost me nothing to resist the warm, rich, employing baker, who would have taken me to his arms and given me of his abundance? Though she have the honesty of toil in her nerve and habit, yet, shut into the dark alcove of inopportunity, is it strange that a girl goes to the winning person of man . . . Moved by the cold, calculating impulses of business, many men now marry for money, and many women for a home, with inevitable disaster to both.

Angela believed that egalitarian love could conquer sexism. In viewing free love and labor as related, both she and Ezra were individualist anarchists. Society could be bettered not through legislation (such as alcohol prohibition) but through increased humanity. Virtue could not be imposed by the government or by other people. Only when individuals controlled sex, through equality, free love, and abolition of marriage, would women have happier, fairer unions and access to contraceptive information. This last idea—the belief that all human beings are sovereign and that no law should privilege or restrict people based on race, gender, or religion—has been called "individualist feminism."

Though later sex radicals, including Ida C. Craddock, viewed women as maternal and less sexual than men, Angela hated stereotypes that depicted women as sex-hating and dispassionate: "If she, as woman, duly gives to man who cometh in unto her, as freely, as equally, as well as he gives her, how shall she be abashed or ashamed of the innermost?" She believed that a woman possessed a "lady-nature," and that "it is the very great *everything* she wants to do *with* man."

Angela and Ezra presented a lecture titled "Love and Marriage" throughout Massachusetts, and she spoke plainly about sexuality. Ezra called her a "coming teacher of wild boys and infuriated husbands" with "well-chosen words and impressive appeals." Naturally, both Heywoods despised Comstock and took frequent aim at him in their paper. Andrews wrote that the Comstock law "outraged the ideas of Mrs. Heywood. She is also equally outraged at the public, and most of all with the women themselv[e]s, for tolerating such legislation." When Comstock tried to organize an anti-vice society in Boston in early 1875, the Heywoods called it "a blind to divert attention from the immoral practices of clergymen" and his law "an outrage on popular liberty."

Cupid's Yokes, published in 1876, harshly criticized the Comstock law and the evils of marriage while advocating women's rights and male continence. The subtitle was *The Binding Forces of Conjugal Life: An Essay to Consider Some Moral and Physiological Phases of Love and Marriage, Wherein Is Asserted the Natural Right and Necessity of Sexual Self-Government*. In the book, which in one estimate sold as many as two hundred thousand copies, the authors defined as altruistic the bonds of affection, or "Cupid's yokes," because the individual in love defers selfish interests to the greater welfare of the loving relationship. In marriage, the bonds were "unreasonable, unconstitutional, unnatural and void" laws and vows.

The Heywoods opposed artificial contraceptives, which they considered "unnatural, injurious or offensive," and which they, like Woodhull, believed let men off the hook. The egalitarian solution to unwanted pregnancy was for women to tell their husbands when they didn't want to have sex. An enlightened man would listen, and obey. Furthermore, a man who loved intelligently would consume less "passional heat" and, as a result, be "a genial, civil, and serviceable being."

Men who could control their desire would not rape their wives, instead viewing them as peers and partners. And if an enlightened couple procreated unintentionally, then the child was meant to come into the world. "More impressive than the theological 'Judgement-day,'" *Cupid's Yokes* stated, "will be the tribunal before which diseased and crime-cursed children summon guilty parents to answer for the sin-begetting use of their reproductive powers."

Who were these "diseased and crime-cursed" children? Like Woodhull, the Heywoods believed in hereditarianism: the idea that fewer unwanted children would purify humanity, because unwanted children were morally or physically defective. Involuntary motherhood produced vice, and controlled conception could abolish it. Beyond this misunderstanding of genetics, Ezra did in fact hold racially prejudiced ideas. In 1877, he wrote that the "foreign element (mostly Irish and French Catholic) is gaining rapidly on all grades of native Protestant stock!"

On sexual health, he and Angela were enlightened and forward-thinking, promoting the idea that women should take good care of themselves throughout pregnancy for the health of the baby. As for contraception, the single form advocated in *Cupid's Yokes* was continence, with other methods, including rhythm, dismissed as "disgusting." Abortion was "a murderous practice . . . unworthy of Free Lovers." The age gaps between the four Heywood children—five, seven, and two years—indicate that the couple probably practiced male continence during some or all of their marriage.

Intriguingly, free lovers who supported continence were not philosophically far from the Comstockians who defended Victorian ideals. Both camps believed in forms of control, though the free lovers thought a person should control him- or herself, while the Comstockians believed that *God* should wield this control. Both idealized a form of "repression" through abstention from orgasm. E. B. Foote, Sr., pointed out in a letter to the *Times* that both Comstock and health editors were engaged in what each regarded "as humanitarian reforms.

He is trying to make people better by reformatory measures, and I by formatory processes; he playing the role of the moralist, and I the part of both moralist and physiologist."

Though the male continence portion of *Cupid's Yokes* was incendiary, it appears to have been the portion on Comstock's law that drew the agent's attention. A progressive movement was forming around several prominent court cases involving radical editors. In Foote's 1876 trial over mailing a contraception pamphlet (*United States v. Foote*), a U.S. Circuit Court judge ruled that an obscenity indictment did not need to give a definite or detailed description of the matter, and that both a written slip of paper sent in reply to a query and sealed, first-class mail were indictable.

Fueled in part by fury over this outcome, a group of liberals opposed to state and federal Comstock laws founded the National Liberal League (NLL) in 1876 in Philadelphia. The league also opposed the National Reform Association, a Presbyterian-led group that sought a constitutional amendment declaring that God reigned over civil government and Christ over all nations. The NLL's freethinking members, who supported separation of church and state, freedom of religion, and freedom of political belief, called the Comstock statutes "subversive of the grand principles of personal and universal liberty upon which our government was founded." The founding document, sent to thousands of doctors and freethinkers across the country, included a petition to overturn Comstock laws.

Ezra wrote in *The Word* that Comstock's pursuit of Woodhull, Foote, and others inspired him to publish *Cupid's Yokes*, which described Comstock as "*a religious mono-maniac*, whom the mistaken will of Congress and the lascivious fanaticism of the Young Men's Christian Association have empowered to use the Federal Courts to suppress free inquiry." It specifically mentioned the Claflin sisters' "Brooklyn Scandal" and encouraged Americans to try "to repeal the National Gag-Law which [Comstock] now administers." Enough supporters agreed that by the conclusion of 1877, Ezra had mailed out a total of five hundred thousand Co-operative Publishing Company titles, one for every ninety-two people in the United States.

When Angela and Ezra were typesetting *Cupid's Yokes*, he remarked to her, "Either Comstockism or this book will go under." He was right.

On November 13, 1877, in response to Comstock's decoy "E. Edgewell" letter, Ezra was arraigned for mailing *Cupid's Yokes* and Trall's *Sexual Physiology*. Comstock used pseudonyms to order everything from pamphlets to contraceptives. His pseudonyms would come to include "Jerry Baxter," "Ella Bender," "E. Semler," "S. Bender," "E. W. Jones," and "J. G. Phillips." In some cases he concocted entire families, individuals sharing a last name, living in the same town. Though his letters were controversial, as decoying was illegal, Comstock defended them as valid, calling them "'test' letters." In *Traps for the Young*, he contended that the real decoy in his cases was *"the circular, advertisement or notice sent out by the vender* to allure youth from the paths of virtue . . . The officer's letter does not cause a scamp to do an act he is not anxiously waiting an opportunity to do."

As the trial date approached, Angela grew increasingly upset. She wrote to her friend the New England Free Love League officer Elizabeth Denton that the "case of the truth as against Christianity becomes to be tried before the Grand Jury of our collective human wits, though the tide in many respects at present is heavily against us, in outward appearances." She added, "I must go wash now, my sleeves are up ready, while I am writing this. I was going straight to the tub but got pushed into the study by the 'fates,' of whatever order that or they may be." Even while coping with the potential imprisonment of her husband, she was busy with housework.

Radicals were infuriated by Ezra's arrest. Foote circulated a petition to overturn the federal Comstock law. "Our short-sighted politicians and statesmen have no right to make a sort of detective and police organization of the post office," he wrote in his *Monthly*. The new American president, Rutherford B. Hayes, inaugurated just six months earlier, was seen as a potential ally. A former Republican congressman and governor of Ohio, he had lost the popular vote but won in the Electoral College, and Democrats agreed that he could be elected if he withdrew U.S. troops from the South, ending Reconstruction.

For Comstock and the NYSSV, Ezra's arrest was a victory. "Another class of publications issued by free-lovers and free-thinkers is in a fair way of being stamped out," Comstock wrote in the NYSSV *Annual Report*. "Under a plausible pretense, men who raise a howl about 'free press,' 'free speech,' etc., ruthlessly trample under feet the most sacred things, breaking down the altars of religion, bursting asunder the ties of home, and seeking to overthrow every social restraint." In his view, free lovers were attacking Victorian values: religion, the home, the family.

After he arrested Ezra, Comstock went to the *Truth Seeker* offices in New York and arrested the publication's editor, Bennett, whom he had lured with a decoy letter into mailing a scientific pamphlet titled *How Do Marsupials Propagate Their Kind?* and a tract called *An Open Letter to Jesus Christ*. The charges were obscenity and blasphemy. Aided by other freethinkers, Bennett was able to get the charges dismissed.

Ezra's trial opened soon thereafter, on January 22, 1878, with Judge Daniel Clark of the U.S. Circuit Court in Boston presiding. Angela felt that few members of the public were sympathetic; their encouragement had "no vital spirit of accord." She realized that her sex writing was considered by most people "a real vulgarism, unwomanly & unfit for their ears," and she was particularly incensed by the women in the courtroom who judged her as "a pitiable object of sex-suppression." Other trial attendees told her that her purpose was to be impregnated "by as many men as could cause my womb to teem with babies' faces."

The district attorney declared that the jury was to answer only two questions: Had Ezra mailed the works? and Were they obscene? Only the titles were delineated in the indictment, although the jury had access to the documents in deliberations. Questioned by J. F. Pickering, one of Ezra's lawyers, Comstock acknowledged sending the Edgewell letter after being alerted by the Princeton post office that *Cupid's Yokes* was obscene. Pickering asked if Comstock had been seeking reprisal for the Heywoods' attacks in *The Word* and *Cupid's Yokes*. Comstock said he was not aware of any such attacks when he commenced the proceedings.

Though Pickering called twenty witnesses to testify on Ezra's behalf, only four were allowed, Angela was excluded, and none could speak to the intent of the two books. In his closing argument, Pickering said that the books were useful and moral, and that the government had not proven that Ezra had actually mailed the books himself. The district attorney responded that free love was dangerous to children, and read excerpts from *Cupid's Yokes* to illustrate his point.

The judge instructed the jury to consider the effect of the mailing of *Cupid's Yokes* on a happy family with happy children. He quoted two paragraphs from one of the books—no record exists of which ones—and asked what could be more indecent. The men of the jury found that *Sexual Physiology* was not obscene, but that *Cupid's Yokes* was. Ezra's lawyers filed motions to set the verdict aside, based on the unconstitutionality of the Comstock law. As a concession, Judge Clark postponed the hearing for several months, because the U.S. Supreme Court was hearing a similar case, *Ex parte Jackson*, which challenged the constitutionality of the law on free speech grounds.

In 1878, *Ex parte Jackson* found that although sealed mail could not be searched without a warrant, the Comstock law itself was constitutional. *Jackson* was a major victory for Comstock, who announced proudly to his YMCA brethren in the *Annual Report* that constitutionality "has long been a mooted question, and one from which the enemy has long drawn comfort, and now by their good service has been settled in our favor."

However, in the spring of 1877, several months before Ezra's arrest, an obscenity case had been tried in England involving the book *Fruits of Philosophy*. The publishers and reformers Charles Bradlaugh and Annie Besant had sought to test obscenity law using the book, which had been written by a Massachusetts country doctor more than forty years earlier. Between their arrest and trial, the couple sold more than 125,000 copies. They were sentenced to six months' imprisonment and fines, but their conviction was overturned on appeal because the indictment had not specified which words were obscene.

Ezra's lawyers decided to waive the question of constitutionality and instead base their appeal on the precedent of Bradlaugh-Besant: his indictment should be thrown out, they argued, because it had failed to specify the alleged obscene matter. The court denied the motion. Pickering pled for the lightest penalty under the law, citing Ezra's good character and sincerity. On June 25, 1878, Ezra's lawyers appealed to the U.S. Supreme Court, but Justice Nathan Clifford denied the appeal. Ezra was sentenced to a fine of $100 (about $2,500 today) and two years in Dedham Jail, in Norfolk County, Massachusetts.

During the sentence, the couple fell behind in their mortgage payments to Ezra's brother Samuel, who opened foreclosure proceedings. Mountain Home went unrented, and Angela took Vesta and Hermes, both under ten, to live with family in Boston. Mountain Home was sold to Samuel at auction in July 1878. Their income from subscriptions and book sales was not enough to make ends meet, and Ezra appealed to *Word* readers for donations.

In prison, Ezra wove bottoms for chairs. He and Angela wrote each other nearly every day. He created a calendar system based on free love: the year the New England Free Love League was founded, 1873, became "Y.L. 1," for "Year of Love 1." *Word* editions from 1879 on were dated according to the "Y.L." calendar: "Y.L. 7," "Y.L. 8," and so on.

A Massachusetts liberal, friend of Ezra, and anti-Comstocker, Alfred E. Giles, wrote that "the articles in [The] Word, which induced [Ezra's] prosecution under the Comstock statutes, were not written by Mr. Heywood but by Mrs. H; and his appreciation of her rights to express her views in the Word, were so delicate that though he would have for himself prefer[r]ed a less objectionable phraseology, he always yielded to her wishes and peculiarities and never disclosed her authorship of them."

After the trial, a reader wrote to Angela that there was "nothing on the earth so low and contemptible as the obscenity that flows from your pen." Initially hurt, Angela developed a tough skin, writing, "Many a thrust which I was 'fated' to suffer pierced me to the heart, while other expressions were simply laughable . . . But *now* I cannot be made to so crisp before any man's or woman's pressure of thought, look, word or deed towards me, but find myself able to work with ease & pleasure at dissecting, analyzing, classifying & recording . . . the right and purpose of way, the actions and reactions of the Penis & Womb." She was impoverished, married to an incarcerated man, and raising two children on her own, but Angela Fiducia Tilton Heywood was discovering her voice.

Madame Restell's arrest, New York Illustrated Times, *February 23, 1878*

7

THE WICKEDEST WOMAN IN NEW YORK

Date:	Feb. 11, 1878
Name:	Ann Lohman
Address:	5th Avenue, N.Y. City
Age:	65
Aliases:	Madame Restell
Nationality:	English
Religion:	?
Education:	Common
Married or Single:	Widow
Occupation:	Abortionist
Offence:	Selling articles for abortion and preventing conception

In January 1878, a few months after attending the free love convention in Boston, Comstock took up a legal challenge in New York. His law had passed nearly five years before, and he had not procured the arrest of one female abortionist on his home turf. This was despite the fact that even abortion opponents called it "a regularly-established money-making trade" throughout the United States.

In 1875, the state Comstock law had been strengthened, allowing NYSSV members to act as police officers—empowering them to arrest alleged violators and bring them before courts or magistrates. But most of those arrested were men, and most abortionists were women, who made more sympathetic defendants. Evidence was difficult to obtain; patients, even those who were injured by the procedure, did not want to go public, and abortionists used aliases, making them hard to find. Even when abortionists were prosecuted, many were found not guilty, while others received suspended sentences and fines. Abortionists' "victims," Comstock wrote in an early *Annual Report* of the society, "are numbered by thousands. But so resolute are the victims to conceal their own lapse from chastity, and so wary and skilled in deception are these self-styled doctors, that few are detected and punished."

Comstock needed a high-profile abortion case, in New York, that would reveal abortionists as the amoral, money-grubbing evildoers he believed they were. By the early 1840s, the decade of his birth, the most famous abortionist in New York was Madame Restell, or Ann Lohman. Known as "the wickedest woman in New York," she was so closely linked to abortion that some referred to the procedure as "Restellism." Her first arrest came in 1841, after a patient named Ann Maria Purdy died in her care, though it was her husband, Charles Lohman, who performed Purdy's abortion. (Charles began as her assistant, preparing nostrums, before he began to provide abortions himself.) The prosecutor in the Purdy case said that "lust, licentiousness, sedition and abortion would be the inevitable occurrences of every day" if Ann Lohman was not stopped. Though a jury found her guilty, the case was overturned in the state supreme court on the grounds that Purdy's dying statements were inadmissible.

The case transformed Madame Restell into a celebrity. In 1844, she appeared in *The Lady in Black: A Story of New York Life, Morals, and Manners*, a novel by Thomas Low Nichols. In "this virtuous New York," he wrote, "we have Restell and others of the same calling. I have watched her to-night and have seen more than one cheek turn pale as death as she passed smilingly around the room."

In 1847, Lohman was prosecuted yet again, charged with second-degree manslaughter for performing an abortion after quickening. The year before, Maria Bodine, an unmarried servant who had been impregnated by her employer, came to Lohman at six months pregnant. Lohman ruptured the amniotic sac and administered pills to cause contractions. Following the abortion, Bodine stayed in bed in a private room, after which Lohman gave her money for travel and taught her how to drain her breast milk. After Bodine contracted pain, chills, a descended uterus, a weak back, trembling, and a burning sensation in her hands, and confessed her abortion to a doctor, Lohman was arrested, convicted, and sent to Blackwell's Island. She was released in 1849.

The Purdy and Bodine stories were disturbing, but until the 1840s, most ordinary Americans held a benign view of abortion. In the early part of the nineteenth century, couples seeking abortions went to (invariably male) doctors. Afterward, the couple would maintain the doctor as their "regular" physician, or family practitioner. But if a doctor refused to perform the procedure, couples turned to "irregulars," who included homeopaths, eclectics (healers who used botanicals), and midwives—mostly women. These irregulars, self-taught or educated at homeopathic colleges, believed in women's rights, including a woman's right to practice medicine.

To understand the mid-nineteenth-century crackdown on abortion, one must understand it as a business that had been dominated by women. Abortion was a specialty and also a service in high demand; the rate had risen from about one abortion for every twenty-five or thirty live births between 1800 and 1830 to one out of every five or six live births during the 1850s and 1860s. As the historian Carroll Smith-Rosenberg has chronicled, to break into the business, male doctors lobbied to found medical societies, create specialization, and make medical school attendance a prerequisite for licensing. If they could control and regulate abortion, they could corner the market on women patients, taking the trade away from women's doctors and women doctors alike.

In 1857, a Boston gynecologist named H. R. Storer persuaded the American Medical Association (AMA) to form a committee on abortion. Equating the procedure with infanticide and murder, he reserved special disdain for those middle- and upper-class women who sought it. Such a woman, the AMA committee wrote in one report, "becomes unmindful of the course made out for her by Providence" and "overlooks the duties imposed on her by the marriage contract." Storer urged other doctors to lobby for stricter abortion laws. At the 1859 AMA convention, an antiabortion resolution was adopted. Clergy joined the call for change, and states created stiffer penalties for patients and abortionists. The medical world as we know it—with medical schools, specializations, and licensing groups—came into existence due to male doctors' fear of being replaced by women homeopaths and midwives. The new American doctor was a specialist, and a man.

The abortion system became two-tiered, with lifesaving abortions ("therapeutic exemptions") offered to middle-class women but not poor women. Those who needed to resort to "irregulars" were now hard-pressed to find them. And yet "women's doctors" continued to practice, doing what they could to stay out of prison. This was Comstock's concern in the first few weeks of 1878.

Ann Trow was born in Painswick, England, on May 6, 1811. When she was about sixteen years old, she married a tailor, Henry Summers. They had a baby, Carrie, in 1830, and then immigrated to New York, where Henry died in 1831 of bilious fever. Ann supported herself and her daughter as a seamstress and in 1836 met Charles Lohman, a freethinker and printer for *The New York Herald*. A Russian immigrant of German ancestry, Charles was tall, handsome, and educated. They were married about a year later.

The Lohmans lived on Chatham Street, on Printing-House Square, where Ann began working for their next-door neighbor, William Evans, an abortionist and druggist who sold quack medicines. Customers often came in for contraceptives, and she developed and began to sell an herbal powder. It must have been somewhat effective, because soon she was able to give up sewing and devote herself to selling her concoction. Though she left behind no letters or diaries, her marriage to a freethinker most likely amplified her initial openness to, and curiosity about, helping women.

She worked out of an office at 148 Greenwich Street from 1839 to 1847, and one on Chambers Street from 1848 until the late 1860s. She also practiced with Charles at 129 Liberty Street. The Lohmans may have learned about abortion from an abortionist or a midwife, from Evans, or from a woman who assisted them in their Greenwich Street office. Ann's first ad, which appeared in *The Sun* in March 1839, was written by Charles. Addressed TO MARRIED WOMEN, it queried:

> Is it moral for parents to increase their families, regardless of consequences to themselves, or the well being of their offspring, when a simple, easy, healthy, and certain remedy is within our control? The advertiser, feeling the importance of this subject, and estimating the vast benefit resulting to thousands by the adoption of means prescribed by her, (introduced by the celebrated midwife and female physician, Mrs. Restell, the grandmother of the advertiser,) and who has made this subject her particular and especial study, has opened an office, where married females can obtain the desired information.

Other ads claimed that "Mrs. Restell" or, later, "Madame Restell" (a name concocted by the Lohmans) had been a physician for thirty years in Vienna and Paris.

A patient who came to her Greenwich Street office would walk up a street of redbrick Federal-style homes with steep roofs. At 148 Greenwich, she would be met by an elderly female assistant. The assistant would lead her past a curtain into a private, dimly lit study with anatomical displays. There, Ann would greet her and discuss her condition, sell her preventive powders, and instruct her in their use. Charles usually kept to the background. As was common for women abortionists of the time, Ann also offered lectures on feminine hygiene and family limitation, or the benefits of smaller families.

In other words, the wickedest woman in New York was also a sex educator.

Though pennyroyal, cedar, and tansy—the ingredients used in contraceptive powders—had spermicidal qualities, some women returned after using Ann's concoction to say they had become pregnant. Masters of branding, the Lohmans would then sell them "Mrs. Restell's Female Monthly Pills." They were said to regulate menses but were actually abortifacients. If the pills were unsuccessful, she offered surgical abortions on a sliding scale from twenty to one hundred dollars.

In 1864, the Lohmans moved into a palatial four-story brownstone at 1 East Fifty-Second Street, at the northeast corner of Fifty-Second Street and Fifth Avenue, which they had built to vex the archbishop of St. Patrick's Cathedral—then under construction just blocks away—who had preached against Mrs. Restell. The parlor floor contained a hall of marble and mirrors, three parlors decorated with yellow, satin wall-hangings, and French mirrors in mosaic gilding. The bathroom was carpeted, with a marble basin and velvet settee.

In May 1867, Ann relocated most of her business to Fifth Avenue, hanging a silver plate with the word OFFICE on the iron railing. The basement office was furnished in green and featured lace curtains, a sewing machine, and a mantelpiece with bronze figurines. Her customers were upper class and wealthy and paid two hundred to two thousand dollars per case, at a time when abortions outside the city cost about ten dollars. She sold her French Female Pills for one dollar, extra-strength for five. Her income was estimated to be thirty thousand dollars a year.

She rode in her carriage in Central Park, her horses decked with silver harnesses, she wrapped in ermine robes if it was cold. At her housewarming party, she wore a Parisian gown with silver brocade, a crown of diamonds in her hair and more at her neck. She was the most visible symbol of abortion in New York—rich, famous, and seemingly unrepentant—and as far as Comstock was concerned, the police were looking the other way.

In the early 1870s, two New York abortionists, Thomas Lookup Evans and Michael A. A. Wolff, were convicted of manslaughter and attempted manslaughter and sent to Sing Sing prison in Westchester County. The *Times*, which had been instrumental in reporting on Boss Tweed's corruption, realized that abortion could be an eye-grabbing investigative topic. In August 1871, a reporter named Augustus St. Clair, accompanied by a female companion, visited a handful of abortionists and wrote an exposé headlined "The Evil of the Age."

St. Clair visited Charles Lohman, who was practicing as "Dr. A. M. Mauriceau" in an office downtown. (Either Charles Lohman or Ann's brother Joseph Trow had used that name to publish a sex education book called *The Married Woman's Private Medical Companion* in 1847.) St. Clair wrote that "Mauriceau" was "of comely exterior, about fifty years of age, and of bland and courteous manner." Charles said he could relieve a lady of a difficulty, and that she would have elegant accommodations uptown. St. Clair noted that Madame Restell was said to be the wife of Dr. Mauriceau.

The reporter went uptown to call on Ann. After he and his companion asked her if she could "relieve a lady of a physical difficulty," she offered to sell them some pills. Perhaps her suspicions had been raised, because she said she could do no more. "All the parties interested," St. Clair wrote, "have the strongest motives to unite in hushing the scandal."

A few days after the *Times* ran "The Evil of the Age," a baggage master at the Hudson River Railroad depot on Thirtieth Street discovered the body of a nude, redheaded girl, Alice Bowlsby, stuffed in a trunk. One of the abortionists in St. Clair's article, a German Jew named Jacob Rosenzweig, was charged with murder: he had given Bowlsby an abortion, she had died, and he tried to get rid of the body. In the next few months, two additional abortionists were arrested for patient deaths, and one was imprisoned. Madame Restell and Dr. Mauriceau's ads disappeared from the *Herald*, although they soon returned.

By early 1878, Ann Lohman was sixty-six and a widow. Charles had died of kidney disease; she was estranged from her daughter, Carrie, but lived in the Fifth Avenue mansion with her adult grandchildren, Caroline and Charlie. Around ten in the morning on January 28, the basement doorbell rang. When Lohman opened the door, she saw a barrel-chested man with red side-whiskers. "Is Madame Restell in?" he asked.

She showed him into her office and asked what his business was. After some discussion of contraception, she said she had a medicine to offer. From another room, she fetched a package containing a ruby-colored fluid, pills, and instructions. She told him that it worked in nine cases out of ten, but that if it didn't, the woman could come to her for an operation and return home on the train the same day. She said the procedure cost two hundred dollars. The man paid her ten dollars for the package and left.

About a week and a half after the first visit, the red-haired man appeared again. She asked about the medicine, and he implied that his friend had miscarried naturally. He told her he wanted medicine to prevent conception, and she brought out a vaginal syringe and a bottle that contained powders in white papers. She demonstrated how to use the syringe, dissolving the powders in water and drawing them into the syringe. "After you do that," she said, "the girl wants to stand up and place this up the parts." She demonstrated how the girl should raise one leg and said that the fluid would "kill the seed." He asked if there was any risk, and she said no. He purchased the products for twenty dollars.

The following Monday, as Lohman was conferring with a customer who wore a heavy black veil, the doorbell rang: the stocky man was back. She waved him in. He signaled behind him with his handkerchief. An officer and a roundsman rushed in, along with two newspaper reporters.

"You have brought quite a party with you," Lohman said.

"Yes, there are several of us," he acknowledged, and revealed that he was Anthony Comstock. He said that a state law empowered him to make arrests and to search homes for articles that caused miscarriage or prevented conception.

"I don't have any articles in the house at all," she said.

"The same as you sold me," he said.

"I have not sold you anything."

"We will see about that."

The evening of January 28, the date Comstock had first visited Lohman, the NYSSV had held its fourth annual meeting in the lecture room of the YMCA on Twenty-Third Street. Comstock's *Annual Report* was read and referred to the Y's executive committee. Over the course of the prior year, 1877, he had seized more than twenty thousand obscene books and two hundred thousand pictures and traveled more than one hundred thousand miles. And he had scored a high-profile arrest with Ezra Heywood.

In a section of the *Annual Report* called "Principles of the Society," Comstock articulated several rules that he had learned in his vice work:

> First. Never arrest a man on suspicion.
>
> Second. Never arrest any person, however guilty, without full and proper evidence necessary to convict.
>
> Third. Treat all persons alike, without regard to riches or position in society, if guilty.
>
> Fourth. Arrest no person from malice.

In the case of Lohman, he would violate each tenet.

In her home, she demanded that he show his shield and warrant, which he did. "I thought Mr. Comstock was a man of dark complexion," she said. "You are fair. Are you the man who was injured in the face by a prisoner?" He said he was.

Comstock went into the waiting room to speak with the woman in the veil, who wept as soon as she saw him. According to Comstock, she told him she was the wife of a prominent merchant and had four children. If word got out that she had seen Madame Restell, she said, she would kill herself. He told her to go.

As he and the officers searched the house, a caged canary began to sing. They started their search in the front of the basement, coming up empty-handed. The kitchen revealed three servants eating lunch. He later noted in his arrest logbook, "Her house is furnished throughout in most elaborate style." Continuing to search the basement, the policemen found a few powders, but it was not until they neared a small, curved room by the office, containing bottles of sherry, port, and champagne, that Lohman appeared nervous. Ransacking closets and drawers, the men turned up what Comstock logged as fifteen bottles of medicine, a hundred boxes of pills, five hundred packages of powders, two hundred fifty circulars, three syringes, and ten dozen condoms. (The quantities cited in Comstock's arrest logbook, nearly always round numbers, were probably partially fabricated.)

"If you would be kind enough to send down to my druggist, he would testify just what those things are," Lohman told Comstock. She might be a snake oil saleswoman, she was saying, but she was not an abortionist.

Caroline appeared, and while she waited with her grandmother, Comstock and the houseboy searched each of the upper floors. The grandson, Charlie, was the only other person home at that time. After the officer arrested Lohman, she said she would take her own carriage. She dressed to go out—in a silk dress and sealskin cape—and an officer sat with her while she ate a plate of oysters. She told Charlie to contact her lawyer, Ambrose H. Purdy, an assemblyman from Westchester who had prosecuted the Claflin sisters' obscenity trial (but had no relation to Ann Maria Purdy). Comstock and an officer accompanied her in the carriage. Pulled by two black horses, it made its way downtown to Jefferson Market Police Court. On the ride, Comstock accused her of performing abortions, and she said that she had not boarded any women on Fifth Avenue since she had moved.

At the police court, dozens of reporters were waiting; Comstock had sent word of the arrest. Lohman was charged with selling articles for purposes of malpractice (which meant abortion) and contraception. Bail was set at ten thousand dollars; she produced bonds worth that amount from her pocketbook. The justice said the bonds had to be in the form of real estate. While Lohman waited in the court squad sergeant's room for Charlie to find property owners who could post bail for her, Comstock sat in an anteroom, pulling at his whiskers and loudly talking to reporters about the arrest. A *Sun* reporter asked if there was someone powerful behind it, and Comstock replied, "Literally no one. I know Restell says there is, but that's bosh. I have done it on my own responsibility."

Madame Restell receiving a meal in her Tombs cell, New York Illustrated Times, *February 23, 1878*

At six, Charlie returned empty-handed. Lohman's coach took her to the Tombs, the nickname for the mausoleum-like city prison at Franklin, Leonard, and Centre Streets that housed those awaiting trial and witnesses deemed to be a flight risk. Before 1889, executions for capital offenses took place in the Tombs; Charles Dickens called it a "dismal-fronted pile of bastard Egyptian, like an enchanter's palace in a melodrama," and the cells "indecent and disgusting dungeons." Lohman had not been inside the Tombs for thirty years.

The following morning, the papers announced Lohman's arrest with headlines such as "A Vile Business Stopped." From the matron's room at the Tombs, Lohman, who was dressed in a fashionable hat, diamond earrings, and a black silk dress, gave an interview to *The Sun*. The reporter wrote that her eyes were "full and sharp" and she came off as "a contented and well-to-do keeper of a fashionable boarding house. She was as calm and mild as a morning in June, betraying no emotion whatever, save now and then a gleam of indignation at 'Comstock's trick,' and regret that her granddaughter should be left alone so long."

During the interview, a woman came in on a tour, and for discretion, Lohman covered her own face under her brown veil. Asked if Comstock had a vendetta against her, Lohman said no. It was doctors who were behind her arrest, she said. "They think if they can get me in trouble and out of the way, they can make a fortune. If the public are determined to push this matter they will have a good laugh when they learn the nature of the terrible items of the preventive prescriptions. Of course, if there's a trial it will all come out." She was speaking to the divide between "regulars" and "irregulars."

Comstock sent a letter to David B. Parker, chief special agent of the Post Office Department in Washington, writing that he could make a stronger case in state court than federal. "She is reputed as being worth $1,500,000," Comstock wrote, "all made in this traffic. It appears that her friends are few . . . Mad. R. lives in a gilded palace on 5th Ave. She has once before been arrested for abortion on a young woman, and sent up for one year, to jail. I think I have a good case."

Lohman was soon released on bail. In the New York Supreme Court on March 5, Purdy said that no offense had been proven against her, since it had not been demonstrated that the items she sold Comstock could prevent conception or produce abortion. Quack medicine was not punishable by law. Two days later, in the presence of Comstock and Lohman, the judge decided she should stand trial, after which she retained a new lawyer, a former judge named Orlando Stewart. In his office, she begged him to take on her case, claiming that she had not provided abortions in twelve years and that the pills were harmless. He instructed her to take down her sign, burn any recipes for medicines, and destroy her instruments. She promised she would. He said he would take the case if the grand jury indicted her, and told her to ride in a coupé, an enclosed carriage, for appearance's sake, and leave her coachman at home.

On March 12, she was indicted under the June 1873 state Comstock law outlawing the sale, advertising, or possession of contraception and abortifacients. A few days later, her granddaughter, Caroline, married a family friend named William P. Shannon. Fearing he was after Caroline's money, Lohman made adjustments to her will—transferring her horses and carriages to Charlie.

Though Stewart reassured her that the case would be thrown out, she was certain that a prior charge against her would be brought up and she would be imprisoned once again. At her arraignment, on Friday, March 29, in the Court of General Sessions, she wore a black velvet bonnet with a black feather, a red cape, and a camel-hair shawl. She sat in the section for women witnesses, restlessly moving a Russian leather wallet between her gloved hands. Stewart entered a plea of not guilty and asked for a postponement so that an expert could analyze the medicines and prove that they were useless, meaning that her only offense would be fraud. Assistant District Attorney Daniel G. Rollins opposed the request for analysis and was sustained by the recorder, but the recorder gave the defense a delay. The trial was set for the following week.

On Saturday, March 30, the case was transferred to the Court of Oyer and Terminer, a higher tribunal, presided over by a supreme judge. Cases that were serious or complicated were tried there several times a year at the request of the defense or the prosecution. Lohman was to appear Monday, April 1, at 2:00 p.m. She was convinced that the venue transfer would lead to conviction. "The papers have persecuted me day after day, and they are determined to send me to prison!" she told Stewart. He reassured her that they would request another postponement and instructed her to meet him in his office on Monday morning at 10:00.

All day Sunday, she wandered the mansion, moaning, "What shall I do? What shall I do? I never done anything to anybody. Why should they bring this trouble on me?" She intoned, "Oh, how I dread two o'clock," and "I cannot go to the court tomorrow."

That night, she went to bed early. At 9:00 p.m., Shannon, her new grandson-in-law, went to check on her and found her talking to Caroline. "How I dread tomorrow!" Lohman exclaimed. "How shall I ever get through that trial? Oh, how I dread two o'clock!"

Caroline left, and Shannon sat with her. "I'm in a little doze," she said, appearing to fall asleep. He tiptoed out.

He set the burglar alarm, a set of bells that ran from her bedroom to the rooms downstairs. The houseboy locked the outside doors, pantries, and cupboards and gave him the keys. Shannon went to Lohman's bedroom, and, as he placed the keys on the nightstand, he noticed she was sleeping. He went to his own room, and then to bed.

At 6:30 the next morning, the chambermaid, Maggie McGrath, went upstairs and noticed that the second-floor bathroom door was ajar. She spotted Lohman's nightgown on a chair and assumed she was taking an early bath. An hour later, she went up and found the nightgown in the same place. She knocked on the bedroom door, and then the bathroom door. Hearing no reply, she entered the bathroom.

The bathtub was toward the left, enclosed in black walnut folding doors, slightly open. Maggie could hear the faucets running. On the edge of the tub, she spotted blood. She threw open the folding doors. Lohman, nude, was immersed in water. One arm was by her side and the other was draped over the edge of the tub. Her head was reclining and her throat was slit from ear to ear, her carotid artery and both jugulars severed. The bathwater from the three-thousand-pound tank on the roof had been running so long that it had turned pink. There was a shallow wound on the right side of her neck, indicating that she had failed at her first attempt. In the water lay a long carving knife, its handle made of ebony.

Maggie shrieked and ran.

At 10:00 a.m., the court convened. Assistant District Attorney William Herring and Comstock were there, but no defendant and no Stewart.

A telegram arrived. The judge and Herring read it and conferred. A second telegram confirmed the news: Madame Restell was dead. At first, Comstock believed it was an April Fool's Day joke.

Reporters who viewed the remains, which lay in an ice chest in the mansion's parlor, wrote that Lohman appeared calm, her brown hair gray-tinged and a thin line across her throat. There was an oil painting above her body, depicting her estranged daughter, Carrie; Carrie's husband, Isaac, who had died; and their four small children, two of whom had died as babies.

Comstock told *The Sun* that she had hired witnesses to give false testimony and discredit him, but said he could not reveal the names. He regretted that the case had not gone to court, as he felt confident of a conviction. In the society's *Annual Report* following the suicide, he defended his deceptive tactics, arguing, "Does [the special agent] seduce

Madame Restell in her bathtub, 1878, as imagined by the New York chief of police George W. Walling in his memoir

this murderess to commit crime? Exactly the opposite. She was waiting in that office that she might commit crime—she had advertised her
place of business and her business. She was willing, for so many dollars, to take a human life. He paid her the dollars, and forever stopped
her pre-natal murders." New York was now "rid of the disgrace of this
woman and her murderous business," which she had flaunted "with
bold defiance on one of the most prominent avenues of the city."

According to D. M. Bennett, in his book *The Champions of the
Church* (published later that year), Comstock told a mutual friend that
the case of Madame Restell was the fifteenth time he had driven a
victim to suicide. Whether or not he actually bragged about causing
suicides, the rumor that he did would dog Comstock the rest of his
life. Having caused suicides was bad enough. To boast about it—as a
Christian—was unconscionable.

Was Madame Restell the wealthy, unrepentant beast the press
made her out to be? By the time Comstock got to her, she was a griev-
ing widow, saddened by her estrangement from her daughter and
providing fewer abortions than she had at an earlier stage of her
career—or none at all, if her claim is credible. At sixty-six, she knew
she would most likely die in prison. Alone in the bathtub, as she realized the first cut of the knife had not done the trick, and slashed her
neck a second time, she was surely aware that many would not be sad
to see her go. And yet she chose the unknown over returning to the
fortress-like stone building on Blackwell's Island. As far as she was
concerned, she would die under miserable circumstances either way.
She chose to end her life, rather than allow Comstock to do the job.

So great was the myth surrounding Madame Restell that many
refused to accept that she was gone. There were rumors that the dead
body was actually that of a patient, and that the abortionist was on her
way to Canada or Europe. Some said she had been murdered by clients afraid of being exposed. *Puck*, a humor magazine, ran a cartoon
showing Fifth Avenue in a post-Restell era, swarming with infants.

The *Times* called her suicide "a fit ending to an odious career." A
Sun editorial defended her, though: "No matter what the wretched

*Cartoon from the
April 17, 1878,
issue of* Puck

woman was who took her life with her own hand yesterday, her death has not freed the world from the last of detestable characters. Whatever she was she had her rights, and the man who cunningly led her into the commission of a misdemeanor acted an unmanly and ignoble part." An editorial in New York's *Daily Graphic* claimed that Comstock had not brought the case out of "public duty," as her medicines were harmless. Instead, he had done it to send a message, because she was wealthy and practiced "her trade openly in this city."

Comstock pasted that editorial in his scrapbook, along with one from a religious paper in Cincinnati that questioned his use of deception when "employed in the category of Christian methods and work." As far as he was concerned, Madame Restell had gotten her just deserts. In the "Remarks" column of the arrest records, he wrote,

"Committed suicide by cutting her throat morning of trial. A Bloody ending to a bloody life."

Around the time Lohman committed suicide, Comstock found himself distracted by liberal attempts in Washington to revise the Comstock law. The House Committee on the Revision of the Laws was hearing speeches from a group affiliated with the National Liberal League. Members circulated a petition for revision that garnered fifty thousand signatures; the paper on which it was written was two thousand feet long. It called the law an invasion of personal and states' rights and argued that Comstock's use of decoy letters constituted a crime. It demanded an amendment confining the law to obscene literature, exempting scientific publications, and prohibiting Comstock from extending his power beyond the YMCA. Congressman Benjamin Butler, who had supported Woodhull's suffrage argument, presented the petition to his colleagues in Congress.

Worse for Comstock, his antagonist, the freethinker Bennett, had written a pamphlet, called *Anthony Comstock: His Career of Cruelty and Crime*, that detailed the censor's ruthlessness, mendaciousness, and frequent decoying. Fifteen thousand copies had been sent to editors around the country, accompanied by blank petitions to be sent to Congress. The pamphlet was also sent to congressmen.

On April 16, a representative of the fifty thousand signers, J. B. Wolff, testified before the Committee on the Revision of the Laws in Washington. Comstock despised the repealers and believed some were out for his life. Regarding his own testimony before the committee, he said, "Everything looked black. I was alone . . . As I entered the Committee room, I found it crowded with the long-haired men and short-haired women, there to defend, obscene publications, abortion implements, and other incentives to come, by repealing the laws. I heard their hiss and curse as I passed through them. I saw their sneers and their looks of derision and contempt."

Comstock thought, "My grace is sufficient," and defended the law. Dr. Ned Foote, whose father had been convicted, said that medical works by reputable physicians were being suppressed and called Comstock's supporters "fanatics and bigots." Comstock repeated his concern that smut dealers obtained school catalogs, with names and addresses of students, and mailed them demoralizing articles, causing both boys and girls to be "ruined."

On May 1, 1878, one month after Ann Lohman slit her throat, the committee unanimously reported to the House that it would take no action regarding the petition. The Post Office, the Committee on the Revision of the Laws stated, "was not established to carry instruments of vice, or obscene writings, indecent pictures, or lewd books. Your Committee believe that the statutes in question do not violate the Constitution of the United States, and ought not to be changed; they recommend, therefore, that the prayer of the said petition be denied."

Madame Restell was dead, and the Comstock law had survived a repeal attempt. Eight days later, perhaps feeling emboldened, Comstock went after another contraceptive dealer in New York, also a woman. She was not nearly as famous as Lohman, but her name would hit the papers when she decided to seek revenge in a highly public way. The press would refer to her as "Mrs. Dr. Sara Blakeslee Chase."

8

THE PHYSIOLOGIST

Date:	May 9, 1878
Name	Sara Blakeslee Chase
Address:	56 West 33rd Street, New York City
Age:	41
Aliases:	S. B. Chase, 111 E. 11 St.
Nationality:	Ohio
Religion:	Spiritualist and Free Lover
Education:	Common
Married or Single:	Married
Children:	1
Occupation:	Lecturer & pretended Physician
Offence:	Selling articles to prevent conception

Weeks after the death of Madame Restell, a physician friend came to Comstock with bad news. He had a patient, he said, with an ulcerated uterus. Three months pregnant and married only three weeks, the patient told the doctor that she had attended a lecture on "prevention of conception" by Dr. Sara Chase, at Ross Street Presbyterian Church in Brooklyn. Chase, a forty-one-year-old single mother, was a homeopathic physician who gave lectures on physiology—which included anatomy, sex education, reproduction, and contraception—to separate groups of women and men at churches and lecture halls such as the Cooper Institute, and in her house on West Thirty-Third Street. After the lecture in question, as Comstock later said he was told, the patient bought an instrument intended to induce abortion.

Comstock spoke with the girl's doctor, and then wrote to David B. Parker, the chief special agent, with whom he had corresponded about Ann Lohman. The young woman, according to Comstock, "had been seduced before marriage, & became diseased as above. [Chase] sold a sponge swab, and syringe, to be used by the woman immediately after copulation, to throw up a solution of sul[f]uric acid to wash out the parts and destroy the sperm, as she said." Various acids were common spermicides, including carbolic acid, household vinegar, and boric acid, though some were painful or dangerous. Based on Comstock's confusing account, Chase likely sold the woman a douching syringe with a more benign spermicidal solution to be used as a postcoital contraceptive—not as an abortifacient. The woman probably became pregnant after the douching did not work, and then underwent a botched abortion, causing the ulceration.

On May 9, 1878, a redheaded man calling himself "Mr. Farnsworth" appeared at Chase's "physiological rooms," where she had boarders and also saw patients. She was dressed in a plain black dress and bonnet. Tall, majestic, and willowy, she had a broad forehead, auburn hair, and large, expressive eyes. The redheaded man presented a letter from his wife, "Mrs. Farnsworth," saying that she had planned to buy a syringe after one of Chase's lectures and was sending her husband to get one. Chase told Mr. Farnsworth that she did not sell or advertise syringes, but manufactured them for her patients.

The next day, Mr. Farnsworth returned with a man who he said needed a syringe for his wife. The second man gave Chase five dollars, and she handed him a syringe wrapped in brown paper. The package may also have contained sulfuric acid; there are conflicting accounts. Mr. Farnsworth asked if she was afraid that she was violating the law. She said she wasn't, as syringes were for cleansing purposes. "It could not by any possible means be used for the production of abortion or any immoral purpose," she said, "and it is what every woman should possess as an adjunct to her toilet, and any druggist has a right to sell them. I would not be afraid to sell one to Anthony Comstock if he should want one."

At this Mr. Farnsworth proclaimed, "I am Anthony Comstock, and I have a warrant here for your arrest." The friend was his assistant Joseph Britton, Comstock's "man Friday." Britton was nearly as loathed as Comstock. *The Truth Seeker* had called Britton the "valuable assistant in the peculiar business conducted by the firm of Britton, Comstock, & God." His aliases included Cohen, Levy, and Andrews, and he was said to be a gambler, a liar, and a perjurer.

Just as Comstock had done with Ann Lohman, he summoned two men, a patrolman and a *Tribune* reporter. He locked Chase's boarders and patients in their rooms and ransacked the house. In Chase's account, while he searched he said, "If I can't hold her on the syringe, I will get her on the *Physiologist*." Chase had recently launched a health journal called *The Physiologist and Family Physician*, which encouraged small family size. "She won't lecture tonight," he said of Chase, "for she will be too late to get bail and will have to lie in the Tombs overnight."

Finding no contraband in the front parlor, Comstock and Britton left Chase and went upstairs. In the *Tribune's* account, she called him a "miscreant" and said, "I am doing God's work. I am preventing poor families from being burdened with children whom they cannot support." The back room contained copies of *The Physiologist and Family Physician*. In a desk drawer and in a closet, the men found six syringes. An officer arrested Chase and took her to the Tombs. She was held on $1,500 bail and charged with selling articles for a criminal purpose under the state Comstock law.

Before Comstock left, he made a thorough search of the house. Among Chase's papers he found a speech she had written called "Foeticide." In it, she advocated for contraception to prevent the tragic consequence of abortion. He snatched it. When he found the "Mrs. Farnsworth" letter, he grabbed that as well.

In the Tombs, according to the *Tribune*, Chase said she had no response to the charges. A friend bailed her out. That night at eight, in the physiological rooms, she delivered her Thursday-night sexology lecture to gentlemen.

Born in Ohio on January 18, 1837, the third of six children, Sara Blakeslee was raised in Broome County, New York, in the northwest part of the state. Her father was a Presbyterian clergyman. She wanted to become a missionary and receive a classical and medical education, and entered Alfred Academy in Allegheny County, where she took three terms of the Preparatory College Course, finishing in 1858. Alfred Academy was the first coeducational college in the state, admitting women in 1836.

After moving to Illinois, on December 11, 1859, she married a medical student named Hazard Chase, and following Hazard's service in the Civil War, they studied homeopathy in Dayton, Ohio. Their daughter, Grace, was born in 1865. In 1870, the Chases graduated from the Cleveland Homeopathic Hospital College. They opened a homeopathy office in Cleveland and later settled in Brownhelm, Ohio, about fifty miles west. Sara was admitted into the Medical Society of Cleveland and the Homeopathic Association of Ohio.

She returned to Cleveland Homeopathic Hospital College to teach anatomy to women students, who preferred a female instructor. In an article advocating medical education for women, she wrote, "I feel deeply the need in our progressive age of having our women practitioners stand high in their profession, and also know the perplexity which arises in the mind in selecting a college wherein can be had thoroughness of instruction, together with pleasing and friendly associations."

By early 1873, she and Hazard had separated; she told a friend he had a mistress. Sara lived with Grace and two servants on a fruit farm between Cleveland and Sandusky, surrounded by Oberlin College graduates, and ran a full practice as the only doctor in town. In the 1870s, she began to lecture on sexual health to women at Cleveland's Euclid Avenue Presbyterian Church. Many women "hygienists" in the postbellum period taught anatomy and sex education, and used terms such as *voluntary motherhood*, which touted the benefits of fewer children for increased health and happiness. They founded physiological societies in cities such as Washington, Brooklyn, Chicago, Philadelphia, and Boston. They spoke in churches to single-sex groups, giving talks that church leaders felt were beneficial to marriage and family.

In 1873, Chase wrote an essay about abortion called "The Great Evil of Society," published in *The Ohio Medical and Surgical Reporter*. She was concerned about women who sought abortions due to sickness, poverty, or unhappy marriages. "There comes from my soul a deep wail of anguish," she wrote, "over the unwritten and inexpressible agony which has here sought relief from its woes." Women, whom she called "the continued progenitor of the race," should have the right to determine for themselves when to become mothers—a radical idea in 1873. And they should not have to consult their husbands before opting for abortion. "The ovum belongs to the mother," Chase declared. "She alone has the right to decide when it shall be impregnated."

She was a supporter of women's rights, speaking at a suffrage convention in Cincinnati with Elizaeth Cady Stanton and Susan B. Anthony in 1874. She also advocated for dress reform, lecturing at the National Convention of the Women's Dress Reform League in Cleveland. Dress reformers believed restrictive clothing such as corsets prevented women from being healthy. Only unrestricted dress would let women compete with men in the workplace and gain equality. After one talk at an Akron college, the young women were so impressed that they immediately took off their corsets and shortened their dresses.

In 1875, Chase and Grace, age ten, moved to New York. On the journey east, Chase made stops to lecture on the relationship between the sexes. She sent recommendation letters from Euclid Avenue Presbyterian to the Church of the Strangers on West Fifty-Seventh Street in New York and became a parishioner there. She opened a facility on West Eleventh Street, advertising "treatment of female diseases." Later she would maintain that she gave information about sex and contraception, but did not provide abortion.

Her rise in New York liberal circles was swift. In July 1875, she booked a speech called "Responsibility of Sex" at the New York Liberal Club. The club had been founded in 1869 and held public lectures on science, suffrage, class, and free speech by prominent thinkers, doctors and professors, authors, editors, journalists, clergymen, and politicians. (A few months after Chase's talk, Stanton would give a speech titled "Rich and Poor.") Chase's "Responsibility of Sex" lecture argued that no one with hereditary diseases should have children. She argued that if women wanted to maximize the "mental and moral endowments of their children," the best fathers were men of "strong frame and noble fashion, vigorous life-force and exalted spirit."

The concept then called *family limitation* or *voluntary motherhood*— which aimed to improve the human race, make for healthier mothers and children, and provide an easier and cheaper life for the family— was gaining traction, among not only liberals but also moral reformers. Both free lovers and conservative women, with vastly different visions of a perfect society, believed in controlled family size, though the contraceptive information given by the latter would be vague. At its first congress in 1873, the Association for the Advancement of Women, a conservative women's rights group, held a session called "Enlightened Motherhood."

After Chase's New York Liberal Club talk, the attendees, including Woodhull's speechwriter Stephen Pearl Andrews, held a vigorous discussion. According to Chase, "Many complimentary remarks were made relative to the character and excellence of the lecture, and but few criticisms were made against it." D. M. Bennett published her speech in a collection of *Truth Seeker* tracts the following year.

As her reputation in New York liberal circles continued to grow, Chase booked such prominent venues as Brooklyn's Williamsburgh Lyceum, the all-girls Packer Institute, and Manhattan's Second Presbyterian Church. To men, she gave speeches titled "Manhood; its Mission and Misuse," "The Relations of Man to the Maladies of Woman," and "What shall we do to improve the Health of our Wives?" She also had a men-only lecture on masturbation, or "the secret vice." One write-up stated, "This talkative lady can tell more unwholesome truth in a given time than any other woman on the planet."

By the late 1870s, she had founded and become corresponding secretary of the New York Physiological Society, based in her home on West Thirty-Third. It was devoted to "the scientific discovery of principles and facts related to the mental and physical progress of mankind through the interchange of ideas." The society offered lectures on Wednesday and Thursday afternoons, at 2:30 p.m. for women and at 8:00 p.m. for men. There was a library, and social and literary events included recitations, music, conversation, and dancing. The lectures were prominent enough to draw such members of the elite class as Police Commissioner Jacob Hess and General Henry A. Barnum, a Civil War veteran, Medal of Honor recipient, and former New York state prison inspector.

In April 1878, Chase edited and published the first edition of *The Physiologist and Family Physician*, her health journal. In her note to readers, Chase wrote, "The only guarantee we can give is earnest effort in the grandest cause that ever attracted the attention of man or woman." Other popular health journals at the time included *Dr. Kinget's Health Journal*, the contested *Dr. Foote's Health Monthly* (which would remain in publication until the late 1890s), and J. W. Stillman's *Boston Agents' Advocate*.

The inaugural issue of the *Physiologist* included articles titled "The Equality of Woman," "When Conception Becomes a Crime," "Constipation," and "Faintness." In "Husbands and Wives," Chase argued that marriage was physically dangerous to women, leading to shorter life spans for wives than for husbands. Marital rape and forced maternity "rendered marriage every thing but the pure and beautiful sacrament which Nature ordained it to be." One regular *Physiologist* contributor was Elmina Drake Slenker, a Quaker-raised atheist in Snowville, Virginia. She published novels with atheistic themes, edited the children's section of the *Boston Investigator*, and had a children's column in *Lucifer, the Light-Bearer*. She believed in a philosophy called "Sexual Temperance." For Slenker, drinking and sex were masculine activities, and alcoholism led to brutish, violent sex; birth defects; and men's dominance over women.

Comstock's visit to Chase came a few weeks after the second issue of the *Physiologist* was published. In the wake of her arrest, the *Tribune* ran an article called "A Rival of Madame Restell: Arrest of Dr. Sara B. Chase, She is Charged with Selling Articles for Criminal Purposes." The article described Chase as resembling "a German, her only bad feature being a large, sensual mouth." It claimed that Comstock had found circulars and a speech called "Foeticide—why it should be done." He had appended the subtitle when he gave his account to the reporter—wholly altering its intent.

In an incensed response to the *Tribune*, Chase wrote, "I am a regularly graduated physician, and have been for years engaged in legitimate medical practice, and in no sense can the reputation of an abortionist be placed to my charge. My public utterances, my private life, my published writings, all attest [to] the falsity of this charge." The "Foeticide" talk, she explained, was "opposed to abortion from every standpoint." She had delivered it at Christian churches and for pastors, who supported her.

The syringe she had sold Comstock, she stated, was for cleanliness and disease prevention. She had never heard of a woman sustaining injuries from a syringe sold by her. She was a victim of a hatchet job: "I would never have complained of any truthful statement of the arrest or what took place publicly in regard to it, but I was not prepared to find that Mr. Comstock's stories could be placed in your columns as though he was one of your staff, and without the slightest inquiry as to their truth." She was "morally and legally innocent, as the result will prove."

When her case was brought before the grand jury, a member of the panel asked Comstock if he wanted her to commit suicide, referring to Madame Restell's death just two months earlier. The jury unanimously decided to dismiss the case. Accompanied by the NYSSV president, the soap magnate Samuel Colgate, Comstock brought new affidavits against Chase to District Attorney Benjamin Phelps, asking permission to go before the grand jury that was in session. Phelps had the affidavits filed in the clerk's office and issued a statement that he did not want to send the case to the grand jury. The indictment failed, he wrote, "not for lack of evidence, but because the Grand Jury did not think it for the public good to order it." In Phelps's mind, a syringe seller was not a criminal.

Comstock was furious. In the arrest logbook, he wrote that he had given the grand jury "all the filthy detail that Chase used in describing this article and its use. That she recommended sul[f]uric acid in water to be thrown up into a woman immediately following the act." Afterward, Comstock swore an affidavit, which he and Colgate took to the recorder. According to Comstock, the recorder told him it was the district attorney's duty to send the case before another grand jury.

The Heywoods defended Chase, having met her at a New England Labor Reform League convention. Uncertain whether she provided abortions, they made it clear that they themselves were opposed to the procedure. But men, they contended, were not to "dictate to women what they shall do with the life-seed they give to or force upon them." Infanticide and abortion were "unnatural inhuman actions, but what shall be said of men who fright a woman with offspring, deprave her to think child-murder right or desirable, and then make laws to punish others for the results of their own lascivious indiscretion?" This argument was not far from Claflin's on abortion: Why should women and abortion providers be punished, when callous or thoughtless men caused unwanted pregnancies?

A few weeks after Chase's case was dismissed, a sympathy meeting was held at Science Hall, a liberal meeting place that also housed *The Truth Seeker*. Chase said the great question on the minds of thinking people "on both sides of the Atlantic, is either abortion or the prevention of conception. This question is forced home especially upon every physician who meets from day to day the demand in his practice." Contraception, or "checks to population," prolonged life, protected the weak, and saved the sickly; it made wars less frequent and bloody, and eliminated famines. Instead of being outlawed, more "enlightened and humanizing" checks were needed, because over-population would lead to poverty and starvation.

The idea that contraception could counter overpopulation was called neo-Malthusianism. Following the Besant-Bradlaugh obscenity trial in 1877, a group called the Malthusian League had been formed in England to advocate for population control, and for the idea that overpopulation was to blame for poverty. The name was a reference to the Reverend Thomas Malthus, who argued in his 1798 *Essay on the Principle of Population* that the human population would one day exceed the food supply.

At the Science Hall meeting, Chase was saying that the United States was behind the times on population control. James McClelland, an attorney who had defended several Comstock targets, also spoke. He told a story about a man who mailed a syringe and was imprisoned for two years, sending his family into poverty and his wife into prostitution. Comstock, he said, was one of the worst men he had ever known. The audience cheered.

On June 12, 1878, a group of Chase's and Ezra Heywood's supporters formed the National Defense Association (NDA) to fight the charges against Chase and try to get Ezra out of prison. An appeal to *Truth Seeker* readers for donations warned that Comstock was going to bring more cases "against Liberals and others." The NDA's executive committee would later include Flora Tilton (Angela's sister) and Ezra. Its constitution stated that it aimed to investigate questionable cases under state and national Comstock laws, help people "unjustly assailed by the enemies of free speech and free press," defend medical doctors and scientists, uphold the right to acquire knowledge of human physiology, and "roll back the wave of intolerance, bigotry, and ignorance" that threatened "cherished liberties." In subsequent years, group members attended local vice society meetings, distributed anti-Comstock literature, and lobbied federally and locally.

Liberals were particularly appalled by Chase's arrest because it came on the heels of a controversy involving contraception and Colgate. His New York–based company, Colgate & Co., had been running

Vaseline ads that claimed the product was effective as a contraceptive: "Vaseline, charged with four or five grains of salicylic acid, will destroy spermatozoa without injury." A man sent away for a Vaseline circular, received it, and took it to a U.S. commissioner, who said the district attorney had to be consulted before warrants for arrest could be issued. U.S. Attorney Stewart L. Woodford of New York's Southern District consulted with Colgate and dismissed the charges, reporting that Colgate had admitted to sending the pamphlet but did not know what was inside it.

In *The Truth Seeker*, Bennett pointed out the NYSSV's hypocrisy:

> The crime which the agent of the Society for the Suppression of Vice charges against Mrs. Chase is that by the syringes which she recommends and sells, she places it in the power of wives to prevent conception. This he holds to be very criminal in any one whom he chooses to make his victim, but when the president of his society, Mr. Samuel Colgate, wishes to engage in the business of selling an article which he recommends as a preventive of conception, he does not interfere in the enterprise.

Bennett was arguing against a medical double standard. In a tract called *An Open Letter to Samuel Colgate*, he declared that "'regular,' aristocratic physicians may prevent conceptions, produce abortions, or do anything else they choose, and your agent will not disturb them." Colgate would not pursue druggists who sold contraceptives, because they were a powerful lobby and "could raise too much money to successfully oppose him." Like Lohman, if less famous, Chase had been targeted not because she sold spermicidal solutions, but because she was an "irregular," a homeopathic physician.

Was Bennett right about this double standard? Between 1880 and 1890, one mail-order company rejected one hundred eighty ads as unfit; a quarter of these were for contraceptive devices. Bennett's ally, E. B. Foote, Sr., had taken to using code in his own journal, advertising his douching syringes during the 1880s as "Sanitary Syringes." Such products were still available in retail stores and by mail, in books and in druggists' catalogs, but one Boston drug firm removed "capotes" (condoms) from its list of items in 1874, 1876, and 1885, though it did mention douching syringes and pessaries. As vendors increasingly feared arrest in the 1870s and 1880s, condoms and diaphragms became more difficult to find in New York, Philadelphia, Boston, and Chicago.

As for Chase, in a startling act of defiance for a Comstock target, and for a woman, she filed a lawsuit against him, seeking ten thousand dollars in damages for false arrest. She charged that he had injured her reputation and profession as a physician, causing the loss of clients and inflicting financial damage. Her complaint alleged that his search of her home and treatment of her were done "willfully, maliciously, wrongfully, and without legal right or authority to do the same, to the great damage of the plaintiff."

On June 25, something remarkable happened. Policemen and a deputy sheriff arrived at the NYSSV office on Nassau Street, and the sheriff arrested Comstock by order of a Supreme Court judge. Comstock was taken to the sheriff's office, where a $2,500 bail was posted by Elbridge T. Gerry, counsel of the Society for the Prevention of Cruelty to Children (and grandson of the Massachusetts governor who invented gerrymandering). Comstock was released on his own recognizance—but Dr. Chase had turned the hunter into the hunted.

Next, Chase used the pages of the *Physiologist* as a mouthpiece for her views on Comstock, the laws, and contraception. She wrote in the June/July issue that Comstock did not understand "the difference between obscenity and science. Everything which pertains to the organs of reproduction, whether presented with a view to instruction in regard to their physiology and hygiene, or to inflame the lewd passions of the lower nature, all to his mind are alike vile, and he forthwith proceeds to exercise the power vested in him, in conformity to his perverted judgment."

In the same issue, an advertisement appeared for a new item. The "'Comstock' Syringe" was "especially adapted to purposes of cleanliness, and the cure and prevention of disease. A necessary adjunct to every lady's toilet. Price, $5, and express charges." A note explained that the syringe was the same one for which Chase had been arrested for selling: "We trust that the sudden popularity brought to this valuable syringe by the benevolent agency of the enterprising Mr. Comstock, will prove to suffering womanhood the most beneficent act of his illustrious life."

Later syringe ads mentioned her lawsuit as a selling point, as though purchasers were taking political action against Comstock and his power:

ANTHONY COMSTOCK

HAS BEEN

ARRESTED AND HELD TO BAIL

To answer the suit of a lady physician of this city for

TEN THOUSAND DOLLARS DAMAGES,

He having tried to suppress the sale of a

CERTAIN SYRINGE

Sold by her.

MARRIED WOMEN

Say it is the most perfect article ever used by their sex for

purposes of purity and the prevention and cure of disease

and for the

JUDICIOUS AND HEALTHY REGULATION OF THE

FEMALE FUNCTIONS,

That it is a Blessing to Womankind. It is now called the

"COMSTOCK" SYRINGE

Undoubtedly apoplectic over the fact that a vaginal syringe was being marketed in his name, Comstock ratcheted up his attacks on Chase. He called her "a notorious abortionist" and claimed there was a conspiracy to have him removed as post office inspector. He drew up two indictments and presented himself to a different grand jury, which granted his request for a hearing. After listening to his statements, they indicted Chase. When Assistant District Attorney Daniel G. Rollins told the facts to the judge and requested a nolle prosequi, the judge granted the motion. Rollins issued a statement admonishing Comstock for not consulting with the district attorney and for failing to inform the new grand jury of the prior dismissal. The *Times* reported, "The action of Mr. Comstock, in his method of approaching the grand jury, has elicited pretty severe criticism."

An irate Comstock sent a lament to the *Tribune*: "Many slurs and insinuations have of late been made against me by the papers of this city. I say to you, as I say to the world at large, if you have any charges against me, submit them to the Executive Committee of the Society for the Suppression of Vice, and you can very easily find out the facts . . . The work must go on. Your attacks only make it more difficult." In the same issue, the *Tribune* published an editorial arguing that NYSSV members had to "either teach Mr. Comstock more discretion or lose a good deal of the cordial support they have hitherto received from the better portion of the public and the press of New-York."

With anger over the Chase and Heywood arrests rising, on the evening of August 1, 1878, the NDA held a massive "indignation meeting" in Boston's Faneuil Hall. It lasted four hours, and six thousand people attended. August 1 was the anniversary of the freeing of the slaves in the British West Indies in 1834, and abolitionists marked the date every year. It is unclear whether Angela attended, but one prominent speaker was Laura Kendrick, formerly Laura Cuppy Smith, the women's rights activist who had spoken at Woodhull's Cooper Institute talk. At Faneuil Hall, Kendrick said, "Vice, my friends, can never be legislated out of the world: our only remedy is education." One day, she said, curiosity would "give place to knowledge, and obscene pictures and literature will have no patrons."

At the meeting, the NDA resolved to call on President Hayes to pardon Ezra. The association resolved that Comstock was abusing his power, suppressing "free thought, free speech, and free press," and "unfit to be entrusted with the execution of any law seriously affecting the liberty of the citizen." The NDA sought "his immediate dismissal from the Government service."

That fall, the NDA amassed six thousand signatures petitioning for Ezra's pardon. Kendrick met with aides to Hayes and members of Congress, and in November the NDA sent her to Washington with the petitions. Angela did not like the idea of another woman speaking for her family, and felt that Kendrick was making her out to be a victim. She therefore wrote to her friend Elizabeth Denton:

> People ought to get it into their heads that "mercy" is simply and purely a matter of Mrs. Heywood's, her want, towards her husband as "his wife," as the mother of her and "his children" etc. And no one or number of ones can in propriety move in such a matter without her voice of consent, and her choice, of person, to represent herself and give her prayer to the President either by her own immediate selection and profound wit or by a united consultation of suggestion and choice . . .
>
> [Kendrick] wrote to Mr. Heywood "she would rather die than not to succeed." These [were] her very words. Release a man, and if possible slay a woman!! . . . I protest against Mrs. Kendrick going on for me, or for "mercy" at all. I am in dead earnest. Do as they please about Mr. Heywood but do not invade my rights, as another person, to accomplish even the "release" of their much beloved prisoner.

Many prominent liberals submitted letters in support of a pardon. Calling the president "Friend Hayes," the *Physiologist* contributor Elmina Slenker argued that Ezra was virtuous, and "if he does not see precisely as thee and I do, in regard to love and marriage relations, why should he be debarred from expressing his honest convictions, especially when he claims to do so in plain, sensible and decent language? There is nothing obscene in his writings . . . Obscenity is far more often found in the reader than it is in the writer."

The secretary of the recently formed New England Society for the Suppression of Vice sent a letter to the U.S. attorney general, Charles Devens, opposing the pardon and offering to amass a counterpetition from Bostonians if requested. The officers and board of the NYSSV sent their own anti-pardon letter, and Comstock and his allies defended the Heywood sentence before a congressional committee.

In a strongly worded affidavit sent to Hayes, Comstock recounted his arrest of Ezra at the free love convention. To make his case for Ezra's continued imprisonment, Comstock quoted *Angela's* talk— specifically her jokes about "jerks." He continued:

> The said [Ezra] Heywood has been in the habit of holding same or similar conventions in different cities and places, and at said conventions selling to young men his obscene book *Cupid's Yokes*, to the manifest injury of their morals . . . [T]his deponent prays if for no other reason than this, that no pardon should be granted to said Heywood: for to do that will be to virtually license his vile book, and encourage and embolden others to scatter the seeds of licentiousness among the young.

He concluded that he "most humbly and earnestly" prayed and protested against "any pardon being granted to said Heywood, or anyone else convicted for dealing in same or similar obscene matter."

Ezra's letter to Hayes stated that he had no criminal intent and had intended to benefit humanity when he wrote *Cupid's Yokes*, and that his sentence was an outrage against freedom of speech and the press. "My helpless family, to whom I am bound by the tenderest ties of love and affection," he wrote, was suffering. The massive effort worked, and Hayes pardoned Ezra on December 16, 1878, after he had served six months of his sentence. The Heywoods were able to repurchase their house and inn, Mountain Home, and sleep in their own beds. Following Chase's lead, Ezra brought suit against Comstock for ten thousand dollars for false arrest, though nothing came of the effort.

Explaining the pardon, Hayes wrote in his diary that the real objection to Ezra's writing was "not that he discussed a question in an objectionable manner, but that he was on the wrong side of the question. That he maintains the wrong side of the question as to marriage, I entertain as little doubt as those who assail me. But it is no crime by the laws of the United States to advocate the abolition of marriage." He concluded that the writings, though objectionable, "were not obscene, lascivious, lewd, or corrupting in the criminal sense."

Comstock felt personally betrayed by the president. "The Pres. Pardons this man on the petition of Infidels and liberals free lovers + Smut dealers," he wrote in the logbook. "This action of Pres. Hayes practically licenses the sale of Cupid's Yokes, and is a strong encouragement for others to violate the law, as well as a great hind[r]ance to the further enforcement of the law."

Despite the high-profile pardon of a free lover, the NYSSV's mission was expanding, and the judicial branch was on its side. *Ex parte Jackson* had upheld the constitutionality of the Comstock law. According to the society's 1879 *Annual Report*, contraception, abortion, and smut ads in the sporting press were on the decline. Anti-vice societies had formed in Boston, Cleveland, St. Louis, Cincinnati, Louisville, and Chicago. Bennett was convicted for selling Heywood's *Cupid's Yokes* in response to a decoy letter from Comstock under the name "G. Brackett." His case made its way up through the courts, with liberals following closely to see how the outcome might affect other freethinkers tried for selling progressive publications. A judge upheld the conviction using the *Hicklin* standard, which prevented those prosecuted under the Comstock law from describing their intent, even if it was social change.

Several months after the Heywood pardon, the Bennett *Cupid's Yokes* case reached its resolution: a three-hundred-dollar fine and thirteen months' hard labor at the Albany Penitentiary. A major freethinker and anti-Comstockian would be imprisoned. (After serving his time, Bennett traveled abroad, continuing his work as a writer and freethinker; he died in 1882, shortly after his return to New York, at nearly sixty-four.) *United States v. Bennett* affirmed that an obscenity indictment did not need to specify the passage or enter the book into evidence if it was "offensive to the court." The defendant did not need to know that the book was obscene; the indicted matter could not be compared with books of "alleged similar character" and "the object of the use of the obscene words" was not to be considered.

As the courts were affirming his power, and the constitutionality of his law, Comstock experienced a personal triumph: he and Maggie became parents again. Around 1879, seven years after their loss of Lillie, Comstock was on a raid in a tenement in Chinatown when he encountered a newborn baby girl lying by her dying mother. When the mother died, he took the baby home to Maggie, never filing formal adoption papers. The baby, near death for months, would have lifelong developmental problems, which may have made Comstock feel more justified in having taken her. His "adoption" of the baby was an act of Christian charity. It also must have been an attempt to repair the pain he had suffered when he came home from school to find his mother dead, near his newborn sister.

Though there is no evidence in his diaries, it is likely that the Comstocks had tried for many years to have a baby after Lillie's death. Given the fact that they had conceived once, Maggie may have been injured during the birth, preventing future pregnancies. Or Lillie may have been an anomaly. Whatever the story, after the pain of their only biological child's death, the Comstocks now had a baby again. They named her Adele.

9

THE COMSTOCK SYRINGE

As though the arrest, the damages case, and the loss of clients were not enough, during the summer of 1878, Dr. Sara B. Chase faced a crisis in her personal life. That year, her husband, Hazard, who had given up homeopathic medicine and was working as a stonecutter, had sued her for divorce. Thanks to the controversy with Comstock, the news was written up in the papers. *The Cleveland Leader* reported that as Chase became known as a lecturer, she moved "to a broader field. She held some rather peculiar views on certain matters and was quite fond of ventilating them. New York was the spot that she settled upon as the field of her future practice." The article mentioned her arrest and the nolle prosequi. On December 28, 1878, Hazard was granted the divorce due to Chase's "willful absence."

The summer after her divorce, she was forced to move; she had lost customers and was struggling to pay the rent. She needed a hundred dollars a month to print the journal and was trying to save money for her suit against Comstock. Samuel H. Preston, a *Physiologist* contributor and Chase's business manager, appealed to the radical press for financial assistance. Meanwhile, Comstock had told a friend of Chase's that he was, in her friend's words, "terribly bitter on you. He says you have placed him in a false position before the country, as he knows you are Restell No. 2, and says he would give $500 for sufficient inculpating evidence to set himself right before the world. Look out for him, as he may have detectives at work."

It was no surprise that Comstock was growing irrational. Every day gave rise to new threats against him. He could withstand antipathy from radicals and smut sellers, but not from mainstream society. In the spring of 1881, in his late thirties, he decided to try to gain entry into the Masons, a fraternal group, only to find that they did not want him. Progressives delighted in his travails. An investigating committee of Masons came to the *Physiologist* offices to inquire about him. Preston and Chase showed them decoy letters he had mailed them—and offered a list of prominent public figures who would swear that he was a liar.

The Masons' committee reported this interview to Comstock, who declared that he "had not got done" with Chase yet. He vowed to ban the syringe, raid the journal offices, and put Chase and Preston behind bars. The duo secured bail and a lawyer. Back at Chase's home, they filled fifteen new orders for the Comstock syringe, which now totaled more than two thousand sales since they first advertised it.

In March, NYSSV members, including Comstock and Colgate, went to Albany to appear before the state legislature's Committee on Religious and Charitable Societies, which was considering a bill that would expand the society's powers and require police and sheriffs to act under its orders. The police superintendent appeared before the committee to oppose the bill; NYSSV officers had raided numbers games, and the police felt that society members were stepping on their toes. An assemblyman professed that Comstock was a dangerous bigot who persecuted people because of their opinions, and that he had entered the New York post office and opened letters. Comstock sprang from his seat and said, "That is an infamous libel, and I will not sit here and listen to it." The assemblyman pointed his finger at him, calling him an "infamous wretch who rejoices in hounding men to death. You, sir, have driven innocent men and women to suicide"—a clear reference to Madame Restell—"but you can't bully me." The vice hunter did not reply; the assemblyman apologized to the committee and closed his argument against the bill. Ultimately, it was defeated.

The April issue of the *Physiologist* reprinted an article from a tabloid newspaper, arguing that the legislature should not give the NYSSV power over public officials. The same issue also contained an original article by Preston, "The Pulp of a Little Pungent Public and Private Opinion," dubbing Comstock "a loathsome mortal leper" and a fraud. Preston wrote that if Comstock were to be admitted to the Masons it "would cast such a reproach upon the craft as to cause every common bricklayer in the country to go and bury his square and compass."

The issue was printed and mailed to the *Physiologist*'s five thousand subscribers. Chase received a letter from H. P. Pearson, postmaster at the Auditor's Office of the First Division in New York, informing her that Washington's first assistant postmaster general, T. L. James, had instructed the New York office to exclude the issue from the mail. Any further issues would have to be submitted for inspection before they could be mailed. Chase was certain Comstock was behind the ban.

The next day, Chase and Slenker, who was now the *Physiologist*'s associate editor, wrote to Postmaster General James, enclosing the April issue and requesting that he point out the page or paragraph that had incited the action. "We claim this right," they wrote, "as the representatives of a free and irrepressible Press, the omnipotent opinion of whose readers determines the duties of presidents and departments. We claim the right to know the particular thing about our print that subjects it to this postal proscription. We claim the common right of criminals to have the charges against us clearly specified." Chase consulted an attorney and, to buy time, launched a new journal called the *Monthly Medical Monitor*.

The Word called the *Physiologist* ban "backstrokes from Comstock's dying power." The tabloid paper *Truth* compared Comstock's work to "Russian censorship." Slenker wrote in *The Truth Seeker* that Chase's journal had been suppressed because it "gave too much useful information to the people . . . Today the great mass of the world's thinkers decide that had [Comstock's] mother given birth to one man (child) less the human race would hav[e] been greatly the gainers thereby."

On May 15, 1881, an indignation meeting was held at Boston's Paine Hall to protest Comstock's suppression of the *Physiologist* and other health journals, including *Dr. Kinget's Health Journal, Boston Agents' Advocate*, and *Dr. Foote's Health Monthly*. The other publications had been informed they could not use second-class postage rates, effectively crippling them. The Paine Hall Liberal League secretary W. S. Bell read a letter from Chase in which she called Comstock an "Autocrat of Vaseline and Vice." The Post Office, she wrote, had "set its inquisitorial foot upon our cherished free press rights." Comstock had recently published his first book, *Frauds Exposed*, a self-congratulatory work summing up his achievements; J. W. Stillman, publisher of *Boston Agents' Advocate*, claimed that the Post Office had banned his journal only after he wrote negative reviews.

The Heywoods' Free Love League met in Boston on May 29 and 30 to protest the *Physiologist* suppression. Liberals established a legal defense fund for Chase. The postal ban was lifted in time for the June issue, though *Dr. Foote's Health Monthly* remained under suppression. Chase and Preston devoted the entire June *Physiologist* to supportive newspaper articles about them. On its penultimate page was a letter to friends, announcing: "Here is our PHYSIOLOGIST. We are happy . . . We want the opinion to become popular in the Post Office that the power that provides for the mail system in this country, and supports its service, is positively opposed to its being prostituted to the spiteful purposes of any spy."

The entire back page was an ad for the ten-dollar Comstock syringe, with testimonials from doctors, editors, and customers. "Anthony Comstock has at least been of some service to humanity in calling public attention to such a blessing as your Syringe," read one.

In July, the bans on *Dr. Foote's Health Monthly* and *Dr. Kinget's Health Journal* were also lifted. The Heywoods wrote, "Comstock's savage effort to so far confirm traditional subjection of woman to man that she shall not even know how to resist male use of her person by preventing conception is illustrated in his base assaults on citizens for selling syringes. Provoked to good works Sarah [*sic*] Chase invented one for this very purpose; he arrested her, but she escaped."

Comstock was rattled by the damages suit and he or Colgate

mentioned it in the 1882 *Annual Report*, claiming that Chase and "others of like infamous character—bad company for our Chief" had sued him. The report claimed there was a conspiracy to injure him and have him removed from his position as post office inspector, "thus seriously crippling our usefulness. In all of this they most signally failed, thanks to the fairness and justice of the faithful and efficient Postmaster General, Hon. Thomas L. James."

Over the next several years, Chase was evidently able to restore her income, through medicine, contraceptive sales, and real estate. In 1886, at forty-nine years old, she placed an advertisement with a matrimonial agency, calling herself a "healthy, middle-aged widow, liberal in religion, a college graduate, with a yearly income of $8,000." She said she wanted to meet a "high-minded, substantial gentleman, of forty-five to sixty years. Wealth not essential, but a competence and business ability essentials." After receiving numerous replies, she entered into a correspondence with a man who came to New York to meet her. She thought he drank too much and was after her money. He went home.

Through a different matrimonial agency, she wrote to a man from Butte, Montana: fifty-nine-year-old Thomas Hookey, a judge. They wrote letters and exchanged photographs. Convinced she was in love, she would walk in her garden, reading "Tommy's letters" and gazing at the moon. One day, while suffering from a severe headache, she rubbed the letters against her head. The pain went away.

A year after they became pen pals, she heard the doorbell ring. A servant opened the door, and when Chase laid eyes on Hookey, who was carrying a valise, an umbrella, and a walking stick, she rushed into his arms and sobbed, "You have come at last, Tom. You have come at last." Soon after his arrival, he prepared a turkey for her. They were married in her home on December 4, 1888, in a ceremony that made national news, due to her arrest by Comstock and the damages suit, which she later dropped.

She entered on the groom's arm, wearing a white silk dress trimmed with black lace and carrying a large bouquet of roses. The couple stood by the piano at one end of the drawing room and clasped hands. He said, "I take thee, Sara B. Chase, as my lawful, wedded wife, proving to you in the presence of these witnesses to be a loving husband in sickness and in health until death do us part." She asked him to remove his glove and said, "I hereby take you, Thomas Hookey, to be my lawful husband and prove to you a faithful, loving wife in sickness and in health until death do us part." He forgot to kiss her, perhaps a bad omen. She turned and kissed Grace. Their marriage contract lay on a table, tied up with a big piece of blue ribbon. General Barnum asked the guests to sign as witnesses.

Explaining her unconventional marriage ceremony to *The Sun*, Chase said she was certain that Hookey was of "the best character," a man she could "trust implicitly." She said they chose a Quaker service because it was the simplest and did not require an officiating clergyman. She decided to keep the last name Chase. Judge Hookey prepared a chicken salad for the wedding lunch.

But only four months later, she told him to leave. They signed, and had notarized, a contract stating that they were separated by mutual consent. Asked by a reporter what had gone wrong, she said, "I thought he loved me, but he did not; it was my money he was after." Once again, she was alone.

Though the ban on the *Physiologist* had been lifted in June 1881, Chase and Preston managed to put out only a few more issues before they folded it due to lack of funds. But that was not the end of the Comstock syringe. Angela and Ezra had been so taken by Chase's case that, three years after the *Physiologist* first advertised a "Comstock syringe," they did the same in the July 1881 issue of *The Word*.

A notice about the syringe, repeating a familiar theme, said, "If Comstock's mother had had a syringe and known how to use it, what a world of woe it would hav[e] saved us!" The August ad stated:

COMSTOCK TRIED to imprison Sarah [*sic*] Chase for selling a syringe; she had him arrested and held for trial, while
the syringe goes "marching on" to hunt down and slay
Comstock himself!

WOMAN'S NATURAL RIGHT to Prevent conception is
unquestionable; to enable her to protect herself against in-
vasive male use of her person the celebrated Comstock Syringe,
designed to prevent disease, promote personal purity and
health, is coming into general use.

They kept advertising it in the next few issues of the paper, and in
December they revised their advertisement, proclaiming that the
product would thereafter be named "The Vaginal Syringe," so that
"its intelligent, humane and worthy mission should no longer be li-
belled by forced association with the pious scamp who thinks Congress gives him legal right of way to and control over every American
Woman's Womb."

As freethinkers were publicly arguing for reproductive rights, physicians lobbying in Albany scored an important victory. That year, the
New York Comstock law was revised to exempt articles or instruments
used by physicians in their practices, or prescribed by physicians, "for
the cure or prevention of disease." Physicians who prescribed them or
directed patients to use them were not committing an offense. The
physician's exemption would become crucial when Margaret Sanger
opened a birth control clinic in Brooklyn thirty-five years later.

Late in 1881, Chase and others spoke at the first public meeting in
New York of a group called the Institute of Heredity. The weather was
rainy and disagreeable, and thirty people congregated at Republican
Hall in Madison Square to discuss the idea that poor, criminal, and
alcoholic people should not have children. Stephen Pearl Andrews spoke
on heredity, and Chase said some women were not fit for motherhood
and should not have children. She then thanked God for old maids, who
became teachers, dressmakers, physicians, artists, and lawyers.

About a month after the Institute of Heredity held its meeting,

Comstock gave an evening talk at the YMCA's Association Hall, ten blocks south. His speech was titled "The Corrupters of our Youth," and the occasion was the ten-year anniversary of his time with the society. He mentioned the NYSSV's current concerns, such as gambling and "flash," or sensational, newspapers targeted at children. He was deeply incensed by the "liberal fraud" against him. The National Liberal League now had two hundred subordinate leagues seeking to repeal the Comstock laws. The league, he contended, was "so liberal that it would give the vilest and lowest of criminals freedom to send their engines of moral death into your very families to destroy your children at your firesides." The room broke into applause.

He was thinking about these "vile" and "low" criminals when, on October 26, 1882, he and a U.S. deputy marshal entered Mountain Home. This time, nearly five years after his first visit, the Heywoods were in. Comstock offered to shake hands with Ezra, and Ezra put his hands behind his back. The Heywoods' daughter Psyche, a toddler, waddled in. Comstock tried to coax her closer.

"Don't pollute her with your caresses," Ezra told him.

He was there to arrest Ezra on four counts of sending obscene matter. Specifically, Ezra was charged with mailing a copy of *Cupid's Yokes*, a special edition of *The Word* (*The Word Extra*) that contained two Walt Whitman poems, and two issues with "Comstock syringe" ads. Some of the material had been sent to a reader named "J. A. Mattocks" in Nyack-on-Hudson, New York. When Comstock logged the arrest in his book, he called Ezra "a notorious offender," adding that he also advertised "an article to prevent conception." Clearly, he could not bring himself to call the article a "Comstock syringe."

It was no surprise that Walt Whitman's poems were appearing in an obscenity indictment, as Comstock had been after the poet for nearly a year. The prior fall, a Boston publishing house had issued an edition of Whitman's landmark and groundbreaking poetry collection *Leaves of Grass*, which included "To a Common Prostitute." Then, in the spring of 1882, due to pressure from Comstock, the Suffolk County district attorney advised the publisher that *Leaves of Grass* was obscene. The publisher asked Whitman to remove the offending verses, but he refused and found a Philadelphia printer for his book, which became a commercial success. The reformer and publisher Benjamin R. Tucker tried to challenge the assault on free expression, obtained copies of the book from Philadelphia, and advertised it for sale in his journal and in the daily Boston papers. According to Tucker, Comstock begged the U.S. district attorney for an indictment, but the request was refused. By the fall of 1882, the book was being sold openly by Boston booksellers. Ezra's approach was to print two of the "objectionable poems": "A Woman Waits for Me" and "To a Common Prostitute." Comstock took no action against Tucker, the New York booksellers who were selling the Philadelphia edition, or the Boston book dealers. Instead, he went after Ezra.

The case was postponed, and Angela argued in *The Word* that the indictments were unjust, specifically on the Comstock syringe ads. A syringe was more than just a syringe, she argued:

> Now, not books merely, but a Syringe is in the fight; *the will of man to impose vs. the Right of Woman to prevent conception is the issue.* The giddy, evasive ways, in which the sexes hav[e], hitherto, met must turn to serious facing of facts. Does not Nature giv[e] *to* woman & install her *in* the right of way to & from her own womb? Shall Heism continue to be imperatively absolute in coition? Should not Sheism hav[e] her way also? Shall we submit to the loathsome impertinence which makes Anthony Comstock inspector and supervisor of American women's wombs? This womb-syringe question is to the North what the Negro question was to the South; as Mr. Heywood stood beside the slave demanding his liberation, so now he voices the emancipation of woman from sensual thral[l]dom. Clergymen tell us we must "bear the cross," that is, the penis; Congressmen vote our persons sluice-ways for irresponsible indulgence,

empower Comstock to search bureaus and closets,—lest
by means of a syringe, or otherwise, we resent the outrage!

She proposed a satirical alternative to the Comstock law: a man
would "flow semen" only when a woman said he could. She suggested
other rules. A man had to keep his penis tied up with what she called
"'continent' twine," which he would have to keep nearby to assure
his virtue. If he were found without the continent twine, he would be
"liable, on conviction by twelve women, to ten years imprisonment
and $5000 fine." She then proposed "that a feminine Comstock shall
go about to examine men's penises and drag them to jail if they dare
disobey the semen-twine 'law'!"

The essay garnered notice. Tucker called it a tract "in which the
sexual organs are spoken of with unusual freedom . . . Still the argument is legitimate, sober, and earnest, and contains nothing lewd or
lascivious in the least, and it would be a most contemptible outrage
to punish any one for circulating it." The *Truth Seeker* editor George
Macdonald, who had taken over after Bennett's death following his
prison release, admonished, "If the social relations of men and women
can be discussed vulgarly, Mrs. Heywood has found the way to do it.
Her writings remind one forcibly of some of the trash found in the Bible, except that she is nasty in pleading for woman's rights, while the
so-called sacred book is obscene in degrading woman."

While Ezra was awaiting trial, his brother Samuel again tried to
wrest the house from the Heywoods, and a jury assessed financial
damages against them. With the threat of foreclosure looming, they
sold Mountain Home to a joint stock corporation of friends and supporters. Angela and the children temporarily moved to Boston with
Angela's sister Josephine.

The trial began in April 1883, in Worcester. Ezra represented himself. Comstock testified that he had penned the "J. A. Mattocks" letters
and said that two other decoys had been written by men he employed.
He claimed he never used more than ten fictitious names and felt

himself to be a Christian. In Ezra's account of the trial, Comstock also admitted that he had, in fact, boasted of the number of victims who, as Ezra put it, "died under his treatment."

Ultimately, the judge threw out the *Word Extra* and *Cupid's Yokes* charges, leaving only those related to the syringe. In his address to the jury, Ezra argued that women had a right to control conception. Free lovers, he noted, did not generally use contraceptive devices, he said, but:

> since Comstockism makes male will, passion and power absolute to impose conception, I stand with women to resent it. The man who would legislate to choke a woman's vagina with semen, who would force a woman to retain his seed, bear children when her own reason and conscience oppose it, would way lay her, seize her by the throat and rape her person. I do not prescribe vaginal syringes; that is woman's affair not mine; but her right to limit the number of children she will bear is unquestionable as her right to walk, eat, breathe or be still.

He quoted from what he described as a jury of sixteen women—including Angela, Elmina Slenker, and the Milwaukee gynecologist and women's rights activist Juliet Severance—saying that they voiced "resolute indignation at vice-society effort to supervise maternal function by act of Congress."

The judge told the jury that the burden was on the government to demonstrate that the syringe was manufactured specifically for the purpose of preventing conception. The jury men were sent out with the Comstock syringe ads and the October *Word* as evidence. The men wanted to acquit from the beginning but also wanted lunch on the government's tab. After eating their meal, they waited until three o'clock to give the verdict: not guilty of obscenity on the remaining charges. Ezra and Angela's supporters burst into applause. In a speech before the New England Society for the Suppression of Vice, Comstock said that the court had "turned into a free-love meeting."

A month after Ezra was acquitted, he was arrested under Massachusetts law for mailing a reprint of several *Word* articles that included Angela's "The Woman's View of It—No. 1," a.k.a. the penis twine essay. Though Angela's words had led to his indictment, Ezra was charged for mailing the reprint. Angela was pregnant with their fourth child, and Ezra thought it would send a strong message if she were put on the stand. He called her "the real person assailed" and wanted her to appear as a witness on "Woman's behalf."

Angela desperately wanted to be held accountable for her writing and told Ezra that if he were imprisoned again, she would not visit him. She didn't want to be perceived, as Andrews wrote, as "a mere wife, following the fate of her husband, instead of a free individual fighting her own battles." Angela called the trial a "male 'obscenity' case" in which a woman had "persistently kept the words Penis and Womb traveling in the U.S. Mails."

The trial was postponed four times due to her pregnancy. During the postponements, the judge died and was replaced by Robert Pitman, who was believed to be more sympathetic to Ezra. Andrews organized a defense fund in Princeton, and a petition circulated calling for the charges to be dismissed. Angelo Heywood was born in the fall of 1883, his birth announced by his father in *The Word*: "Our baby Boy came Sept. 14, weighted 10 lbs., & seems all right, physically and mentally . . . Mrs. H is about house but not very stout yet." The baby made Angela reflect on sex inequality: "As I look upon my baby-boy and forecast his future, I am moved, more deeply and firmly than ever, to see to it that this Sex Question, in all its impressive bearings, is set in the light of searching Intelligence."

The penis twine essay case came up when Angelo was still an infant. The new presiding judge, Pitman, ruled that the prosecutors had to charge and prove a *willful* intent to corrupt the morals of youth, which he did not believe had been the case. He dismissed the charges. Ezra was free.

In *The Word*, Angela began to use even franker, bolder language to advance her idea that there was nothing shameful about sex, and that so-called moralists such as Comstock were the ones making it dirty. In a piece called "Sex-Nomenclature—Plain English," she wrote, "Cock is a fowl but not a *foul* word; upright, integral, insisting truth is the soul of it, sex-wise." In "The Ethics of Touch—Sex-Unity," she mused, "Such graceful terms as hearing, seeing, smelling, tasting, fucking, throbbing, kissing, and kin words, are telephone expressions, light-houses of intercourse centrally immutable to the situation; their apt-ness, euphony and serviceable persistence make it as impossible and undesirable to put them out of pure use as it would be to take oxygen out of air."

In one article, she argued in favor of abortion following a rape: "Women do not like rape, and have a right to resist its results. To cut a child up in a woman, procure abortion, is a most fearful, tragic deed; but *even that* does not call for man's arbitrary jurisdiction over woman's womb." She believed that the marriage contract robbed women of the "power to resist rape even, inside the marital cage, while the married penis becomes an active creator of 'prostitutes,'—married men being the most constant & lucrative patrons of houses of ill-fame!"

But none of these strongly worded pieces were indicted. Instead, it would be the penis twine article that landed the Heywoods in court for the third and final time. In the spring of 1890, more than twelve years after his first arrest at the Nassau Hall free love convention, Ezra was arrested again. He was indicted by a federal jury in Boston on three counts of obscenity published in *The Word*. Two were for explicit letters about sex sent by readers, and one was for an April 1889 reprint of Angela's penis twine essay. Throughout the trial, Angela, who sat with one of the children on her lap, kept her gaze fixed on Ezra's face.

She was the only character witness for him that the judge would allow. For the first time in her life, she was able to testify about her writing. "I am the wife of defendant," she said. "I wrote the matter set out in the third count of the indictment beginning 'Now to books merely' et cetera." She wanted her article to be understood as polit-ical speech, but District Attorney Frank D. Allen instructed Ezra's lawyers "that the motive and purpose or object for which the article was printed are entirely immaterial and that the defendant and they will not be permitted to give any evidence tending to show what the motive, purpose, or object of the publication was."

The jury found Ezra guilty on two charges, one involving a letter, the other Angela's penis twine article. Ezra's attorneys moved to quash the indictment on the grounds that (1) there was no offense, (2) the statute was unconstitutional, and (3) the indictment contained no allegation that Ezra had known the papers were lewd, obscene, and lascivious. They were overruled.

At the sentencing, on July 24, 1890, District Attorney Allen moved for five thousand dollars or imprisonment for at least five years. Judge George M. Carpenter asked Ezra if he had anything to say. Angela's sister Josephine rose to her feet. "Men of Massachusetts!" she cried. "In the name of the rights of man, I protest against this proceeding. I ask you if you countenance a court that does not aid justice, that does not weigh equity?"

"Take her out of court," Judge Carpenter ordered.

"That does not countenance liberty," she replied.

"Remove her," said the judge.

Ezra began to deliver a statement but was cut off. Angela asked, "Your Honor, may I say a few words?"

"No," Judge Carpenter replied. Ezra was sentenced to two years' hard labor in Charlestown State Prison. As one newspaper reported, Angela and Josephine "made the corridors ring with their shouts of denunciation."

Angela later wrote that "the *he* was imprisoned in part to shut up the *she* tongue-pen-wise. But I am still at it; penis, womb, vagina, semen are classic terms, well-revered in usage; other words, of equal dignity and trenchant familiarity form the clear-cut vocabulary in common use."

In another piece, she declared,

> I am not ashamed of myself—or of you either. I come at this critical hour unto yourselves as well for your sakes as

for the sake of Mr. Heywood, the chosen father of my four children . . . I come openly, frankly to *converse* about man, as seriously, as impassionately, as though my subject were the stars above our heads or the rocks beneath our feet . . .

I am told that the words are "obsolete," by persons who dislike them because they are in such common use! The words are pounced upon by the Vice Society and "indicted" as "obscene," though classic literature, scientific authority, learned men, and all the standard English dictionaries give them to me, and my purpose in use of them is always good.

In the same issue of *The Word*, the Heywoods' friend Lucian V. Pinney wrote that Angela believed "that Mr. Heywood is right, that with him she has a serious life work to perform and that she should do her full share of the labor cheerfully, suffering any sort of deprivation necessary to help him develop new ideals. Her intelligence, breadth, and clearness of vision are shown in her leaflet literature, where on the difficult and intricate subject of sex she has said some of the best things that have yet appeared in print, without saying any of the worst."

Ida C. Craddock

10

A NEW SECRETARY

Just a few months before Comstock's second attempt to nab Ezra on obscenity charges, Ida Craddock received some disappointing news. At the age of twenty-four, in the summer of 1882, while living at home with her mother and teaching stenography at Girard College, she had decided to try to get admitted into the University of Pennsylvania's liberal arts program. There was only one problem: though Vassar, Wellesley, and Smith admitted women, a woman seeking an Ivy League education faced a challenge. Barnard was not founded until 1889; Radcliffe, 1894. The Penn board requested that Craddock take the exams—four days on geography, math, grammar, Latin, and Greek, and an oral exam on Cicero and Horace. She passed "very satisfactorily," according to the Faculty of the Arts board, which recommended to the Penn board that she be admitted. *The Philadelphia Inquirer* reported that a decision on her admission would "define the future policy of the institution in regard to the admission of women students."

The Board Committee on the Department of Arts, to which she was applying, met the following month to consider Craddock's application. One board member, a trustee and former state senator named Frederick Fraley, submitted detailed plans for women's admission to the college, recommending that the plan be adopted at the opening of the next term. Craddock was to be provided with "all of the facilities that may be practicable for carrying on her stud-ies" before this "women's section" opened. But at the next trustees' meeting, a bishop named William Bacon Stevens brought forth a resolution opposing any admission of women to the Department of Arts. The resolution passed. After two other women tried to be admitted the same month, Craddock's case was used as justification to reject them.

Proponents of women's education petitioned the trustees, asking them to "open the doors of the University to women on the same terms as to men." It was signed by Board of Education member Si-mon Gratz; Dr. Henrietta Payne Westbrook, one of the first women in Philadelphia with a medical degree; and her husband, Richard Westbrook, a clergyman turned radical lawyer. It was also signed by Craddock's former teacher Annie Shoemaker, principal of the girls' department at Friends' Central.

Even Susan B. Anthony mentioned Craddock in a speech hosted by the Woman Suffrage Association at Spring Garden Unitarian Church, to which Craddock and her mother belonged. The *Inquirer* re-ported that Anthony spoke with enthusiasm about coeducation, "ex-pressing her hearty approval of the recent efforts of Miss Craddock to open to young women the doors of the University of Pennsylvania." Anthony was still advocating for suffrage and other women's rights causes nearly a decade after the Supreme Court decided in *Minor v. Happersett* that citizenship did not give women the right to vote, and that suffrage was under state jurisdiction. The movement's most sig-nificant recent victory was that the House and Senate had, that year, appointed select committees on Woman Suffrage.

Craddock tried at least three other times to gain admission to Penn, with no success. At the 1883 commencement, the university granted its first "bachelor of laws" to a woman named Caroline (Carrie) Burnham Kilgore; she became the first woman permitted to practice law before the Supreme Court of Pennsylvania. But Crad-dock was half a century ahead of her time: it would be more than fifty years before the University of Pennsylvania College for Women was formed.

Ida Celanire Craddock was born on August 1, 1857, to a secular father, Joseph Craddock, and a domineering, French-born mother, Lizzie, who would become active in the Women's Christian Temperance Union. An earlier baby girl, also named Ida, had died in infancy. Joseph sold patent medicines, including cannabis, and died of consumption when Ida was six months old. After his death, Lizzie took over the business. She then married a produce merchant, who also died, leaving his estate to Lizzie. Her third husband, Thomas B. Decker, lived with her from 1878 to 1886, after which he died or left.

Lizzie was an active writer and reader and wanted Ida to become an author. Ida had been bright from the start, learning to read at two and a half. As a schoolgirl, she excelled at Friends' Central, graduating second in her class. She studied French, German, and Latin, and afterward studied classics privately with a professor. After graduation, she wrote short stories under the name "Celanire" in *Potter's American Monthly* and *The Saturday Evening Post*. An indication of her future path as a sexologist came in a story called "An Old Maid's Reverie." It was an account of an unattractive young woman, Edna Ripley, whose crush marries one of Edna's friends. To forget her heartache, Edna starts a sewing school, a reading circle, and an art club, but she is bored living in her small country village. She moves to the city—a fictional indication, perhaps, of Craddock's hunger to be known on a grand scale. Edna writes essays and books and meets cultured men and women. As Craddock wrote in Edna's voice, "The old, aching pain at my heart began to cease. I learned to take joy in life, just as it was."

It was likely due to frustration over her middling freelance writing career that she decided to try to get into Penn. The rejection hit her hard, and she struggled to find new ways to use her intelligence. About a year after her fourth failed attempt to gain admission, Richard Westbrook, the attorney who had signed her petition and a proponent of church-state separation, became a trustee of the Wagner Free Institute of Science, a natural history museum that provided free science education to Philadelphians. Westbrook, who had a strong, clean-shaven face and gray hair, brought Craddock on for an administrative position. She worked with tenants of the institute, which rented out row houses for income. For unknown reasons, she resigned after only five months.

Lizzie Decker may have wanted her daughter to break the gender barrier at Penn, but she also wanted her to find a husband, and so in the summer of 1884 she decided to take her on a group trip out west. Their train stopped in the Royal Gorge of Arkansas, where Craddock joined a few others in climbing up the hillside. She returned to the train full of energy and proud of her fortitude, but as she was passing through one of the train cars, she overheard two married society women on the trip gossiping about her. "With all her intellect," said one, "she lacks in femininity."

Though she kept her head high, she was rankled. What was so unfeminine about her? She sat one car ahead of them, thinking. She knew she was attracted to men; as a teenager she flirted with a businessman friend of her mother when he came to visit. He would call her "Miss Ida" and give her a book or piece of music, or sit and chat. She would darn stockings and talk with him, and he would stare at her inscrutably. Later he professed love and proposed marriage, but she refused, viewing him as a friend. He died young, of tuberculosis.

On the train, she determined to be more of a flirt. Flirting, she wrote years later in her mini-memoir, "Story of My Life," was "going dangerously near to the verge of allowing a man to take liberties in terms of caresses, and yet never overstepping that verge by criminal act." As men from her trip passed through her car, she looked at each one, trying to determine if she was attracted to any of them. Finally, an older man caught her eye. She had met him earlier on the trip and found him handsome. He, too, lived in Philadelphia. She began a conversation with him, and he lingered. As they kept talking, he took the seat next to her.

When they returned east, they courted, but Craddock recounted, "He refrained, honorably, from taking advantage of my very evident disposition to fling myself at him. If he had been anything else than the honorable man and gentleman that he was, I might have gone into my grave as his mistress, so infatuated was I with him. Yet I knew somewhere within me that he was not my true mate." She decided to break off her relationship with the "cut-and-dried bachelor." Instead, she wanted to find a husband for whom her soul and body cried out.

But to find that intimacy, she had to get out from Decker's clutches. Craddock's primary bone of contention was that Decker would not clean the house sufficiently to allow her to hold an intellectual salon where she could gather with like-minded people to discuss religion, belief, and women's rights. A day after they returned from their trip out west, mother and daughter argued. Decker came into her room and "got me up at the head of the bed," Craddock recalled in "Story of My Life," "between the bed and the wall, and with flaming eyes and disheveled hair, came at me in a way which made me suppose my last hour had come." Craddock told Decker she reminded her of a hag character in a popular play. Decker, who had whipped Craddock throughout her childhood and into her adulthood, struck her, bruising Craddock's hand with her ring; she then pressed her against the wall and made her promise not to speak that way again. To end the argument, Craddock promised. But she resolved to depart; she had had enough. Leaving her job at Girard College, she moved to California around 1887.

In San Francisco, Craddock found a job in a bank. She enrolled in an adult education class at a church, where she read Herbert Spencer's *Principles of Psychology*, an influential contribution to evolutionary theory and natural selection, and learned about psychology and sociology. She felt smarter than her classmates, writing to her childhood friend Katie Wood, "I can say truly, without the least egotism, that I have never yet been in any class or club that went quite fast enough for me." She also became interested in the occult, which would lay the groundwork for her later work as a sexologist.

She read *Open Door*, by the Scottish novelist Margaret Oliphant, which suggested that inert objects could contain their own sounds. "Not only is my horizon of scientific knowledge widening," Craddock wrote Wood, "not only is my mode of thinking becoming more consecutive and logical; but my sense of the nearness of God, of the truth of the assertion that in him we live and move and have our being, grows daily more vivid." But she had a hard time making money and felt frustrated by her lack of higher education. If she had a university degree or normal school (teacher training) certificate, she told Wood, she could have had her pick of positions.

Later in life, she would write a deeply personal essay, "Telepathy Between the Sexes," about an experience she had in California and women's mental power to resist sexual assault. To make extra money she had taken a position as a canvassing agent, selling copies of *The History of California* door-to-door. She visited a small town a few miles away from San Francisco and rented a room in a lodging house. As she knocked on doors, canvassing, she grew despondent. If she stuck with canvassing, she would become "hard, unfeminine, and possibly, unwomanly to some extent." This conflict, and her fear of being unfeminine, would be central to her personal and professional life.

But the town was charming, and as she walked through it she fantasized about becoming a servant in one of the cottages. When she returned to her lodging house, she met the brother of the hotel keeper, who was the bartender. He asked how she had done with the book canvassing. She laughed and said she'd had no success, and asked him to send the bill to her room.

A little later, while inside her room, she heard a knock. Her arms were folded and she wore a shawl, and she was pacing to keep warm. When she opened the door, the bartender came in, without taking off his hat. She asked if he knew a place in town where she could get a job as a governess, chambermaid, or waiter girl. Suddenly he lunged at her, hands raised, and grabbed her shoulders. Without unfolding her arms, she wiggled free. She was certain that he was going to rape her, and that she had to assert her superiority in order to avoid attack.

Taking on a cold, contemptuous voice, she said, "As I was saying, sir, I am very desirous of finding work." He backed all the way to the wall, his face white, his limbs trembling, and removed his hat.

"Oh, Madam," he said. "I see that I have made a mistake. I hope you will forgive me." She said she did, and suggested he leave. Alone, she locked the door, threw herself onto her knees, "and burst into tears of mingled terror and thankfulness." For years she would try to understand how women might have, and wield, power over men—despite the fact that men had the power to rape.

Back in San Francisco, she grew increasingly demoralized by her professional options, writing Wood, "I have begun to question why it is that I, who am capable and industrious, should be foredoomed to a life of drudgery—especially when my life could be made a real blessing to the world." She wanted to be a blessing to the world; she just had to figure out how to do it.

The summer of 1889 was pivotal. Craddock's bank employer in San Francisco offered to take her along on a trip to Alaska; he was writing a compendium on Alaska and its resources. The trip transformed her views on sex and religion. In Sitka, she saw glaciers, icebergs, and religious symbols, including human figures carved from wood. One was a male figure holding a fish—a phallic idol. Other phallic symbols included totem poles, and obelisks and oval-topped slabs on Christian graves. She was so inspired that she wrote an article on Alaskan mythology, which was published in *The Truth Seeker's Annual & Freethinkers' Almanac*. It was a stamp of approval from the free thought world and a validation after her unsuccessful quest to get into Penn. Soon after her return to San Francisco from Alaska, she received an intriguing job offer from Richard Westbrook, who was now the newly elected president of the American Secular Union (ASU).

Some of the more radical members of the National Liberal League had recently spun off and formed the ASU. The shift was linguistic, in part; the word *liberal* had become a point of controversy because members believed it was too easily associated with certain branches of Christianity, such as Unitarianism (thus, *Secular*). *Union* was to indicate a collaboration between American and Canadian secularists. The ASU formed two hundred fifty auxiliary chapters to campaign for secularization within their states. In 1886, ten thousand people signed a petition to keep the Metropolitan Museum of Art open on Sundays.

When Westbrook invited Craddock to join him as corresponding secretary at the ASU, the group was in a moment of transition. Westbrook wanted it to appeal to agnostics, Spiritualists, evangelicals, Universalists, Unitarians, Free Religionists, and ex-Catholics. To manage this, he wanted new officers, people unknown in freethinker circles. Craddock certainly fit. She decided to return to Philadelphia to take the position. But she did not want to stay long in Decker's house. She wrote Wood that she wanted her own apartment, which she would transform into a gathering place "for the bright intellects and liberal and cultured minds of the city . . . I shall have my salon yet before I die."

She took the secretary post, briefly staying with the Westbrooks before moving back in with Decker. She returned to teaching at Girard College to bring in money. Philadelphia in the late 1880s was an exciting place to be a radical, especially a radical woman. One of the better known of these, with whom Craddock crossed paths, was Voltairine de Cleyre, a freethinker who would go on to found the Ladies' Liberal League. An offshoot of the Friendship Liberal League, it was a venue to host intellectual discussions on sex, political ideas, and revolution. There were talks and lectures for anarchists, freethinkers, and free lovers, all opposed to the Comstock laws.

In her ASU work, Craddock soon found "that the secretary of a national society has practically to run the whole thing." She swiftly made new friends within the ASU. One member who attended a convention in Philadelphia took a seat in the hall and was immediately asked, "Do you think Miss Craddock is pretty?" He answered that she was certainly charming, and in an article about the convention called her

> a young lady of attractive appearance, intellectual gifts
> and refined manners, who brings both ornament and aid

to the cause she has espoused . . . She invariably proved her claims and manifested both accuracy and courage. Her eager voice, flashing eye, expressive face, graceful attitudes and dramatic gestures were the most interesting features of the occasion; and when I was invited to go to the theatre in the evening I declined for the reason that I would not obliterate the impression of the genuine action of Ida Craddock by witnessing the feigned acting of any dramatic star.

As corresponding secretary, she read radical papers every week and learned about atheism and materialism. In a piece for the *Boston Investigator* called "How to Make Freethinkers of the Young," she argued for free thought Sunday schools that would teach a variety of views. She wrote a few dozen articles for free thought publications between 1889 and 1891, and delivered talks on the separation of church and state. Still, even as she expanded her knowledge of other religions, she continued to identify as a Liberal Unitarian and belonged to Spring Garden Unitarian Church. Unlike liberal purists who advocated secularism over any religion, she wanted more unity between freethinkers and religious people, like Spiritualists, who supported progressive causes; a broad base had the best chance of influencing politics.

During Craddock's time at the ASU, her interest in women's rights intensified. When the Woman's National Liberal Union was formed by the radical feminist and suffragist Matilda Joslyn Gage in February 1890, Craddock offered the ASU's support. She wanted liberals to recognize that women's rights aligned with their overall platforms on civil and religious liberties. Her tenure at the ASU also coincided with an important advance for suffrage: in 1890, the NWSA and the AWSA merged, forming a new suffrage group, the National American Woman Suffrage Association, with Elizabeth Cady Stanton as its first president. Its mission was to achieve suffrage through the states; when Wyoming entered the union, its constitution was the first to include it.

Craddock was reelected to her secretary position after a year, but the next year, in October 1891, after the annual congress in

Philadelphia, she and Westbrook resigned. Both had come to feel that the ASU was too aligned with free love, she recalled later:

> Free-Lovers and other ultra members wished to force us to take up the defense of radicals who were prosecuted for sending so-called "obscene literature" through the mails, and we would not; neither would [we] encourage Free-Love. In those days, I drew my dress very carefully aside from all such questions, and was exceedingly prim and proper in all my public expression, and careful not to give the slightest encouragement to the left wing of Radicalism.

The new postmaster general in Washington was the Philadelphia-born merchant and civic leader John Wanamaker, who had been appointed by President Benjamin Harrison. Wanamaker was said to have bought himself the job. He banned Leo Tolstoy's novel *The Kreutzer Sonata* from the mail on obscenity grounds because his department store had not secured the discount he wanted in order to stock it.

Even before Wanamaker, recent years had seen a series of high-profile arrests of free lovers under the Comstock law. In 1887, the *Physiologist* associate editor Elmina Slenker had been tried for obscenity in Virginia for mailing sexually explicit "leaflets"—brief sex memoirs, though not her own—to a group of freethinkers and physicians. The National Defence Association, which had close ties to the ASU, raised money for her, and she was acquitted. Around the same time, the *Lucifer* editor Moses Harman was tried for publishing a letter that had references to oral sex, bestiality, and homosexuality and was sentenced to a year in the Kansas penitentiary. After the sentence was delayed, there was a massive effort in the "ultra wing" to protest the sentence.

Just before Craddock ended her stint with the ASU, she bought a Ouija board, which would upend her ideas about free love and almost everything else in the world. Having been curious about Spiritualism since she was a teen, she experimented with the board, trying to feel an otherworldly presence. One day, she did. Certain that unseen intelligences were moving the planchette, over time she tried using a Daestu, or automatic writing machine, to make them heard (these allowed spirits to communicate in strange handwriting), and tracing parts of sentences on her knee using her finger. The unseen intelligences told her to listen for the spoken voice. She heard what she called an "interior voice" rising from her solar plexus, and four spirits announced themselves: her father, Joseph; Nana, a new name for her dead infant sister; Nana's husband, Iases, who said he had passed away six hundred years before; and a young man who called himself Soph. Soph turned out to be the ghost of her mother's businessman friend, the one with whom Craddock had flirted as a girl. Soph told her he had acquired his new name (Greek for *shrewd*) in heaven.

Over the ensuing months, the affection between Soph and Craddock grew deep and playful. He called her "treasure-trove," "Pussy," and "Little womb-man" She called him "Cupid," comparing him to the painting *L'Amour et Psyche, enfants* by William-Adolphe Bouguereau, which had been displayed in the Salon of Paris. She had never been happier. Over the course of eight years, she would write hundreds of pages about their sexual and emotional relationship in a manuscript she called "Diary of Psychical Experiences." In October 1892, he proposed marriage. At first, the idea of marrying an "unseen spirit lover" seemed amusing to her. But "it fired up the latent feminine love of romance." Finally, she agreed to be his wife, "on the Borderland of the two worlds."

The Borderland was the place where she and the ghosts could meet, and where she and Soph could make love. She called her ghosts her "people." They gave her life advice and taught her to be a good person—to exhibit self-control and be amiable, selfless, and loving. After she told the Westbrooks about her new friends, Richard remarked that she was changing for the better and had become more easygoing. But her mother was horrified. Decker had no patience for irrationality. If Craddock believed in ghosts, then surely she was insane.

Soph and Craddock were "married" on Saturday, November 12, 1892, in a Borderland ceremony officiated by Iases. Just a few days earlier, Grover Cleveland was elected, defeating Benjamin Harrison and James B. Weaver to land what would be his second, nonconsecutive term as president. The wedding to Soph was ecstatic for Craddock. Night after night, he lay down beside her and "made love to [her] more ardently and tenderly than ever." When friends pressed her to admit that she had a human, living lover, Craddock denied it vehemently. She would hold this position until her death.

In the first few months of marriage, Soph was invisible, visiting only at night. But one morning in her bed in the living room of her mother's house on Race Street, she awoke shortly before daybreak. Iases told her she would be able to see him:

> Suddenly, as I lay on my side, looking upward, I saw, standing beside the bed, my husband. He was visible only to about the waist, and was dressed as I never saw him on earth—in an evening dress suit of exquisitely fine black broadcloth. He was leaning forward and looking at me, and held in his hand a black silk handkerchief . . . He was standing in a strange light which seemed quite as material as sunshine.

The following summer, when she went off to see the belly dancers in Chicago, she did so as a married woman who was experiencing electrifying sex (with a ghost). For her, the dance was not intellectual. It was personal. After *The New York World* ran her danse du ventre essay, she decided to transform it into a book, printing a short, mimeographed pamphlet called *The Danse du Ventre (Dance of the Abdomen) as performed in the Cairo Street Theatre, Midway Plaisance, Chicago: Its Value as an Educator in Marital Duties.* Less about belly dancing than about better sex, it advocated male continence as the purest form of sex, because the technique led to fewer unwanted pregnancies. Professing humility, she called it a "little pamphlet, as an entering wedge for detailed scientific instruction from those sexologists who are more widely conversant with the matter than I."

Why did she choose a belly-dancing essay to spread the idea of male continence, a technique she herself did not need, given that Soph was a ghost? She wanted a name in the liberal world and saw an opening for a progressive sex educator, or sexologist (a term already in use by the time she visited the World's Fair). Her line of work would come to be known as "marriage reform."

She began selling the book by mail order and in person and pitching it to liberal journals for reviews. She wanted to appeal to respectable people—temperance activists and churchgoers, ordinary Americans seeking no-nonsense advice. But as she sent out more copies, she realized that she was in a bind. Legally, she was unmarried. If she was a virgin, how could she possibly know so much about sex? And if she knew so much about sex, how could she possibly be a virgin?

She decided to pin an extra paragraph to the end of the book:

> I would say that I speak from the standpoint of a wife. My husband, however, is in the world beyond the grave, and had been for many years previous to our union . . . How far the reader may value my testimony as being the result of my personal experience, he will decide of course according to his bias for or against the possibility of communicating with our deceased friends beyond the grave. However, whether my psychical be a fact or a hallucination, I can truthfully say that I have gained from it a knowledge of sexual relations which many years of reading and discussions with other people never brought me.

She had come out as the wife of a ghost.

Aware that this was a risky move in rationalist, atheist circles, when she sent the revised book to Ned Foote at *Dr. Foote's Health Monthly*, she informed him that the extra paragraph was for those "interested in knowing upon what authority I, an unmarried woman, presume to express an opinion on the duties of the marital relation. You are at liberty to refer to the circumstance or not in your Monthly, as you may see fit." She might have been a Spiritualist, but she had marketing savvy.

Foote printed her essay in the September issue, calling her a "clear-headed and clean-minded writer." The *Truth Seeker* editor, George Macdonald, was less kind, calling her "deranged" and concluding, "Let the dead marry the dead." Harman published the piece in *Lucifer*, saying that she had placed herself "in the front rank of thoughtful and fearless investigators into or upon the causes that underlie the inequalities, the vices[,] the diseases, the insanities, the crimes and miseries everywhere prevalent in our so-called society." He also noted that the belly dance had "excited the displeasure of the American censor of morals, Anthony Comstock." Thus, Craddock found herself anointed as an anti-Comstockian by one of the most famous free lovers in the nation, a man who had been sentenced under the Comstock law himself for mailing obscenity in his role as *Lucifer* editor.

Between her former position in the ASU, her freethinker articles, the belly-dancing piece, and the book, she was building a name in radical circles. Now she had to make money, which was the only way to move out of her mother's house permanently. She began pitching herself as an expert on "phallic worship" to liberal outlets in the Northeast, and waited to see who would bite.

11

HELPS TO HAPPY WEDLOCK

Date:	Dec. 4, 1893
Name:	Zera Zeiman
Aliases:	Streets of Cairo dancers,
	Crystal Palace, Lexington Ave & 42 St.
Age:	18
Nationality:	Turkey
Religion:	Heathen
Married or Single:	S
Occupation:	Hip dancer
Offence:	Obscene & indecent exhibition

Date:	Dec. 4, 1893
Name:	Fatima Mesigish
Aliases:	Streets of Cairo dancers,
	Crystal Palace, Lexington Ave & 42 St.
Age:	18
Nationality:	Turkey
Religion:	Heathen
Married or Single:	S
Occupation:	Hip dancer
Offence:	Obscene & indecent exhibition

Date:	Dec. 4, 1893
Name:	Zelika Zieman
Aliases:	Streets of Cairo dancers,
	Crystal Palace, Lexington Ave & 42 St.
Age:	21
Nationality:	Turkey
Religion:	Heathen
Married or Single:	S
Occupation:	Hip dancer
Offence:	Obscene & indecent exhibition

As Craddock was sending out pitch letters about her belly-dancing expertise, New York was being invaded by the dancers themselves. In December 1893, after the conclusion of the World's Fair, four Cairo Street dancers booked an engagement at the Grand Central Palace on Lexington Avenue, the city's premier exhibition hall. Its Crystal Theater seated two hundred, but demand was so high that thousands of people waited outside and spectators wrecked the ticket office in their attempts to obtain tickets.

The dancers—Zora Zeimman, Zuleika Zeimman, Fatima Missgisch, and Farida Mahzar (the newspapers had many spellings of their names)—put on five performances a night, each forty-five minutes long. Red-and-white-striped Turkish cloths draped the stage. Farida, the wife of a Cairo physician, had "a pretty face and large, lustrous black eyes." One article noted Zuleika's "marvellous control over the abdominal muscles." *The Sun* reported that the audience contained men and women, some of them gray-haired, and that the "number of disreputable-looking persons in the crowd was proportionately much less than gathers at the average respectable theatrical performance."

For four nights, beginning on November 29, the women performed without incident. On Sunday, December 3, a headline in the

World asked, "Danse du Ventre in New York: Where Is Anthony Comstock?" That was all the invitation he needed. He instructed Police Inspector Alexander S. Williams, Captain William C. F. Berghold, and two plainclothes detectives to attend the next show. In the final minutes, as Farida performed, Inspector Williams forced his way through the crowd, crying, "Stop that!" He repeated himself as the musicians played on, and finally she ceased. The dancers looked at Williams in amazement.

He put his hand on the footlights and shouted, "This performance cannot go on!" Some cheered, while others rose to their feet, upset. "This may be all right for Chicago," Williams cried, "but it can't go in New York." The management said the show would stop but those who wanted refunds would get them. It took half an hour to clear the room.

After the show was shuttered, the dancers' manager, Adolph Delacroix, issued a statement: "This dance has been in existence over three hundred years and is of a religious character. It has been performed before prophets and soothsayers, and is replete with poetry and grace. Surely if it has commended itself to the religious sentiment of the Orient it cannot be very immoral." Delacroix wanted to ask for an injunction, and his press representative offered to have the women perform for a committee of clergymen. In the meantime, the dancers would do more shows—twelve a day.

On Tuesday, they all danced again, except Farida, who, *The New York Herald* reported, had been frightened off. Captain Berghold was again in the audience. At the show's conclusion, he announced that all three dancers were under arrest. They were charged with a misdemeanor: violating the "immoral conduct" section of the state penal code. The women seemed to treat the affair as a joke. Peals of laughter could be heard coming from their dressing room. Comstock recorded their arrests in the NYSSV logbook.

They were taken in carriages to the Yorkville Police Court in the East Thirties, where they were held on bail. Delacroix retained the Claflin sisters' lawyer, Abe Hummel, who said the dance had been performed all over Europe and at the World's Fair, including "before ladies and gentlemen and members of the clergy." Hummel said he would waive examination and have the case tried in the Court of Special Sessions, which adjudicated six to seven thousand misdemeanor cases per year. Three police justices presided over cases in that court and could either decide the case themselves or transfer it.

Comstock visited Williams at police headquarters to congratulate him on his judgment. The post office inspector agreed the dance was sufficient to create indignation in all decent citizens. In their own countries, he was certain, the dancers would be beheaded if they displayed themselves the way they had in New York.

For the trial, the justices Patrick Divver, Martin McMahon, and Joseph Koch sat on the bench. The women entered the courtroom in their stage costumes, concealed by stylish English cloaks. Zuleika and Zora wore pink slippers, bonnets on their heads, and short veils that partially hid their faces. On the stand, a policeman demonstrated the dance, prompting a spate of laughter from the spectators. Delacroix testified that it was traditional and had been performed for ministers and merchants; Zuleika said that she had been performing it since she was twelve. Hummel asked if she would show the court the dance. She started to move, as though to remove her coat. *The Brooklyn Daily Eagle* reported, "The scar on Anthony Comstock's face assumed a livid color." Justice Koch waved his hand and said, "No, no, Mr. Hummel," to Comstock's and Williams's visible relief. A group at the rear of the courtroom departed.

After a pause, Comstock rose from his seat and began to address the court, standing near Hummel. "Your Honors," he said. "I have seen this dance in Chicago, too. I know and I can prove—"

"Oh! Oh! Now this cannot be allowed," Hummel cut in. "I insist that the Court needs no instruction. You mustn't, Mr. Comstock."

In a higher-pitched voice, Comstock said, "But if evidence to show—"

"That will do," Justice McMahon said. "The Court has already made up its mind."

"I am the friend of American womanhood!" shouted Comstock.

"So am I," replied Hummel.

Justice McMahon found the women guilty and fined them fifty dollars each. Hummel said he would appeal. Delacroix said he would take his show elsewhere. The four women went out into what one newspaper called the "cold unwriggling world."

The women went on to successful burlesque careers, touring the country with their dance. The Hoochy-Koochy became a craze at side-shows and theaters, and at the Coney Island amusement parks, Steeple-chase, Luna Park, and Dreamland. Due to its popularity, every carnival in the country soon had a Street of Cairo. Comstock had exacted his revenge on the dancers, but belly dancing was in the country to stay.

A few months after the belly dancers' trial in New York, Craddock's self-promotional efforts paid off. She booked a speaking gig with the Manhattan Liberal Club at the German Masonic Temple in the Gramercy section of Manhattan; her talk was titled "Survivals of Sex Worship in Christianity and in Paganism." The club held discussions on scientific, social, political, and religious problems. Ned Foote, the club's president, had given a speech on contraception at the New York Liberal Club (the same club at which Chase had delivered her "Responsibility of Sex" talk nearly twenty years earlier). Afterward, he organized the Manhattan Liberal Club, which gave voice to the city's most prominent radicals, including Stephen Pearl Andrews and Walt Whitman. When Craddock learned that Morrill Goddard, editor of the Sunday World, might attend, she wrote to Foote, "I dare say you will rejoice, as we Liberals are usually thankful for being advertised, since it helps to spread the Gospel of Freethought."

After Craddock finished her talk, an officer of the club, Emma Beckwith, rushed to the front, flushed and excited, and said the meeting should adjourn for the sake of the club's good name. She was over-ruled, and the group held a vigorous discussion. In the World article about Craddock's speech, Goddard wrote, "It is fair to say that no such debate ever before followed a lecture delivered before a mixed audience in this town." He mentioned that Craddock handed out copies of her book *The Danse du Ventre*, whose contents he described as "unprintable."

A few weeks after the Manhattan Liberal Club lecture, back at home in Philadelphia, Craddock received a disturbing phone call from the Philadelphia post office inspector Warren P. Edgarton, who told her that *The Danse du Ventre* violated the Comstock law and could not be mailed. She was certain Edgarton had read the *World* article about her talk. When Decker found out, she was so worried that she began making plans to lock Craddock in an asylum.

Craddock soon caught wind of Decker's plans. She was terrified of asylums, imagining bromides, cold-water douches, and electrotherapy, and she fled to the Westbrooks' house. Richard Westbrook wrote Ned Foote a letter that called her a "perfect Monomaniac on all questions pertaining to sex" and "a very unhappy girl." When he wrote this, she was thirty-six years old. He said he had opposed "her silly delusions in regard to the Spirit Husband," and had warned her that *The Danse du Ventre* would be banned. "I have my fears for the future," he concluded. "I have exacted from her a promise to utterly drop all sex questions for at least three months, but I fear she will not do it."

From the Westbrooks', Craddock contacted Carrie Burnham Kilgore, one of the only women lawyers in the city. Kilgore, who had received her law degree from Penn after Craddock was rejected, was a Spiritualist, which Craddock believed would make her sympathetic to the case. But Kilgore did not have good news, telling Craddock that if she were institutionalized and demanded a court appearance, she might never be released. The sexologist was left with only one option: to leave town.

Probably through freethinker circles, Craddock had met the Englishman William T. Stead, editor of London's *Review of Reviews* and author of the bestselling exposé *If Christ Came to Chicago!*, which revealed deep political corruption in the Windy City. Stead had recently launched a London-based journal called *Borderland*, and happened to be in Philadelphia before his planned return to England. He offered Craddock a yearlong position as his secretary in London but insisted she say nothing about *The Danse du Ventre*, or Soph, without his permission. He had two other stipulations: that she go by a pseudonym and pretend to be married. A married father, he was concerned that his wife, Emma Stead, might not like the idea of a single, attractive sexologist working as her husband's secretary.

Craddock visited Stead at his Philadelphia hotel, where they discussed pseudonyms. Though married, Stead had a ghostly lover himself, an American journalist named Julia Ames with whom he communicated through automatic writing. Ames had "written" that Craddock was to be "Mistress Roberts" and wear a ring. Craddock chose the name "Mrs. Irene Sophie Roberts," the middle name an homage to Soph. It must have thrilled her to be able to go by "Mrs.," a validation of the love she felt for her husband.

The next morning, she received a letter from her friend Katie Wood's father, a doctor, asking Craddock to come to his house. Convinced that he was in cahoots with Decker to institutionalize her, she determined to get to England as quickly as possible. She sent her trunks and Remington typewriter to New York, stayed in a Jersey City hotel, and checked into the Astor House in New York under a different pseudonym. Detectives chased her to Jersey City, but she made it onto the ship—which she boarded under her real name. Then she learned that it was an American ship, and became convinced that her roommate was a plainclothes detective. She didn't breathe freely until she stepped off the boat in Southampton. Mrs. Irene Sophie Roberts had arrived in England.

London in the 1890s was a haven for a budding medium such as Craddock. She studied witchcraft, mysticism, hypnotism, crystal gazing, telepathy, automatic writing, and levitation, and visited the Theosophical Society, formerly run by the Russian occultist Madame Helena Blavatsky, who had died a few years before Craddock's arrival. She started to write a manuscript called *Heavenly Bridegrooms*, a scholarly tome on the documented relationships between humans and angels, which also described her relationship with Soph. She studied yoga, beginning to understand the connection between the poses, the body, and spirituality. She learned that *yoga* meant "union" and had the same root as the English word *yoke*. She fantasized about moving to Ceylon to study with a Buddhist monk. In India, she thought, sex was not considered "nasty," but was "reverenced by the wisest of Brahmins as pure."

She also spent time with Alma Gillen, a teacher from the school known as New Thought, a form of mental healing that had grown popular in the United States. Its ministers were primarily women. Gillen practiced a New Thought offshoot called "Divine Science." She taught her students mantras such as "I am spirit; the physical is under my control. I am part of God, and can create outward conditions as I wish." Craddock's ghostly entourage soon expanded from four to six, with the additions of Socrates, whom she called "Head Master of the occultists," and Iason (pronounced "Yahsone"), a German physician who said he had been her guide throughout her childhood and youth.

But her most potent and moving relationship was with Soph. She filled her diary with accounts of their sex sessions, dubbing them "wissenings," for "growing wise." She tried to have sex only when mentally prepared. She bathed beforehand and abstained during her period. They only did it at night, and when Soph took her from behind, she cushioned her breasts with a pillow. She wrote about the wissenings with the detail, and occasional banality, of any sex diarist. "When indications of sex union began to be a bit more promising," went one account, "I asked if I might turn over on my face." "Wednesday night was appointed for union, but I did not feel sufficiently fresh; ditto, last night. Hope to try this evening."

Though one might think that ghostly sex would be perfect by its nature, it wasn't. One session, she fretted, was "more prolonged than has been our wont." And in keeping with then-prevalent views about the clitoris, she often judged her own orgasms. Even a decade before Freud's theories crossed the Atlantic, many sex writers viewed clitoral stimulation as immoral, because it conveyed homosexuality, in the clitoris's resemblance to a penis, or masturbation. Craddock was not immune to this way of thinking. As she was "going over the brink" one night with Soph, she realized that he had moved from her vagina to her clitoris. Then he "seemed to return to the entrance; but it was only to deceive me; just as I began to go off in the height of the orgasm, joyously happy in his presence, I found he was away at the clitoris. Well, I stopped short off, on the very second, hurt at his behavior."

In later books, she would instruct men never to "use the hand to arouse excitement at the woman's genitals." Only vaginal stimulation was truly satisfying to women, she believed, because it brought out their sweet, maternal instincts. The clitoris "should be simply saluted, at most, in passing, and afterwards ignored as far as possible." Clitoral orgasms evoked "a rudimentary male magnetism in the woman, which appears to pervert the act of intercourse." Freud would have agreed with the fiction that only vaginal orgasms were "mature."

After a frustrating wissening in which she did not have a spiritual orgasm, she wrote it off as "a failure." But whatever she felt was partly due to her "own sub-consciousness, which was partially hypnotized by [herself] into a sort of mental masturbation." She may have believed that spiritual orgasms with Soph, which she defined as vaginal, were purer than masturbatory, clitoral orgasms.

While trying to understand more about sex, she read a book on oral sex, as well as Pierre Garnier's *Onanisme*, which argued that masturbation led to poor health. As her views about human sexuality expanded, she saw a new opportunity. "My education has been in so many respects wider than that of most women," she wrote in her diary, "and even wider than that of many men, especially in the direction of the study of sex-ology. It really seems as though my whole life . . . had been one steady preparation for my work."

In the summer of 1895, after about a year in London, she returned to Philadelphia. The trolleys had run on only a few streets when she left, she wrote Stead, but now they were everywhere, extending miles into the country. Their speed helped her understand her ghosts, who could go from one place to another at the speed of thought. She felt new energy in the city; women were becoming more vocal about their rights. A friend had seen a trolley containing only young women, all dressed in white, waving handkerchiefs and singing. Craddock called this vision a "triumphal procession of goddesses of liberty." Despite this spirit of liberty pervading the city, she moved in with her mother once again. Given Decker's antipathy to Soph, Craddock instructed friends to address her in letters as "Miss" and not "Mrs." She wrote Stead that her mother occupied every corner of the home "with her personality, if not with her possessions."

There was also a new complication. In London, she had had her own flat, and privacy. Now Decker was around. "Last Saturday and Sunday, Mother was out of town," she wrote, "and the servant being out on both evenings until about 9.30, I had a good chance to try a vigorous danse du ventre with Soph, with no danger of the creaking of the bed being overheard."

To try to save money for an apartment, Craddock took a job as a stenographer at the Bureau of Highways. She wrote her second sex book, *Helps to Happy Wedlock No. 1 For Husbands*. On the title page she called herself a "Lecturer and Correspondent on Social Purity." In *Helps to Happy Wedlock*, she expanded on prior writings about male continence to include female continence. In her view, the woman, in addition to the man, "should learn to suppress or to induce her orgasm at will," and to pass through orgasms by using self-control. In raising the subject of female orgasm, she was acknowledging that women could and should climax. But in ideal sex, she argued, *both* parties ought to practice continence for better sex and connection. As for withdrawal, she called it "degrading" and said that it did not "properly satisfy either party."

Like John Humphrey Noyes and the Heywoods, Craddock advocated continence as a form of contraception. It was best if children were a minimum of three years apart in age, in the interest of the health of the mother, who should "not be burdened at the time of gestation and lactation with the care of other small children." The only time a man should ejaculate during intercourse was for procreation.

Like Woodhull, who had spoken out against the evil of marital rape, Craddock wrote that a husband should never use his wife "as a convenience for himself, even if she amiably consent to allow herself to be thus used." Unless a woman truly desired "union," the husband was to "refrain from sexual approach. A woman should be as much queen of her own person after marriage as she was while still a maiden." *Helps to Happy Wedlock* was a sex guide, but it also advanced bold ideas about women's rights: women, not only men, could experience sexual pleasure; not every sexual union had to be procreative; pregnancies should be infrequent for maternal health; and marital rape was wrong.

One afternoon in November 1896, about a year after her return to Philadelphia from London, she received another call from Inspector Edgarton. In his office, he informed her that, under the Comstock law, no pamphlet that described the sexual act could be mailed, regardless of the author's intention. Though she decided immediately to stop mailing *Helps to Happy Wedlock*, the visit left her shaken, unsure of the legal status of the other books.

At home she cried for hours, worried that even private letters were indictable:

> Can I give advice by mail, as a correspondent, to people seeking to live aright? Can I write to a friend, say to any one from whom I might seek advice, at some crisis of my life—for instance, in such an ordeal as I lately passed through—if the advice sought has to do in any way with the marital relations of my spirit husband and my self on the sexual plane? Apparently not . . . I feel, at times, as though I were being shut out by a prison wall from all my friends.

She considered suicide, writing, "I don't care tuppence for my life right now. I will lay it down gladly for the cause of preaching right sexual living." If she did take her life, it would be in a way that advertised widely "the great wrong to liberty which chokes my soul's freedom of speech . . . But I cannot and I will not be silenced! If not in life, then in death, this gospel *shall* be preached throughout the world."

While Craddock was contemplating suicide in the "cubicle" at Decker's house, Comstock was celebrating the twenty-fifth anniversary of the NYSSV at Carnegie Hall. Before a packed auditorium of supporters, the NYSSV president, Morris K. Jesup, recalled the day he had met Comstock at the dry goods firm. "I have learned to love this man Comstock," he said. "I believe he is one of the bravest men that God ever raised up for any work." The audience erupted in applause.

Comstock, just a few days shy of fifty-four, was at the peak of his career. He recounted the unsuccessful attempts by liberals to repeal the Comstock law. "Notwithstanding all the combinations of evil men against me," he said, "no weapon formed against us has prospered, and every tongue that has risen in judgment against us has been condemned." The Mendelssohn Quartette Club sang "Blue Bells of Scotland," and the Reverend William C. Faunce pronounced the benediction.

A few months later, Comstock received a check from the society incorporators for $5,000, in recognition of its silver anniversary—about $140,000 today. By this time, he and Maggie were living comfortably. Along with Adele, now about eighteen, and Maggie's sister Jennie, they had moved from Brooklyn to Summit, New Jersey. Many prominent residents of Brooklyn, such as A. F. Libby, a member of the Comstocks' former church, had relocated there. About twenty-five miles from Manhattan, Summit had many churches and private schools, and dated its founding to the American Revolution.

Comstock always had a coach with a team of horses; the couple had joined a new house of worship, Central Presbyterian Church; and they lived in a Queen Anne named Breeze Crest. It was a large, three-story shingled house with a round corner turret, on a two-acre lot. Comstock kept a few tame squirrels in a big cage in the backyard and took pleasure in watching them run on a treadmill. The house held sixteen rooms, including quarters for servants (the Comstocks had three), and a large porch with rocking chairs. One of their favorite pastimes was cribbage in the card room. The kitchen had a modern oil stove. Among their artworks were paintings depicting the signing of the Declaration of Independence and the signing of the Magna Carta. He was a middle-aged family man and a suburbanite. If, over the course of the NYSSV's twenty-five-year history, he had made some enemies among "moral cancer-planters," it was only proof that he was engaged in the promulgation of good.

And yet American views on sex and contraception were changing. In 1897, the National Congress of Mothers (a forerunner of the PTA) heard addresses such as "Moral Responsibility of Women in Heredity," which took a positive view of contraception and eugenics. In an 1890s meeting of the Woman's National Council of the United States, the term *scientific motherhood* was used to describe the benefits of controlled conception. Temperance activists argued that alcohol led to unintended pregnancies, and that voluntary mothers (who were considered morally upright) produced healthier babies than involuntary ones. The Woman's National Council president and former Women's Christian Temperance Union leader Frances Willard predicted, "We are going to have, ere long, a scientific motherhood. Children will be born of set purpose and will cut their teeth according to a plan . . . The best work of the mother will be intelligently done, on the bases of heredity, pre-natal influence, and devout obedience to the laws of health." She did not specify contraceptive methods, but the message was clear: contraception could *help* a woman be a better mother, not provide an excuse for her to shirk her maternal duties.

Back in Philadelphia, after Craddock's harrowing visit to Inspector Edgarton, Craddock turned to Soph for support. He told her that she should teach orally and only to women, agreeing with Craddock's belief that oral instruction, as opposed to written, was protected by the First Amendment and not indictable under the Comstock law. Women made better students anyway, she felt, because they were "less hysterical over sexual matters than are men."

Because there was no way she could see sex clients in her mother's house, she decided to rent a small office. Offices in the city went for about $12.50 a month—too high for her civil servant salary. One day, Soph said to her, "Little Woman, would you be willing to pay seven dollars for an office on Arch Street?" The location was convenient to home and work. While she was walking in the area, Soph indicated a building, 1230 Arch, on a block parallel to the Race Street house. The landlord's wife showed Craddock to a small room, number 6, on the second floor. On the way upstairs Craddock told her a little about her work. The woman was sympathetic; she had heard of "prenatal culture," or prenatal health. The office was a former bathroom, from which the bathtub had been taken out. The walls were papered with pale blue felt paper and the floor stained. It faced east and had a skylight and a large window. Feeling it was "a dear little box of a room," Craddock took it.

She placed advertisements in *The Philadelphia Inquirer* and printed business cards listing her course offerings: "Scientific Motherhood, Pre-Natal Culture, Right Living in the Marital Relation." She charged five dollars for individual lessons and six dollars for couples, with price drops for larger groups. A letter of advice, which clients across the country could solicit, cost one dollar. Because of the mail, she could earn money from people all over the nation.

She called her technique of male and female continence "Divine Science," the name of the New Thought branch of mental healing, but it was her own invention. A woman enrolled in her Divine Science course would have learned something like this: *At the point of orgasm, the man and woman are to turn their thoughts away from bodily sensations and pray to God. If they keep their mind on a high plane, their orgasms can be repressed at will, with no ill effects on the body. This allows sex to be prolonged long enough for the woman to climax, which takes approximately half an hour to an hour after entrance.*

In her mail-order course "Regeneration and Rejuvenation of Men and Women Through the Right Use of the Sexual Function," participants filled out a diagnostic questionnaire and she followed up with advice letters (costing five dollars each). The questionnaire for men—all that survives of it—included ninety-eight questions, such as "Do you usually sleep on your side or on your back?," "Can you prolong the act of coition after entrance sufficiently to arouse an orgasm in your wife?," and

> Do you consider [sex] as a nasty act; or as a pleasurable act of which you are afterwards so ashamed that you could either kick the woman or kick yourself; or as a bodily necessity of a natural sort, akin to the relief felt after urinating or ejaculating your faeces; or as the satisfaction of a healthy, natural appetite, similar to the satisfaction of the appetite of hunger by food; or as a sensuous pleasure which is upon the plane of the sensuous delight to be had in feasting the eye upon beautiful forms and colors, and the ear upon joyous or soothing melodies, and the sense of smell upon delicious or stimulating perfumes?

As she taught more students, in person and through the mail, she gathered enough material to pen two new books: *Advice to a Bridegroom* and *Letter to a Prospective Bride*. In *Advice to a Bridegroom*, she advocated naked sex over clothed. She wrote that foreplay, which she called "love-making," should last between fifteen minutes and half an hour. This was an important idea: couples could be intimate without having intercourse. On the wedding night, "if the entrance be small, lubricate the bride's genitals and your own with some simple ointment—petroleum is as good as any. Be patient. Do as you would with a glove that has a finger a trifle small for you."

In *Letter to a Prospective Bride*, she reassured couples that the wife might not be lubricated the first time. And if a couple was too tired to have sex after the wedding, they should "go straight to sleep like two tired children. Never, upon any account, allow sexual union to take place when either of you is physically weary or mentally fagged out." While she wanted anxious virgins to feel unashamed, she also had complimentary words for women with high libidos. Women who were unwilling to let their pleasure be known by wriggling their hips violated "natural law" and became "abnormal and debased conveniences for their husbands."

A century before second-wave feminists taught the same concept, she argued that women should be responsible for their own orgasms. Further, they had an obligation to make sex pleasurable for men. She would never state it explicitly in one of her books, but she understood that the wriggling of hips would enhance the bride's pleasure because of clitoral stimulation.

Letter to a Prospective Bride was reviewed in Philadelphia's *Medical World*, yet another indication that the self-taught, virgin sexologist's ideas held currency with the medical community. The reviewer called it "both direct and delicate . . . While it may be difficult to talk to a prospective bride, it is easy to hand a little book to her and ask her to read it." Capitalizing off the review, Craddock advertised *Letter to a Prospective Bride* heavily and began to get orders from readers. She also sold on commission the Illinois gynecologist Dr. Alice Stockham's *Karezza*, a guide to better sex, marital pleasure, and limitation of pregnancy.

On November 13, 1897, Craddock mailed *Helps to Happy Wedlock* and *Letter to a Prospective Bride* to a woman named Mary J. Parsons in Philadelphia. A few days later, Philadelphia's *Evening Bulletin* reported that Craddock's boss, Director of Public Works Thomas M. Thompson, came to his desk and found a typewritten sheet of paper. After reading it, he realized that it "treated with startling frankness a physiological subject which is never discussed in public." He asked his assistant, Harry Quick, where the page came from.

"The Highway Bureau," Quick replied.

"What man is bringing matter of that kind into this office?" Thompson asked.

"It is not a man, but a woman," said Quick.

According to the *Bulletin*, Thompson learned that Craddock had written similar pages while at work. He asked her to resign, which she did. Craddock, whom the *Bulletin* described as "a modest-looking, lady-like woman who is evidently intelligent and well educated," told the reporter she was trying to enlighten mankind. "It was plain to be seen," the *Bulletin* wrote, "that she regarded herself as a martyr."

In Craddock's version of events, a colleague ratted her out because she did not pay political assessments to the Republican Party boss Matthew Quay, a senator from Pennsylvania and one of the nation's most powerful men, known for taking graft. When John Wanamaker ran against him unsuccessfully for his Senate seat, he campaigned against "Quayism," or corruption. Whatever the facts, Craddock persuaded Thompson to write her a letter saying the *Bulletin* story was wrong. She considered suing for reinstatement under civil service rules, but soon abandoned the idea. Once she decided to drop the matter, Edgarton was willing to let her off with a warning if she stopped mailing *Letter to a Prospective Bride* and *Karezza*.

She did so immediately and then learned, possibly from Edgarton, that *Helps* was also unmailable. Day after day, she returned remittances, fearing prosecution. She could not tell potential readers how else to obtain her books or what they cost; to do so was a crime under state and federal Comstock laws. By December, with her book income dwindling and her day job gone, she had written a letter to her patrons, citing positive write-ups of *Letter to a Prospective Bride* and asking supporters to take her classes in oral instruction. She begged for "financial, social and legal support," entreating them to try to persuade Philadelphia postal authorities to revoke their decision. "ALL THESE THINGS ARE IMPORTANT," she concluded, "IF THE WORK IS TO CONTINUE UPON A SOUND BUSINESS BASIS. WILL YOU HELP?"

But her woes persisted when, several months later, in April 1898, *The Bookseller and Newsman* ran an article mentioning Craddock's troubles at the Bureau of Highways:

Miss Craddock may not be prudent at all times in her writings, but any one who has the honor of her acquaintance understands the purity of her motives and her loyalty to truth. The title of her last book has startled many of her friends, but it is having an immense sale. "Advice to a Bridegroom" is sold openly, and Miss Craddock claims that some of the most eminently respected people in Philadelphia have sanctioned its publication.

When she read the mention, she knew her "days were numbered."

She soon received a written request from Professor Otis Mason of Washington, DC, seeking information on her books. (Mason was an ethnologist and curator at the Smithsonian Institution who, by coincidence, had overseen the cultural design of the Midway Plaisance at the World's Fair.) She enclosed three circulars for the books and mailed them on May 7. The letter and circulars eventually found their way to Craddock's U.S. Post Office case record. On the stamped envelope she sent to Mason, someone wrote, "Respectfully referred to the Postmaster General."

A month later, she received another request, this time from a Wilbur J. Farnsworth of Philadelphia—the last name Comstock had used with Dr. Sara B. Chase—for *Advice to a Bridegroom* and *The Danse du Ventre*. She mailed "Farnsworth" the two books. A few weeks later, the Philadelphia post office sub-inspector Wallace Moore called Craddock, telling her that "instructions had come from headquarters in Washington." He instructed her to come to the U.S. commissioner William W. Craig's office for a hearing. There, she was arrested on federal obscenity charges. It was May 27, 1898.

The day Sub-Inspector Moore called Craddock in Philadelphia, Comstock entered her name in the NYSSV logbook for the first time. In the column labeled "Offence," he wrote "obscene by mail," with the comment "supposed to be insane." It did not matter to him that she considered her work an aid to young married couples. "Science is dragged down by these advocates," he had written of free lovers such as the Heywoods, "and made a pretended foundation for their argument, while their foul utterances are sought to be palmed off upon the public as scientific efforts to elevate mankind."

In Commissioner Craig's office, Craddock was charged with violating the postal laws by mailing *Letter to a Prospective Bride*, *Advice to a Bridegroom*, and *The Danse du Ventre* to "Wilbur J. Farnsworth" in May and to Mary J. Parsons the previous November. Craig set bail at one hundred dollars, but Craddock told him she would not dream of asking a friend to post it. He agreed to release her for a few days on her own recognizance, after which Decker posted bail. Craddock was set to be indicted two and a half months later.

She gave up her office and decided to flee to Chicago, which she called "that Mecca of Freethought." She had been exposed to the rich culture of Chicago—its religions, ideas, and belly dancing—at the World's Fair five years earlier. She had friends with connections in the Windy City and asked Ned Foote to make introductions on her behalf. Moses Harman of *Lucifer, the Light-Bearer* had moved to Chicago after serving five years in the Kansas penitentiary for violating the Comstock law.

In Chicago, as Craddock wrote Foote, she would give only oral instruction. In a new city, she would reinvent herself as mainstream:

> I am hoping to reach some of the church people and similar sorts who would shrink from me with horror if they heard anything about my being a writer of (so-called) "indecent literature." The less said, the less handle it gives them against me, in case I should chance to run across a prude of either sex. I'm going to try to be swell and toney—as far as my little store of money will permit me to.

Chicago would also allow her, finally, to take on the identity of a wife, in the public's eyes as well as in her own: "I intend to be *Mrs.* Craddock in Chicago and from now on." The question of "Miss" versus "Mrs."

had long been crucial to her; she declared to her friend Katie Wood that it was "very evident that I know by experience of the marital relation, so everybody says. I positively insist that this experience was gained on the Borderland worlds . . . [O]n the other hand, the moment I let fall remarks which show that I know by personal experience what marriage is, I should be looked on with suspicion, if I were known only as 'Miss.'"

As she was preparing to make her escape to Chicago, Decker intervened once again. On June 10, Craddock was eating breakfast with her when a strange man came into the house. He grabbed Craddock by the arm. She ran into the hallway and screamed for the tenant, Mrs. Troth; scribbling down the Westbrooks' and Stead's addresses, she thrust the paper toward Mrs. Troth. Decker snatched the paper away and threatened to have Mrs. Troth arrested. Another man arrived, and with the first man he took Craddock by carriage to the Friends Asylum in nearby Frankford. Her nightmare was coming true. Decker had contacted the Philadelphia assistant district attorney Thomas Barlow, a Comstock supporter, and arranged to have her daughter institutionalized.

With Craddock in the asylum, Decker had a locksmith break into her office. She took all of Craddock's letters and turned them over to Barlow. Decker told a friend she was relieved that Craddock was in an asylum, because she had feared her daughter would be raped and impregnated by a wicked man.

In the asylum, Craddock made fourteen attempts to contact Henrietta Westbrook, and also cabled Stead in London. The first few days were agonizing. "Had I had the slightest tendency to insanity," she wrote Wood, "I should have gone stark, staring mad, with the shock and the horror of it." Because she had told her friends that she was shortly bound for Chicago, she knew none of them would search for her for weeks or even months.

The Friends Asylum superintendent, Dr. Robert H. Chase (no relation to Dr. Sara B. Chase), turned out to be partially sympathetic to her plight. (No official records of her institutionalizations survive, only her own letters and diary entries.) He told her that *The Danse du Ventre* would have been acceptable had it been written by a man—a physician or a scientist—and the paragraph about the spirit husband omitted. He said that the only explanation for her knowledge was either "illicit experience" (premarital sex), which Craddock denied, or insanity. Craddock felt there was a legal double standard for physicians and non-physicians when it came to sexology. Physicians had asked her questions in letters, visited her for oral instruction, and purchased her books. "Is the literature any less obscene because it has the signature of 'M. D.' or any more obscene because a layman, and not a physician, has written it?" she wondered. Dr. Chase called Assistant District Attorney Barlow to say that he did not consider her insane and wanted to release her to her mother. Barlow threatened criminal action. The asylum's board of directors met and agreed to transfer her to the Pennsylvania Hospital for the Insane.

When the hospital's superintendent, Dr. John Chapin, whom Craddock described as "a bigot upon both sex and religion," asked about her spirit husband, she suspected he was trying to build an insanity diagnosis. He told her, "The whole subject with which you have been dealing, Miss Craddock, is unclean." When he inquired whether a husband and dead wife could communicate, she said, "I positively would not discuss my religious belief with any but intimate friends or those especially interested in it."

While locked up, she was able to reach Carrie Burnham Kilgore, her former attorney, who brokered a deal with the district attorney's office: if the court ordered the hospital to free Craddock and not remand her to prison, Craddock would stop selling the indicted books. On September 7, 1898, after three months in the hospital, Craddock was released. On September 8, the district attorney and the clerk entered a motion to let her go on her own recognizance for one hundred dollars.

But after she became convinced that Decker was going to try to put her back in an asylum, she left Race Street for Kilgore's house. Her lawyer advised her to leave the state as soon as possible. She fled to a friend's home in Delaware and had her trunk and Remington shipped. That winter, she went to London again. Stead, traveling in Rome, offered her another secretarial job at *The Review of Reviews*. While he was away, his manager opened a letter that Decker had written to Stead, in which Decker appealed to him not to let Craddock call herself "Mrs. Craddock." The manager gave the letter to Stead's son, who discussed it with his mother, Emma. When Stead returned from his travels, he had an uncomfortable talk with his family. Now that Mrs. Stead knew Craddock was unmarried, she did not understand how she could know so much about marital relations. Stead told Craddock that she had to go. Had Decker not sent the letter, Craddock wrote Wood, "I should very likely have remained for [some time] in Mr. Stead's employ."

Craddock imagined that she would "become a wanderer on the face of the earth, pursued by my mother's vindictiveness—and why? Because I am trying to help people to a knowledge of chaste, self-controlled, happy marital living." She told Wood to contact her at her friend Dr. Alice Stockham's address in Chicago, so her mother would not find her. She bought a ticket on the White Star Line, sailing to New York on Friday, December 30, 1898, just a few weeks after the end of the Spanish-American War.

Craddock's plan was to stay at a Turkish bath in Brooklyn Heights, see friends, and eventually go on to Chicago. If it all worked out according to plan, she would soon land in the very city where she and Comstock had witnessed the danse du ventre five years before.

12

THE CHURCH OF YOGA

When Craddock arrived at the beginning of 1899, Chicago was the largest city in the Midwest and the second largest in the country. The population had exploded from around 300,000 in 1870 to 1.1 million in 1890. To serve poor residents suffering from disease and overcrowding, Jane Addams had founded Hull House, which was now thirteen years old, a standard-bearer for the progressive settlement movement, seeking to enrich and improve the lives of the urban poor. The city had recovered from the Great Fire of 1871 and was facing an influx of new residents. It was also home to a thriving radical scene. The year Craddock arrived, Emma Goldman would spend a month in the city, lecturing on religion and the emancipation of women. Religions of all types found followers, as newspaper announcements attested: services were offered by Jews, Spiritualists, Christian Scientists, Episcopalians, Methodists, Rosicrucians, the Second Eclectic Society of Spiritual Culture, the Vedanta Society, and the Independent Church for Students of Nature. As a Spiritualist fascinated by world religions, Craddock would be right at home.

She rented a room from a French professor on Dearborn Street, for classes, lectures, and Sunday meetings. For her office, she took two rooms in Handel Hall in the Loop. Formerly home to the Western News Company, it contained an active recital hall on the second floor, with a gallery for receptions. As a sign of the progressive world's respect, Harman noted her arrival and address in *Lucifer* and listed her courses. He urged readers to write to her for circulars or information.

Her business card identified her as "Mrs. Ida C. Craddock," offering "Instruction given upon Marriage." She had separate lessons for mothers, wives, and widows; unmarried women; and men. She also gave lectures to individuals and groups, similar to those Sara B. Chase had given, with titles such as "The Wife Should be Queen of her own Person." Anyone under twenty-one had to provide written permission from a parent or guardian.

Ida C. Craddock's business card (front) Ida C. Craddock's business card (back)

Though she made no mention of it in her diary, in March 1899, Craddock returned to Philadelphia to take care of unfinished business. She appeared in court on her nine-month-old federal obscenity charges. The U.S. attorney decided to throw out the case, went before the judge, and made a motion for a nolle prosequi. Craddock was discharged. The Philadelphia post office sub-inspector Wallace Moore wrote in her record, "The reason assigned by the U.S. Attorney for the above action was the impaired mental condition of the defendant." She no longer had federal obscenity charges hanging over her head.

Back in Chicago, she built a steady business of in-person sex pupils. She tracked them in a typed set of sheets she called "Records of Cases in Marital Reform Work." Male students outnumbered female about three to one. One unfortunate peril of being a vibrant, comely sex teacher was that male clients often hit on her. Case 1, a redheaded divorce lawyer with a mustache, confessed that he ejaculated too quickly. Craddock told him to stay in the vagina for thirty to sixty minutes. The man, she noted, "smiled, as though I were telling him something absurdly impossible."

Case 18, a forty-six-year-old married lawyer with a putty face, gray mustache, and jet-black hair, said his wife was unwilling to perform her conjugal duty. Craddock gave him a lesson and he returned later that day, asking her to repeat it. She said she never gave the same lecture twice. He "planked down" another dollar. As she continued, he interrupted to say he had an erection. She "froze to a white heat," no doubt recalling her near-rape in the Northern California inn. After apologizing for offending her, he said he had never seen a woman's genitals and would give ten dollars for the chance. She told him "harlots could doubtless be bought" and advised him to get a divorce.

Not all of her male pupils were heterosexual. One man confessed he was in love with a male friend, and frequently hugged him affectionately in his sleep and ejaculated on him. She advised him to love his friend inwardly and talk to his minister. Her women pupils gave her less trouble. A married Roman Catholic Polish woman, Case 5, told her she had masturbated since the age of four, after discovering that she could stimulate herself by clinging to the side of a door. The woman had confessed to her priest, who told her to stop. Ever since, she had been wracked by bad headaches. The solution, Craddock said, was for "her to unite with God during the act."

At night, Craddock's own sexual education continued. She believed God was present in her lovemaking with Soph. Some wissenings were so powerful they left her ecstatically happy:

> When having union with my husband, I was asking God
> to enter me through my husband's organ, and to abide
> in me and ride my husband's organ; when suddenly a vi-
> sion flashed before me of a rushing mountain torrent such
> as one feels is dangerous to step into, lest one be carried

away . . . I felt that I wanted to dare to enter this mightily rushing stream, and that it was God Itself. And so, for some moments, I passed through a thrilling sexual struggle as though my husband and I and God were all one in this whirl of watery forces.

Another night she made love with Soph, turned over on her face. She began to have an orgasm, but he told her she was only allowed to have an "astral" orgasm. They stopped. As she was drifting off, she felt poetry vibrating in her body. Soon lines came to her: "But still my faithful vigil I am keeping / Beside her, who is all the world to me." She knew Soph was thinking those words, and it meant more to her "than any sex union could have."

Seeking to expand her sex clientele, she wrote an article called "Right Marital Living," in which she expounded on her continence philosophy. She sent it to *The Chicago Clinic*, a prominent medical magazine, which printed it in its May issue. The piece advocated self-control through prayer to God at the moment of orgasm. Responding to those who believed right marital living (RML) would lead to illicit unions, she stated that RML-practicing men were unlikely to be libertines, and that partners who practiced self-control possessed an unbreakable bond. To those who claimed that RML would make married people stop procreating, she answered that women were naturally maternal and would always want children; RML would increase fertility due to the "conservation of the male principle." Fewer ejaculations could increase sperm count—an idea that has scientific credibility today. She also supported the idea of hereditarianism, contending that "the quality of children" born to RML-practicing parents would be "superior to that of children who are the result of accident or of lust."

The most provocative idea in "Right Marital Living" was that couples could have sex for pleasure and not procreation, when they exchanged sex magnetism. Less evolved than Victoria Woodhull or Angela Heywood on the subject of female desire, Craddock believed that men were sexually passionate, while women were maternal and "affectional." This was for the best, however, for if women were as sexually driven as men, the world would be filled with sexual vice. Sex magnetism (sex with continence) would free men from their lustful urges. To Craddock's mind, amative, non-procreative sex was necessary to satisfy men's lust, not women's.

After "Right Marital Living" was published, doctors urged her to print it as a book. She did, using money loaned to her by Stead. In her book version, she denigrated "preventives to conception," which she called "always wrong," "distinctly injurious," and "abominable and degrading." Condoms, womb veils, and pessaries rendered sex masturbatory, because they interposed a foreign tissue between the genitals. Withdrawal was "an act of onanism" and "morally degrading." The rhythm method was unreliable. Her stated opposition to physical contraception may have been a way to avoid prosecution under the Comstock law, but it was in keeping with her spiritual beliefs. Anything artificial interfered with the bonds between husband and wife.

In the book version, she used bolder language than ever: *vagina, male organ, ejaculation of semen,* and *emission from the woman.* One passage instructed the bride to visit a doctor before the wedding night, and, if the hymen was tough, to have it snipped with surgical scissors, after which it would shrivel away. Then she was to tell her groom about the visit, so he would not wrongly suspect that she was not a virgin. If a groom felt it was his conjugal right to break the hymen, "it would be as well for the bride to find it out before she marries him."

In another explicit section, she wrote that if a woman's "orifice" was small in relation to the penis, "Nature will, indeed, furnish a natural lubricant in the woman's own emission after awhile; but at first, it is well to have the ointment at hand." She suggested forms of petroleum: petrolatum, cosmoline, or Vaseline. Depending on the bodies of the bride and groom, she advised, missionary was not always the best position. If a man was very heavy, or for other reasons, "it is sometimes better for the woman to mount the man. Again, there are various side positions, which different couples can find out for themselves, by experimentation."

Medical journals in Chicago, New York, and Syracuse gave *Right Marital Living* positive reviews. Byron Robinson, a leading gynecologist, wrote her, "The young woman is the subject who especially requires sexual instruction, whereas, in the present state of society, she receives almost none. I hope that sooner or later sexual instruction for the young will become more general." But as orders for the new book streamed in, Craddock remained wary of the Comstock law. After receiving a request for two copies, along with one dollar, by registered mail from "George H. Vorst" in Crawfordsville, Indiana, she asked for proof that he was older than twenty-one. He responded that he could only provide his own written statement. She returned his money and never sent the books.

That summer, she mailed a copy of *Right Marital Living* to *The Woman's Journal* in Boston, hoping to get a review. The *Journal* had been co-founded in 1870 by Lucy Stone, a founder of the American Woman Suffrage Association. After Stone's death in 1893, her widower, fellow suffragist Henry Blackwell, had taken over. Craddock was unaware that a wolf could come in suffragist's garb. Though progressive on some women's issues, Blackwell, then seventy-four, was disgusted by the notion of non-procreative sex and shortly alerted the authorities to Craddock's book.

The morning of October 27, after she finished a lesson with a slender, refined Christian client, she received a visit from Walter S. Mayer, postal inspector, and Robert McAfee, general agent of the Western Society for the Suppression of Vice and local postal inspector. She admitted to having mailed *Right Marital Living* to Blackwell. Though she told the men that she had been arrested in Philadelphia for mailing three books and had stopped mailing them, she was arrested and indicted before the grand jury for having sent *Right Marital Living* to Blackwell. The indictment named "a certain pamphlet which contained obscene, lewd and la[s]civious matters of an indecent character."

While speaking with Assistant District Attorney Oliver Pagin, Craddock mentioned that she only mailed *Right Marital Living* to people who had convinced her they weren't minors. He said that McAfee had tried to get the book but "could not do it without satisfying your conditions." Pagin also informed her that McAfee lived in Crawfordsville. Craddock realized that "George Vorst" had been Agent McAfee.

Clarence Darrow

In need of a lawyer, she reached out to a rising progressive attorney by the name of Clarence Darrow. He was forty-two, the same age as Craddock, and recently divorced. He was living in a coed commune and having an affair with the journalist Ruby Hamerstrom, age twenty-six, who was engaged to another man. Darrow had published an essay called "Woman" in the free love journal *To-Morrow* that depicted marriage as an institution of control. He had become interested in sex and free speech after he was consulted for legal advice by a Cook County gynecologist who was trying to persuade the American Medical Association to publish a paper on the physiology of sex. Darrow assisted the gynecologist, but the association rejected the paper over concerns about the Comstock law. In another twenty-five years or so, Darrow would rise to fame as the "attorney for the damned," defending Nathan Leopold and Richard Loeb in their murder trial and the teacher John T. Scopes in the "Scopes Monkey Trial." But when Craddock met him, he was primarily a labor lawyer; her case would require him to learn some new legal strategies.

When he received her call, he posted the five-hundred-dollar bail himself and agreed to defend her pro bono. The future attorney of the damned advised her to take a plea to avoid a conviction and prison sentence. She said she had the names of physicians who would testify that *Right Marital Living* was wholesome and helpful, but, according to Craddock, he "said it would not matter who testified on behalf of the book; I was sure to be convicted." She did persuade him to enter a "not guilty" plea. Darrow subpoenaed Blackwell, Postal Inspector Mayer, and Comstock himself.

Longing for a showdown with the man whose law had caused her so much anxiety during the five years since she first received a call from the Philadelphia postal inspector, she wrote Darrow a long letter about her defense. If prosecutors claimed her books promoted contraception, she would explain that self-control, or continence, did not involve a barrier and, as such, was not contraception. If they inquired as to her spirit husband, she would say that she had been married and her husband was dead. If she were asked whether she had intercourse with a ghost, Darrow was to say the question was an invasion of privacy.

Though she had been mocked and pathologized by some radicals for her Spiritualism, she understood that, from a legal perspective, it could help her. If her books were an expression of religious belief, they were protected under the Constitution. Having heard that the judge in her case, Christian C. Kohlsaat, was a "somewhat narrow churchman," she suggested to Darrow that he draw attention to the religious aspects of *Right Marital Living*. She told him, "Union with that Ultimate Force, with that Divine Power, is the very kernel of my teaching. My teaching, therefore, is religious." If the Comstock law was invoked, Darrow was to raise the First Amendment.

But if she was the idealist, champing at the bit to face Comstock in court, Darrow was the pragmatist, repeatedly advocating that she take a plea. She finally agreed. Only later was she able to reflect, "I had not yet awakened to the possibility of taking stand on high ground; was still apologetic; only dimly feeling my way to standing on my religious rights and in the right of the common people to receive sexual enlightenment in print and in clear language."

The district attorney told Darrow that he would not pursue the case if Craddock turned over *Right Marital Living* and the three previously indicted books, and if she agreed not to print any more copies. On December 9, 1899, she took her books to the Post Office Department to be burned. Though it brought her absolute grief, she felt it was the safest solution. Kohlsaat sentenced her to three months' imprisonment in Cook County Jail, with the sentence suspended pending good behavior. She appeared in court with a woman doctor, identified as "Mrs. Dr. Dickinson" in the postal records. Dr. Dickinson said she would take Craddock under treatment and see if her condition could be improved. She was likely Frances Dickinson, a graduate of Northwestern University Woman's Medical School and a member of the Board of Lady Managers at the Chicago World's Fair.

Low on cash, Craddock moved into a smaller room in the office suite on Dearborn Street. Without income from her books, she could not repay Stead's printing loan. She wrote in "Diary of Psychical Experiences," "It seemed to me my work had come to an end." But the ghosts did not agree, telling her that to abandon her work would be a desertion of duty.

Soon, a new set of notices appeared in the Chicago papers. The Dearborn Street office was now the "Church of Yoga." No longer a marriage instructor named "Mrs. Ida C. Craddock," now she was "Ida C. Craddock, Pastor." Her first advertised lecture at the Church of Yoga was held at 11:00 a.m. on Sunday, December 17, 1899, and titled "Man and Woman as They Were, as They Are, as They Ought to Be." One attendee was a Zoroastrian priest who went by the name Otoman Zar-Adusht Hanish. The founder of Chicago's Mazdaznan Temple, Hanish claimed to be of Persian descent. Surely enchanted by his connection to the East, Craddock brought him on as a collaborator. One Sunday she would give a lecture titled "Marriage and Divorce in the Light of Yoga," and a few hours later Hanish would offer "Birth and Childhood of Jesus of Nazareth." They talked with each other about yoga teachings and exchanged ideas.

In 1904, one of Hanish's followers went insane after fasting according to Hanish's direction, and Hanish was arrested for practicing medicine without a license. In 1913, a postal inspector wrote him a decoy letter and he was arrested under the Comstock law for mailing his book *Inner Studies*, which advocated nude sunbathing. He was sentenced to six months in prison. His father would out him as Otto Hanisch, the son of German immigrants in Milwaukee.

But Craddock seems to have been unaware of her friend's real identity during her time in Chicago. Soon after she dubbed herself pastor of the church of yoga, Craddock developed a new course that was part yoga, part sexology: "Yoga Applied to the Married Life." In a circular describing the course, she explained that yoga taught people to enter a state of oneness with the Divine Force of the Universe. This would "secure them both spiritual bliss and power over their bodies." She was wholly remaking her sex teachings as religious.

Perhaps realizing this would narrow her audience to those swell, "toney" church people she had been seeking in Chicago, she decided to publish a revised edition of *Right Marital Living* that she hoped would be unindictable. After drafting a new introduction, she visited a well-known defense attorney, Captain William P. Black, a Civil War veteran who had defended those charged with inciting the Haymarket Riot in 1886. He told Craddock that he and his wife approved of all four of her books, finding them helpful and useful.

Her new, sixteen-page introduction called Comstockism "an institution resembling the Holy Inquisition of mediaeval times." Instead of heresy, modern Americans were being tried for obscene literature. She faulted "'Societies for the Suppression of Vice,' the original one of which was founded by Anthony Comstock. They are four in number, the New York, the New England, the Western, and the California Societies, respectively; they are independent of one another, but they all work together, and maintain a 'lion's mouth' in the Post Office, into which 'confidential information' against a citizen may be thrown." When Craddock asked Black if he thought she could be sued for libel, he said no. He did suggest several edits, all of which she accepted: she changed *semen* to *generative fluid* and cut the portions on hymen-snipping, anointing the vagina, and sexual positions.

She paid for the second edition with money she earned by editing for Stead, and optimistically wrote him that she was hoping for newspaper coverage, ads, and increased sales if the new edition was not suppressed. But to her disappointment, sales were slow. Her health deteriorated. She had catarrh and was exhausted by the "heavy lowland atmosphere" of Chicago. The ghosts told her to move to Denver, write a big book, and then move to Washington, DC.

In Denver, she saw sex students with no interference from the law. She even went on a date with one, a married lawyer, because she was in need of a good square meal, "and had a satisfying dinner of spring chicken." She agreed to have lunch with him another time, but "our conversation was cold and somewhat dull that day, I fear; and he hasn't called since. I am just as glad that he has not."

In her new city, she wrote a new book, *The Wedding Night*. It contained several incendiary passages, which would define her, her relationship with Comstock, and her future. The first was a section on how a groom should enter a virgin bride without causing pain (by kissing and caressing her at the throat and bosom). There would be "reflex action from the bosom to the genitals," and the bride would seek closer and closer contact until the couple melted "into one another's embrace." Then, the groom would find his bride's "genitals so well lubricated with an emission from her glands of Bartholin, and, possibly, also from her vagina, that [his] gradual entrance [could] be affected not only without pain to her, but with a rapture so exquisite to her, that she will be more ready to invite [his] entrance upon a future occasion."

The second explosive passage was about Comstock himself:

I would add that the habit of using a wife as a convenience for a man's easing himself of a fluid which is looked on as an excretion, is chiefly responsible for the widespread idea that the sex relation is unclean, and for the growth of Comstockism, with its baneful efforts at suppression of all enlightening literature upon the details of coition as being "obscene, lewd, lascivious." The sex relation is indeed unclean, when made use of by a man for the purpose of easing himself of a supposed excretion; and the details of such a union are truly "obscene, lewd, lascivious."

She was linking Comstock's attitude about sex with that of men who used their wives and did not care about their pleasure. To Craddock, he was just another man among far too many who treated women as objects. The only solution was to live by a higher law, "genital union in self-control and aspiration to the Divine." Her divinity was not Comstock's, but both believed deeply in the power of God.

The third incendiary passage in the book covered the virtues of performing the danse du ventre during sex, the very subject that had first enthralled her at the Cairo Street Theatre. A wife had a duty to perform pelvic movements during "the embrace, riding [her] husband's organ gently, and, at times, passionately, with various movements, up and down, sideways, and with a semi-rotary movement, resembling the movement of the thread of a screw upon a screw. These movements will add very greatly to [her] own passion and [her] own pleasure."

Though she had written explicit pieces of advice in other works, The Wedding Night went into extreme detail about anatomy. "Sometimes the man's organ," she stated, "which in a state of activity should be about six inches in length, is much longer and proportionately large; and if the woman's orifice and vagina chance to be unusually small, great suffering will result unless one party or the other has been cautioned and knows what to do." She told of a woman who almost died on her wedding night due to her husband's large penis. The family physician insisted that he wear a padded ring, after which the couple was happy and had several children. In situations where the man was too small, she recommended he undergo electrical treatment.

She printed the first edition of The Wedding Night in August 1900. In reviewing the book, Moses Harman told his readers that it had been written "from the standpoint of a physiologist and humanitarian" and noted that it was useful for "every woman and man contemplating the marital relation, whether that relation be in accord with conventional morality or not." Denver was uneventful enough that she stayed until the spring of 1901, when the ghosts advised her to move to Washington, DC. She found an apartment, did research at the Library of Congress on a manuscript for Stead, and mailed books. She was not in the capital one month before she was arrested by two police detectives for hand-selling "certain obscene books or pamphlets." The law in the District of Columbia had been revised to prohibit distributing obscenity by hand as well as by mail. She was held overnight in the House of Detention and in the morning was arraigned in police court. *The Washington Times* wrote that she claimed "to be the pastor of the 'Church of Zaza.'"

Newspapers printed her name and address and the charge (circulating indecent literature), so the courtroom was full of, in Craddock's words, "people who came prepared to hear something spicy." Unable to afford a lawyer, she represented herself. She asked the women to leave the room because the subject matter was "too delicate for discussion in a mixed audience." All the women left, except Craddock. *The Washington Times* called her "a pre-possessing elderly woman, with grey hair and an earnestness and evident purity of purpose that commanded the respect and consideration of the usual mixed assemblage of the Police Court."

Craddock said she should be encouraged in her work, and not hounded as a criminal. When Assistant District Attorney Alexander Mullowny said her books promoted preventives, Craddock explained the difference between physical contraception and her method. In her closing argument, she defended her religious rights under the First Amendment. The judge said he would not decide on the worthiness of her aims or the good of her work, only on whether she had violated the statute. He thought it should proceed to the grand jury, and put her under bail for three hundred dollars for six months to await the jury's action. Then an agent of the Prisoners' Aid Society whispered a question to Mullowny: Could Craddock leave town instead of being sent to jail? Mullowny approached the judge, who said he would accept her personal bond for the bail. She could leave the district, though the court could not compel her to. She left the court, according to an article in Washington's *Evening Star*, "followed by a number of sympathizers." In an interview for that article, she said, "I do not for an instant admit that I have done anything wrong or that my doctrine and my literature are obscene, but I must bow to superior force."

She soon received a card from a lawyer offering to defend her pro bono before the Supreme Court, to test the constitutionality of the Comstock law, but she decided not to pursue the matter. She was worried she would not be able to make ends meet if the case dragged out. She agreed to leave Washington two days later.

She had escaped imprisonment, though not institutionalization, three times in three years in three cities. Comstock already had her name in his arrest logbook in New York, as though waiting for her to appear. Though he knew about her writings, he had never set eyes on her. That was about to change.

Anthony Comstock in his New York office

13

COMSTOCK VERSUS CRADDOCK

Date:	Feb. 5, 1902
Name:	Ida C. Craddock
Address:	134 W. 23, N.Y. City
Age:	45
Aliases:	Pastor of Church of Yoga
Nationality:	Philadelphia
Religion:	?
Married or Single:	S
No. of Children:	0
Occupation:	Lecturer of filth
Offence:	Obscene book by mail

The sign on Craddock's office door read "Ida C. Craddock, Room 5, fourth floor, instructor in Divine Science." It was in the rear part of the top floor at 134 West Twenty-Third Street, in what was then the theater district. Determined to make money through oral instruction, she placed ads in *The Evening Telegram*. Students came, but many claimed they could not pay her full fees. She started to pray for pupils with money, calling this "ringing up the Central Telephone of the Universe." In July, to save cash, she moved to her office from a doctor friend's home uptown. She made a bed for herself on the floor: three blankets in a muslin bag. She wrote Katie Wood that she felt like the princess from "The Princess and the Pea." A stack of envelope boxes served as her dresser, and flowered burlap curtains hid her personal items from her sex students.

The weather was achingly humid. That summer would see the worst heat wave in U.S. history until the 1930s, with an estimated death toll of nearly ten thousand people. Many New York doctors, on whom Craddock relied for patient referrals, were away on vacation. She wrote letters to "customers" and visited those physicians who were in town, on days when the weather was not too warm. She made ends meet doing research for Stead, but, desperate for income, she issued new print runs of some of her books. "Just as soon as I am on my feet financially," she wrote Wood, "with enough pupils to keep me going, I intend to refuse my books absolutely to all applicants."

Each time she mailed a book to a customer, her mind wandered to Comstock, whose Nassau Street office was only three miles away. She fretted to Stead:

> I am now an old offender, and likely to receive a severe penalty, if hauled up. If there were anything to be gained by being arrested, it would be another matter; but, judging from past experiences, I think there is everything to lose, with the added danger of being immured along with convicts for perhaps several years, and having my life-work suppressed during that time, and then coming out under a stigma of impurity, penniless and helpless.

Suffering from heat exhaustion, poor and demoralized, she wrote her mother to ask if she could come home for the rest of the summer. Decker said yes—but only if Craddock rented a post office box so none of her sex mail would come to the house. Craddock decided to stay in New York.

As she was figuring out how to circulate her teachings in New York, the nation was in the midst of a population shift. Birth rates were on the decline; college-educated women married later and less often and produced smaller families. Birth rates of white women had decreased: 45 live births per thousand in 1870, 42 in 1880, 38 in 1890, and 36 in 1900. The Black birth rate was also declining. Though accurate statistics were not available until the early twentieth century, demographers' estimates put it at around 55 births per thousand for 1870–1879 and 48 for 1890–1894. This decline was attributed to post–Civil War movement of African Americans from rural to urbanized areas. Among all classes, illegal abortion remained common. By 1900, the only country with a lower birth rate than the United States was France, where contraception was legal.

New immigrants were a subject of much concern for nativists who, in the face of large families born to new Americans, feared "race suicide" due to white Protestants undergoing abortions and using birth control. This was not based on accurate statistics, as immigrants' birth rates fell the longer they were in the United States. But the concern was that native-born whites would soon be outnumbered by immigrant families.

Ordinary American families increasingly believed in their own right to make reproductive choices. Juries were less and less inclined to view contraceptive sellers as evil. From 1890 to 1910, the number of employed women doubled from four to eight million. Many, like Craddock, were unmarried and lived away from home. This gave rise to YWCAs and boardinghouses that sought to protect these women, the same way the YMCA had sought to protect men such as Comstock upon his arrival in New York.

As the historian Linda Gordon has chronicled, Greenwich Village attracted young people, with young women sharing apartments, outnumbering single men, and working in jobs where they could not easily meet men. Premarital sex became more acceptable, and women needed contraception, as did new wives who sought economic freedom for themselves and their families. Bohemians sought to rethink marriage and family, and were deeply connected to labor rights and unionism. There was a burgeoning art and literary scene in the Village, with modernists such as T. S. Eliot, Georgia O'Keeffe, and Alfred Stieglitz gaining worldwide attention. A new leftist community was being born, not spread throughout the country like the nineteenth-century free lovers, but centralized in New York. Meanwhile, the Victorian *denial* of pleasure was fading, replaced by a focus on its *pursuit*: "pleasure-seeking." From 1900 to 1910, Coney Island brought in six million people per year, and young men and women were spending time together, courting.

Were Craddock not poor and anxious, she might have felt at home in New York. But so obsessed was she with thoughts of prosecution and penury that she thought of Comstock all the time. One Saturday, after a wissening with Soph, she felt the nearness of God and fantasized that she would write a book about her marriage. Then her mind wandered to the post office inspector. "I thought of Anthony Comstock," she wrote in her diary, "and how he would and could check any widespread efforts of mine at putting my experiences into printed form for circulation. And all the while the desire burned and glowed within me, at a sort of white heat."

By August 1, her forty-fourth birthday, she had $6.96 to her name. She was afraid to leave her office even for a moment during office hours, lest she miss a pupil. When the weather was unbearably hot, she went to Coney Island to swim in the ocean, or across the Twenty-Third Street ferry to Jersey City—three cents each direction—to catch a breeze. In Jersey City, she would spend fifteen cents on a pint of ice cream, take it home, bathe, eat the ice cream to cool her stomach, and doze near a fan to sleep.

One afternoon, a big man with no mustache walked into the office and said, "What can you give me for a dollar?" He said that it was "worth something just to see the writer of those books." Angry but desperate, she agreed to give him a lesson. She felt that he was looking at her like a monkey in a show. She took the dollar and tried to draw out his problems. When she asked if he could orgasm without ejaculating, he said no. As she walked to her chart on mental self-control and pointed to it with her left hand, he grabbed her right.

She pulled it away. "I am not here to be touched," she said. "I am here to teach. That is all, sir." He drew back, but a few minutes later he said he was excited and had to leave. As she walked him out, she was furious, but she felt it would be impolite not to shake his hand, so she reached out to do so. He grabbed her hand and pulled it close. She tore it from him. In her case records she ranted:

> Lord! If I could only have castrated that beast, then and there, with what joy I would have done it! But I had to control my boiling indignation, and frigidly ignore his remark; in fact, I didn't quite know what to say; such a thing is not wont to happen to me . . . I felt afterward as though his dollar note, which was clean and new, was foul with rotting mud of unnamable impurity, and I shall be chary, after this, about shaking hands on saying farewell to my male pupils, especially when I loathe them.

One day in August, she gave a lesson about which she thought so little that she never wrote it up in her records. It was for the son of her landlord and two of his college friends. When the landlord, E. D. Garnsey, learned of it, he was appalled. A lay Baptist preacher, he was afraid that Comstock would find out about Craddock and impugn him in the Baptist community. He told her to secure another place to live. She begged him to let her stay, and he agreed to a compromise: if Comstock would endorse her books, she could stay.

She decided to send Comstock her books and ask whether she could sell them in New York. Did she believe he would say yes? She sought closure, consciously or unconsciously aware that New York would be her last stop. She was not going to run from him, or his laws, again.

That fall, as Craddock was figuring out how to boost support for her works, President William McKinley was shot in Buffalo by a young self-proclaimed anarchist named Leon Czolgosz. Police claimed that Czolgosz was inspired by one of Emma Goldman's lectures. McKinley died on September 14, 1901, eight days after he was shot, and his vice president, Theodore Roosevelt, became the twenty-sixth president. Goldman was arrested by Chicago police, with her bail set at twenty thousand dollars. After her release, the case against her was dropped, but she took the pseudonym "E. G. Smith" and avoided public appearances. Czolgosz was executed on October 29, 1901.

McKinley's assassination passed without a mention in Craddock's diary, as she was monomaniacally focused on staying solvent and finding a way to sell her books. To boost the argument that her work was educational, she mailed *The Wedding Night* and other books to the Reverend William S. Rainsford, rector of St. George's Church, who was known to be opposed to the Comstock law. He wrote her a complimentary letter, approving of much of the material, but added, "I do not feel that I could [e]ndorse all that the little books contain. This much I will say. I am sure if all young people read carefully 'The [Wedding] Night' much misery, sorrow, and disappointment could be avoided."

She also sought support from Dr. Robert W. Shufeldt, a former army surgeon and medical writer, mailing him *The Wedding Night* and *Right Marital Living*. "You are evidently pounding away at the very root, the primal cause of ninety per cent of the domestic unhappiness, social ignorance, and the death of everything that is good in the world," he wrote back.

She mailed Comstock a package including the Rainsford and Shufeldt letters, *Right Marital Living*, *The Wedding Night*, and several of her circulars. Around the time she moved to New York, Comstock was still railing against the NDA and its members, writing in an *Annual Report* that "time and time again they have tried to impeach our Secretary, Mr. Comstock, in the Courts, and through the press by false and malicious methods."

A few days after she sent the package, Craddock received a letter from "Frank Lea" in Long Branch, New Jersey. Lea wanted *The Wedding Night*, enclosing the fifty-cent cost. She went to the Madison Square post office on East Twenty-Third Street and mailed it, along with *Right Marital Living*, a circular on oral instruction, and her diagnostic questionnaire for men.

She swiftly received a letter from Comstock that stated her books and circular were "within the purview of the Statutes," meaning indictable. He continued:

> Will you please inform me if it is not a fact that the Courts have already passed upon some of these books in Chicago? I am so informed . . .
>
> The complaints that have been sent to this office, by mothers who have been to your lectures, describe them as gross and very improper for young people.
>
> You are not allowed in this State, either verbally or by printed matter, to debauch the minds of the young or place in their hands, matters which suggest lewd and libidinous thoughts.
>
> Since you have written to me for an opinion, I must not hesitate to give you what my opinion and conviction is, concerning your publications.

Certain she would be arrested, Craddock went to meet a prominent radical lawyer, Hugh Pentecost, in his office in the New York Life Insurance Building. Afterward, they went for a walk and Pentecost told her that at any moment Comstock could have her sent to prison. Pentecost said she was free to stop mailing her books. "But if I should be arrested my propaganda will stop!" she replied.

But Pentecost was right to be concerned: the Frank Lea books wound up in Comstock's possession immediately. Comstock informed Henrietta Westbrook in a letter, "I personally secured from Ida C. Craddock, the foul stuff which she was sending through the mails in violation of the law." Judging from the New Jersey postmark and the pun in the name, "Frank Lea" was almost certainly a Comstock decoy.

Comstock now had Craddock for a federal offense—mailing her

books—but he wanted to nab her in state court as well. To do that, he had to catch her selling in New York. On February 1, 1902, he sent the NYSSV agent James Deering to her office undercover. She sold him *Right Marital Living* and *The Wedding Night*.

A few days later, she received a letter from a girl calling herself "Frankie Streeter." It was written on cream-colored stationery, and at the top was printed "Breeze Crest, Summit, NJ." The letter read, "Would you oblige me with a copy of your 'Wedding Night.' I enclose half a dollar. Do you admit young girls to your lectures? What do you charge for two chums who would like to come together? I am past 17 years. Please seal tight and oblige me. Address plain Miss Frankie Streeter. Post office box 201."

In eight and a half years of sex reform work, Craddock had never before received a request for books from a young girl. Determined to keep her books away from minors, Craddock returned the fifty cents, with a twenty-five-hundred-word letter to Miss Streeter, explaining that she could not send her work to minors without signed and notarized parental permission. She wrote that some books might "fill your mind with memories and thoughts which would disturb you emotionally, and perhaps eventually render you less the pure and delicate young girl which I trust you are to-day." And "Frankie" best not forge her parents' signatures, because it would be a crime punishable by law and "no sensible young person would risk anything of the sort."

A day after Craddock sent her reply to Frankie, she opened the door to her fourth-floor office and found herself face-to-face with Anthony Comstock. It was the first time she had seen him in person. His eyes were squinty and his top lip curled out over the bottom. He was in his late fifties, with steely blue eyes, his hair white. He was accompanied by three deputies, and he had a warrant for her arrest. She demanded to see the warrant up close. It named only *The Wedding Night*—no other books. As she examined the handwriting on the warrant—she was a shorthand expert, after all—she realized that what she would term the "crabbed handwriting of an elderly person" was identical to Frankie Streeter's. This was why the single book requested in the letter was the same book named in her arrest warrant.

At Craddock's bookshelf, Comstock began to comb through her books and pamphlets. Then he began to whistle. Within a few seconds, she realized the melody was familiar. It was the "Hoochy-Koochy," the belly-dancing song that Sol Bloom had improvised in Chicago—the theme to the danse du ventre, the dance that had first drawn his story close with hers at the World's Fair. "This is the gentleman who poses as an apostle of purity, the protector of innocent youth from the corrupting influences of books which instruct adults in the laws of a chaste and wholesome marriage relation before God," she wrote later.

When he asked for her books, she said she would not turn anything over without a search warrant. A deputy marshal arrested her. Comstock accompanied them to Ludlow Street Jail by elevated train, along with two of the three deputies. As she sat quietly in her corner of the seat, he showered her with what she called "opprobrious epithets" and loudly told the other passengers that she wrote filthy books.

"Really, Mr. Comstock," she said. "I should think that a public conveyance is not a place for the discussion of such subjects."

He ignored her.

She said, "Will you kindly cease from this discussion?"

He finally stopped crowing.

While Craddock was in custody, Comstock secured a search warrant and a warrant to apprehend her in state court. He went back to the apartment and seized what he logged as "51 books and 536 circulars." He entered her in the NYSSV arrest log, naming her occupation "lecturer of filth." Then he began to build his federal case. In a letter to the New York postal inspector T. W. Swift, he requested the records from her Washington trial. He added, "I would like this to use in the Final adjudication of this matter in her case in this City. I would also request that this case may be jacketed and numbered, and that hereafter the case may be known by that jacket number, so as to keep a record of it in the P.O. Department at Washington." Craddock became Special Case 1755C.

She was committed to Ludlow Street Jail in default of $2,500 bail. It was posted, probably by her mother, and she returned to Twenty-Third Street. After retaining Pentecost as her attorney, she told him that they should take their stand on the First Amendment, which guaranteed her religious freedom, freedom of speech, and freedom of the press. "He should be forced into respecting *all* the sections of this Constitutional Amendment, if he be thus willing to respect one part of same," she instructed him. "I wish to fight right through to a finish, and in the most effective way. Use me as a battering-ram against Comstock; pour out my life like water, relentlessly, in this fight."

On February 18, she was charged before the federal grand jury with mailing *The Wedding Night* to Frank Lea. Afterward, Comstock told *The Sun*, "She calls herself Pastor of the Holy Church of Yoga. I believe she herself is pastor, congregation, Yoga and everything else. She says that she has a familiar spirit who visits her twice a week and who instructs her in her work." He claimed that she had a plan to distribute her books when class let out at girls' high schools, and that a businessman had told him that she had accosted his sixteen-year-old daughter and a young friend and forced a book into their hands.

Enraged, Craddock wrote a letter to *The Sun* denying that she had ever sold books to minors. Printed beneath the headline "Mrs. Craddock on Her Recent Arrest," the letter claimed that Comstock's statements were false. She said she taught no evening classes, never knowingly handed circulars to girls under sixteen, never went to high schools to distribute her literature, and didn't even know where city high schools were located. The only request from a minor she had received in her marriage reform work, she contended, came from the Frankie Streeter letter. As for his dig about her being "pastor of the Holy Church of Yoga," she wrote, "Does either law or custom prohibit one from being the pastor of a congregation of readers?" She theorized that Comstock was desperate for victims because he was growing old: "He probably is hungry for a fresh victim—as hungry as a Jersey mosquito."

Craddock's many friends in liberal circles took to her defense. Ned Foote wrote a circular, "Comstock Versus Craddock," that was published in *Lucifer* and *The Truth Seeker* and widely distributed. He said that she worked "quietly and inoffensively" and her mission was among adults. But Foote added that he had advised her to desist from the religious aspect of her teachings, in part because she was a woman: "The world is not yet entirely reconciled to hear women talk religion from pulpits or politics from platforms, and the prejudice against her entering the field of remodeling the marital manners of men is simply insuperable." To claim authority on sex as a doctor or a man was one thing. To claim such authority as a Spiritualist and a woman was another.

To strengthen her federal and New York cases, Craddock tried to gain support from physicians. Shufeldt told her he would testify on her behalf but counseled her not to bring up Soph. She was beginning to feel that any discussion of Soph could lead her to another asylum. "I have a horror of the insane asylum," she wrote Pentecost, "better, far better the penitentiary for me! I wanted you to know what Comstock might possibly bring up against me as a last resort, so that you, as my lawyer, should not be taken by surprise. But if we can keep it out, and object to its being put in evidence, either spirit husband or charge of insanity, I should heartily rejoice and co-operate in this." If she pled not guilty by reason of insanity, she could be acquitted but institutionalized. She was saying she preferred to go to prison. She also wrote to the physician Clark Bell, a lawyer and editor of New York's *Medico Legal Journal*, who agreed to testify on her behalf.

While Craddock was working to strengthen her case, Decker secretly wrote Pentecost to urge him to change her daughter's plea to "not guilty by reason of insanity." He responded that he would not do so without Craddock's permission, as he had never betrayed a client. Taking a different tack, Henrietta Westbrook tried to convince

Comstock in a letter that Craddock's books were not obscene. He responded that "no decent man or woman" would pass along her books. "It is not a question of sentiment; it is not a question of sympathy, or lack of sympathy for this poor woman. But it is a question of preventing the youth of this great country, from being debauched in mind, body and soul."

The New York case against Craddock for hand-selling *The Wedding Night* to Deering opened on Friday, March 14, 1902, in the Court of Special Sessions, for a panel of justices. Decker did not come, but prominent liberals such as Ned Foote and the attorney Edward Chamberlain, who had defended the atheist Elmina Slenker in her trial and been involved in Ezra Heywood's and Moses Harman's legal defenses as well, were in attendance. The justices were Elizur Brace Hinsdale and John Bell McKean, both in their seventies, and Julius Marshuetz Mayer, thirty-six. Hinsdale was a strict Presbyterian who had sentenced the anarchist Johann Most to a year's imprisonment for an article that had been published shortly before President McKinley's assassination; Most collapsed on his way to the Tombs. McKean was an Irish Catholic descendant of Andrew Jackson. Mayer, a Jew, would later become the New York district attorney, but at the time he was only two months into his tenure at the Court of Special Sessions.

Foote provided an account of the trial in *The Truth Seeker*. Comstock testified that Craddock had told him she had sold the books, and that they should be read by young men and young girls. Pentecost put Shufeldt on the stand and asked, "Is the book indicted a book that you would offer to your patients? Are the information and instruction contained in it useful and desirable? Is the book, in your opinion, moral or immoral? Is it not a fact that the suppression of such knowledge as is contained in the two paragraphs upon which the prosecution is based is conducive to adultery on the part of the husband?" Hinsdale threw out all of the questions.

Craddock was so worked up that she, as Shufeldt described it, rose "to her feet with all excitement" and asked him if he believed, as a psychiatrist, that the failure on the part of wives to satisfy their husbands sexually was responsible for at least 75 percent of divorces. Hinsdale would not permit Shufeldt to answer; Shufeldt later wrote that he would have said yes.

Pentecost then tried to introduce the testimony of another doctor, but Hinsdale said there was no point in bringing more witnesses, as he would not let the second doctor answer anything that Shufeldt was not permitted to answer. "The book is not obscene," Pentecost argued, continuing:

> When Mr. Comstock undertakes to suppress books and pictures manufactured for the purpose of exciting the passions of men, he is within his province. But here is a lady of good character, who has held many honorable positions, and she has written a book for the purpose of correcting lasciviousness and promoting morality. I know that there is a prejudice against the sex question, but the discussion of sex matters is legitimate. Is it not terrible to take a lady of refinement and education and put her in prison among depraved people, when she devotes her energies to the elevation of men?

Pentecost wanted to introduce Rainsford's letter of support, but Hinsdale would not admit it, because Rainsford only agreed to endorse portions of *The Wedding Night*. The only letter of support that Hinsdale allowed was from Stead to Craddock. In it, Stead mentioned her "high moral character, which is unimpeached and unimpeachable" and "lofty religious motives," concluding:

> That you who have dedicated your whole life, regardless of all personal risk, to promoting what, rightly or wrongly, you are profoundly convinced is a loftier standard of ethics than that which is generally accepted, should be prosecuted as if you were a wil[l]ful corrupter of public morals and a disseminator of obscene literature—even if some of

your phrases may have been ill chosen—seems to me an outrage abhorrent to the principles of religious liberty and of the freedom of the press which are guaranteed in the American Constitution.

He was one of Craddock's many male mentors who endorsed her only partway, slapping her on the hand while praising her motives—protective and paternalistic.

Pentecost submitted all of Craddock's books to the court, but Comstock said on the stand that the question was whether the tendency of the books, "when put in indiscriminate circulation," was to debauch. Pentecost said it was not, and that there was no evidence of indiscriminate circulation. Comstock then brought up her prior arrest and suspended sentence in Chicago. Mayer responded, "You have no business to tell the court anything of the kind." Comstock went on, and Mayer told him politely but firmly to be quiet.

In his closing argument, Pentecost revealed that Decker had committed Craddock to an asylum, and said that only an insane person would publish such a book. A rationalist through and through, he was never comfortable with his client's Spiritualism. And yet he chose not to plead insanity, perhaps due to Craddock's insistence. In essence, he was registering a nonexistent plea: "*guilty* by reason of insanity."

Throughout the case, there was a conflation of obscenity and blasphemy, an indication of the broad hostility among conservative Christians such as McKean and Hinsdale toward those with unconventional religious opinions. McKean said that he regarded *The Wedding Night* as "blasphemous" even though Rainsford had endorsed it. But Craddock was not being tried for blasphemy, which had not been prosecuted in the state of New York since 1811, though it was still a crime in some states. In its coverage, *The Sun* referred to it as the "book of the Church of Yoga."

While Craddock made her concluding remarks, Comstock stood close beside her. She said, "I am not ashamed to speak plain truths plainly. I seek to advance the principles of truth and morality in marriage. My arrest is an outrage to those principles."

After two days of testimony, Hinsdale pronounced:

> This is the most awful case that ever came into this court. I have never before known of such indescribable filth. I cannot believe that this woman is in her right mind, no woman in her right mind, gentle born and well educated, as the literary style of this book shows, could conceive such filthy phrases. She has caused just such trouble as this in Chicago, Washington and Philadelphia before she came to this city. We consider her a danger to the public morals.

Hinsdale said that due to Craddock's suspended sentence in Chicago, she should be sentenced in New York. She was given three months in the Women's Workhouse on Blackwell's Island.

Craddock, silent, looked straight ahead as she was led across the bridge to the Tombs. As Foote reported, Comstock "exulted with savage glee when he had winged his bird and bagged his game."

14

THE FEMININITY OF THE UNIVERSE

Certain that she knew what was best for her daughter, Lizzie Decker chastised the lawyer Hugh Pentecost for not pleading insanity, writing him that Craddock's "fault was in the head and not the heart . . . Hers is no ordinary case. Instead of punishing the body, we should administer to the brain . . . Were she *your daughter* would you send her to jail or to an asylum? Give your candid opinion to a heartbroken mother."

Though Craddock had said she would prefer the penitentiary to an asylum, she was unprepared for the reality of prison life. At the Women's Workhouse, she had to wear thin skirts that exposed her knees, and she immediately came down with a sore throat. She feared pneumonia. She faced overcrowding, limited toilets, little running water, inadequate heat, unclean blankets, and vermin. Prisoners had to lie among swarms of cockroaches, with no windows and sparse ventilation.

Convinced that she had not received a fair trial, she wanted Pentecost to demand a new one and have her released on a writ of error. She believed that Comstock had made a false statement in saying she had received a suspended sentence, as opposed to a suspended decision, in Chicago. (The postal records indicate that she did receive a suspended sentence, but Darrow may not have explained that this could create problems for her later.) She wanted the new trial to be moved to the Court of General Sessions, where she could be tried by jury. When Decker visited her at the workhouse, Craddock said she would make a speech in her next trial and "roast Comstock."

"Poor dear girl," Decker wrote to Ned Foote, "I fear for her in need. I trouble to think of the effect, when one fully understands she will never be allowed again to publish her books or continue her teaching . . . I fail to see the wisdom of punishing the body, and degrading the spirit for a weakness of the brain. That girl is no more responsible for what she is doing than a two year old child."

While Craddock was in prison, Henrietta Westbrook wrote to New York's governor, Benjamin Odell, to request clemency. His office requested the court papers from the judges, but Hinsdale wrote that they could not be sent by mail. He sent only *The Wedding Night*; the governor's office took no action. Stead wrote to the U.S. attorney general, Philander Knox, calling Craddock "the stuff of which enthusiasts and martyrs are made," also to no avail.

She was released in June, and a new group called the Free Speech League (FSL) feted her at the Clarendon Hotel on Eighteenth Street and Fourth Avenue. The dinner was the group's first official event. It had been organized in response to an increase in legislation repressing political speech following the McKinley assassination, legislation that would become a major blow to U.S. citizens' right to speak against their own government. During Craddock's imprisonment, the New York legislature had passed the New York Criminal Anarchy Law, which made it a crime to advocate the violent overthrow of the government. It was the first in the twentieth century to criminalize political speech and agitation and was a model for similar laws across the nation. FSL members were opposed to the new law and sought "to maintain the right of free speech against all encroachments." An ACLU founder, Roger Baldwin, referred to FSL members as "the anarchists, the agnostics or atheists, the birth-controllers and the apostles of a once slightly 'fashionable' cult on the left, the free lovers." It was significant that the group's first honoree was a woman, and a woman who had been imprisoned for sex writing. This was a bold step for a free speech group that was seeking a broad base of support.

The Manhattan Liberal Club's president, Edwin C. Walker, was provisional president of the FSL, and Foote was its treasurer. A hundred

people came to the dinner in Craddock's honor, and many prominent freethinkers spoke in her defense. Though food was provided,
the only drink was ice water. "All those whose hearts beat with the
spirit of liberty," Walker said, "not only welcome Mrs. Craddock, but
protest against the laws that led to her conviction." Not offering full
support, Foote said that the future would decide whether she was
doing good work. At the close of the remarks, their honoree said
she was deeply touched and hoped to be vindicated at her federal
trial. She kept her comments vague and uncontroversial: she had
confidence in the success of liberalism and free thought and promised "to join the Free Speech League in the struggle for freedom."

Ruminating on her prison experience, she wrote an exposé for
The New York World called "Horrors of the Women's Workhouse on
Blackwell's Island," documenting the inhumane conditions she had
encountered, including insufficient food and risk of consumption,
smallpox, and other diseases. As after any meaningful experience, she
could not avoid writing.

Eight days after her release, desperate for money, she treated a
sex pupil, a Boston nurse named Eunice O. Parsons who was anxious
about sex with her fiancé; Craddock also gave lessons to him. Other
visitors that summer included a man who was impotent (advice: nude
sunbathing) and a gray-haired man who wanted to know how he
could tell if a woman had venereal disease (advice: find a new partner,
and avoid affairs).

With the federal trial looming, she vacillated between depression
and optimism. In July, she told her ghosts that she did not want to
live. She began to plan how to get her papers and letters to Stead. She
tried to be hopeful about the future. "I am getting a better grasp of
myself," she wrote in her diary. "The depressions of the past year are
now passing away; I think I must have been worn by the Washington
episode, too, as well as by the Workhouse confinement. But now I begin to see daylight ahead, in the possibility of my Appeal resulting in
a large number of letters of protest being sent to the Attorney General
at Washington."

The problem was that Pentecost did not want to defend her—he believed she would lose. In a letter to Foote, she considered retaining Howe and Hummel, or Pentecost's law partner. Pointing out a divide between prosecuted marriage reform writers and even the most radical lawyers, she wrote, "We Liberals have never had a fair chance at our sex literature cases because our lawyers have always been so apologetic for us, and have tried to make us out insane or to apologize for us in some other fashion. We have never had a chance to contest the issue on high ground, on the merits of the case."

She decided to hire Edward Chamberlain, the well-known radical lawyer who had attended her trial in the Court of Special Sessions, and who had dubbed Comstock "Smutty Tony." She told him she was considering a trip to Philadelphia to visit Decker. He wrote back, "The only advice I can give you is the conservative advice not to be caught in a trap." She did not go.

Craddock's federal trial opened on October 10, 1902. Judge Edward B. Thomas, a Republican, was to preside over a twelve-man jury. According to the indictment, *The Wedding Night* contained three incriminating passages, which were delineated by line numbers, page numbers, and a few words. It added that a "more minute description of the said obscene, lewd and lascivious language, appearing upon the several pages herein before enumerated, would be offensive to the Court, and improper to be spread upon the records of the Court." The sections were on how a groom should enter a virgin bride; how Comstockism was similar to marital rape; and why pelvic movements were beneficial for sexual partners.

The proceedings were as much of a sham as those in the Court of Special Sessions. Chamberlain was not allowed to admit Craddock's older books, which stated that parental consent was required for all underage students. Craddock was allowed to read from various paragraphs of *The Wedding Night* but could not comment on the book. She was permitted to make a speech to the jury, in which she said she had written and circulated the book for educational and philanthropic reasons.

When Comstock was on the stand, Chamberlain introduced Exhibit A, the Frankie Streeter letter. Comstock admitted instantly that he had written it, but he denied receiving Craddock's refusal. He pushed his claim that Craddock sold to minors, saying, "The janitress of the building was horrified to find that Mrs. Craddock's books had been given to her daughter." (The building had no janitress.)

Like the other obscenity judges, Thomas instructed the jury to decide only whether or not she had mailed the book. Without rising, the men found her guilty. Craddock declared that she was a "martyr to Comstockism" and that she would continue in her educational mission "in spite of a dozen Comstocks." Edwin Walker, president of the Manhattan Liberal Club, argued in a tract called *Who Is the Enemy; Anthony Comstock or You?* that Judge Thomas had assumed the authority to find *The Wedding Night* obscene, "indisputably usurping the functions of the jury and refusing to the defendant the opportunity to 'go to the country' with her cause on matters of fact."

Chamberlain said he would appeal. Liberal friends wrote and visited Thomas to protest the verdict. Thomas told a Craddock supporter, never named, that he intended to send her to prison for a long term. The news got back to her, and she became convinced that she would get the maximum sentence under the Comstock law—five years or a five-thousand-dollar fine, or both.

Her sentencing date was set for Friday, October 17, at 11:00 a.m. Decker arrived from Philadelphia on Tuesday the fourteenth. Craddock told Decker she expected to die in prison, but her mood improved as they packed her things, and she began to joke around. On Thursday, Craddock visited Chamberlain at his home on West Forty-Second Street. He found her more cheerful than she had been in months. Just before she left, she said, "If I don't choose to escape in the meantime, I'll see you in court tomorrow." That night, she and Decker went to dinner. Craddock told Decker she would finish

packing on her own. In her room on Twenty-Third Street, she sat for
hours, typing on her Remington.

On Friday, Decker was supposed to meet Craddock for breakfast before court, but Craddock never appeared at the restaurant. Concerned,
Decker went to the apartment building but found Craddock's door
locked and noticed a strong odor of gas. She could not see through the
keyhole. She fetched the janitor, who summoned two police officers.

An officer kicked down a panel on the door and found Craddock
in her nightgown, dead, with shallow cuts to her right wrist, and
her arm above a pail that collected her dripping blood. The *Tribune*
reported that a long rubber tube extended from a gas jet to her
mouth. The official cause of death was "illuminating gas poisoning
and hemorrhage from incised wound of right arm." The room was
littered with books and papers; she had been writing to friends and
relatives.

Among her belongings was a long letter she had written to Decker
that alternately attacked and forgave her for their tortured relationship. Though her mother had controlled her, rejected her teachings,
institutionalized her against her will, conspired with a district attorney, and tried to plot her legal defense behind her back, Craddock
wanted to meet her in heaven. She wrote:

> Some day you'll be proud of me. You will understand that
> what I have done has been done because you and my father
> prepared me for just such a propaganda to humanity. You
> may ask why I did not give it up and come home to live with
> you, resuming my name of "Miss Craddock," and taking
> up other work. But, dear mother, I could be of no possible
> help to you, with the shadow of reproach which bigots and
> impure-minded people have put on me. I should be only a
> hindrance to your respectability . . .

The real Ida, your own daughter, loves you and waits for you to come soon over to join her in the beautiful blessed world beyond the grave, where Anthony Comstocks and corrupt judges and impure-minded people are not known. We shall be very happy together some day, you and I, dear mother; there will be a blessed reality for us both at last.

The suicide made national news, with headlines such as "Priestess of Yoga a Suicide" and "Death, not Prison—Miss Craddock, Yoga Priestess, Kills Herself." In an indication of her longtime identity struggle, some articles called her "Miss," while others called her "Mrs." William Stead compared her to Socrates and Jesus. (Stead himself would die ten years later on the *Titanic*, one of the most famous Englishmen aboard.) Pentecost maintained his belief in her insanity, while Macdonald wrote in *The Truth Seeker*, "Whatever doubts she may have had about another world—of that she seems to have had none—she knew it could not be worse than this while the Vice Society exists here. As to her sanity, I cannot deem a person insane who chooses the devil before Anthony Comstock." Walker told *The New York Herald* that no rational person "could have read her books and held that her purpose was anything but worthy and pure."

Just before she took her life, she mailed a letter to Chamberlain, addressed "to the public." He received it the day her body was discovered, and portions of it made that day's papers. With the authority of a sexologist, she declared that Comstock was a "sex pervert" and a "Sadist—namely a person in whom the impulses of cruelty arise concurrently with the stirring of sex emotion." She went on:

I resolved, when I came to New York, that if again attacked by Comstockism, I would stand my ground and fight to the death. Perhaps it may be that in my death more than in my life, the American people may be shocked into investigating the dreadful state of affairs which permits that unctuous sexual hypocrite, Anthony Comstock, to wax fat and arrogant, and to trample upon the liberties of the people, invading, in my own case, both my right to freedom of religion and to freedom of the press . . .

I earnestly hope that the American public will awaken to a sense of the danger which threatens it from Comstockism, and that it will demand that Mr. Comstock shall no longer be permitted to suppress works on sexology. The American people have a right to seek and to obtain knowledge upon right living in the marriage relation, either orally or in print, without molestation by this paid informer, Anthony Comstock, or by anybody else.

She ended with an entreaty to the public to demand her one non-indicted book, *Right Marital Living*, so as to discourage Comstock from outlawing it.

When Comstock learned of Craddock's suicide, he told *The Sun* he was greatly surprised and repeated his claim that she had sold a book to an underage girl. He had wanted New York to see the final disposition of Craddock's case, and so it had come to pass. He filed the *Sun* article about her suicide ("Escapes Jail by Death") with her other court papers and sent them to the post office inspector in charge for New York, along with a letter recounting her prior arrests and prosecutions. His letter concluded that she was "remanded for sentence October 17, 1902, upon which day she took her own life, before the hour of going to Court. I therefore recommend that this case be closed."

Craddock was buried in Woodlands Cemetery in Philadelphia on October 20, 1902. Decker made the funeral arrangements and chose the Spring Garden Unitarian Church pastor, Frederic Hinckley, to preside. Several days later, a memorial for Craddock in Chicago's Handel Hall drew twelve hundred people and was covered by the *Chicago American*. Elizabeth Cady Stanton had died about a week after Craddock, but those who eulogized Craddock focused exclusively on her. The women's rights activist and gynecologist Juliet Severance said, "Let a woman write a book calling in question the teachings of the ignorant past and behold prison doors fly open to receive her, and her only escape is through the portal of death. How long, oh, how long, will such things continue?"

Dr. Alice Stockham, author of *Tokology* and *Karezza*, similarly defended the value of Craddock's sexology:

> Miss Craddock elects to devote her life to instruction upon tabooed subjects. She believed that people were unnecessarily ignorant and that they suffered from that ignorance. Anthony Comstock failed to distinguish between literature which is demoralizing in intent and the literature that Miss Craddock wrote. Her writings taught scientific facts and were prepared and promoted with the intention of enlightenment.
>
> Honestly, and with the faith of a martyr, she gave her time, talent, ardor and enthusiasm to the enlightenment of men and women. She pleaded that the heart life, the real life, should become manifest in thought and word and deed.

Three years later, in May 1905, Stockham would be fined for mailing a circular and a fifteen-page pamphlet she had written, also titled *The Wedding Night*, to a man in Crawfordsville—surely McAfee, the Western Society general agent and postal inspector. Stockham was also defended by Darrow; she later criticized him for providing a poor defense.

Craddock's death energized the progressive community. The Philadelphia activist Voltairine de Cleyre, using the pseudonym "Flora W. Fox," wrote to *Lucifer* that the suicide offered liberals "a [G]atling gun loaded with legitimate condemnation—facts and righteous indignation against Comstockism for the increasing number of reformers who are being driven to the graves . . . The tide of Freedom and Progress rolls onward with the ripening of old mother earth. A repeal of the Comstock laws is now in order!"

But initially, at least, Comstock's society stood behind him. At the monthly meeting of the NYSSV weeks after the suicide, members discussed the Craddock case. A committee member told a *Sun* reporter, "Whatever Mr. Comstock does is all right with us." Comstock announced that the executive committee had "[e]ndorsed his course" unqualifiedly.

The popular press was not as kind. *The Brooklyn Daily Eagle* claimed the suicide was a sign that Comstock's activities needed to be restrained. He responded with a long letter, calling the book "inexcusably nasty" and "the licentious utterances of a disordered mind." Its contents, he continued, were

> a disgrace to her sex, and an outrageous blasphemy upon the sacredness of the marriage bed. It must be remembered I did not condemn this book. I tried to restrain it by my letter of appeal to her. When nothing else would avail I brought her before the courts to have the question judicially determined. Two courts condemned it as obscene. I am not responsible that she resolved to take her life if she could not parade her filthy books before the public.

He suggested that Chamberlain could have raised the issue of "her disordered mind."

On a Sunday afternoon in December, he went to the assembly hall of the Brooklyn Philosophical Association in Williamsburg to defend himself before hundreds of her friends. He summed up his decades of anti-vice work and said that Craddock had received justice. The attendees, who included Pentecost and Walker, shouted at Comstock that he had lied on the stand and hounded Craddock to death. "Let him find two filthy passages from the book," Walker said, "and I'll read fifty from the Bible." The freethinker, writer, and minister Moncure D. Conway brought up the Frankie Streeter letter, and Craddock's "powerful letter" refusing to send her work. Comstock said, "The society I represent does not use decoy letters. It uses test letters." Laughter filled the hall. Conway pressed, "When you write the test letters you refer to, is it not wrong for you to write under an assumed name?"

"If it is right to use false initials or names to advertisements in newspapers," Comstock replied, "which is done every day, it is right in our case." (Craddock had never advertised her books under anyone else's name.) A dozen men and women jumped to their feet, and the din grew louder. Comstock became pale with rage. The association's chairman, Herbert Casson, tried to quiet the room, denouncing the audience's conduct as the most disgraceful he had witnessed in the history of the association. When Comstock left the podium, audience members continued to shout and jeer.

But he would not let the Craddockites get the last word. In his 1903 *Annual Report*, he wrote a long section on Craddock's case in which he compared her to a mad dog, perhaps thinking of the one he had shot long ago in Winnipauk. "To all those who realize the effect of a mad dog's bite," he wrote, "it is imperative that mad dogs of all sizes should be killed, before the children are bitten. Moral: Stop all *obscene books*, whether by women or men, before the children are cursed by them." He then filled six pages with letters testifying to his own noble character. One was from Thomas Barlow, the assistant district attorney in Philadelphia who had helped Decker institutionalize Craddock. Barlow wrote that Craddock had "for years fixed delusions, and she was a nymphomaniac, writing things and saying things which were lewd and obscene, the expressions of a disordered mind." It was as though frank sex writing itself were a form of insanity, no matter how beneficial the information. To be a marriage reformer and a woman was to be a delusional nymphomaniac.

Shufeldt published an article in the *Boston Investigator* stating that he had decided Craddock was insane. In his mind, "she was irresistibly impelled to make the constant attempt to combine religious fanaticism with her otherwise quite natural and correct views of sexology." He wrote that her suicide was inevitable. In his view, her religious ideas invalidated the fact that she had practical, even scientific knowledge about sex. So extreme was his disdain for her Spiritualism that he could not properly credit her for her sex guides.

Nearly two years after Craddock's suicide, the U.S. attorney for the District of Columbia, Morgan H. Beach, suggested that the government abandon the prosecutions of twenty-two cases that had been pending on the criminal dockets for two or three years. The cases were called before a justice in September 1904, and Beach directed a nolle prosequi in each one. Craddock's DC case was officially thrown out, along with cases involving larceny, perjury, and highway robbery.

Craddock laid the groundwork for birth control activism, even though she limited her talk of it to continence. Her books taught the values of sexual pleasure for women, understanding between couples, non-intercourse-oriented sexual intimacy, and child spacing to support maternal health. If fear of prosecution, lack of personal experience, or moral objection stopped her from discussing condoms, womb veils, and pessaries, she nonetheless did more than any other sex radical of her era to bring female pleasure into the conversation. More important, her work, her trial, and her death laid the foundation for the twentieth-century birth controllers. They would pick up where Craddock left off.

Comstock was having problems of his own. Contributions to the NYSSV declined from about $4,800 in 1902 to $3,800 in 1903. Two months after Craddock's suicide, the controller of the Treasury Department, Marshal Henkel, informed Comstock that the federal government would no longer pay his witness fees, mileage, and per diem. The fees were considerable because he traveled so often to testify, and he was paid to commute by ferry from Summit to the Nassau Street office daily.

In the fall of 1903, he accompanied a U.S. marshal and deputy sheriff to the home of a New Haven doctor who had allegedly violated the Comstock law. Comstock left the marshal and deputy sheriff outside. Inside, the doctor tried to dash upstairs. Comstock stopped him and seized his coat, and they tumbled down a flight of stairs. Both men weighed more than two hundred pounds, and Comstock landed on the bottom. He sustained fractured ribs and internal injuries. He reached his home late that night, accompanied by his family physician, and was confined to his room under a nurse's care for nearly a month. Against his doctor's advice, he returned to work in early December, but within a few weeks he was seriously ill. "During Holiday week his life was despaired of," the 1904 *Annual Report* noted. According to his doctor, the New Haven accident changed him; after that point, he became "more quickly excitable, more easily unnerved," and weaker.

Lucifer used the stair-tumbling to praise the New Haven doctor and roast Comstock: "The way Comstock has turned the incident to account by advertising his injuries just at the time his annual meeting is due shows that he will never take a kick for a hint. Comstockism is the thing to kick, and it can be reached without soiling a boot on the person of Comstock."

One night in August, a few months before Craddock journeyed to the Borderland to be with Soph forever, the two had an ecstatic wissening. It was the kind of uplifting, mind-boggling sex that makes a person think the world is as it should be. For the first time she could feel his penis against her womb. She wrote in her diary that she thought of the "Great Penis and the Great Vagina of the Universe" connecting through them. Usually, she thought alternately "of the Masculinity, again of the Femininity of the Universe, but of late, I have begun to think of them both together, and in action, through us . . . I was in full control of myself, as queen of myself, and I WAS A WOMAN! A woman, for the first time in my life."

Emma Goldman

15

WHAT EVERY GIRL SHOULD KNOW

About a month after Craddock's memorial in Handel Hall, Emma Goldman was to speak in the same location on modern anarchism, as part of a tour about an agrarian crisis in Russia. But when the hall managers heard of the program, they summoned the Chicago police, two hundred of whom showed up to bar her from speaking. Over the next few weeks, the police followed her from venue to venue. In a letter to *Lucifer, the Light-Bearer*, Goldman compared the Chicago police to the Russian tsar Nicholas II, arguing that there "must be something wrong with the American Institutions of today; something terribly black and corrupt, if they cannot stand the light of criticism; if they can thrive only when physical force is used to defend them against the light of free discussion."

Goldman already had firm support in Chicago, having known the *Lucifer* editor Moses Harman since the late 1890s. In 1899, just before Craddock's arrival, Goldman visited Harman and, as she recalled in her memoir, *Living My Life*, expressed doubt as to whether the "coarse and vulgar" American approach to sex was likely to change. Harman told her, "I am convinced we are not far now from a real revolution in the economic and social status of woman in the United States." Still doubting, she raised the issue of the growing power of Comstockism, and Harman told her he had faith in those who had been fighting it for years, likely mentioning the Heywoods. In this meeting, a bridge was built between anti-Comstockism and the new social movements beginning to flower: anarchism, labor rights, and birth control. In the early stages of each, the most visible representative would be Emma Goldman.

Emma Goldman was born to poor Orthodox Jewish parents in Kovno in the Russian Empire, on June 27, 1869, with two older half sisters from her mother's previous marriage, and three brothers born after Goldman. When her authoritarian father, Abraham Goldman, tried to marry her off at age fifteen, she begged him to let her continue her studies instead. He responded by tossing one of her books into the fire. At sixteen, she persuaded him to let her go to America with one of her half sisters—after she threatened to jump into the Neva River if he said no. She emigrated to Rochester, New York, with five dollars and a sewing machine. Alarmed by the living and working conditions of Jewish immigrants employed in sweatshops there, she became involved in the German socialist scene. She read about, and was invigorated by, anarchism, which she defined as a new social order based on liberty and unrestricted by man-made law.

Goldman married a fellow sweatshop worker; he turned out to be impotent, and she divorced him. He threatened to commit suicide and they remarried, but in 1889, at age twenty, she left him for good and moved to New York. She became a well-known speaker, and after she gave a speech in Union Square in 1893, she was charged with incitement to riot.

While she was awaiting trial in the Tombs, the famous investigative journalist Nellie Bly interviewed her for *The New York World*. Their conversation covered a variety of subjects. On free love, Goldman professed, "I believe in the marriage of affection. That is the only true marriage. If two people care for each other they have a right to live together so long as that love exists." She called the marriage ceremony "a terrible thing." She urged "voluntary affection," which she said would strengthen families by decreasing unwanted pregnancies. If this happened, "we would never have diseased or disabled children from careless and incompetent mothers." Like the free lovers, she was a eugenicist, but she also linked social problems caused by poverty to the lack of options. Contraception would liberate poor families from economic oppression and make it easier for working-class people to find jobs.

The questions of motherhood and women's autonomy were also deeply personal. In her early twenties, Goldman visited a doctor who told her that if she wanted to conceive, she needed surgery for an inverted womb. The doctor told her she would never be free from pain, nor experience full sexual release, unless she had the surgery. Even though a doctor friend urged her to have the operation, she decided not to. The reason was her political commitment: "I would find an outlet for my mother-need in the love of all children." When she later experienced love with an Austrian anarchist named Ed Brady, he urged her to try to conceive. However, motherhood, she felt, required the "absorption in one human being to the exclusion of the rest of humanity. I would never give up the one for the other. But I would give him my love and devotion."

At the conclusion of her trial for incitement to riot, she was imprisoned on Blackwell's Island, and while in prison she received instruction in practical nursing. Following her release, a prison doctor helped her get nursing work, though she had no degree. She studied in Vienna for a year, obtaining diplomas in nursing and midwifery, and became a practicing midwife on the East Side (now called the Lower East Side), where she found that most of her women patients dreaded conception. When they became pregnant, she wrote, "their alarm and worry would result in the determination to get rid of their expected offspring." She encountered women who jumped off tables, rolled on the floor, and used blunt instruments to abort. "I would return home sick and distressed," she recounted, "hating the men responsible for the frightful condition of their wives and children, hating myself most of all because I did not know how to help them."

In the late 1890s, she frequently lectured and published on women's issues. In an October 1897 talk in Chicago with Harman's group Lucifer Circle, she spoke against "sexual slavery" and the rule of authority in private sex lives. Her support for legal contraception in the United States grew stronger after she attended the small, secret Neo-Malthusian Congress in Paris in 1900 and returned to the United States with birth control literature and supplies.

Emma Goldman had penetrating blue eyes, only a hint of an accent, and a low, melodious voice that a longtime lover once compared to that of "the angel Gabriel." A government agent sent to one of her speeches wrote that she was "womanly, a remarkable orator, tremendously sincere, and carries conviction. If she is allowed to continue here she cannot help but have great influence." People who heard her lecture said she had changed their lives. "Life takes on an intenser quality when she is present," said the editor Margaret Anderson. Goldman "remov[ed] despair from those who would otherwise be hopeless," wrote the Greenwich Village chronicler Hutchins Hapgood. "Those who would otherwise regard themselves as outcasts, after hearing Emma, often felt a new hope."

Goldman was central to the civil liberties movement that coalesced around political speech in the fall of 1903. An English anarchist named John Turner was arrested after a talk in Manhattan and charged with promoting anarchism and with violating alien labor laws. The federal government had recently passed the Anarchist Exclusion Act, barring those with anarchist views from entering the country—thus restricting immigration on the basis of belief. Turner was detained for deportation on Ellis Island.

Incensed by his arrest and the passage of the act, Goldman went on a northeastern lecture tour to support him, backed by the Free Speech League, which had feted Craddock upon her workhouse release. Throughout her speaking and writing career, Goldman would be closely connected to the FSL, contributing lecture proceeds, raising money, and raising awareness of its activities. In turn, the league gave her legal and financial support, defending her when her talks were squelched by local governments and police.

The league built on the success of nineteenth-century libertarian radicals but had the potential to draw broad support from free speech advocates, including those not focused on the Comstock laws. According to the free speech historian David M. Rabban, it was only with the creation of the FSL that an organization advocated freedom of speech and the press "for viewpoints its members opposed." The FSL was the throughline between the McKinley assassination, Craddock, Goldman, and what would become the free speech movement.

The John Turner case made its way to the Supreme Court, and the justices ruled that Congress had unlimited power to exclude aliens and to deport those who entered illegally, including those who believed in anarchism. In the wake of this repression, leftist actions gained national attention. Goldman hosted two members of the Russian Social Revolutionary Party who sought political freedom in Russia. One of the largest reported New York City anarchist meetings was held in support of Russian anarchists. The Industrial Workers of the World (IWW), which supported workers' control of their wages and labor conditions, was established in Chicago.

Goldman and her allies, who believed in civil liberties, labor rights, and contraception, had numerous enemies in the first decade of the twentieth century. As pro-labor, anti-government voices were seeking to redefine the social order, those in power were worried. Immigration was rising, and the face of an "American" was changing. In an address to the National Congress of Mothers, President Theodore Roosevelt lamented "race suicide," predicting that if the average American family contained two children, the nation would reach extinction in two or three generations. A race that practiced race suicide, he said, would prove that "it was unfit to exist." Within a few years of this speech, the NYSSV would include in its *Annual Report*, for the first time, a table called "Nationality and Religious Creed of Persons Arrested." Each table indicated the increase or decrease in nationalities and religions of arrestees over the most recent period, compared with March 1872–June 1884 and June 1884–May 1895. The same few sentences would precede each table: "The following tabulated statement may help thoughtful men to realize what we are up against, and sound an alarm call for the future. The fact of the large increase of Foreigners . . . should go very far in sustaining our noble Commissioner of Immigration in his heroic efforts to keep undesirable classes from our shores." The society's new mandate was to protect not only American values, but Americanness itself.

In March 1906, Goldman decided to launch a journal called *Mother Earth* as a mouthpiece for her bold new ideas. Its inaugural issue came soon after Roosevelt began his first full term as president. The new magazine would "endeavour to attract and appeal to all those who oppose encroachment on public and individual life . . . The Earth free for the free individual!" Within the very first pages, Goldman lambasted Comstock. In an editorial, she cited censorship in Russia, critiquing the hypocrisy of American journalists: "Have they forgotten the censor here? . . . Have they forgotten that every line they write is dictated by the political color of the paper they write for; by the advertising firms; by the money power; by the power of respectability; by Comstock?"

Soon after the first edition was published, Goldman was crisscrossing the country, lecturing on topics including contraception and women's liberation in talks with titles such as "Crimes of Parents and Education" and "The Woman in the Future." In her vision of womanhood, women accepted marriage because they were focused on internal tyrants. Until a woman could defy them and listen to her own inner voice, whether it called for love for a man or for "her most glorious privilege, the right to give birth to a child," she could not call herself emancipated. This was a new take on women's liberation; equality could not be attained solely through suffrage. To Goldman, women's rights included a broad range of issues, and single-issue suffragists were largely anti-labor and bourgeois.

As she spoke about women's independence, she herself would soon become embroiled in a personal conflict. At age thirty-nine, in Chicago, Goldman met Ben Reitman, ten years her junior. Known as the "Hobo King," Reitman was a physician to the poor, specializing in gynecology and venereal disease. He had a mass of curly black hair and full lips, and Goldman thought him "a handsome brute." After he offered to arrange a speaking engagement for her, he quickly became her manager and lover. Exceedingly good at drawing publicity, he expanded her audience and increased her pamphlet sales. On one tour she lectured to twenty-five thousand paying audience members, in thirty-seven cities, and sold ten thousand pieces of literature. She later estimated that she spoke to between fifty thousand and seventy-five thousand people a year.

The sexual chemistry between Reitman and Goldman shook her to the core. He called her his "blue-eyed Mommy." She called him "Hobo" and "baby mine." They wrote of his "willie," her "joy Mountains," her "t.b." (treasure box), his "fountain of life." "I press you to my body close with my hot burning legs. I embrace your precious head," she wrote, and wanted to "put my teeth into your flesh and make you groan like a wounded animal."

Though they had a strong sexual connection, he was unfaithful. After her talks, she would speak with the press, and he would sneak off to seduce other women. He lied constantly and stole money from her to support his mother. She agonized over his infidelity, writing him that his promiscuity tore at her. "Oh, Ben, Ben, give me peace, give me rest," she lamented. "Tell me, what does your love mean to you?"

Her romantic turmoil was deepened by her belief in free love. "Dearest, I wish I could still be an

Ben Reitman

arch-varietist," she wrote. "I fear that is gone, for now at any rate, maybe forever . . . Do you believe that one who has known all the madness, of a wild, barbarian primitive love, can reconcile oneself to any relationship under civilization? I believe you have unfitted me for that." She worried he was using her to bed other women, writing him that one of his lovers thought "that the man who is loved by [Emma Goldman] can be trusted, must be big, and honest."

Woodhull had proclaimed her varietism in public; Goldman struggled with the possibility that she loved only one man. In one of her most popular speeches, "Marriage and Love," listeners were moved to tears as she urged them to confront societal constrictions so they could truly be free. She called marriage similar to "that other paternal arrangement—capitalism." Her radical views about relations between men and women were coupled with provocative ideas about homosexuality. She opposed "the social ostracism of the invert," as gays and lesbians were then called, and believed anarchism was "a living influence to free us from inhibitions." There is evidence that she herself had at least one lesbian affair later in life.

Privately, she was wrestling with love and commitment, writing to Reitman, "'Marriage & Love' is hateful to me, hateful because my faith in the power of love has been shattered. I used to think it could perform miracles, poor fool that I was . . . I therefore hope, that when we meet again, you will not use the methods you employ with other women, coerce me, drive me, force me back into a relationship." Goldman's cynicism was personal. Was it men who were disappointing, or *her* man?

The Postal Service Appropriation Act of May 27, 1908, expanded the meaning of the term *indecent*, as used in the federal Comstock law to describe excluded mail. Now it also encompassed "matter of a character tending to incite arson, murder, or assassination." Initially novel for defining contraception as obscene, the Comstock law now defined anti-government writing as indecent. The law was evolving to meet the times, and activists such as Goldman would be targeted on two levels.

As for New York's state Comstock law, in the first decade of the twentieth century, it was also stiffened to punish a person who "gives information orally, stating when, where, how, of whom, or by what means such an instrument, article, recipe, drug or medicine can be purchased or obtained." To *speak* about birth control—not only to sell it, mail it, or print information about it—was now a crime. Craddock had shifted to oral instruction following her move to New York, believing it to be safer, but that was indictable, too. Every time Goldman spoke on birth control, she was putting herself at risk of imprisonment. "I did not discuss methods," she wrote, "because the question of limiting offspring represented in my estimation only one aspect of the social struggle and I did not care to risk arrest for it. Moreover, I was so continually on the brink of prison because of my general activities that it seemed unjustifiable to court extra trouble. Information on methods I gave only when privately requested for it."

In the spring of 1909, she gave a lecture at the Sunrise Club, a discussion group founded by Edwin Walker that met every other Monday at an East Village café. Outside the restaurant, an inspector and policemen were ready to break in if her talk covered anarchism. With an audience of three hundred, her engagement was the best attended in the history of the dinner series.

She delivered a speech titled "The Hypocrisy of Puritanism," calling Comstock "the loud expression of the Puritanism bred in the Anglo-Saxon blood, and from whose thralldom even liberals have not succeeded in fully emancipating themselves." Puritanism, she contended, condemned women to celibacy, "indiscriminate breeding of a diseased race," or prostitution. The stigmatization of sex led women to become depressed, neurasthenic, and obsessed with "sexual desires and imaginings." In her view, Comstockism harmed women, its Victorian ideals about the purity of womanhood notwithstanding.

A few days after the "Hypocrisy of Puritanism" talk, she had arranged to speak on modern drama at her weekly Sunday lecture at the Harlem Masonic Temple. Several hundred people had gathered, but the police prevented her from entering. They tried to disperse the crowd, leading to two arrests. After that, no hall owner would let her deliver a Sunday lecture; they were afraid they would be imprisoned if they booked her, as Alexander "Sasha" Berkman, Goldman's ex-lover, collaborator, and *Mother Earth* manager, told the press. The FSL's president, Leonard D. Abbott, wrote a manifesto called "A Demand for Free Speech," protesting the infringement on Goldman's rights. "It is not necessary to approve or share Miss Goldman's ideas to recognize the importance of the issue raised by this kind of tyranny," the manifesto declared.

It was only a matter of time before Comstock would try to interfere with *Mother Earth*. One of Goldman's speech topics was prostitution, and her lecture "The White Slave Traffic" discussed the economic ills that led women to sell their bodies. *White slavery* was a euphemism for prostitution. She had encountered many prostitutes while working as a nurse on the East Side and while imprisoned on Blackwell's Island. In her speech, she argued that the "respectable" class had ushered in prostitution, "from Moses to Trinity Church." Women were reared as sexual commodities but kept ignorant about sex.

Prostitution was thriving, with the support of corrupt politicians. In New York, the Committee of Fifteen, most of its members prominent businessmen, was leading an effort to eliminate the sex trade. Meanwhile, federal legislation such as interstate commerce laws and the Pure Food and Drug Act were Comstockian in their ideals, controlling individual choice and access to pornography or "unsafe" food and drugs. President William Taft would sign the Mann Act into law in 1910, criminalizing interstate trafficking of prostitutes. In an NYSSV *Annual Report* around that time, Comstock wrote that prostitutes could trace their downfalls to a glance at a dirty book or picture. This led to "a life of pleasure-seeking, and soon the victim is inoculated with the moral contagion that makes her reckless, lost to shame, and filled with the idea of nothing to do but follow the crowd, regardless of what the results may be."

After Goldman published "The White Slave Traffic" in the January 1910 issue of *Mother Earth*, she and Reitman received complaints from people who had not received the issue. Berkman wrote to the New York postmaster to find out what had happened. He was told that the January issue had been held as unmailable, and that the matter had been referred to the post office inspector in charge, Walter Mayer. Eighty pounds of the issue were held by the post office. Goldman and Berkman wanted to find out why it had been suppressed. Based on pencil marks made on the article in postal records, the passages that drew notice were one statement that prostitutes were common among the Jews in antiquity, and another to the effect that Moses had observed Jewish young men having sex with foreign prostitutes. Some nativists were concerned that a high proportion of young women immigrants were prostitutes, due to innate moral corruption, and Goldman was questioning this stereotype. She called the history of the Christian church "a history of prostitution, since the two always went hand in hand and furnished thereby great revenues for the Church."

Goldman was on tour at the time, and when Berkman learned that the magazine was being held on a complaint lodged by Comstock, he went to the NYSSV office on Nassau Street. Comstock told him that the unmailable matter was Goldman's "The White Slave Traffic." In *The New York Times* the next day, Comstock claimed that he had not made any complaint against *Mother Earth* and that the magazine had not been suppressed. When Berkman called him, Comstock said the reporters had made up the story, and hung up. Finally, on January 29, the copies were released.

Due to the popularity of both Goldman and her magazine, her high-profile speaking career (which included birth control talks), and her status as an anarchist Russian Jewish immigrant, Comstock was surely aware of her by the time Berkman came to his office regarding the ban. But it was not until later that year that Comstock and the anarchist would have what appears to have been their first face-to-face interaction. On a Tuesday night in the fall of 1910, Comstock came to speak at the recently founded Labor Temple, inside the former

Fourteenth Street Presbyterian Church in the East Village. A nonsectarian gathering place where anyone could make their opinions heard, the temple was popular with labor activists, socialists, and anarchists. Goldman and Reitman planted themselves in the audience to hear Comstock go on at length about the passage of the Comstock law. He referenced the unsuccessful attempts by "so-called liberals, free thinkers, and free lovers" to repeal it. When he finished, the Labor Temple's founder, the Reverend Charles Stelzle, asked for questions.

"Is it true that you have sent a thousand people to jail for spreading necessary information about sex?" Reitman asked.

"No," Comstock answered.

"Yes," shouted Goldman.

"And drove as many to suicide?" Reitman asked.

"I have acted only according to the rules of law."

Goldman rose to her feet with a long list of questions. "Do you believe it is honest for you to assume, in your investigations, [a] fictitious name?" she asked. Comstock had written a decoy letter under a pseudonym, from "P. O. Box 201, Summit, N.J."—the same post office box he had used in his decoy letter to Craddock—to a German American anarchist named George Bauer. In the letter, Comstock requested memorial pictures of the executed Spanish anarchist and educator Francisco Ferrer, one of which displayed a drawing of a nude woman to represent humanity breaking free. After Bauer sent them, he was arrested and sent to the Tombs, but the grand jury declined to indict him.

In the Labor Temple, Comstock replied, "As a Post Office inspector I am entitled to any name I please. I am not too stupid as to write to a publisher and say I am a Post Office inspector and will you please forward to me any obscene books you may be sending out?" There was a roar of laughter.

Goldman shouted, "Do you realize purity is truth?"

"Who do you represent?" someone called out to her.

"I represent the truth," Goldman said. She asked how Comstock's mind could remain pure when he had been inspecting obscene literature for forty years.

"A man can remain pure if he keeps his will under subjection, and obeys always the laws of God and morality," he said.

A shouting match about the nature of obscenity ensued. Comstock said he had eliminated half of the obscene literature in New York. Reitman tried to ask a question, but Stelzle wouldn't recognize him, and Comstock threatened to have him arrested. "Go ahead!" said Reitman.

"And you call this an open forum!" Goldman chimed in. Stelzle closed the meeting, and Comstock missed the train home to Summit.

Months after the Labor Temple meeting, Goldman suffered a personal tragedy. Early in 1911, she believed she had become pregnant by Reitman, who already had a daughter from a past marriage. When she discovered a few months later that she was not pregnant, she was devastated. Reitman later wrote, "I've been in jail with her a dozen times, and have seen the mob howling for her blood, and she never lost her poise or her courage. I only saw her weep once, and that was when she learned that she was not pregnant. For several months she had had the hope that we would have a child and she was so happy about it." She was not meant to be a mother, she felt, but that did not diminish her pain.

In December 1910, a young couple with two children moved into a railroad tenement on West 135th Street in Manhattan. Their names were Margaret and Bill Sanger. They had moved to the city to be near the art scene in Greenwich Village. He was an artist, an architect, and a stained-glass designer, and, like many, he wanted a studio in which he could develop his talent.

There are conflicting stories as to how Margaret met Bill. It was the spring of 1902, and Margaret had been working as a nurse at White Plains Hospital. In one version Bill came in to have something removed from his eye. In another they met when he came to show house plans to a doctor friend of hers. Regardless, they fell in love instantly and were married that summer. After several years in

Hastings-on-Hudson, in Westchester County, they decided to rent out their house and relocate to the city.

Margaret Higgins was born in Corning, New York, on September 14, 1879, thirty-five years after Comstock was born and about six years after the passage of his law. She was the sixth child of an Irish stonecutter, Michael, and his wife, Anne, a religious Catholic. Anne died at fifty of consumption, after having borne eleven children. Margaret cared for her ill mother and wanted to become a doctor, but the family doctor smiled and said, "You'll probably get over it." A year after her mother's death, she entered White Plains Hospital as a nurse.

Within her first year of marriage to Bill, Margaret became pregnant. By the time they moved to New York City, they were parents to two sons, Stuart and Grant. A daughter, Peggy, was born in 1909. Already involved in socialist politics, the Sangers joined a local chapter. In 1912, the Socialist Party had about 118,000 members, up from 10,000 in 1901. About 6 percent of people voted Socialist in 1912, a year in which the party had twelve hundred public officials in office. Bill ran for alderman, and Margaret was recruited for the party's women's committee. She was small and lithe, with green and amber eyes, shiny auburn hair, a warm smile, and high spirits. Men adored her, and she had a fiery temper. When she had an idea in a meeting, Bill would wave his hand and say, "Margaret has something to say on that. Have you heard Margaret?" But Hutchins Hapgood recalled that Margaret "seemed to grant little value to her husband." Though there was debate within the Socialist Party on birth control, the party's strength laid the groundwork for the emergence of the movement during the 1910s.

The Sangers frequently had activists over to their apartment, and while Bill's mother took care of the children, guests would debate the pressing issues of the day. Bill Haywood, an IWW organizer, was often present, along with the reporter John Reed (who would later write *Ten Days That Shook the World*, about the October Revolution in Russia), the attorney and socialist Jessie Ashley, Berkman, and Goldman.

Goldman and Sanger met in 1911 or 1912, at the art patron Mabel

Dodge Luhan's famed Village salon. In her autobiography, Sanger described the scene in Luhan's spacious drawing room: "Cross-legged on the floor, in the best Bohemian tradition, were Wobblies with uncut hair, unshaven faces, leaning against valuable draperies." As for Goldman, Sanger wrote, "Short, stocky, even stout, a true Russian peasant type, her figure indicated strength of body and strength of character, and this impression was enhanced by her firm step and reliant walk. Though I disliked both her ideas and her methods I admired her."

Sanger took a part-time job with Lillian Wald's Visiting Nurse Association on the East Side, in part to bring in money while Bill focused on his art. Like Goldman, Sanger was enraged by the ignorance she saw around pregnancy and abortion. On Saturday nights she saw "groups of from fifty to one hundred with their shawls over their heads waiting outside the office of a five-dollar abortionist." In 1913, as she recounted on a later speaking tour, she was tending to a young Russian Jewish woman in her late twenties named Sadie Sachs—possibly a composite—in an East Side tenement. The husband, "Jake Sachs," a truck driver, had come home to find the three children crying and Sadie unconscious after a self-induced abortion. He called the doctor, who sent for Sanger. With the doctor, Sanger fought Sadie's bacterial infection septicemia as the hot days and nights melted "into a torpid inferno." When Sadie recovered, she asked the doctor how she could avoid such an illness, from a self-induced abortion, in the future. He laughed good-naturedly, as Sanger described it, and said, "Tell Jake to sleep on the roof."

Sanger spoke to her about condoms and withdrawal, but Sachs did not like either, because they relied too much on the man's agency. Three months later, Sanger received a call from Jake Sachs, summoning her to the tenement. "[Sadie] Sachs was in a coma and died within ten minutes," Sanger recalled. Sanger left Jake, who was sobbing as though he had lost his mind, and paced through the streets for hours. She went to bed having decided she "was finished with palliatives and superficial cures; I was resolved to seek out the root of evil, to do something to change the destiny of mothers whose miseries were vast as the sky."

Through her work and activism, Sanger became awakened to the catastrophic effect of the Comstock laws on American women, believing that he "caused the death of untold thousands." Even those who survived botched abortions were suffering. The Comstock laws were "directly responsible for the deplorable condition of a whole generation of women left physically damaged and spiritually crippled from the results of abortion. No group of women had yet locked horns with this public enemy." Of course, that was not true—free lovers such as Angela Heywood had, and Craddock had, of course, but Sanger was not yet informed about nineteenth-century activists.

When she was working as a nurse on the East Side, the medical establishment was coming out firmly on the side of birth control. In 1912, Abraham Jacobi was elected president of the American Medical Association, and he advocated for public health, venereal disease testing, and birth control, citing a double standard between the wealthy and non-wealthy. He was influenced by a doctor named William J. Robinson, who edited and published many works on birth control, which he believed would lead to sexual liberation. Pro–birth control physicians rejected "continence" as a contraceptive strategy and believed that frequent, non-procreative sex was good and healthy. The male libido was to be accepted, as was greater sexual permissiveness in general.

It was in this climate that Sanger's birth control views evolved, and Robinson would become a significant ally. In 1911 and 1912, she lectured for audiences of Socialist Party women, frequently discussing the problems of poor immigrant women. In 1912, John and Anita Block, editors of the socialist daily *The New York Call*, asked her to write a column on sex education and health for the national Sunday women's page. The column, "What Every Girl Should Know," was to include twelve pieces. The first one ran on November 17, 1912. Dedicated to "The Working Girls of the World," the articles included descriptions of anatomy, reproduction, sexuality, abortion, menstruation, masturbation, and loss of virginity. She advocated access to contraception, though she was not specific, and sex education for all women.

At first, she did not use the word *penis*, referring to *sex glands* instead. Even so, the series was controversial. Some *Call* readers even canceled their subscriptions. A woman in Greenpoint, Brooklyn, wrote, "I for one condemn the idea where a mother should show through the columns of a newspaper her nakedness to her children."

Sanger criticized the concept of marriage in one of her columns: "All over the civilized world today girls are being given and taken in marriage with but one purpose in view; to be well-supported by the man who takes her . . . When women gain their economic freedom they will cease being playthings and utilities for men, but will assert themselves and choose the father of their offspring." Marriage was a personal matter to Margaret, as there were tensions with Bill. He did not like her traveling, and jealously watched her develop warm friendships with Haywood, Reed, and Berkman. Anita Block, who edited the page on which Sanger's column appeared, spoke to gender tension within the socialist movement when she wrote that most radicals were "unmoved by the Socialist call to women to revolt from sex slavery . . . They are still too oversexed, too tainted with the sins of their fathers, to be able to look upon women's claims as their own." To be married was to be economically enslaved, and class liberation would liberate women from their husbands.

Sanger's final column in the series, "Some Consequences of Ignorance and Silence," about the risks to women of syphilis and gonorrhea, was published in the February 8, 1913, issue. She recounted the story of a syphilitic woman in her care who had lost her hair, eyebrows, eyelashes, nose, upper lip, and teeth. Doctors were often unsympathetic, Sanger declared, and harmed public health by charging too much and causing those with venereal disease to forgo treatment or to turn to quack treatments. In the concluding paragraphs, she blamed the economic system. Until capitalism was eliminated, mothers could not develop as individuals; prostitution would never cease. "There is no hope for a strong race as long as general diseases exist," she wrote. "And they will exist until women rise in one big sisterhood to fight this capitalist society which compels a woman to serve as a sex implement for man's use."

New York Call *front page column, February 9, 1913*

After the paper was sent out, Comstock learned of the column and tipped off the Post Office, which sent the *Call* a warning that the series violated state and federal laws. Subscribers did not receive their issues. On February 9, the editors printed "What Every Girl Should Know—NOTHING! By order of the Post Office Department" in the column space. Two weeks later, the ban was lifted and the full article appeared in the March 2 issue. During World War I, Sanger's portion on venereal disease was officially reprinted (though without credit) and distributed among soldiers.

When a group of New Jersey silk workers went on strike in February 1913, the workers asked for help from the IWW, and Sanger went to Paterson, New Jersey, to organize picket lines. The strike failed in the summer, but Sanger's interest in birth control bloomed again when she sailed for Europe in the fall with Bill and the children. There she would realize that the French were far more advanced in their beliefs about sex, the body, and the role of women.

As Sanger's columns were appearing in the *Call*, some of the board members of the NYSSV were growing concerned about the society's future. One of them, C. Clarence Swift, went to see a lawyer named John S. Sumner in April 1913. He told Sumner that Comstock, sixty-seven, was growing old and that the board had been questioning his judgment. To prepare for the society's future, Swift wanted someone to take on the duties of associate secretary. In 1906, Comstock had shamed the society by arresting a young secretary at the Art Students League and seizing its catalog, which contained nude drawings. Public uproar ensued; the event made the NYSSV look out of touch and cruel.

Sumner studied the issues of the *Annual Report*, talked to his wife, and decided to accept the job. When he went to Nassau Street to meet Comstock, he found him alone in the outer office. "I had been advised that he was rather a brusque character and that he had expressed the opinion that he needed no help," Sumner wrote in his autobiography. He found Comstock seated near a pail of hot water, soaking photographic glass plates and scraping film off them with a putty knife. Sumner introduced himself, noting of Comstock that "although he was not cordial, he was not antagonistic." Comstock told Sumner that each plate could create hundreds or thousands of obscene pictures, that the defendant had been convicted, and that the district attorney had instructed Comstock to destroy them. Sumner learned later that the clean glass panes were sent to a brother of Comstock, who had a greenhouse in Connecticut.

Sumner took the associate secretary position, quickly eclipsing

Comstock. At the NYSSV fortieth anniversary celebration in December 1913, Sumner, not Comstock, was a featured speaker. In later arrest logbook entries, Comstock seemed irritated by Sumner's encroachment, writing, "Sumner took case into state court without my being consulted."

Though Comstock's star might have been waning in 1913, Charles Trumbull published his hagiographic biography, *Anthony Comstock, Fighter,* that year. Summing up Comstock's work, he wrote that the seized matters "would require sixteen freight cars, fifteen loaded with ten tons each, and the other nearly full. If the persons arrested were to be transported, sixty-one passenger coaches would be needed, each with a seating capacity of sixty persons, sixty cars filled, and the other nearly full." Comstock's era of power was coming to an end. Records were being kept of his progress, for posterity.

16

WHY AND HOW THE POOR SHOULD NOT HAVE MANY CHILDREN

In the fall of 1913, Sanger began researching birth control with doctors, midwives, and pharmacists in Europe, finding that it was widely accepted there. Bill decided to stay in Europe and pursue his painting while Margaret took the children home; she had been having an affair, and their marriage was already strained. "I'm sure I mean something in your life," Bill wrote her. "I feel now that nobody can take you away from me." Her emotional life during the marriage is harder to gauge, as Bill destroyed all of her letters.

On the way back from France, she walked around on the deck and came up with the idea for a new magazine, *The Woman Rebel*, "dedicated to the interests of working women." It would, in Sanger's words, "express with white hot intensity the conviction that they must be empowered to decide for themselves when they should fulfill the supreme function of motherhood. They had to be made aware of how they were being shackled, and roused to mutiny." It combined the direct action strategy she had learned in the IWW with her belief in contraception as a radical cause.

The first issue of *The Woman Rebel* was eight pages and was published in March 1914, forty-one years after the passage of the Comstock law. NO GODS NO MASTERS was printed under the title, from the IWW slogan. It included Goldman's "Love and Marriage" and also contained a piece by Sanger, "The Prevention of Conception," which argued that widespread use of contraception would help to reduce poverty and increase wages. She asked readers, "Is it not time to defy [the Comstock] law?"

One morning, after Sanger had washed and dressed the children and sent them to school, she looked over her mail. There was an unstamped envelope from the New York post office, with a letter from the postmaster in New York, E. M. Morgan, informing her that the March issue of *The Woman Rebel* was unmailable under Section 211 of the criminal code, in the Postal Laws and Regulations. The U.S. Post Office Department had seized the entire stock. In the postal records, the marked portions include the magazine's manifesto, which stated that its aim was "to advocate the prevention of conception and to impart such knowledge" to its readers; Goldman's "Love and Marriage"; "The Prevention of Conception"; a poem saying a rebel woman had a "right to be an unmarried mother"; portions of articles that urged strikes and violence to advance political causes; and an unbylined piece titled "A Woman's Duty." The piece reads, in its entirety, "To look the whole world in the face with a go-to-hell look in the eyes; to have an ideal; to speak and act in defiance of convention."

When Goldman learned of the ban, she wrote to Sanger,

> My dear Margaret: So the thing has happened before you have at all started on the way! But then, we might have expected it, from the stupidity of the postal department . . . I know you will be amused to learn that most of the women are up in arms against your paper; mostly women, of course, whose emancipation has been on paper and not in reality. I am kept busy answering questions as to your "brazen" method.

Goldman asked for more copies of *The Woman Rebel* to sell; she was already working as an agent.

In New York, Sanger kept working on the paper and became convinced that contraception needed a new name, one that could convey its social and personal significance. One night, she brainstormed with friends in her apartment. They tried *voluntary parenthood, voluntary motherhood, the new motherhood, constructive generation,* and *new generation.* Sanger felt *neo-Malthusianism, family limitation,* and *conscious generation* "were stuffy and lacked popular appeal." Then Sanger's friend Otto Bobsein suggested *birth control.* In that moment, a movement was launched. Contraception had been repositioned as a social issue and a family right.

The March ban of *The Woman Rebel* was only the first of several suppressions. Before the April issue had been printed, the U.S. Post Office instructed Sanger not to send it. She paid no heed. In ensuing issues, she urged subscribers to fight Comstockism, encouraging them to join neo-Malthusian or birth control leagues, with information about such organizations to be provided by the magazine. The May issue included articles advocating birth control to help the poor and to preserve maternal health.

Goldman was complimentary of *The Woman Rebel*, writing Sanger that it "sells better than anything we have." She suggested that Sanger tour, talk about preventives, organize leagues, and distribute the magazine. "I am inclined to think you'd have a tremendous success," Goldman wrote. "You have no idea what the personal element means in reaching people."

In August, Sanger was arrested and charged with four criminal counts of sending non-mailable matter in the form of the May issue of *The Woman Rebel*, carrying a maximum sentence of forty-five years. The named articles were a notice of the formation of the Birth Control League of America; an essay calling the marriage bed "the most degenerating influence of the social order"; an essay by Sanger called "Are Preventive Means Injurious?"; and an article by Herbert A. Thorpe titled "A Defense of Assassination," which advocated for "the removal of the tiger, the savage, the political or industrial tyrant." Archduke Franz Ferdinand had been assassinated on June 28 in Sarajevo—world war was looming. The indictment called the issue "obscene, lewd, and lascivious" and the Thorpe article "so indecent by reason of its character tending to incite murder and assassination."

In total, six out of the seven issues had been suppressed in the mail. Two postal inspectors came to visit Sanger to tell her she had been indicted. She spent three hours with them, presenting "some of the tragic stories of conscript motherhood," as she put it, and in the end they agreed that the law was wrong. When she met with the judge, he released her on her own recognizance, and the case was adjourned until late October.

Sanger printed a circular, "The Suppressed 'Obscene' Articles," which included all the articles named in the indictments. When Congress was authorized in the Constitution to establish the mail, she wrote, "it was never intended that the latter should pass upon the political, religious or moral opinions of the matter to be conveyed . . . *The Woman Rebel* was a voice trying to deliver a message to the working women of America. That message—Birth Control—was objected to by officialism running riot."

Despite her encouraging letters to Sanger, Goldman did not address the *Woman Rebel* postal bans in *Mother Earth*. Wounded, Sanger wrote an angry letter to the journal: "I expect very little publicity on this 'delicate subject' from the capitalist press, but naturally I look for an attitude of solidarity and comradeship from the radical press." Goldman replied in *Mother Earth* that she had pushed *The Woman Rebel* and discussed Sanger's case in front of thousands of people. The attack was "very unfair . . . But then it is human to feel neglected when one faces one's first great battle with the powers that be, in behalf of an unpopular cause."

The summer of Sanger's indictment, Americans' attention was drawn to events abroad. President Woodrow Wilson had declared U.S. neutrality; Germany and Britain were at war. By the close of the summer, World War I was under way. The pacifist Sanger had included anti-war statements in *The Woman Rebel*, writing, "Exponents of birth-control have long pointed out why nations need men—why rulers need them. Now every woman can see this in the savage slaughter of the children she brings into the world." If women controlled their fertility, they would reduce the supply of "cannon fodder," meaning the sacrifice of working-class men who were drafted to fight. Goldman, too, frequently lectured on anti-militarism.

While Sanger was awaiting her trial date, it became clear that her marriage to Bill had fallen apart. For some time, he had been unwilling to accept that it was broken. "I shall always consider it a marvelous privilege to sit beside you obediently that you might express the best that is you," he had written. She replied that she wanted an open marriage. "I am essentially a monogamist," he wrote back, "and that's why women don't understand me. I cannot adapt to new personalities."

Not sure how she would plead in her case or whether she would wind up imprisoned, Sanger wrote a sixteen-page pamphlet, *Family Limitation*, which outlined common forms of birth control, including withdrawal, condoms, douches, plugs, suppositories, and pessaries. It called special attention to a rubber pessary, popular in Europe, that blocked the cervix. She included diagrams of women's anatomy. With a far bolder style than in her *Call* columns, she used the terms *penis*, *vagina*, *uterus*, and *semen*. Like Angela Heywood, Sanger believed in plain language as an educational and political tool.

Family Limitation also defended women's right to abortion. From a leftist perspective, Sanger argued that working people "produce the surplus number of wage-earners that overflows the labor market. It is up to the women of the world—the vast majority of whom necessarily are working women—to see that the human material for exploiters and militarists is curtailed in the interests of all useful and productive members of society."

After several postponements, Sanger's trial was set for October 20, 1914. She took a train to Montreal and fled to Europe under a false passport, believing that, with Americans focused on the war, she would not receive adequate publicity for her cause, which would harm her chances at trial. Bill came back to New York to be with the younger children, Grant and Peggy; Stuart, ten, was enrolled at a boarding school on Long Island.

Sailing to England on the RMS *Virginian*, Margaret cabled Bill

Shatoff, a New Jersey printer and radical, telling him to distribute one hundred thousand pre-addressed copies of *Family Limitation*. The money came from a free speech lawyer, Theodore Schroeder, who managed a fund left behind by Dr. Ned Foote, who had died in 1912—to whom Sanger referred in her autobiography as "a certain Dr. Foote," unaware that he had been an important contraceptive activist. Before she left, she sent a letter to "Comrades and Friends." As she waited to learn whether she would be imprisoned, she wrote, she would "attempt to nullify the law by direct action and attend to the consequences later."

The trip to England changed Sanger politically and personally. Once settled in her hotel, she wrote Bill to ask for a divorce. She met the married Spanish radical Lorenzo Portet at the intellectual Clarion Cafe in Liverpool, and they became lovers. But a week before Christmas, in Brixton, she met another man, one who would become a major influence on the modern American birth control movement.

Havelock Ellis had white hair and a long white beard and was fifty-six years old, to Sanger's thirty-five. She had read his books before she arrived and became captivated by his thinking and philosophy. They discussed his *Studies in the Psychology of Sex* (1910), which had been censored in England, as well as birth control methods, including male continence. Ellis believed that liberation from taboos would lead to increased happiness and fulfillment. He imagined an independent, free woman who delayed childbirth until she was ready. He felt that the male partners of non-orgasmic women were insufficiently educated on how to bring them pleasure. His rationale for birth control was "social hygiene," the idea that regulated reproduction would improve humanity. He came to the theory through socialist beliefs. To Ellis, women—not men—ought to control reproduction, because they had the power to procreate. Empowering women to reduce population growth would benefit the environment and create more jobs by decreasing competition for labor.

Ellis fell in love with Sanger, calling her "my little rebel" and "you wicked woman" in love letters. He could not sustain an erection, but years after their affair, Sanger wrote that he was "alert to all physical impulses and delights." Personally and politically, she was expanding. She was now certain that the United States was behind the rest of the world on birth control. In the Netherlands, she learned about clinics that provided contraceptive and gynecological information and devices for contraception. The wheels started to turn in her mind: Could such clinics ever exist in the United States?

Less than a week after Sanger met Ellis in his Brixton home, Bill had a visitor at his art studio on East Fifteenth Street in Gramercy. It was December 18, 1914, and so early in the morning that Bill was still in his pajamas. A man calling himself "Heller" arrived at the studio. The man said he was interested in Margaret's writing and asked for a copy of *Family Limitation*. Recalling that Margaret had mentioned a "Heller" in the Socialist Party, Bill found one of the pamphlets on the library table and gave it to him.

On January 19, 1915, about a month later, the same man appeared in the studio and asked where he could buy Margaret's books. Bill named a store on Grand Street. At that point, as Bill described it, "a grey haired, side whiskered, five foot ass presented himself." That "five foot ass" was Comstock.

The first man, "Heller," was Comstock's assistant Charles Bamberger, who always wore

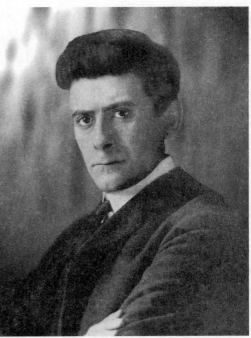

William Sanger

a bowler hat and had previously helped reel in perpetrators through undercover work. Comstock carried an arrest warrant and began to open the desk and seize papers, finding two other pamphlets. He advised Bill to plead guilty, offering to recommend a suspended sentence; Bill refused. Comstock asked Bill if he and Margaret were living together or separately, but Bill refused to answer. Comstock tried to learn Margaret's whereabouts, to no avail. "When I confronted him with the statement that he had no legal or moral right to ask me that question," Bill recounted, "there was no reply, but a cynical smile." On the way to be arraigned, Bill asked Comstock what sentence a birth control author would receive, and Comstock said he would recommend the maximum, five years of hard labor.

Bill was arraigned in Yorkville Court (where the belly dancers had been taken) with bail set at five hundred dollars. He pled not guilty. The case was sent to the Court of Special Sessions. The FSL, which was raising legal objections to suppressions of Goldman's speeches all over the country, sent out a letter seeking support for Bill. The case "raised the questions: How much longer will liberty-loving men and women submit to 'Comstockery'? How much longer will Comstock be given the right to pry into the most private affairs of men and women, and to determine what they shall and shall not read?"

From London, Margaret wrote to her supporters, thanking them for buying *Family Limitation* and noting that Bill could receive up to a year's imprisonment and a one-thousand-dollar fine. She claimed that she had wanted to keep him and close friends ignorant of the pamphlet. She said Bill's arrest was a trap by the government, to get her to return to the United States and to "silence the propaganda of birth control."

Knowing that Margaret was weighing when—and whether—to return to the States, the FSL's president, Leonard Abbott, wrote to tell her that Bill's lawyer believed she was likely to get a long sentence. National newspapers carried the story of both Sangers' indictments, and socialist groups and IWW locals distributed Margaret's pamphlets. Offering to help Bill were prominent radicals such as Goldman,

Berkman, Robinson, Ashley, and the labor activist Elizabeth Gurley Flynn. In a sign of the changing popular sentiment, popular magazines were covering birth control; forty-seven articles about birth control were indexed in the *Reader's Guide to Periodical Literature* from 1915 to 1919, the majority before World War I. *Harper's Weekly* and *The New Republic* each ran a series on birth control. *The New Republic* compared the United States unfavorably to France, Germany, England, Austria, and other countries regarding legalized birth control, stating, "Not more babies but better babies cared for is to be the ideal." Women wanted "a life beyond childbearing," and one day, birth by sexual impulse would "give way increasingly to birth by human design."

In May 1915, *Harper's Weekly* ran an interview with Comstock conducted by Mary Alden Hopkins, an activist and a suffragist reporter in her thirties. A photo of Comstock accompanied the piece; his white muttonchops extended a few inches past his chin. He wore a bowler hat and looked old and tired. He gave his usual quotes about obscenity's danger to children. "I was somewhat confused at first that Mr. Comstock should class contraceptives with pornographic objects which debauch children's fancies," Hopkins wrote, "for I knew that the European scientists who advocate their use have no desire at all to debauch children. When I asked Mr. Comstock about this, he replied—with scant patience of 'theorizers' who do not know human nature: 'If you open the door to anything, the filth will all pour in and the degradation of youth will follow.'"

Raising a common criticism of the Comstock laws, she pointed out that they handicapped physicians, the same criticism brought up in the debate preceding the federal law's passage. "They do not," Comstock told her. "No reputable physician has ever been prosecuted under these laws . . . Only infamous doctors who advertise or send their foul matter by mail. A reputable doctor may tell his patient in his office what is necessary, and a druggist may sell on a doctor's written prescription drugs which he would not be allowed to sell otherwise." He was tacitly acknowledging that the law had been intended to punish women physicians and women's physicians, not "regular" male doctors. The "infamous doctors" could only be midwives and women's doctors such as Chase and Restell.

Indicating that he did, in fact, find the withdrawal and rhythm methods acceptable, he said, referring to couples, "Can they not use self-control? Or must they sink to the level of the beasts?"

"But if the parents lack that self-control," Hopkins answered, "the punishment falls upon the child."

"It does not. The punishment falls upon the parents," he rejoined. "The prevention of conception would work the greatest demoralization. God has set certain natural barriers. If you turn loose the passions and break down the fear you bring worse disaster than the war. It would debase sacred things, break down the health of women and disseminate a greater curse than the plagues and diseases of Europe." By "natural barriers" he seemed to be indicating the rhythm method. This was a seismic shift from his previous statements, an admission that families could take charge of their own size. And yet he still opposed artificial contraception, as he had back in 1873.

A month after *Harper's* ran its piece, *The New York Times* printed a story suggesting that Comstock was going to lose his job as post office inspector. He told the *Times* the next day that he was the victim of a conspiracy: "This is not the first attempt that has been made to relieve me of my commission . . . Do you know that I could be worth $1,000,000 today if I had listened to the bribers who have tried to stop my crusade against vice in this city?" The *New-York Tribune* reported that Sumner was running the NYSSV and that Comstock no longer represented its interests. It claimed that the NYSSV had backed away from its mission of protecting young people, and that the society was focused too much on art, as exemplified by an embarrassing case involving the painting *September Morn*, a portrait of a nude young woman by the French painter Paul Émile Chabas. The executive committee had been seeking to decrease Comstock's power, the *Tribune* announced, and intended to "drop him from its rolls." Comstock would keep his five-thousand-dollar salary as NYSSV secretary but soon retire on pension.

The rumors about his job loss turned out to be false. Washington's new Post Office Department chief inspector, Carter Keene, said the government supported Comstock's work. Comstock told the *Times*, "I knew all along the plans of the miserable schemers, plotting to out me, would fail." He then recounted the number of indecent picture arrests and book and pamphlet confiscations the NYSSV had made that year.

With Comstock's power apparently on the wane, and the birth control movement gaining power, Goldman became bolder in her attempts to flout the law. At one of the biweekly Sunrise Club dinners in the spring of 1915, she chose to discuss birth control, chronicling in her memoir that she was "intending openly to discuss methods of contraception." Word got out, and six hundred people showed up. She was so certain that she would be arrested that friends came with bail money, and she carried along a book in case she had to spend the night in the station house.

In her talk, Goldman reviewed the history of birth control and discussed the use and effects of various contraceptives. "I spoke in the direct and frank manner that I should use in dealing with ordinary disinfection and prophylaxis," she recalled. Afterward, physicians complimented her on having presented the delicate subject in a "clean and natural manner." To her surprise, there were no police waiting outside the café. Bill Sanger had been arrested for selling a pamphlet he had not written; she had spoken openly about birth control and nothing had happened. "Comstock's failure to act," she surmised, "was due to the fact that he knew that those who were in the habit of attending the Sunrise Club gatherings were probably already in possession of contraceptives."

To test the authorities again, she decided to deliver the lecture at her own Sunday meeting. The Harlem Masonic Temple was packed with young people, including Columbia University students, who asked direct, personal questions. Again there was no arrest, though a dozen detectives were in the audience. Comstock had "discovered that by persecution of the Sangers, he has stepped into a hornet's nest," she wrote in *Mother Earth*. "That may explain his timidity as regards [me]. My own belief is that energetic and defiant proclamation in behalf of contracepts would put St. Anthony and his regime out of commission very soon."

That August, in Portland, Oregon, after Goldman began a birth control speech, she and Reitman were arrested under a state law for distributing birth control literature. She was released and fined, and the chief of police said she would not be allowed to speak again in Portland, but she gave a talk called "The Intermediate Sex" later that night and two more lectures the next day. Emboldened, she and Reitman released a four-page pamphlet, possibly penned by William J. Robinson, titled *Why and How the Poor Should Not Have Many Children*. It described condoms, pessaries (to be fitted by a physician), suppositories, douches, and a cotton ball in borated Vaseline. It also gave a political justification for birth control: that poor children were "not only a burden to their mothers and families, but also glut the labor market, tend to lower wages, and are a menace to the welfare of the working class . . . If you think that the teaching of prevention of conception will help working men and women, spread the glad tidings."

As she continued to deliver lectures with titles such as "Man: Monogamist or Varietist," "Freedom," and "Jealousy: Its Cause and Possible Cure" all over the country, she and Reitman were struggling. She was unaware that he had struck up an affair with a British suffragist named Anna Martindale. He had become infatuated with Anna and longed for a married life with children. Goldman and Reitman's days as a couple were coming to an end.

Emma Goldman speaking at a birth control rally in Union Square, May 1916

17

I AM GLAD AND PROUD TO BE A CRIMINAL

Just before Bill Sanger's trial opened in the fall of 1915, Comstock went to San Francisco to attend the ninth annual International Purity Congress, having been appointed the U.S. delegate by President Wilson. According to John Sumner, "Comstock was as active as ever[,] literally throwing his weight around with the vigor of a man ten years younger. He may have been annoyed at rumors that he was to be deprived of his Post Office Inspectorship but did not show it." Four thousand people attended the Congress. At the opening session, after Comstock had finished a half-hour lecture on his work, reciting statistics to show how he had driven obscene books and pictures out of New York, a protester named Leon Malmed stood up and questioned him about Bill Sanger's arrest. Malmed, an Albany anarchist and friend of Goldman, asked if Comstock had used "subterfuge" to obtain the copy of *Family Limitation*.

"I consider that question very impertinent at a meeting of this kind," Comstock answered angrily.

Three sergeants at arms rushed Malmed and threatened to arrest him. A San Francisco medical student named William C. Hall stood up, mentioned Havelock Ellis's and Richard von Krafft-Ebing's books on sex, and asked Comstock, "Are you assuming that to those of pure mind books on the body and sex are gangrened and rotten?" The audience broke into an uproar, and the sergeants silenced Hall.

When Comstock returned from the Purity Congress to New York, he appeared to have lost weight and vitality, according to Sumner. At home in Summit, he contracted pneumonia. In the September issue of the socialist newspaper *The Masses*, a political cartoonist named Robert Minor depicted Comstock dragging a helpless young woman in front of a judge. The caption read, "Your honor, this woman gave birth to a naked child!" The message was clear: Comstock was out of touch with American values.

THE MASSES

Drawn by Robert Minor.

"Your Honor, this woman gave birth to a naked child!"

The Masses *magazine cartoon by Robert Minor, September 1915*

Bill and his lawyers tried and failed to get him a jury trial, and when his trial opened on September 3, he decided to defend himself, hoping to challenge the constitutionality of the Comstock law. He was twenty-nine years old. In an interview he gave to *The New York Call* the night before, Bill urged supporters to rally for Margaret when she returned to face her own charges. "I hope the searchlight of truth and day will be turned on Comstock and Comstockery," he said, "on the post office and on the post office ring, which have prevented the dissemination of literature on vital information for forty years."

In the Court of Special Sessions, a hundred supporters were present, including Berkman, Flynn, Abbott, and the anarchist Carlo Tresca, plus a hundred more outside. On the stand, Bill said, "I admit that I broke the law, and yet I claim that, in every real sense, it is the law, and not I, that is on trial today." He called Comstock a "self-appointed censor of our morality," and a victim of "incurable sexphobia" who could not "distinguish between pornography and scientific information."

Throughout the trial, Comstock engaged in shouting matches with activists. He said he had been told that if he prosecuted the case he would be shot, but had disregarded the threat. He spoke out of turn and was rebuked by the presiding justice, James J. McInerney. Charles Bamberger had to accompany Comstock wherever he went and see him to the Barclay Street ferry every night on his way home. Over Labor Day weekend, Comstock tried to recuperate but ran a high temperature.

McInerney pronounced Bill guilty after five days of testimony, on September 10, 1915. He told Bill, "There are too many now who believe it is a crime to have children. If some of the women who are going around and advocating equal suffrage would go around and advocate women having children they would do a greater service." He sentenced him to a $150 fine or thirty days in the city prison. Bill took the thirty days and said, "I would rather be in jail with my ideals and convictions intact, than out of it, stripped of my self respect and manhood." Men and women rose in their seats, shrieked, cursed, and cheered. They threw hats into the air, and screams could be heard all over the building and in the street.

When Bill was removed from the courtroom, supporters waved hats and handkerchiefs. In the hallway, Abbott said one thousand dollars had been raised toward another edition of *Family Limitation*. Margaret wrote of her husband, "It was one of life's sharpest ironies that, despite our separation, he should have been drawn into my battle, and go to prison for it."

The next day, Comstock's pneumonia became acute. *The New York Times* seemed to trace it to the dramatic trial, reporting, "The day after this scene in court Mr. Comstock was ill of an intermittent fever, which finally caused pneumonia." Doctors and the minister attended to him, Maggie by his bedside. On Saturday, September 18, 1915, Sumner visited him, bringing a letter requesting that Comstock turn over the office keys to the NYSSV. Sumner read the letter aloud, and Comstock told Maggie to get the keys. Before his successor left, Comstock said, "Sumner, I hope that you will be very successful."

Comstock recovered briefly on September 20 and dictated notes to a stenographer, but the next evening, September 21, he shrieked from his upstairs bedroom, "Doctor! Doctor!" and died. Though "lobar pneumonia" was written on his death certificate as the official cause, the contributory cause was "exhaustion from over work & mental strain."

Sumner was appointed acting executive secretary and took over the logbook. The last arrest in which Comstock assisted, entered in his own handwriting, was on September 3, 1915, the day Bill's trial opened. Seventeen-year-old Herbert Wheatley, of 128 East 123rd Street, had allegedly mailed obscene writing. Young Herbert received a suspended sentence.

Comstock was buried next to his daughter, Lillie, in Brooklyn's Evergreens Cemetery. On his tombstone was written "In memory of a fearless witness" and a quote from Hebrews 12: "Lay aside every weight—looking unto Jesus—despising the shame." After his death, the *Times* proclaimed:

> That Mr. Comstock never made mistakes, that he did not sometimes allow himself to be carried away by excessive zeal, that he was not an occasional persecutor as well as a frequent prosecutor, not even his best friends and most sincere appreciators could truthfully deny, and they do not. They can and do claim for him the credit due to a thoroughly honest

man who through a long life, for the scantiest of material re-
wards, devoted his courage and energy to the protection of
society from a detestable and dangerous group of enemies.

Sumner wrote that Comstock's "faults were the faults of a zealot—a
lack of tact, and, on occasion, of self-control. Any criticism of the man
was largely due to those failings, magnified by his enemies and regretted by friends."

Mother Earth (probably Berkman writing) remembered him this
way: "While less subtle crusaders were crying for honesty and frankness and openness in sexual relations, he wisely realized the extreme
value of suppression, secrecy, illicitness. These measures . . . were
quite necessary to keep alive the feeble flames of passion and animal-
ity in a society that has rapidly become impotent through the efforts
of [u]nattractive suffragists and feminists."

Suffrage was indeed drawing national attention, with Alice Paul
leading a suffrage delegation to President Wilson, petitions from all
over the country being presented to Congress, and the Senate voting for the first time since 1887 on a federal amendment, though the
measure was defeated. The week before Comstock died, the Congressional Union for Woman's Suffrage organized the first Woman Voters
Convention with delegates from states that already allowed women
to vote. At the Panama Pacific International Exposition, half a million
signatures were collected on a suffrage petition taken to Congress and
to Wilson. American women were getting closer to the vote, though
exactly how close they were still depended on race and ethnicity.

When Comstock died, the nation was focused on international
events. In early 1916, the bloody Battle of Verdun began; it would rage
on till year's end. With Americans alert to tension abroad, the new
NYSSV secretary, Sumner, wrote in a report:

Such a condition of mind cannot exist where the moral
tone is low, mercenary and vicious. It follows that by carrying out our work, improving the moral tone and removing

that which contaminates the minds of the rising generation, we are indirectly bringing about that state of mind
whereby the country may be saved in any future emer-
gency and its traditions preserved to posterity.

In Sumner's view, patriotism required morality. Weak morals (a category
that included obscenity and birth control advocacy) would weaken
a nation, and immigrants, who were threats to American strength,
were the new enemies of society.

Citing a mixed year on convictions of contraceptive sellers and
quietly acknowledging the publicity surrounding Bill Sanger's case,
Sumner wrote that there was some difference of opinion on "the
provisions of the law" in regard to birth control. Still, he contended,
"while there is something to be said in favor of a more liberal construction, at the same time the weight of opinion and the weight of
morality is on the side of the enforcement of the law as it now stands."

With Comstock dead, Margaret Sanger decided to return to the
States to stand trial. She had come to believe that she had to advocate
birth control as a single issue and a gender issue; if she pursued other
causes alongside birth control, her commitment would be compro-
mised. She ceased to identify as a radical or socialist. After the United
States entered World War I and a friend showed up at her apartment
in uniform, having just been commissioned as a lieutenant, she said,
"I'm against all war . . . just as all my friends and associates are—but
if I take a stand against it, become an active pacifist, the Birth Control
movement will suffer. I cannot let this happen just as I have gotten
order out of chaos."

Her legal advisers debated for months over whether she should
plead not guilty—risking a long sentence—or take a plea. She arrived
in New York a few days before Bill was to be released from prison, but
instead of visiting him, she spent time with her children and alerted
the authorities that she was in New York. After his release, they met at
her hotel. They argued bitterly. Later she wrote him that she wanted

a divorce, but she would not secure one until the fall of 1921, six years after her first request, on grounds of desertion.

A month after Margaret's return to American soil, Peggy Sanger, age five, caught pneumonia and died with her mother at her side in Mount Sinai Hospital. The death was a pivotal moment in Sanger's development as an activist. She blamed herself and her long absence for the death, and had new doubts about the trial. A severe prison sentence would keep her away from her two surviving children.

She was flooded with support from *Woman Rebel* subscribers, who sent sympathy letters and locks of hair and photos of their own babies who had died. Goldman wrote from Chicago, promising to use all her birth control lectures to raise money for her. About Peggy's death, Goldman wrote:

> I really think it is [un]pardonable on your part to blame yourself for the death of Peggy. I am sure that it is due only to your depressed state of mind as I cannot imagine anyone with your intelligence to hold herself responsible for something that could not possibly have been in your power . . . Please, dear, don't think me heartless. I feel deeply with your loss but I also feel that you owe it to yourself and the work you have before you to collect your strength.

Having learned that Sanger's lawyer, the Free Speech League secretary Theodore Schroeder, was trying to persuade her to plead guilty, Goldman then wrote to Sanger:

> Just kill the movement you have helped to advance [for] 50 years[.] I hope you will do no such thing. That you will be brave as you have so far[.]
>
> Dear dear Girl, I appreciate your state of mind[.] I feel deeply all you have gone through since you began your work. But at the same time I feel that it would be a great

[un]pardonable error were you now [to] allow yourself to be beaten . . .

You have aroused the interest, as no one ever has. Think of losing it all by declaring yourself guilty. Don't do it[.]

Then she suggested that Sanger come away with her on vacation to Lakewood, New Jersey, for a few weeks. "We'd both gain much," she wrote, "and I would help you find yourself."

Margaret was focused on Stuart and Grant and unable to think clearly. But she finally decided to plead not guilty. She wrote a letter addressed "To My Friends and Comrades," informing them she had made her decision because "the issue involved is to raise the entire question of birth control out of the gutter of obscenity and into the light of understanding." She pled with supporters to write to newspapers, hold protest meetings, send resolutions to Washington, and raise money for publicity. In a *Mother Earth* essay, she explained that she sought to separate birth control "from the gutter of slime and filth where the lily-livered legislators have placed it, under the direction of the late unlamented Anthony Comstock, and in which the forces of reaction are still attempting to hold it."

Meanwhile, Goldman was continuing to speak out on birth control. Two days before Sanger's trial was to open, Goldman gave a talk called "The Child's Right Not to be Born" in the Harlem Masonic Temple. She said that if "every one followed the injunction of the Bible and Theodore Roosevelt to 'Be fruitful and multiply,' every tenement house would be turned into a lunatic asylum by the excessive number of children." The *Times* ran the story under the headline "T. R. Wrong, Says Anarchist."

The evening that article ran, a dinner was held for Sanger at the Hotel Brevoort, among the best in New York. During her European travels, a committee called the National Birth Control League (NBCL) had formed; its members were a group of agitators who wanted to reform federal and state Comstock laws. But the NBCL did not believe in breaking the law. Its leader was the Bostonian Mary Ware Dennett, a divorced woman who had cut her activist teeth in the National

American Woman Suffrage Association. Attendees at the dinner in-cluded wealthy lawyers, doctors and judges with Ivy League degrees, and graduates of prestigious women's colleges.

While Sanger was building upper-middle-class support for birth control, Goldman was delivering lectures to poor, immigrant Jew-ish women, because "the women on the East Side needed that infor-mation most. Even if I were not vitally interested in the matter, the conviction of William Sanger and his condemnation to prison would have impelled me to take up the question . . . His bold defence in court earned him the deserved appreciation of all right-thinking people." On February 11, after Goldman had delivered her birth control lec-ture eight times in New York alone, she was arrested while walking into Forward Hall to give a speech on atheism. A thousand people were waiting, and five hundred people followed her out, cheering her on. The charge regarded an earlier speech in Harlem. She was transported to Clinton Street Jail, where she was, as she reported, "searched in the most vulgar manner by a coarse looking matron in the presence of two detectives, a thing which would outrage the most hardened criminal." Then she was locked up until her bondsman re-leased her on five-hundred-dollar bail. She decided to use the arrest to spark a national publicity campaign in support of birth control. She would fight "for the right of the masses, and especially women, to de-cide whether or not they shall bring forth life in a system which rests on the degradation and humiliation as well as the destruction of life."

On February 18, 1916, while Goldman was awaiting her own trial, the government dropped all charges against Sanger; her indictment at that point was two years old. Goldman felt the government's lax attitude toward Sanger was due to the "fashionable women" who sup-ported her, women who used their "position including their sex to hypnotize men in office in order to have a case dismissed," adding that Sanger "did not disapprove" of such behavior.

Tension continued to brew between birth control's most prom-inent advocates. On Sunday, February 20, a celebration was held in honor of the dropped charges against Sanger. Robert Minor, who had drawn the Comstock cartoon for *The Masses*, thought there should be discussion of Goldman's case at the celebration, and made a motion that Goldman be summoned from the Harlem Masonic Temple, where she was giving her Sunday lecture. The audience applauded, but no one sustained his proposition, the chairwoman continued the meeting, and Sanger, on the platform, did not speak up.

When Goldman learned of this, she wrote to her anarchist friend W. S. Van Valkenburgh, "If you ever thought for a moment that the people who backed Margaret Sanger in her struggle will do anything in my case, please get that out of your head. They have demonstrated that last night at the so called 'Jubilee' meeting for Margaret Sanger that they are not really interested in birth control or if they are it is only when it can be kept within respectable channels." She told Valkenburgh that Sanger's treatment of her proved "the anarchists are merely used to fetch the chestnuts out of the fire and that when they are in trouble they need not hope for any support from those who pose as liberals and radicals."

At a birth control mass meeting on March 1, which Sanger did not attend, claiming recurrent grippe, the venue was filled into the galleries with about four thousand men and women, girls and boys. A letter was read in which the state health commissioner, Dr. Hermann Biggs, argued that the law should allow birth control literature to be distributed. Women wore scarlet ribbons that read "Birth Control" across their bosoms. Ben Reitman sold pamphlets. Goldman said, "This movement has been brewing for a hundred and fifty years. It is the greatest movement of the age, and in the last three years it has furnished direct action . . . Women are doing more work than the soldiers in Europe." As Goldman spoke, four police stenographers and plainclothes detectives listened for violation of the penal code. She declared, "Police and the press, you can arrest me, but what will you do with the women who decline to be coerced? Are you going to place detectives in their homes to compel them?"

On April 20, the first day of Goldman's trial, hundreds were prevented from entering the Court of Special Sessions, but many birth control activists were inside. Abbott wrote that "it was as if a gust of fresh air had blown into a musty room." A man carrying a bouquet of American Beauty roses for Goldman was not allowed in.

Goldman opted to defend herself before the three judges. She asked for a dismissal of the indictment because birth control information was "merely part of a vast movement which is backed [by] certain social and economic reasons." She cited hunger, poverty, and infant mortality, and said she was propagating the ideas "to bring to women the light and knowledge and opportunity to know under what conditions and by what means to bring children who are of quality to the race, instead of quantity, into the world." She called the birth control movement

> one phase in the larger social struggle . . . a war for a seat at the table of life on the part of the people, the masses who create, who build the world and who have nothing in return. I look upon Birth Control as only one phase of that vast movement, and if I, through my agitation,—through my education, I should rather say,—can indicate a way towards the betterment of that human race, towards a finer quality, children who should have a joyous and glorious childhood, and women who shall have a healthy motherhood, if that is a crime, Your Honor, I am glad and proud to be a Criminal.

At this point the courtroom crowd broke out into applause. Justice George J. O'Keefe offered a fine of one hundred dollars or fifteen days in the workhouse. "I'll take the Workhouse, Your Honor," Goldman replied. As she was rushed out toward the pen, friends waved their hands and stuck their fingers through the wire grating of the runway. She tried to touch them back, her face lit up with enthusiasm.

She was taken to Queens County Jail in Long Island City. A thousand letters of protest were sent to the district attorney and judges. While in prison, Goldman befriended fellow inmates and persuaded the warden to allow the girls and women to remain in the hallway until 6:00 p.m. instead of 4:00. In jail, she read, wrote, and made notes for lectures. She wrote to a woman friend that the jail term gave her an opportunity to diet. Upon her release, when a yellow automobile containing Reitman and others arrived to take her to the *Mother Earth* offices, she had it go around the corner so she could wave goodbye to her fellow inmates through the iron bars.

On Saturday, May 20, 1916, there was a mass open-air meeting about birth control in Union Square. Two thousand people gathered to hear Goldman, Abbott, Hall, Ashley, and Ida Rauh Eastman speak from a touring car. Goldman told the crowd that the prosecution of those engaged in distributing birth control knowledge should halt, and the people cheered loudly. Abbott said there was a "double standard of laws— one for the rich, one for the poor." He said the group would make a test of police enforcement and distribute birth control literature. Thirty plainclothes police officers attended. After the speeches, Ashley and Eastman, standing in the open-air car, as well as young women on the outskirts of the crowd, handed out *Why and How the Poor Should Not Have Many Children*. *The New York Herald* reported, "Boys and young girls struggled roughly with elder persons in the fight to obtain the literature," which did not bear the name of a printer, a publisher, or an author.

Goldman's and Reitman's arrests had led to protests all over the country. Forty San Francisco women signed a letter sent to the judge in Goldman's case; they wrote, "We are going to break your law and break it so thoroughly, so completely that the future will find it without form." Educated and working-class women attended rallies, kissing the hands of those distributing birth control pamphlets. The socialist Agnes Inglis had a clinic running in Ann Arbor, Michigan, and St. Paul socialist women planned a clinic as well.

On April 1, 1916, Sanger launched a national speaking tour. Covered positively by the press, she spoke of free speech and sexual liberation, delivering the same speech 199 times, and she was jailed in Portland for distributing *Family Limitation*. Goldman claimed that while touring the country, Sanger "would not even mention my approaching trial . . . From numerous places friends wrote me that she considered [birth control] as her own private concern. Subsequently,

Mr. and Mrs. Sanger publicly repudiated birth-control leagues organized by us, as well as our entire campaign for family limitation."

On her lecture trail, Sanger arrived at the idea of opening a clinic to provide birth control and information to poor women. After she learned that the local medical society in New York would not interfere if she had a licensed physician on staff—due to the physician's exemption in the New York Comstock law—she decided to put her plan into action. With fifty dollars from a supporter, she rented a street-level storefront in Brownsville, Brooklyn, a Jewish and Italian slum. Working with her sister, Ethel Byrne, a nurse, and with Fania Mindell, a receptionist and translator, she distributed handbills in English, Yiddish, and Italian: "MOTHERS! Can you afford to have a large family? Do you want any more children? If not, why do you have them? DO NOT KILL, DO NOT TAKE LIFE! BUT PREVENT!" It gave the address on Amboy Street and offered "Safe, Harmless Information." "Would the women come?" Sanger asked in her autobiography. "Nothing, not even the ghost of Anthony Comstock, could have kept them away."

The Sanger Clinic

On October 16, 1916, the women opened the clinic on 46 Amboy Street. Sanger never found a doctor and instead staffed Byrne;

Mindell, who spoke three languages; and a social worker with Assisted Charities of New York. The intention was not to fit women with pessaries, Sanger claimed, but to show them samples and, to leave no loophole for testing the Comstock law, "only give the principles of contraception, show [a pessary] to the women, explain that if they had had two children they should have one size, and if more a larger one." A common device, the Mizpah Pessary, was marketed at pharmacies as "womb support," but also worked as contraception.

By the time the clinic opened, there were lines of women on the street. Files were created for almost five hundred women. Each consultation cost ten cents. Nine days after the clinic opened, a large, wealthy-seeming woman came in. She paid two dollars for a sex education pamphlet that cost ten cents. Mindell pinned the money to the wall with a note reading "received from Mrs. _____ of the Police Department as her contribution."

The next day, the woman returned—as Officer Margaret Whitehurst—and arrested Sanger, Byrne, and Mindell. As Whitehurst placed Sanger under arrest, Sanger shrieked, "You dirty thing. You are not a woman. You are a dog."

"Tell that to the judge in the morning," said Whitehurst.

"No. I'll tell it to you, now, you dog, and you have two ears to hear me too!" Sanger and Mindell were reportedly "dragged" to a patrol wagon, a group of Brownsville mothers trailing in support. As the word spread of the arrests, a crowd of a thousand gathered on Amboy Street.

Sanger and Mindell chose to stay in the filthy, vermin-infested Raymond Street Jail overnight. "The mattresses were spotted and smelly," Sanger wrote, "the blankets stiff with dirt and grime. The stench nauseated me." She lay on top of the covers and wrapped her coat around her.

The police seized case histories, pamphlets, and supplies. The next day, Friday, October 27, 1916, Sanger and Mindell were released on bail. Goldman, who had been testifying in the trial of a friend, was arrested and held at Yorkville Court for disseminating birth control information at the Union Square demonstration, a charge she denied. "Three birth control advocates were released on bail yesterday," reported the

Times, "pending trial on the charge of disseminating information on birth control, and another, Emma Goldman, Anarchist, was held [on] $500 [actually $1,000] on the same charge, for which she served a term in the Queens County Penitentiary last Spring." The two most prominent birth control activists in the nation were in jail on the same day.

After a few weeks, Sanger reopened her clinic, but it was shuttered once again and she was charged with maintaining a public nuisance. Brownsville mothers were subpoenaed for Sanger's trial, appearing with bread, fruit, pacifiers, and diapers for their babies. Sanger's testimony focused on whether she had fitted clients with pessaries, about which there were conflicting accounts. Her attorney, Jonah J. Goldstein, argued that the state Comstock law's medical exception impeded the constitutional rights of poor people by denying them the right to family limitation, but upheld the rights of middle-class people with private doctors. Sanger was found guilty, the judge pronouncing that women did not have "the right to copulate with a feeling of security that there will be no resulting conception."

Sanger served thirty days in the workhouse at Blackwell's Island, passing her time reading to illiterate women on her corridor, many of them prostitutes and convicted drug addicts, lecturing them on sex and birth control. When she was released, the guards tried to force her hands down to be fingerprinted, but she resisted. She emerged to a group of friends and supporters who referred to the event as "Margaret's coming out party." They included her sister, Byrne; her attorney, Goldstein; a group from the Women's City Club of New York, which had recently formed a birth control committee; and a Russian Jewish woman named Rose Halpern, who presented her with a bouquet on behalf of the mothers of Brownsville. The assembled group began to sing "La Marseillaise," the French national anthem:

> Ye sons of Freedom, wake to glory
> Hark! hark! What myriads bid you rise!
> You children, wives and grandsires hoary,
> Behold their tears, and hear their cries!

From the windows above, the women prisoners sang along. Sanger "plunged down the stairs and into the car which stood ready" for her.

When Goldman's case on the Union Square rally came up in January, the evidence that she had distributed birth control pamphlets collapsed, and she was acquitted. The hearings and trials related to birth control, Goldman wrote, "proved that at least the judges were being educated." One judge in a case involving a woman with a large family—she had been charged with theft—mentioned that many European nations had adopted birth control with excellent results. He added, "We are living in an age of ignorance, which at some future time will be looked upon aghast as we now look back on the dark ages." As legal sentiment appeared to be shifting to her side, Goldman mused, "We had reason to feel it was worth going to jail if the urgency of limiting offspring was getting to be admitted even by the bench. Direct action, and not parlour discussion, was responsible for these results."

Over the course of 1916 and 1917, at least twenty activists in addition to Sanger were arrested and imprisoned on federal charges related to birth control action. Goldman soon faced legal problems as a result of her views on World War I, not her birth control activism,

Margaret Sanger, 1916

but she had laid the groundwork for one of the most powerful social movements of the twentieth century.

In the ultimate decision in the Brownsville clinic case, Judge

Frederick Crane upheld Sanger's conviction and affirmed the state's right to limit contraception distribution, but said the physician's exception was "broad enough to protect the physician who in good faith gives such help or advice to a married person to cure or prevent disease," which he defined as "an alteration in the state of the body" that could cause or threaten pain and sickness. This protection would also extend to druggists or vendors filling prescriptions for physicians. The finding would affect later state appeals and was a step toward the dismantling of the birth control provision in the Comstock laws.

The issue of credit for birth control agitation lingered during the decades following Goldman's and Sanger's imprisonments. In 1929, Sanger wrote, "Everyone knew that Miss Goldman was first, last and all the time an anarchist and not a birth control advocate." She was right, in that she herself had decided to be single-issue on birth control, while Goldman fought for many leftist causes, ultimately paying a brutal price for this choice. Goldman, for her part, wrote that Sanger was "not big enough to give credit to those who have paved the way for her."

This question was important to Goldman. In *Living My Life*, she described the nineteenth-century roots of the birth control movement, mentioning Ezra Heywood, though not Angela, and Moses Harman. But she also mentioned a sex radical whose conflict with Comstock led her to a tragic ending. "Neither my birth-control discussion nor Margaret Sanger's efforts were pioneer work," Goldman wrote. "Ida Craddock, one of the bravest champions of women's emancipation, had paid the supreme price. Hounded by Comstock and faced with a five-year sentence, she had taken her own life. She was one of the pioneers and heroes of the battle for free motherhood, for the right of the child to be born well."

In the Borderland, Craddock would have smiled. She had been recognized as a pioneer by the woman who made birth control an American cause.

Margaret Sanger emerging from the Brooklyn Court of Special Sessions during the Brownsville clinic trials, January 7, 1917

18

BREACH IN THE ENEMY'S LINES

Anthony Comstock's reign was devastating to American women, but his era was a thrilling period of transformative feminist activism. Woodhull, Claflin, Lohman, Chase, Heywood, Craddock, Goldman, and Sanger placed women's bodies, and pleasure, at the center of the debate over sexuality and obscenity. Woodhull and Claflin took on powerful church-state allegiances, redefined womanhood, and used Wall Street and publishing alike as platforms for social change. Women needed the right to vote, not only because it was wrong for them to be disenfranchised but also because they would *vote for better candidates*. Lohman and Chase sought to help women in need, lecturing to them as well as providing contraception, and were arrested and imprisoned for these actions. Heywood used whimsical, incendiary speech to take on Comstock and to protest governmental control of women's bodies. Craddock fused sexology, spirituality, and women's rights into her own quirky philosophy, hoping to improve the marriages of her students and readers by educating them about sex. And Goldman and Sanger founded the modern birth control movement, which led to the Planned Parenthood Federation of America, the overturning of the Comstock law's birth control restrictions, and *Roe v. Wade*.

The sex radicals' faith in the possibility of control—of marriage and of sex—aligned them with Comstock, their enemy. He wanted to assert control over sex to strengthen the family, while they wanted women to wield their own control over sex for the purpose of strengthening love. He wanted marriage to preserve traditional ideals. They wanted marriage to boost intimacy and, hence, equality. Each recognized the importance of private institutions to the public discourse.

The sex radicals' work for reproductive rights led to important gains in civil liberties in the twentieth century. One cannot look at the history of the ACLU without looking at its predecessor, the FSL, first formed to welcome Craddock out of the Women's Workhouse. To oppose the Comstock laws was to oppose all restriction on speech.

The federal Comstock law itself is remarkable for its linkage of obscenity and contraception. An abortifacient powder was as filthy and debased as a stereoscopic view of dirty pictures on a postcard. Comstock's genius was in his understanding of the power of communication—the mail. By controlling access to information, he could limit women's options. A woman who could not easily find out where to get an abortion would likely still get one, but his hope was that some would be forced to reconsider. And surely hundreds of thousands did.

The sex radicals' legacy lies in their use of speech to fight the repression of speech. Craddock, for example, used religious speech, which was supposed to be constitutionally protected, to educate about sex. In an era when sound information was increasingly difficult to find, they kept women informed about vital matters. Many of their methods are used by today's young radicals. As the free love historian Hal Sears pointed out, the sex radicals' playbook included using the power of their pens to fight an oppressive society, courting publicity to control the narrative, and maximizing the power of the legal system to alter public opinion. Even without the vote, they made their voices heard. The Comstock era revealed the power of radical organizing, direct action, lobbying, and publishing to change public opinion.

The sex radicals had allies along the way—progressive men such as Stephen Pearl Andrews, the doctors Foote, Ezra Heywood, D. M. Bennett, Moses Harman, William Stead, Ben Reitman, Sasha

Berkman, Bill Sanger, and Leonard Abbott—who elevated them and recognized that women were better advocates for birth control than men, even though some of these men were ambivalent in their support. The women also benefited from the power, and reach, of the radical press. Today's radical publications, even online, are stymied by lack of funding and have circulations much smaller than those of *Lucifer*, *The Truth Seeker*, and *Mother Earth*, to name just a few. Gone are the days when provocative, left-leaning journals had hundreds of thousands of engaged subscribers all around the country, engaging in civil debate in their "Letters" sections.

As one of the most powerful and single-minded men of his time, Comstock dealt a near-century-long blow to women's health. In his unflagging commitment to restrictive ideas of womanhood, family, religion, and national identity, he was a symbol of the nation's Puritan founding. Yet his attitudes cannot be understood separately from the era in which he lived. He was antebellum and postbellum America— from his haloed view of his Congregationalist mother, to his rural childhood, to his brother's death in the Civil War, to his arrival as a single man in vice-ridden Gilded Age New York.

He saw himself as a guardian of women. The death of his mother, Polly, only strengthened his belief in the power of God, and in the religious imperative to be fruitful and multiply. The center of life was the family, and the locus of the family was the mother. He believed that he revered women, but he felt that *he* should dictate how they should conduct their lives, and that *he* was the protector of women's natural innocence. When cultural norms began to shift, when single men and women were interacting in large cities, when prostitution led to disease and death, when industrialization changed the nature of work, he dug in the heels of his size-thirteen boots to face all perceived threats. Comstockism's mutability gave it staying power. It cycled from obscene speech to contraception to gambling to immigration to political speech to immigration (again) to patriotism. As the face of America's enemies changed, Comstockism moved its targets.

Under John Sumner's more low-key leadership, the NYSSV continued to draw financial support after Comstock's death and well into the twentieth century. It was renamed the Society to Maintain Public Decency in 1947; when Sumner retired in 1950, it effectively disbanded. The obscenity portion of the Comstock law was tested in several major cases, beginning in 1933. The U.S. District Court case *United States v. One Book Called Ulysses* (1933) resulted when the *Little Review* journal editor Margaret Anderson published a portion of James Joyce's *Ulysses*. The Post Office burned all of the *Little Review* copies sent by mail, and Sumner had her indicted for publishing indecent matter. A Manhattan federal judge ruled in 1933 that the book, though graphic in parts, was "not pornographic" or obscene "in its entirety." In *Roth v. United States* (1957), involving a New York bookseller named Samuel Roth, the court found that obscene material had to be "utterly without redeeming social importance." In its companion case, *Alberts v. California* (1957), Justice William J. Brennan, Jr., wrote that lower courts should no longer rely on the English case *The Queen v. Hicklin* but instead test whether an average person applying "contemporary community standards" would find the dominant theme of the material as a whole appealing to "prurient interest."

The first major legal blow to the birth control provision of the Comstock law was struck in 1936. In 1932, Margaret Sanger ordered a package of contraceptives from a Japanese physician whom she had met at an international birth control conference. The package was intercepted by U.S. Customs. Sanger requested that the package be mailed again, this time having it addressed to Dr. Hannah Stone, a doctor who supported birth control. The case led to *United States v. One Package Containing 120, more or less, Rubber Pessaries to Prevent Conception* (1936), a Second Circuit Court decision finding that doctors could send contraception to their patients through the mail.

But it was not until 1965 that birth control activists delivered another significant kick to the Comstock statutes. When, in the 1960s, Planned Parenthood sought a test case to legalize contraception, its leaders wanted it to take place in Connecticut because of that state's restrictive laws. In *Griswold v. Connecticut* (1965), the Supreme Court invalidated the Connecticut law on the grounds that it violated the right to marital privacy, thus guaranteeing married women the right to receive contraception from their doctors. It took until 1972 for single women to be able to do so, making contraception legal throughout the country for all women—ninety-nine years after President Grant signed the Comstock Act into law.

In New York, the city that shaped Comstock and introduced him to the influential scions at the YMCA, it was not until 1971 that contraception was removed from the law's prohibitions. A customs officer forced a New York woman to throw her diaphragm into the harbor before she reentered the country. She went to her state representative, James H. Scheuer, to protest, and in 1965, a bill to amend the law got out of committee. Passed by Mayor Robert Wagner, the new law nonetheless maintained certain restrictions on the display of contraceptives in drugstores and the sale of contraceptives to minors.

The Comstock era revealed the danger that ensues when a virulent, well-funded, highly connected, determined man gains access to political power and will stop at nothing to keep it. Today, one hundred fifty years after Comstock prayed to God for his bill to pass, we are still fighting over women's bodies. While most Americans support abortion, states have passed ever-more-restrictive abortion laws. State abortion restrictions already impact the availability of medication abortion (abortion by pill); minors' access to abortion; use of ultrasound; and abortion options in the second and third trimesters of pregnancy. It may be years, not centuries, before new Madame Restells find a market in illegal abortion. Reproductive rights, freedom of speech, and freedom of the press are again under assault. Three antiabortion Supreme Court justices have been appointed in recent years. States such as Alabama have passed unconstitutional, near-total abortion bans, without exceptions for rape or incest. That state's chemical endangerment law currently extends to fetuses; the life of a pregnant woman is viewed as less important than that of the viable or nonviable fetus she might be carrying.

Wombs are still a battleground because of what they represent. Who owns women's bodies? Who should decide their fate? What are the economic costs of unwanted motherhood? How does childbearing impact women's ability to make and sustain a living? And what does it mean for men? Reproductive freedom has never been about reproduction alone. It is about labor, power, economics, and opportunity.

The sex radicals understood this. Yet despite their centrality to the sexual revolution and modern-day feminism, they are largely forgotten. They were born too late to be at Seneca Falls and (most of them) too early to chain themselves to Wilson's White House gate. Greater historical awareness of the sex radicals can make them provocative role models for women emboldened by today's #MeToo movement and outraged by the twenty-first-century rise of nativist, sexist demagogues who want to turn back the clock to the Comstock era. It is important to remember, and retell, the stories of women's rights advocates who were not part of any "wave" at all, who posited the brave and explosive idea that women should be able to have sex without the ever-present terror of pregnancy and dangerous childbirth.

The diversity of the sex radicals' views proves that productive feminism encompasses a wide range of opinions about marriage, love, relationships, work, money, sexuality, motherhood, and family. The idea of women's independence was not born in the suffrage movement or in the pages of *Ms.* magazine. To overthrow the patriarchy, then as now, women must write, write more, and shout. They must be open to working for a common goal, alongside those with divergent ideas.

And while they speak out about suffering and pain, they must also speak out about pleasure and hope. A victim-oriented feminism is limited, inciting phobia and panic, turning sex into something that is only ugly, only dark, only violent. A pluralistic feminism recognizes the horror of unwanted sex, but also recognizes that sex can and should be consensual and pleasurable to women. Victim-oriented feminism robs women of their strength and robs the movement of the diversity that made way for the sex radicals. Their vision of sex was optimistic at a time when ordinary women were subjected to forced marriage, marital rape, and repeated unwanted childbirths. The Comstock women believed that better sex made for a more equal society.

Pleasure is key to contemporary feminism, yet many run from discussing it. With no talk of it, we cannot examine the very real problems of twenty-first-century sex. Why do women orgasm less frequently than men? Why do so many heterosexual couples still define only intercourse as sex when sex can, and should, encompass much more? And why is there so much sexual panic? Why is it still so difficult for men and women (not only young people) to communicate openly about what sex is, and could be? Only when we can answer these questions with candor can we have a feminist movement for this century and beyond.

The sex radicals would not have all liked each other, or even have wanted to be in the same room, but the diversity of their views and their free exchange of ideas are testament to a rich time in progressive history. A sex radical might have disagreed with another woman on such subjects as amative versus procreative sex, or women's "innate" morality or libido, but that did not make the dissenter an "Anthony Comstock," or an enemy of women's rights. The sex radicals knew the difference.

As feminists living in the current political era find gains of the past century dialed back, we must face the difficult truth that our efforts may not pay off in our own lifetimes. We must fight not for ourselves, but for our daughters, granddaughters, and great-granddaughters, and all the women who have not yet been born. As Ida C. Craddock wrote more than a hundred years ago, "I would lay down my life for the cause of sex reform; but I don't want to be swept away, a useless sacrifice. I want to make a breach in the enemy's lines before I pass in my checks."

Emma Goldman, 1917

EPILOGUE

Victoria Woodhull (1838–1927)

When Woodhull and her sister Tennessee Claflin moved to England in 1877 (where they were later joined by other family members, including Woodhull's son, Byron), they had been greatly diminished by the obscenity and libel cases, which caused financial problems, illness, and a decline in their popularity. In 1883, Woodhull married John Biddulph Martin, a banker. She published a magazine called *The Humanitarian* and rewrote her past, denying that she had been a free lover. She wrote prolifically about the benefits of monogamy and had the British Museum remove books that contained what she considered unfavorable depictions of herself. After Martin died in 1897, Victoria moved to the country and began to work for educational reform, building a school with Claflin and with her daughter, Zula. When the Nineteenth Amendment passed in 1920, she was written out of suffrage history, despite the fact that she had been the primary point of attraction at four suffrage conventions. She died in Worcestershire, England.

Tennessee Claflin (1844–1923)

After Cornelius Vanderbilt died in 1877, papers reported that he had left behind $100 million. Ninety-seven percent went to one son. The children who had received only a small percentage—and Claflin—contested the will. Rumors circulated that the family had paid the sisters to go to London while the will was contested. Claflin lost interest in the will after she met a businessman named Sir Francis Cook, a married man in his sixties with three grown children. Cook became the sisters' protector. Following the death of Mrs. Cook in 1884, Claflin and Cook married and he later became a baronet. After he died in 1901, she founded a bank, Lady Cook & Co.

Angela Heywood (1840–1935)

Throughout Ezra Heywood's incarceration in Charlestown State Prison in 1891 and 1892, Angela wrote for *The Word*. Ezra was finally released in May 1892. About a year later, he died of an illness most likely contracted in prison. Angela was unable to keep printing *The Word*, and its last issue appeared the following April, after a twenty-one-year run. By 1900, she was living in Cambridge, Massachusetts, with the four children. On a census she identified her occupation as "Capitalist," perhaps a joke on the census taker. On election night of 1908, as Taft defeated Bryan, Mountain Home caught fire and burned to the ground—with all of the family's papers inside. Angela moved to Seattle with her mother and then journeyed to Kellogg, Idaho. She took a job working in the Bunker Hill and Sullivan mine, the largest lead-silver mine in the world. At age seventy, she worked nine hours a day, including Sundays. "I am very well," she wrote her friend Elizabeth Denton, "but find self always full of work (which I think is good for me)." She died in Brookline, Massachusetts, at the age of ninety-four. She had outlived her beloved husband by more than four decades.

Dr. Sara B. Chase (1837–1914)

In June 1893, Chase was convicted of manslaughter in New York, in relation to a young woman patient named Margaret Manzoni. Following a botched abortion, Manzoni was transferred to Chase and then died. Chase was sentenced to nine years and eight months in the State Prison for Women in Auburn, New York. It was the first prison for female felons in New York. She was released in the fall of 1899, with time off for good behavior, and decided to stay in Auburn, giving her single-sex lectures. Though she drew large audiences, she could not support herself and did needlework for families.

After relocating to Alford, Pennsylvania, about a hundred miles south of Auburn, she mailed a syringe to a decoy writer who worked for a deputy marshal. Comstock helped the deputy marshal track her to Elmora, New Jersey. In June 1900 she was arrested. In Newark, she was held on $2,500 bail and charged with being a fugitive from justice and sending improper medical advertisements. There are three examination dates listed in Comstock's logbook, but the case never went to trial, likely because the grand jury declined to prosecute a sixty-three-year-old woman who had recently been released from prison.

Chase moved to Kansas City, Missouri, along with her daughter, Grace, and Grace's husband. She abandoned contraceptive sales and lectures, instead making art pieces out of human hair. She died in Kansas City, at seventy-three. On her death certificate, her occupation was listed as "physician."

From prison, Chase had corresponded with Moses Harman. In one letter, she wrote, "The need of reform is to be seen on every hand yet *all* do not see it, and those who do are unable to resist the innate hatred of injustice and wrong that impels them to try to remedy the evils that lie in their way. They do not stop to count the cost. They only say 'this work must be done and I must help to do it,' and there is no *choice* in the matter."

Emma Goldman (1869–1940)

In the June 1917 issue of *Mother Earth*, Goldman wrote articles urging men to resist the draft, and was charged with sedition. She was sentenced to two years in the Missouri State Penitentiary for Women by Julius Marshuetz Mayer, one of the judges in Craddock's New York case. Sasha Berkman was also imprisoned. Released in the fall of 1919, she and Berkman were rearrested and brought to court by J. Edgar Hoover, head of the General Intelligence Division of the Bureau of Investigation. He persuaded the Justice Department to begin deportation hearings against them. Goldman filed appeals to no avail. On December 21, she and 247 other immigrant radicals were put on a leaky ship called the *Buford* and taken to Russia. While on Ellis Island awaiting deportation, she wrote a letter to Ben Reitman: "I really owe much to you. During our years together, I have done my best and most valuable work . . . Your devotion, your untiring work, your tremendous energy. If I owe also much heartache, much soul tearing misery to you, what of it? Nothing in life can be achieved without pain."

In Russia, when Lenin began to round up anarchists, she fled for Riga, Latvia. She moved to Berlin, and later London, and began work on her memoir, *Living My Life*, in 1928. Peggy Guggenheim helped her settle in a cottage in Saint-Tropez, where she completed the book. She returned to New York in February 1934 to lecture on drama and her memoir. When her visa expired, she went to Toronto and filed another request to enter the United States. It was denied.

When a second world war grew increasingly inevitable, Goldman was convinced that Britain and France had not done enough to oppose fascism. On February 17, 1940, working in Toronto to support Spanish anarchists, she suffered a stroke and was unable to speak. As she was pulled out on a stretcher, she managed the small gesture of pulling her skirt down below her knee. Another stroke soon followed. She died that May and was buried in Waldheim Cemetery in Chicago.

Margaret Sanger (1879–1966)

Among Sanger's achievements were her monthly journal, *The Birth Control Review*, which she founded in 1917, and her organization of the first American birth control conference in New York, in 1921. In 1923, she opened the Birth Control Clinical Research Bureau, which became the American model for clinics staffed by doctors during the 1920s and 1930s.

In 1922, she married a wealthy oilman, James Noah H. Slee, but insisted on sexual autonomy. Their marriage ended with his death in 1943. Continuing her activism in the 1940s, she helped form the Planned Parenthood Federation of America and, during World War II, the International Planned Parenthood Federation. Her work with the reproductive expert Dr. Gregory Pincus led to the FDA's approval of

Enovid, the first oral contraceptive, in 1960. She died in Tucson, Arizona, at eighty-six years old.

In recent years, her legacy has been reevaluated with regard to her views on disability, race, and heredity. There is no doubt that she had eugenicist supporters, and she recorded her patients' nationality, heredity, religion, occupation, and union affiliation. But in the 1920s, eugenics was considered scientifically sound, even by some African American leaders. Moreover, Sanger opposed the primary goal of American eugenics: to increase childbearing among the middle and upper classes.

In the 1920s and 1930s, she endorsed the sterilization of institutionalized people, to prevent those with developmental disabilities from passing on their genes, an appalling position that nonetheless had mainstream support. She praised Germany's sterilization program in 1934, which she called "sterilization of the unfit," but added that "if 'unfit' refers to races or religions, then that is another matter, which I frankly deplore." Her work on African American women's reproductive health was supported by W. E. B. Du Bois and Dr. Martin Luther King, Jr., and there is no evidence that she wanted to coerce Black women into using birth control or to reduce the African American population. Still, in 2020, Planned Parenthood of Greater New York removed her name from its building "to reckon with [the organization's] legacy and acknowledge Planned Parenthood's contributions to historical reproductive harm within communities of color."

Sanger's rationale for birth control changed over time as she sought to achieve a broad base of support; like the other sex radicals, she was complex and held some views that are repellent in modern times. But her goal was to restore the right of the individual woman to determine her reproductive future, and to promote happier and healthier families. She believed every woman should be liberated from unwanted pregnancy and should have access to birth control. A woman's ultimate duty, she believed until the end, was not to the state. It was to herself.

Notes

A note on sourcing: Sources are given for direct quotations (identified by the first few words), for numbers and statistics, and for certain facts. In the text, direct quotations with no note are cited to the preceding source in that paragraph. Most sources used only once do not appear in the bibliography; nor do newspaper articles. Abbreviations for archival sources and periodicals can be found in the bibliography.

ABBREVIATIONS OF NAMES

Ida C. Craddock (ICC)
William T. Stead (WTS)
E. B. "Ned" Foote, Jr. (EBF)
Anthony Comstock (AC)
Margaret Sanger (MS)
Victoria C. Woodhull (VCW)
Tennessee C. Claflin (TCC)
Ezra H. Heywood (EHH)
Angela T. Heywood (ATH)
Stephen Pearl Andrews (SPA)
Elizabeth Denton (ED)
Dr. Sara B. Chase (SBC)
Catherine "Katie" Wood (KW)
Hugh Pentecost (HP)
Lizzie Decker (LD)
Emma Goldman (EG)

1. THE DANSE DU VENTRE

3   *twelve of them*: Donna Carlton, *Looking for Little Egypt* (Bloomington, IN: IDD Books, 1994), 40.

4   *"Disgusting!"*: ICC, *The Danse du Ventre (Dance of the Abdomen)*, 2nd ed., rev. (Philadelphia: 1897), 16, B 2, F 2, RGP.

4   *"the cubicle"*: ICC to WTS, July 11, 1895, S 1, B 1, F 1, ICP.

4   *Ridgway Library*: ICC, "Sex Worship, Continued," 124–25, S 2, B 2, F 5, ICP. Thanks to Leigh Eric Schmidt for this reference.

4   *"sex worship"*: ICC to EBF, Nov. 22, 1893, S 1, B 1, F 1, ICP.

4   *written a book*: ICC, *Primary Phonography, an Introduction* (Philadelphia: 1882).

4   *"Girls, whenever I take up"*: ICC, "Story of My Life in Regard to Sex and Occult Teaching," 1, B 2, F 2, RGP.

5   *"If you knew what"*: "Opinions on the Danse du Ventre," *NYW*, Aug. 13, 1893.

5   *28 million*: Norman Bolotin with Christine Laing, *Chicago's Grand Midway: A Walk Around the World at the Columbian Exposition* (Urbana: University of Illinois Press, 2017), 4.

5   *Ferris wheel*: Carlton, *Looking for Little Egypt*, 14.

6   *"a masterpiece of rhythm"*: Sol Bloom, *The Autobiography of Sol Bloom* (New York: G. P. Putnam's Sons, 1948), 135.

7   *inspired the hokey pokey*: Carlton, *Looking for Little Egypt*, 59.

7   hochequeue: Ibid., 57.

7   *a few hundred thousand*: Bloom, *The Autobiography of Sol Bloom*, 135.

7   *"they delightedly concluded"*: Ibid.

7   *"abomination"*: "Seen by the Wayside," *Princeton (Minnesota) Union*, July 27, 1893.

7   *"veiled wickedness"*: "Citizen Train in the Van," *NYW*, Aug. 17, 1893.

7   *"a depraved and immoral"*: "Dancing Masters Enter a Protest," *CT*, July 23, 1893.

7   *"The dusky beauties"*: George E. Elliot, "The Cairo Street at the Columbian Exposition," *Frank Leslie's Illustrated Weekly*, Aug. 24, 1893.

7   *Forty-nine years old*: John Adams Comstock, *A History and Genealogy of the Comstock Family in America* (Los Angeles: Privately printed for the author by Commonwealth Press, 1949), 99.

8   *"a New Englander who eats pie"*: "Anthony Comstock to Retire After 40 Years Service," unknown paper, Feb. 7, 1913, B 10, F 4, RGP.

8   *"Don't you know who I am?"*: Heywood Broun and Margaret Leech, *Anthony Comstock: Roundsman of the Lord* (hereafter *Roundsman*) (New York: A. & C. Boni, 1927), 145.

8   *"Probably"*: Ibid., 252.

8   *Monona Lake Assembly*: "Comstock Shocked: Tells What He Saw in the Midway Plaisance," *New York Recorder*, Aug. 7, 1893.

8   *"The Foes of Society"*: "Methods Discussed at the Monona Lake Assembly," *Inter Ocean* (Chicago), July 28, 1893.

9   *"That's one of the cases"*: Charles Gallaudet Trumbull, *Anthony Comstock, Fighter* (New York: Fleming H. Revell Company, 1913), 187–88.

9   *August 1*: "Comstock at the World's Fair," *NYW*, Aug. 2, 1893.

9   *"It was thought by the agent"*: *Annual Report of the New York Society for the Suppression of Vice Presented at New York January 16, 1894* (hereafter *Annual* and year), 16.

9   *"hydra-headed monster"*: AC, *Frauds Exposed; Or, How the People Are Deceived and Robbed, and Youth Corrupted* (New York: J. Howard Brown, 1880), 389.

9   *"any drug or medicine"*: "An Act for the Suppression of Trade in and Circulation of obscene Literature and Articles of immoral Use," 42nd Cong., Sess. III, Ch. 258, Mar. 3, 1873, at 598.

9   *Connecticut's*: Mary Ware Dennett, *Birth Control Laws: Shall We Keep Them, Change Them, or Abolish Them* (New York: Grafton Press, 1926), 10.

10   *In the twenty years*: *Annual 1894*, 20–21.

10   *"Mr. Comstock's Society"*: "The Suppression of Vice," *NYT*, Jan. 12, 1877.

10   *far more men*: Elizabeth Bainum Hovey, "Stamping Out Smut: The Enforcement of Obscenity Laws, 1872–1915" (PhD diss., Columbia University, 1998), 432.

10   *he often conflated*: Ibid., 133. Hovey mentions that Comstock used the term *abortionist* to refer to contraceptive sellers, citing multiple entries in the NYSSV arrest logbooks.

11   *"the most shameless exhibition"*: "Comstock Shocked."

11   *"pestilential places"*: *Annual 1894*, 16.

11   *"I would sooner lay"*: "Cairo Dances to Go," *NYW*, Aug. 5, 1893.

11   *"the magnificence of that Columbian"*: Ibid.

12   *a year earlier*: Dr. Richard von Krafft-Ebing, *Psychopathia Sexualis, with Especial Reference to Contrary Sexual Instinct: A Medica-Legal Study*, 7th ed. rev., trans. Charles Gilbert Chaddock, MD (Philadelphia: The F. A. Davis Co., 1892).

12   *a volume on human*: Havelock Ellis, *Man and Woman: A Study of Human Secondary Sexual Characters* (London: W. Scott, 1894).

12   *anatomical details . . . strategies*: Alice B. Stockham, *Tokology: A Book for Every Woman* (Chicago: Sanitary Publishing Co., 1885), 9–21, 171–77. (The page numbers given here are from the 35th edition of this work.)

13   *"complex marriage"*: John Humphrey Noyes, *Male Continence* (Oneida, NY: Oneida Community, 1872), 16.

13   *"propagative" or "amative"*: Ibid., 11–16.

13   *"from the curses"*: Ibid., 13.

14   *euphemism for* sexual: Linda Gordon, *Woman's Body, Woman's Right: A Social History of Birth Control in America* (New York: Penguin Books, 1977), 116.

14   *aligned with free lovers*: Hal D. Sears, *The Sex Radicals: Free Love in High Victorian America* (Lawrence: Regents Press of Kansas, 1977), 26–27, 208.

14   *"graceful pantomime"*: "Opinions on the Danse du Ventre."

14   *"self-control and purity of life"*: Ibid.

16   *coined the phrase*: MS, *Margaret Sanger: An Autobiography* (New York: W. W. Norton, 1938), 108.

17   Boston Investigator . . . Free Enquirer: Tom Flynn, ed., *The New Encyclopedia of Unbelief* (Amherst, NY: Prometheus Books, 2007), 150, 341.

19   *dubbed* magnetation: Albert Chavannes, *Magnetation, and Its Relation to Health and Character* (Knoxville, TN: 1899).

19   *"libertarian radicals"*: David M. Rabban, "The Free Speech League, the ACLU, and Changing Conceptions of Free Speech in American History," *Stanford Law Review* 45, no. 1 (Nov. 1992): 53.

2. VICELAND

21   *fourth of ten*: John Adams Comstock, *A History and Genealogy*, 99. John Adams Comstock lists eight children for Polly, but Trumbull cites ten (*Anthony Comstock, Fighter*, 23).

21   *third to survive*: John Adams Comstock, *A History and Genealogy*, 99.

21   *"She looked upon"*: Trumbull, *Anthony Comstock, Fighter*, 27.

22   *excerpts of his Civil War*: Anthony Comstock's 1927 biographers, Heywood Broun and Margaret Leech, had access to his early diaries, but the diaries themselves appear to be lost.

22   *"the loveliest mother"*: AC, "The Work of the New York Society for the Prevention of Vice, and its Bearings on the Morals of the Young: An address before the Conference on Child Welfare at Clark University, Worcester, July, 1909," in G. Stanley Hall, *The Pedagogical Seminary: A Quarterly* 16, no. 3 (Sept. 1909): 405.

22   *"flooding"*: Polly Ann Comstock, Mar. 17, 1854, *Deaths, 1852–1900*, Office of the Town Clerk and Registrar of Vital Statistics, New Canaan Town Hall, New Canaan, CT.

22   *the day she gave birth*: John Adams Comstock, *A History and Genealogy*, 99.

22   *At sixteen*: "Sketch of Life of Anthony Comstock taken down stenographically, from his own words, on Friday evening, December 17, 1886, at the Massasoit House, Springfield, Massachusetts," 1, B 10, F 7, RGP.

23   *nearly three months*: Comstock, Samuel, Co. CH, 17th Connecticut Infantry, RG 94, E 519-CT, NARA.

23   *Seventeenth*: Ibid.

23   *"obscene book, pamphlet"*: 38th Cong., Sess. II, Chap. 89, Sec. 16, Mar. 3, 1865, at 507, 661 (1865).

23   *November 1864*: CMSR for Comstock, Anthony, Co. H, 17th Connecticut Infantry, RG 94, E 519-CT, NARA.

24   *medical problems*: Comstock, Anthony, Carded Medical, 17th Connecticut Infantry, RG 94, E 534, B 88, NARA.

24   *"Seems to be a feeling"*: AC war diary quoted in Broun and Leech, *Roundsman*, 54.

24   *"O I deplore"*: Ibid., 56.

24 *1867*: AC, "The Work of Suppressing Vice: Chapter II," *Golden Rule* 15, no. 17 (Dec. 19, 1889): 188.

25 *"Go to New York"*: "Sketch of Life," 1.

25 *$3.45*: Ibid.

25 *"locomotive"*: George Francis Train quoted in Ric Burns and James Sanders, *New York: An Illustrated History* (New York: Alfred A. Knopf, 1999), 137.

25 *nearly three hundred*: "History," Trinity Church Wall Street website, https://www.trinitywallstreet.org/about/history.

25 *"It is said that New York"*: James D. McCabe, *New York by Sunlight and Gaslight* (Philadelphia: Hubbard Brothers, 1881), 59.

26 *"Half the passers"*: Ibid., 277.

26 *"the Associated Female Press"*: Donna Dennis, *Licentious Gotham* (Cambridge, MA: Harvard University Press, 2009), 211.

26 *"stanch, well-constructed"*: AC, *Traps for the Young* (New York: Funk & Wagnalls, 1883), 17.

26 The New York Herald *and the* New-York Tribune: James C. Mohr, *Abortion in America* (New York: Oxford University Press, 1978), 47.

27 *Pearl Street*: Trumbull, *Anthony Comstock, Fighter*, 45.

27 *46 percent*: "A Memorandum Respecting New-York as a Field for Moral and Christian Effort Among Young Men; Its Present Neglected Condition; and the Fitness of the New-York Young Men's Christian Association as a Principal Agency for Its Due Cultivation" (New York: The Association, 1866), 3, Records of the YMCA of the City of New York (hereafter YMCA CNY), B 1279, F 8, KFYA.

27 *"Inexperienced young men"*: *A Selection from the Late Correspondence of the New-York Young Men's Christian Association, tending to Illustrate its Mode of Working, and Show its Efficiency; and Supplemental to "A Memorandum" Heretofore Published* (New York: The Association, 1866), 8, YMCA CNY, B 1279, F 8, KFYA.

27 *"pretty waiter girl"*: Luc Sante, *Low Life: Lures and Snares of Old New York* (New York: Farrar, Straus and Giroux, 2003), 184, 110–11.

28 *"It is a safe conclusion"*: William F. Howe, *In Danger; or, Life in New York* (Chicago: J. S. Ogilvie & Company, 1888), 42.

28 *"After dark"*: Walt Whitman, "On Vice," *Daily Times (Brooklyn)*, June 20, 1857.

28 *twenty thousand*: Timothy J. Gilfoyle, *City of Eros: New York City, Prostitution, and the Commercialization of Sex, 1790–1920* (New York: W. W. Norton, 1992), 58.

28 *"the Black Crook" and "the Gem"*: Sante, *Low Life*, 183.

28 *"the Queen of Cherry Street"*: Gilfoyle, *City of Eros*, 218.

28 *under twenty-three*: Ibid., 62.

28 *5 and 10 percent*: Ibid., 59.

28 *thirty dollars a night*: William W. Sanger, *History of Prostitution: Its Extent, Causes, and Effects throughout the World* (New York: Harper & Brothers, 1858), 523.

29 *at least 40 percent*: Ibid., 487.

29 *"gonorrhea bags"*: Charles Goodyear, *Gum-Elastic and Its Varieties, with a Detailed Account of Its Applications and Uses and the Discovery of Vulcanization* (New Haven, CT: Published for the author, 1853), 172–73.

29 *1885 model*: Janet Farrell Brodie, *Contraception and Abortion in Nineteenth-Century America* (Ithaca, NY: Cornell University Press, 1994), 70.

29 *intervals twice as far apart*: Ibid., 73.

30 *"quickening"*: Ibid., 254.

30 *1845 New York state law*: N.Y. Laws Ch. 260, §1, 2, at 285–86 (1845).

30 *White, Protestant*: Mohr, *Abortion in America*, 46–47.

30 *Physicians complained*: Carroll Smith-Rosenberg, *Disorderly Conduct: Visions of Gender in Victorian America* (New York: Alfred A. Knopf, 1985), 221.

30 *"one of the first specialties"*: Mohr, *Abortion in America*, 47.

31 *Ammidon, Lane*: "Sketch of Life," 2 (AC's stenographer misspelled the name).

31 *"Multitudes of young men"*: Verranus Morse, *The Work of the Young Men's Christian Association: What It Is, and How to Do It*, 2nd ed. (New York: The Association, 1865), 3, YMCA CNY, B 1279, F 8, KFYA.

32 *"spiritual, mental"*: Terry Donoghue, *An Event on Mercer Street: A Brief History of the YMCA of the City of New York* (New York: Privately printed, 1952), 22.

32 *1866*: *Fourteenth Annual Report of the Young Men's Christian Association of the City of New York, 1865–66* (New York: The Association, 1866), 83.

32 *"A Memorandum Respecting"*: "A Memorandum," title page.

32 *"feeders for brothels"*: Ibid., 5.

33 *"to waste their time"*: Morse, *The Work of the Young Men's Christian Association*, 8.

33 *Committee on Obscene*: Cephas Brainerd to Mr. [J. F.] Bowne, Oct. 22, 1901, YMCA biographical files, B 38, F Anthony Comstock, KFYA.

33 *Obscene Literature Act*: New York, "Obscene Literature Act," NY Laws Ch. 430 at 856 (1868).

33 *"any obscene and indecent book"*: Ibid.

33 *Michigan and New Jersey*: Hovey, *Stamping Out Smut*, 422.

33 *"obscene and indecent articles"*: New York, "Obscene Literature Act."

33 "the great thoroughfare": AC, *Frauds Exposed*, 391.

34 *"the tendency of the matter"*: *The Queen v. Hicklin*, L.R. 3 Q.B. 360 (1868).

34 *"falling like autumn leaves"*: AC, "The Work of the New York Society," 411.

34 *"been led astray"*: Trumbull, *Anthony Comstock, Fighter*, 51.

35 *The same year*: T. J. Stiles, *The First Tycoon: The Epic Life of Cornelius Vanderbilt* (New York: Alfred A. Knopf, 2009), 484.

3. THE BEWITCHING BROKERS

37 *"Demosthenes"*: Theodore Tilton, *Biography of Victoria C. Woodhull* (New York: Golden Age, 1871), 12.

37 *At Forty-Second Street*: Barbara Goldsmith, *Other Powers: The Age of Suffrage, Spiritualism, and the Scandalous Victoria Woodhull* (New York: Alfred A. Knopf, 1998), 142.

38 *"Oh, you've come about the rooms"*: Ibid., 147.

38 *selected a book*: Tilton, *Biography of Victoria C. Woodhull*, 12.

38 *September 23, 1838*: Charles Henry Wight, *Genealogy of the Claflin Family* (New York: Press of William Green, 1903), 256.

38 *sixth of ten children*: Ibid., 125.

38 *a dollar a head*: Ann Braude, *Radical Spirits: Spiritualism and Women's Rights in Nineteenth-Century America*, 2nd ed. (Bloomington: Indiana University Press, 2001), 16.

38 *estimates*: Ibid., 25.

39 *"promised that the same"*: Sears, *The Sex Radicals*, 20.

39 *Utica . . . 1843, and Tennessee . . . 1845*: Wight, *Genealogy of the Claflin Family*, 125; Myra MacPherson, *The Scarlet Sisters: Sex, Suffrage, and Scandal in the Gilded Age* (New York: Twelve, 2014), 5.

40 *November 20, 1853*: Mary Gabriel, *Notorious Victoria: The Life of Victoria Woodhull, Uncensored* (Chapel Hill: Algonquin Books of Chapel Hill, 1998), 12.

40 *"a cloak made"*: "Proceedings of the Tenth Annual Convention of the American Association of Spiritualists," *WCW* 6, no. 20 (Oct. 18, 1873): 12.

40 *"impacted mass"*: Ibid.

40 *"Victoria, come home"*: Tilton, *Biography of Victoria C. Woodhull*, 18.

40 *a hundred thousand dollars*: Ibid., 20.

40 *Zula Maud*: Wight, *Genealogy of the Claflin Family*, 257. Wight misspells Zula as "Zulu."

41 *twenty-thousand-dollar payment*: Emanie Sachs, *"The Terrible Siren": Victoria Woodhull (1838–1927)* (New York: Harper Brothers, 1928), 39.

41 *"There may be prostitution"*: VCW, "Tried as by Fire; or, The True and the False Socially" (New York: Woodhull & Claflin, 1874), 31.

41 *"the powers of the air"*: Tilton, *Biography of Victoria C. Woodhull*, 24.

42 *"Madam Harvey"*: Sachs, *"The Terrible Siren,"* 45.

42 *July 14, 1866*: Ibid., 46.

42 *Greenbacking*: Ibid., 43.

42 *"Ample" . . . "the old goat"*: Goldsmith, *Other Powers*, 158.

43 *"A thousand"*: Ibid.

43 *"Do as I do"*: Vanderbilt in 1870 *NYTrib* interview, cited in Goldsmith, *Other Powers*, xi.

43 *"I beg your pardon"*: Sachs, *"The Terrible Siren,"* 63.

43 *"Now, waiter"*: Ibid.

43   *"a new evangel"*: Elizabeth Cady Stanton, "The Destructive Male," speech given at Women's Suffrage Convention, Jan. 1, 1868, Washington, DC.

44   *"a commanding intellect"*: "The Coming Woman," *Evening Star* (Washington, DC), Jan. 21, 1869.

45   *"Mrs. Woodhull takes"*: "The Coming Woman," *NYW*, Jan. 28, 1869, quoted in VCW and TCC, *The Human Body the Temple of God* (London: 1890), 271.

45   *seven hundred thousand dollars*: "The Queens of Finance," *NYH*, Jan. 22, 1870.

45   *15 East Thirty-Eighth Street*: Goldsmith, *Other Powers*, 209.

45   *"A Modern Palace Beautiful"*: Madeleine B. Stern, *The Pantarch: A Biography of Stephen Pearl Andrews* (Austin: University of Texas Press, 1968), 112–13.

45   *$2,500 a month*: "The Queens of Finance."

46   *"the Club"*: Stern, *The Pantarch*, 87–88.

46   *"secret society"*: "Free-Love in New-York," *NYTrib*, Oct. 16, 1855.

46   *"resembled the salon"*: *Theodore Tilton v. Henry Ward Beecher, III*, 292, in Stern, *The Pantarch*, 113.

46   *"Queens of Finance"*: "The Queens of Finance."

46   *Randall Foote*: Lois Beachy Underhill, *The Woman Who Ran for President* (Bridgehampton, NY: Bridge Works Publishing Company, 1995), 69.

46   *1967*: "Big Board Gets First Woman," *Miami News*, Dec. 29, 1967.

47   *"the censure or approval"*: "The Bewitching Brokers," *NYH*, Feb. 13, 1870.

47   *seven-thousand-dollar gift*: "Woman's Investment Invasion," *Wall Street Journal*, Aug. 11, 1927.

47   *a hundred policemen*: Goldsmith, *Other Powers*, 191.

47   *"bewitching brokers"*: "The Bewitching Brokers."

47   *"money in their pockets"*: "The 'Working Woman,'" *Revolution* 5, no. 10 (Mar. 10, 1870): 155.

47   *Andrews was likely*: Stern, *The Pantarch*, 117.

47   *"the most prominent"*: "The Coming Woman," *NYH*, Apr. 2, 1870.

48   *"a great undercurrent"*: Ibid.

48   *"enter an enlarged"*: "Woman's Position," *WCW* 1, no. 1 (May 14, 1870): 9.

48   *"without correction or amendment"*: Tilton, *Biography of Victoria C. Woodhull*, 25.

49   *"has no terror"*: "Legality and Morality," *WCW* 1, no. 2 (May 21, 1870): 9.

49   *"consigned many a youth"*: "Medical Literature," *WCW* 7, no. 18 (Apr. 4, 1874): 9.

49   *"Who proposes to"*: TCC, "My Word on Abortion, and Other Things," *WCW* 3, no. 19 (Sept. 23, 1871): 9.

49   *"a symptom of"*: Ibid.

50   *"for all child-bearing"*: "Stirpiculture," *WCW* 8, no. 17 (Sept. 26, 1874): 9.

50   *"The mother who produces"*: "Maternity," *WCW* 1, no. 20 (Oct. 1, 1870): 10.

50   *"Hereditarian thought"*: Gordon, *Woman's Body, Woman's Right*, 120–21.

51   *"the special and distinctive"*: "The Sixteenth Amendment," *WCW* 1, no. 14 (Aug. 13, 1870): 4.

51   *"little woman"*: *Evening Post*, Jan. 9, 1873, in VCW and TCC, *The Human Body the Temple of God*, 373.

52   *"Victoria League"*: Stern, *The Pantarch*, 117–18.

52   *"We are plotting"*: Paulina W. Davis, compiler, *A History of the National Woman's Rights Movement, for Twenty Years* (New York: Journeymen Printers' Cooperative Association, 1871), 118.

52   *"sick, ailing"*: "Mrs. Woodhull and her Critics," *NYT*, May 22, 1871.

53   *May 1871*: MacPherson, *The Scarlet Sisters*, 116.

53   *"I mean you"*: "The Beecher-Tilton Scandal Case," *WCW* 5, no. 7 (Nov. 2, 1872): 11.

54   *"a tomb"*: J.W.H. [Julia Ward Howe], "End of the Beecher-Tilton Controversy," *Woman's Journal* 5, no. 34 (Aug. 22, 1874): 270.

54   *"social problem"*: "The Beecher-Tilton Scandal Case," 12.

55   *"I should sink"*: Ibid.

55   *"The Woodhull"*: "Victoria and Theodore," *NYH*, Nov. 21, 1871.

55   *"A hundred ravenous"*: Ibid.

55   *"How can people"*: VCW, *"And the Truth shall make you Free": A Speech on the Principles of Social Freedom, delivered in Steinway Hall, Monday, Nov. 20, 1871* (New York: Woodhull, Claflin & Co., 1871), 19.

55   *"Their entire system"*: Ibid., 35.

55   *"Are you a free lover?"*: Ibid., 23.

55   *"Yes, I am a free lover"*: Ibid., 23.

57   *"Be Saved by Free Love"*: *Harper's Weekly* 16, no. 789 (Feb. 17, 1872): 140.

4. THE SENSATIONAL COMEDY OF FREE LOVE

58   *"Date: Nov. 2, 1872"*: *Report of persons Arrested, under the Auspices of the "Committee for the Suppression of Vice," of the Young Mens [sic] Christian Association of New York City during the year 1872* (hereafter *AR* and year), 13, #38, #39.

59   *one year younger*: Margaret Comstock, *1875 U.S. Census, Brooklyn Ward 07, Kings, New York* (database online), Ancestry.com.

59   *eighty-two pounds*: Broun and Leech, *Roundsman*, 15.

59   *"fussy"*: Ruth C. Sperry to Mr. [Ralph] Ginzburg, Mar. 30, 1960, B 10, F 7, RGP.

59   *six thousand dollars*: AC, "The Work of the New York Society," 410.

59   *January 25, 1871*: Margaret Hamilton, *U.S., Presbyterian Church Records, 1701–1907* (database online), Ancestry.com.

59   *"my darling is"*: AC diary quoted in Broun and Leech, *Roundsman*, 62.

59   *"beauty and grandeur"*: Ibid., 65.

59   *"dear M"*: Ibid.

59   *Clinton Avenue Congregational*: "Sketch of Life," 5.

60   *"Trade still holds dull"*: AC diary quoted in Broun and Leech, *Roundsman*, 70.

60   *"A little daughter"*: Ibid., 67.

60   *Almost five thousand*: Donoghue, *An Event on Mercer Street*, 49.

60   *Twenty-Third Street and Fourth Avenue*: Ibid., 46.

60   *"not adequate"*: AC, "The Work of the New York Society," 414.

60   *seven arrests*: AR 1872, 3–4, #1–7.

60   *"In order to secure"*: "Arrest of Dealers in Obscene Literature," *NYT*, Mar. 4, 1872.

61   *"Comstock is after you"*: Name and description of Persons dealing in Obscene Literature, not Arrested but from whom stock was seized during the year 1872, 2.

61   *"three publishers"*: "Improper Books, Prints, etc.," pamphlet enclosed with *Annual 1875*, 10, bound with *Annual 1875*.

61   *$450*: Trumbull, *Anthony Comstock, Fighter*, 69.

61   *"My private resources"*: AC to R. R. McBurney, Mar. 23, 1872, YMCA of Greater New York, B 180, *Ledgerbook Letters 1870–1904*, KFYA.

61   *"Mr. Comstock impressed me"*: Annual 1897, 28.

62   *thirty to forty thousand*: Ibid., 69.

62   *"without it being publicly"*: L. L. Doggett, *Life of Robert R. McBurney* (Cleveland: F. M. Barton, 1902), 108.

62   *a hundred dollars a month*: "Sketch of Life," 3.

62   *Obscene Literature Act*: NY Laws Ch. 747 at 1795–96 (1872).

62   *"upon which scurrilous"*: 42nd Cong., Sess. II, Ch. 335, Sec. 148, June 8, 1872, at 302.

63   *five hundred dollars*: Sachs, "The Terrible Siren," 164–65.

63   *Ezra Hervey Heywood*: "The Biter Bit," WCW 5, no. 7 (Nov. 2, 1872): 2.

63   *"which we have never"*: "A Word to the Press," WCW 5, no. 8 (Dec. 28, 1872): 14.

63   *"We recognize"*: "Official Report of the Equal Rights Convention, Held in New York City, on the Ninth, Tenth, and Eleventh of May, 1872," WCW 5, no. 2 (May 25, 1872): 3.

64   *"I propose the name"*: Ibid., 7.

64   *"distinguished representatives"*: "Official Report of the Equal Rights Convention," 8.

65   *a few days later*: Amanda Frisken, *Victoria Woodhull's Sexual Revolution: Political Theater and the Popular Press in Nineteenth-Century America* (Philadelphia: University of Pennsylvania Press, 2004), 174.

65   *"equal rights"*: Sachs, "The Terrible Siren," 161.

65   *"accept the colonelcy"*: "The Modern Joan D'Arc," *Sun* (New York), June 14, 1872.

65   *three to one*: Frisken, *Victoria Woodhull's Sexual Revolution*, 80.

66   *June 28, 1872*: "The Obscene Literature Traffic," *NYH*, June 29, 1872.

66   *cholera infantum*: "following from records relating to plot #95 Sumachs in Evergreen Cemetery, Bklyn," B 9, F 12, RGP.

66   *"The Lord's will"*: Trumbull, *Anthony Comstock, Fighter*, 151.

66   *William Horace Wood*: "The Obscene Literature Case," *BDE*, July 2, 1872.

66   *Gilsey House*: "The Philosophy of Modern Hypocrisy—Mr. L. C. Challis the Illustration," *WCW* 5, no. 7 (Nov. 2, 1872): 14.

66   *"If you go off"*: Sachs, *"The Terrible Siren,"* 167.

66   *"we hold social theories"*: "The Philosophy of Modern Hypocrisy," 14.

66   *"Will you lend me"*: "The Great Social Earthquake," *Daily Graphic* (New York), reprinted in *WCW* 8, no. 14 (Sept. 5, 1874): 13.

67   *"Mrs. Woodhull tossed"*: *Memphis Appeal* in "The Spirit of the Press," *WCW* 5, no. 8 (Dec. 28, 1872): 12.

67   *"The Beecher-Tilton Scandal Case"*: "The Beecher-Tilton Scandal Case," 9.

67   *"immense physical potency"*: Ibid., 13.

67   *"not infidelity to the old"*: Ibid., 11.

67   *"sickly religious literature"*: Ibid., 12.

67   *"The Philosophy"*: "The Philosophy of Modern Hypocrisy," 13.

68   *"And this scoundrel Challis"*: Ibid., 14.

69   *two hundred dollars*: "The Claflin Family," *NYT*, Nov. 3, 1872.

69   *150,000*: "To the Press," *WCW* 5, no. 8 (Dec. 28, 1872): 8.

69   *forty dollars . . . one dollar a day*: "The Progress of the Revolution," *WCW* 5, no. 8 (Dec. 28, 1872): 10.

69   *"M. Hamilton"*: "Circuit Court of the US of A for the SDNY, Second Circuit, third Monday of Oct. 1872–Nov. 4, 1872," B 20, F 12, RGP.

69   *November 2*: "Woodhull-Beecher-Claflin-Tilton," *NYH*, Nov. 3, 1872.

70   *"I know no Beecher"*: AC diary quoted in Broun and Leech, *Roundsman*, 123.

70   *"Tennie was flushed"*: *New-York Dispatch* quoted in Underhill, *The Woman Who Ran for President*, 229–30.

70   *"a most abominable"*: "Woodhull-Beecher-Claflin-Tilton."

70   *"An example is needed"*: Sachs, *"The Terrible Siren,"* 180.

70   *eight thousand dollars each*: "Woodhull-Beecher-Claflin-Tilton."

70   *"Fifth Avenue"*: Ibid.

71   *"private malice"*: "Woodhull-Claflin-Blood," *NYH*, Nov. 5, 1872.

71   *"a certain obscene"*: "Circuit Court of the US of A for the SDNY."

71   *"sensational comedy"*: *NYH* in *Tribune* (Lawrence, KS), Nov. 17, 1872.

71   *"Without having generally"*: "The Scandal and the Blunder Again," *BDE*, Nov. 19, 1872.

71   *"prosecutor and world wide"*: "A False Witness on the Blunder and Scandal," *BDE*, Nov. 23, 1872.

72   *"at the back"*: *Sunday Mercury*, Jan. 12, 1873, in VCW and TCC, *The Human Body the Temple of God*, 375.

72   *"mean and diabolical"*: *Word* 1, no. 3 (Dec. 1872): 2.

72   *"I desire that"*: "Woodhull's Defiance," *NYH*, Nov. 20, 1872.

72   *"illiterate puppy"*: "The New Office of Literary Censor," *WCW* 5, no. 11 (Feb. 15, 1873): 9.

72   *"the special"*: "The Progress of the Revolution," 10.

72   *"the Young Men's Christian"*: "The New Office of Literary Censor."

73   *"J. Beardsley"*: "Woodhull and Claflin Free," *Sun* (New York), June 28, 1873.

73   *"were about six"*: AC diary quoted in Broun and Leech, *Roundsman*, 117.

73   *"a cross between"*: "Woodhull and Blood," *BDE*, Jan. 10, 1873.

73   *about a thousand*: "Arrest of Mrs. Victoria C. Woodhull at the Cooper Institute Last Night," *NYT*, Jan. 10, 1873.

74   *"martyr"*: "The Female Agitators," *NYW*, Jan. 10, 1873.

74   *"Is this a free country?"*: "Woodhull and Blood."

74   *"a cell in the American"*: "Victoria C. Woodhull's Address," *WCW* 5, no. 9 (Jan. 25, 1873): 3.

74   *"an overwhelming"*: *Evening Post*, Jan. 9, 1873, quoted in VCW and TCC, *The Human Body the Temple of God*, 371.

74   *"not half so bad"*: "Victoria C. Woodhull's Address," 4.

74   *"be arrested"*: Ibid., 6.

5. MR. COMSTOCK GOES TO WASHINGTON

76   *"something for Jesus"*: AC diary quoted in Broun and Leech, *Roundsman*, 116.

76   *$1,950*: "Treasurer's Report, Committee of Y.M.C. Association of New York for the Suppression of Vice, in account with J. F. Wyckoff, Treasurer, New York, Jan. 28, 1874" (hereafter "Treasurer's Report 1874").

76   *"There are scores"*: AC to Clinton L. Merriam, Jan. 18, 1873, quoted in "Obscene Literature," *NYT*, Mar. 15, 1873.

77   *two providers*: AR 1873, 21, #69, 70.

77   *"infamous outrage"*: AC diary quoted in Broun and Leech, *Roundsman*, 168.

77   *"a conspiracy to put"*: "Blood-Woodhull-Claflin," *NYH*, Jan. 11, 1873.

78   *A body of case law*: Hovey, *Stamping Out Smut*, 240.

78   *Deuteronomy*: NYH did not mention the specific verse to which Howe was referring, but it is Deuteronomy 22:15.

78   *"a man of literary turn"*: "Blood-Woodhull-Claflin."

78   *"were very anxious"*: AC diary quoted in Broun and Leech, *Roundsman*, 119.

78   *"I am quite clear"*: "Woodhull and Claflin Held for Trial," *Sun* (New York), Feb. 4, 1873.

79   *"At first, a few"*: AC, "The Work of Suppressing Vice: Chapter V," *Golden Rule* 15, no. 21 (Jan. 16, 1890): 251.

79   *"might ask for"*: AC diary quoted in Broun and Leech, *Roundsman*, 131.

79   *"obscene, lewd or lascivious"*: "An Act for the Suppression."

80 *$3,425*: Broun and Leech, *Roundsman*, 136.

80 *"We should no more think"*: "Beecher, Tilton, Bowen," WCW 5, no. 9 (Feb. 8, 1873): 12.

80 *"bouquet to the Comstockians"*: "The Retort Courteous," WCW 5, no. 10 (Feb. 15, 1873): 14.

80 *"on a prescription"*: 42nd Cong., Sess. III, Part II, Feb. 18, 1873, at 1436.

80 *"Has he friends"*: AC diary quoted in Broun and Leech, *Roundsman*, 135.

81 *"I do not want"*: Ibid., 137.

81 *$60,000*: "Woodhull, Claflin, and Blood Again Released on Bail," NYT, Jan. 23, 1873.

81 *"frankly accord"*: "Moral Cowardice & Modern Hypocrisy," WCW 5, no. 8 (Dec. 28, 1872): 3.

81 *$250*: EHH, "Free Speech and the Right of Association—Their Latest Denial," TS 5, no. 19 (May 11, 1878): 299.

82 *Angela Heywood*: "The Beginning of the End," WCW 5, no. 18 (Apr. 5, 1873): 4.

82 *"Men assailing"*: AC diary quoted in Broun and Leech, *Roundsman*, 138.

82 *"the stress"*: Trumbull, *Anthony Comstock, Fighter*, 95.

82 *"beset by the Devil"*: AC diary quoted in Broun and Leech, *Roundsman*, 141.

82 *"but over and above"*: Trumbull, *Anthony Comstock, Fighter*, 96.

82 *"Your bill passed"*: AC, "The Work of Suppressing Vice: Chapter V."

83 *thirty votes against it*: Broun and Leech, *Roundsman*, 141.

83 *"The purity and beauty"*: Appendix to the *Congressional Globe*, Mar. 1, 1873, 168.

83 *"There were four"*: Ibid., 169.

83 *March 3, 1873*: "An Act for the Suppression."

83 Angel of Peace: AC diary quoted in Broun and Leech, *Roundsman*, 143.

83 *"Something will be forgiven"*: Ibid., 144.

84 *"have brought ruin"*: "Obscene Literature," NYT, Mar. 12, 1873.

84 *"Who shall say"*: AC diary quoted in Broun and Leech, *Roundsman*, 146.

84 *"the odium"*: William Adams Brown, *Morris Ketchum Jesup: A Character Sketch* (New York: Charles Scribner's Sons, 1910), 56.

84 *May 16, 1873*: NY Laws Ch. 527 at 828 (1873).

84 *two years . . . five thousand dollars*: NY Laws Ch. 777 at 1183–85 (1873).

84 *up to twenty*: NY Laws Ch. 181 at 509 (1872).

84 *In the twelve years*: Brodie, *Contraception and Abortion*, 257.

85 *"None of them"*: AC diary quoted in Broun and Leech, *Roundsman*, 152.

85 *"The judge seems"*: Ibid., 121–22.

86 *"Anthony J. Comstock"*: "Mrs. Woodhull in Court," NYTrib, Jan. 11, 1873.

86 *"an Inglorious Failure"*: "Woodhull, Claflin and Blood": BDE, June 27, 1873.

86 *"to limit freedom"*: "Leveling Harangues," Word 2, no. 2 (June 1873): 1.

86   *"outrage"*: AR 1872, 14.

86   *Peter Dwyer*: AR 1873, 23–24, #78.

87   *50 percent*: "Treasurer's Report 1874."

87   *"atrocious attack"*: D. M. Bennett, *An Open Letter to Samuel Colgate* (New York: D. M. Bennett, Liberal Publisher, 1879), 72.

87   *"Scar-faced Tony"*: "From the Gospel According to Saint Anthony," *TS* 5, no. 3 (Jan. 19, 1878): 46.

87   *"I say damn"*: "The Scare-Crows of Sexual Slavery," *WCW* 6, no. 17 (Sept. 27, 1873): 14.

87   *"of all the infernal"*: Ibid., 7.

88   *one hundred fifty times*: VCW, "Tried as by Fire," title page.

88   *Court of General Sessions*: Cait Murphy, *Scoundrels in Law: The Trials of Howe & Hummel, Lawyers to the Gangsters, Cops, Starlets, and Rakes Who Made the Gilded Age* (New York: Smithsonian Books, 2010), 270.

88   *"character and tendency"*: "The Woodhull Libel," *NYT*, Mar. 15, 1874.

88   *"It is the most outrageous"*: "The Woodhull Libel," *Evening Telegram*, Mar. 14, 1874.

88   *"against the practices"*: "Vindication," *WCW* 7, no. 17 (Mar. 28, 1874): 9.

89   *only ten days*: Sears, *The Sex Radicals*, 89.

89   *"promiscuity of sexual intercourse"*: "Victoria C. Woodhull," *Buffalo Sunday Morning News*, Dec. 5, 1875.

89   *"Why does the wit"*: "Love's Lesson," *Word* 4, no. 9 (Jan. 1876): 2.

6. THE BINDING FORCES OF CONJUGAL LIFE

91   *"Date: Nov. 2, 1877"*: AR 1877, 103, #51.

91   *"Reason, Knowledge"*: EHH, *Cupid's Yokes: or The Binding Forces of Conjugal Life* (Princeton, MA: Co-operative Publishing Co., [1877]), 19.

92   *"Press on"*: E. Edgewell, letter to the editor, *Word* 6, no. 6 (Oct. 1877): 3.

92   *frank medical books*: Brodie, *Contraception and Abortion*, 180–81. For more about Charles Knowlton, see Amy Sohn, "Charles Knowlton, the Father of American Birth Control," *JSTOR Daily*, Mar. 21, 2018, https://daily.jstor.org/charles-knowlton-the-father-of-american-birth-control/.

92   *"narcotic drugs"*: Brodie, *Contraception and Abortion*, 148.

92   *$3,500*: "A Physician Fined $3,500," *NYT*, July 12, 1876.

92   *$5,000*: Sears, *The Sex Radicals*, 195.

92   *following the passage*: Brodie, *Contraception and Abortion*, 281–86.

93   *"an enervated"*: AC, *Traps for the Young*, 163.

93   *"love is lust"*: Ibid., 159.

94   *"railing at"*: Ibid., 163.

95   *"I am going"*: "Affidavit of Anthony Comstock, Sworn to Nov. 20, 1878," *In Re Application for Pardon of Ezra H. Heywood Filed Nov 25, 1878*, RG 204, B 121, NACP.

95   *the word* penis: ATH, "Sex-Nomenclature—Plain English," *Word* 15, no. 6 (Apr. 1887): 2.

95   *"caricatures of everything"*: AC diary quoted in Broun and Leech, *Rounds-man*, 134.

95   *"chieftain's wife"*: AC, *Traps for the Young*, 164.

96   *"Is your name"*: Ibid., 164. Comstock omitted Heywood's name, writing, "There is no occasion for advertising him."

96   *"felt obliged"*: Ibid., 165.

97   *"experienced the anxiety"*: D. M. Bennett, *The Champions of the Church: Their Crimes and Persecutions* (New York: D. M. Bennett, Liberal and Scientific Publishing House, 1878), 1069–70.

97   *"rude stranger"*: EHH, "The Impolicy of Repression," *Index* 8, no. 414 (Nov. 29, 1877): 573.

97   *"like leaving Joan"*: [Lucian V. Pinney], "The Man and the Woman of Princeton," *Word* 19, no. 2 (June 1890): 1.

98   *May 1, 1840*: Daniel Aaron Bradshaw, *U.S., Sons of the American Revolution Membership Applications, 1889–1970* (database online), Ancestry.com.

98   *John Locke*: ATH, "The Woman's View of It—No. 2," *Word* 11, no. 10 (Feb. 1883): 2.

98   *fourth of six*: Angela F. Tilton, *1850 U.S. Census, Deerfield, Rockingham, New Hampshire* (database online), Ancestry.com.

98   *When Angela was ten*: Wendy McElroy, *Individualist Feminism of the Nineteenth Century: Collected Writings and Biographical Profiles* (Jefferson, NC: McFarland, 2001), 22.

98   *"never to defer"*: ATH, "The Woman's View of It—No. 2," 2.

98   *"whole soul revolted"*: SPA, "The Heywoods, Princeton, Worcester County, and Massachusetts," *TS* 10, no. 32 (Aug. 11, 1883): 498.

98   *"they might have palpable"*: ATH, "The Sex-Education of Children," *Word* 13, no. 1 (May 1884): 2.

99   *"the auction-block"*: ATH, "The Ethics of Sexuality," *Word* 9, no. 12 (Apr. 1881): 3.

99   *"an iconoclast"*: SPA, "The Heywoods," 498.

99   *1869*: Vesta V. Heywood, *1900 U.S. Census, Danvers, Essex, Massachusetts* (database online), Ancestry.com.

99   *1871*: EHH, "Debt—A Lesson in Equity," *Word* 16, no. 8 (Mar. 1888): 2.

100   *"abolition of speculative"*: "The Word," *Word* 2, no. 2 (Dec. 1873): 1.

100   *"the regulation of the affections"*: *Word* 4, no. 3 (July 1875): 1.

100   *"Girls and Women"*: "CANVASSING AGENTS," *Word* 1, no. 12 (Apr. 1873): 2.

100   *"call his idle curiosity"*: *Word* 4, no. 1 (May 1875): 2.

101   *"Is Mr. Hull's sister"*: ATH, "Correspondence," *Word* 2, no. 10 (Feb. 1874): 3.

101   *"in a very high degree"*: SPA, "The Heywoods," 498.

101   *"She has visions"*: [Pinney], "The Man and the Woman of Princeton," 1.

101   *forty-two-room inn*: [Psyche] Ceres Bradshaw to Agnes Inglis, Apr. 10, 1948, Joseph A. Labadie Collection, Special Collections Library, University of Michigan.

101   *"The large airy rooms"*: Jay Chaapel, *Mind and Matter*, July 14, 1880, quoted in *Word* 9, no. 5 (Sept. 1880): 3.

101   *"Psyche Ceres Soul and Body Heywood"*: "phone call 1 Aug 60 to Mrs. Herbert Houghton," B 13, F1, RGP.

101   *"king of brutes"*: "The Ethics of Sexuality," 3.

102   *"They're no more lovers"*: "Original Communications," *BI* 51, no. 22 (Sept. 14, 1881): 2.

102   *"sexual love"*: EHH, *Cupid's Yokes*, 14.

102   *eighty thousand*: EHH, letter to the editor, *LLB*, Aug. 15, 1890.

102   TO THE WOMAN: EHH, *Uncivil Liberty: An Essay to Show the Injustice and Impolicy of Ruling Woman Without her Consent* (Princeton, MA: Co-operative Publishing Company, 1872), dedication page.

102   *"intellect, conscience"*: Ibid., 7.

103   *"a devouring usurpation"*: ATH, "Woman's Love: Its Relations to Man and Society," *Word* 5, no. 3 (July 1876): 1.

103   *"When hungry"*: ATH, "Love and Labor," *Word* 5, no. 6 (Oct. 1876): 1.

103   *"individualist feminism"*: McElroy, *Individualist Feminism of the Nineteenth Century*, 1.

103   *"If she, as woman"*: "The Ethics of Sexuality."

104   *"coming teacher"*: *Word* 5, no. 1 (May 1876): 2.

104   *"outraged the ideas"*: SPA, "The Heywoods," 498.

104   *"a blind"*: "Preachers of the Word," *Word* 3, no. 10 (Feb. 1875): 2.

104   *two hundred thousand*: Samuel P. Putnam, *400 Years of Freethought* (New York: Truth Seeker Company, 1894), 537.

104   *"unreasonable, unconstitutional"*: EHH, *Cupid's Yokes*, 22.

104   *"unnatural, injurious"*: Ibid., 20.

104   *"passional heat"*: Ibid., 9.

105   *"More impressive"*: Ibid., 16–17.

105   *"foreign element"*: "Editorial Notes," *Word*, Oct. 1877, 2.

105   *"disgusting"*: EHH, *Cupid's Yokes*, 20.

105   *"as humanitarian reforms"*: E. B. Foote, "A Conflict of Reformers," *NYT*, Apr. 14, 1876.

106   *"subversive of the grand principles"*: National Liberal League Charter, Philadelphia, 1876, quoted in Anna Louise Bates, *Weeder in the Garden of the Lord: Anthony Comstock's Life and Career* (Lanham, MD: University Press of America, 1995), 129.

106   "a religious mono-maniac": EHH, *Cupid's Yokes*, 12.

106   *five hundred thousand*: EHH, "Debt—A Lesson in Equity."

107   *"Either Comstockism"*: ATH, "The Woman's View of It—No. 1," *Word* 11, no. 9 (Jan. 1883): 2.

107   *November 13, 1877*: EHH, "The Impolicy of Repression," 573.

107   *His pseudonyms would come*: Bennett, *Champions of the Church*, 1019, 1032, 1024, 1062, 1084.

107   *"'test' letters"*: AC, *Traps for the Young*, 232.

107   "the circular": Ibid., 232–33.

107   *"case of the truth"*: ATH to ED, Dec. 24, 1877, DFP-WHS.

107   *"Our short-sighted"*: "The Obscene Literature Law," *DFHM* 3, no. 1 (Jan. 1878): 3.

108   *"Another class"*: *Annual 1878*, 7.

108   *"no vital spirit"*: ATH, "The Woman's View of It—No. 5," *Word* 12, no. 1 (May 1883): 2.

109   *two paragraphs*: "The Heywood Trial," *Index*, Jan. 31, 1878, 52.

109   *Ezra's lawyers filed*: "The Result," *Word* 7, no. 4 (Aug. 1878): 2.

109   *"has long been"*: *Annual 1879*, 14.

110   *June 25, 1878: United States v. Ezra Heywood*, Circuit Court Federal Records, vol. 78, 1877–1878, 696, U.S. District Court of Massachusetts, National Archives at Boston.

110   *July 1878*: EHH to ED, July 27, 1878, Denton Family Papers, Joseph A. Labadie Collection.

110   *nearly every day*: EHH to ED, Dec. 14, 1878, Joseph A. Labadie Collection.

110   *"the articles in"*: A. E. Giles to Prof. Wm. C. Poland, June 11, 1893, Letters Pertaining to Ezra Hervey Heywood, Special Collections, John Hay Library, Brown University.

111   *"nothing on the earth"*: ATH, "The Woman's View of It—No. 5."

7. THE WICKEDEST WOMAN IN NEW YORK

113   *"Date: Feb. 11, 1878"*: *AR 1878*, 111, #4.

113   *"a regularly-established"*: Mohr, *Abortion in America*, 48.

113   *In 1875*: NY Criminal Code Ch. 777, Sec. 1145 at 1183 (1875).

114   "victims": *Annual 1876*, 9.

114   "the wickedest woman in New York": See, for example, George Ellington, *The Women of New York* (New York: The New York Book Company, 1869), 406.

114   *"Restellism"*: Mohr, *Abortion in America*, 94.

114   *Ann Maria Purdy*: Clifford Browder, *The Wickedest Woman in New York: Madame Restell, the Abortionist* (Hamden, CT: Archon Books, 1988), 31–32.

114   *"lust, licentiousness"*: *Trial of Madame Restell, Alias Ann Lohman, for Abortion and Causing the Death of Mrs. Purdy; Being a Full Account of All the Proceedings on the Trial, Together with the Suppressed Evidence and Editorial Remarks* (New York: 1841), 11.

114   *"this virtuous New York"*: Thomas L. Nichols, *The Lady in Black: A Story of New York Life, Morals, and Manners* (New York: 1844), 15.

115   *one out of every five or six*: Mohr, *Abortion in America*, 50.

115   *to break into the business*: Smith-Rosenberg, *Disorderly Conduct*, 230–36.

116   *"becomes unmindful"*: Dominick A. O'Donnell and Washington Atlee, "Report on Criminal Abortion," *Transactions of the American Medical Association* 22 (1871): 241.

116   *"therapeutic exemptions"*: Brodie, *Contraception and Abortion*, 286–87.

116   *May 6, 1811*: Ann Summers Lohman, *U.S. Find a Grave Index, 1600s–Current* (database online), Ancestry.com.

116   *bilious fever*: Browder, *The Wickedest Woman in New York*, 4.

117   *129 Liberty Street*: A. M. Mauriceau, *The Married Woman's Private Medical Companion* (New York: 1852), title page.

117   *written by Charles*: Browder, *The Wickedest Woman in New York*, 10.

117   *"Is it moral for"*: Sun (New York), Mar. 27, 1839.

117   *Vienna and Paris*: Boston Daily Times, Jan. 2, 1845.

117   *feminine hygiene*: NYH, Mar. 26, 1841, in Browder, *The Wickedest Woman in New York*, 14–15.

118   *said to regulate menses*: Sun (New York), Mar. 3, 1846.

118   *upper class and wealthy*: Browder, *The Wickedest Woman in New York*, 125.

118   *one dollar . . . five*: Ibid., 125–26.

119   *"The Evil of the Age"*: "The Evil of the Age," NYT, Aug. 23, 1871.

119   *Either Charles Lohman*: Mauriceau, *The Married Woman's Private Medical Companion*, copyright page. The book is copyrighted by Joseph Trow, Ann's brother.

119   *"of comely exterior"*: "The Evil of the Age."

119   *"relieve a lady"*: Ibid.

120   *"Is Madame Restell in?"*: The People on the Complaint of Anthony Comstock v. Ann Lohman Before Hon. J. K. Kilbreth, Justice, February 23, 1878 (hereafter People v. Lohman and date), 2, Court Records of Madame Restell, 1839–1878, Schlesinger Library.

120   *"After you do that"*: People v. Lohman, Feb. 27, 1878, 36.

120   *twenty dollars*: Ibid., 37.

120   *"You have brought"*: People v. Lohman, Feb. 23, 1878, 12.

121   *January 28*: Annual 1878, [3].

121   *"First. Never arrest a man"*: Ibid., 6.

121   *"I thought Mr. Comstock"*: People v. Lohman, Feb. 23, 1878, 28.

122   *"Her house is furnished"*: AR 1878, 112, #4.

122   *"If you would be kind"*: People v. Lohman, Feb. 27, 1878, 39.

123   *"Literally no one"*: "Madam Restell Still in Prison," Sun (New York), Feb. 13, 1878.

123   *"dismal-fronted pile"*: Charles Dickens, *American Notes for General Circulation* (London: Chapman & Hall, 1913), 71, 77.

123   *thirty years*: Charles V. Smith, *Madame Restell, with an Account of her Professional Career, and Secret Practices* (New York: 1847), 22.

123   *"A Vile Business"*: "A Vile Business Stopped," NYTrib, Feb. 12, 1878.

124   *"full and sharp"*: "Madam Restell Still in Prison."

124   *"They think if they can"*: Ibid.

124   *"She is reputed"*: AC to David B. Parker, Feb. 13, 1878, RG 28, E 1, B 23, F Ann Lohman, Feb. 1878, NARA.

125   *Court of Oyer and Terminer*: Murphy, *Scoundrels in Law*, 270.

125   *"The papers have"*: "Her Last Appeal," *NYH*, Apr. 2, 1878.

125   *"What shall I do?"*: "Madam Restell's Suicide," *Sun* (New York), Apr. 2, 1878.

127   *April Fool's Day joke*: "Her Last Appeal."

127   *"Does [the special agent] seduce"*: *Annual 1879*, 11.

128   *"rid of the disgrace"*: Ibid., 13.

128   *fifteenth time*: Bennett, *Champions of the Church*, 1070.

128   *a cartoon*: Puck 3, no. 58 (Apr. 17, 1878): 16.

128   *"a fit ending"*: "The Death of 'Mme. Restell,'" *NYT*, Apr. 2, 1878.

128   *"No matter what"*: "Doing Evil That Good May Come," *Sun* (New York), Apr. 2, 1878.

129   *"public duty"*: *Daily Graphic* (New York) quoted in "The City Press on the Restell Affair," *TS* 5, no. 15 (Apr. 13, 1878): 238.

129   *"employed in"*: *Herald Presbyter* quoted in Broun and Leech, *Roundsman*, 158.

130   *"Committed suicide"*: *AR 1878*, 112, #4.

130   *two thousand feet*: AC, *Traps for the Young*, 191–92.

130   *Fifteen thousand copies*: *Annual 1879*, 6.

130   *J. B. Wolff*: "The Infamous 'Comstock Law,'" *Selinsgrove (Pennsylvania) Times-Tribune*, Apr. 19, 1878.

130   *"Everything looked black"*: AC, *Frauds Exposed*, 424.

130   *"My grace is sufficient"*: Ibid., 425.

131   *"fanatics and bigots"*: Ibid., 426.

131   *"ruined"*: Ibid., 427.

131   *"was not established"*: *Annual 1879*, 7–8.

8. THE PHYSIOLOGIST

132   *"Date: May 9, 1878"*: *AR 1878*, 117, #18.

132   *"prevention of conception"*: Ibid., 118.

133   *"had been seduced"*: AC to David B. Parker, June 1, 1878, RG 28, E 1, B 27, F 92, NARA.

133   *"Mr. Farnsworth"*: Bennett, *Champions of the Church*, 1074–1075.

133   *"It could not by any"*: "The NY Physiological Society," *PFP* 1, nos. 3 and 4 (June and July 1878): 42.

134   *"I am Anthony Comstock"*: Ibid.

134   *"man Friday"*: Benjamin R. Tucker, *Proceedings of the Indignation Meeting Held in Faneuil Hall, Thursday Evening August 1, 1878, to Protest Against the Injury Done to the Freedom of the Press by the Conviction and Imprisonment of Ezra H. Heywood* (Boston: Benj. R. Tucker, 1878), 49.

134   *"valuable assistant"*: "More Comstockism," *TS* 5, no. 20 (May 18, 1878): 313.

134   *Cohen, Levy, and Andrews*: Bennett, *An Open Letter*, 47–48.

134   *"If I can't hold her"*: "The N.Y. Physiological Society," 42.

134   *"miscreant"*: "A Rival of Madame Restell," *NYTrib*, May 10, 1878.

134   *$1,500*: Ibid.

134   *"Foeticide"*: "More Comstockism."

135   *January 18, 1837*: Sarah B. Hookey, *Missouri Death Certificates, 1910–1963* (database online), Ancestry.com.

135   *third of six children*: Sara Ann Blakeslee, *1850 U.S. Census, Nanticoke, Broome, New York* (database online), Ancestry.com.

135   *1858*: *Catalogue of the Officers and Students of Alfred University and Alfred Academy for the Year Ending June 30, 1858* (Elmira, NY: Fairman &. Co's, 1858), 21.

135   *December 11, 1859*: Sarah A. Blakeslee, *Illinois, Marriage Index, 1860–1920* (database online), Ancestry.com.

135   *1865*: Grace Chase, *1870 U.S. Census, Cleveland Ward 1, Cuyahoga, Ohio* (database online), Ancestry.com.

135   *1870*: Egbert Cleave, *Cleave's Biographical Cyclopædia of Homœopathic Physicians and Surgeons* (Philadelphia: Galaxy Publishing Company, 1873), 395.

135   *"I feel deeply"*: D. H. Beckwith, *History of the Cleveland Homeopathic College 1850 to 1880* (Cleveland: 1880), 49–50.

135   *By early 1873*: "The Career of Dr. Sara B. Chase," *NYTrib*, May 13, 1878.

135   *"hygienists"*: William Leach, *True Love and Perfect Union: The Feminist Reform of Sex and Society* (Middletown, CT: Wesleyan University Press, 1989), 54.

136   *"There comes from"*: SBC, "The Great Evil of Society," *Ohio Medical and Surgical Reporter* 7, no. 1 (Jan. 1873): 39.

136   *"The ovum belongs"*: Ibid., 40.

136   *1874*: "Woman Suffrage Convention," *Cleveland Daily Herald*, July 7, 1874.

136   *talk at an Akron college*: "Tea Table Gossip," *Daily Observer* (Utica, NY), Mar. 4, 1875.

136   *Church of the Strangers*: SBC letter to the editor, *NYTrib*, May 11, 1878.

136   *West Eleventh*: "A Rival of Madame Restell," *NYTrib*, May 10, 1878.

137   *July 1875*: "New York Liberal Club 30th Meeting, held at 30 Stuyvesant street, Friday Evening, July 9, 1875," New York Liberal Club Records 1869–1877, New York State Library.

137   *"Rich and Poor"*: "New York Liberal Club 35th Meeting, held at 30 Stuyvesant street, Friday Evening, October 15, 1875," New York Liberal Club Records.

137   *"mental and moral"; "strong frame"*: SBC, "Responsibility of Sex," in D. M. Bennett, ed., *Truth Seeker Tracts, Upon a Variety of Subjects Vol. III* (New York: Liberal and Scientific Publishing House, 1876), 7, 6.

137   *"Many complimentary"*: Ibid., 13.

137   *"Manhood; its Mission"*: "Programme of Weekly Lectures," *PFP* 1, no. 2 (May 1878): 31.

137 *"the secret vice"*: New York Supreme Court, *The People of the State of New York Against Sara B. Chase* (hereafter *People v. Chase*) (New York: C. G. Burgoyne, 1894), 33.

138 *"This talkative lady"*: "Dr. Sara B. Chase has her say," *New York Evening Express*, Feb. 4, 1879.

138 *Hess . . . Barnum:* J. O. Barrett, "The Inquisition Revived," *Progressive Age*, in *Alfred Sun*, Sept. 12, 1895.

138 *"The only guarantee"*: Editorial note, *PFP* 1, no. 1 (Apr. 1878): 9.

138 *"The Equality of Woman"*: *PFP* 1, no. 1 (Apr. 1878).

138 *"rendered marriage"*: SBC, "Husbands and Wives," *PFP* 1, no. 1 (Apr. 1878): 4.

138 *"Sexual Temperance"*: Elmina Drake Slenker, letter to the editor, *TS* 8, no. 3 (Jan. 15, 1881): 45.

139 *"a German"*: "A Rival of Madame Restell."

139 *"I am a regularly"*: SBC, letter to the editor, *NYTrib*.

139 *"I would never"*: Ibid.

139 *wanted her to commit suicide:* Bennett, *Champions of the Church*, 1080.

140 *"not for lack of evidence"*: "Sharp Practice by Mr. Comstock," *NYT*, July 11, 1878.

140 *"all the filthy"*: *AR 1878*, 118.

140 *"dictate to women"*: "Irresponsible Parentage," *Word* 7, no. 6 (June 1878): 2.

140 *"on both sides"*: "Science Hall, Saturday Eve., May 25th," *TS* 5, no. 22 (June 1, 1878): 345.

141 *June 12, 1878:* Putnam, *400 Years of Freethought*, 538.

141 *"against Liberals"*: "The National Defense Association," *TS* 5, no. 29 (July 20, 1878): 453.

141 *"unjustly assailed"*: Putnam, *400 Years of Freethought*, 538.

142 *"Vaseline, charged"*: T. B. Wakeman, "Liberty and Purity," *TS* 8, no. 19 (May 7, 1881): 290.

142 *"The crime which"*: "More Comstockism."

142 *"'regular,' aristocratic"*: Bennett, *An Open Letter to Samuel Colgate*, 11.

142 *Between 1880 and 1890:* Brodie, *Contraception and Abortion*, 281.

143 *"capotes"*: Ibid., 282.

143 *ten thousand dollars:* "Anthony Comstock Arrested," *NYT*, June 26, 1878.

143 *"willfully, maliciously"*: "Comstock Arrested," *New York Evening Express*, June 26, 1878.

143 *June 25:* "Anthony Comstock Arrested."

143 *"the difference between"*: "The N.Y. Physiological Society," 43.

143 *"especially adapted"*: "Improved Female Syringe," *PFP* 1, nos. 3 and 4 (June and July 1878): 51.

144 *"We trust that"*: "Special Notices," *PFP* 1, nos. 3 and 4 (June and July 1878): 50.

144   "ANTHONY COMSTOCK": "Anthony Comstock Has Been," *PFP* 2, nos. 1 and 2 (Apr. and May 1879): 32.

144   *"a notorious abortionist"*: *Annual 1882*, 15.

145   *"The action of"*: "Sharp Practice by Mr. Comstock."

145   *"Many slurs and insinuations"*: AC, letter to the editor, *NYTrib*, July 11, 1878.

145   *"either teach"*: "The Tribune has again . . . ," *NYTrib*, July 11, 1878.

145   *six thousand people*: "Mr. Heywood's Case," *DFHM* 8, no. 5 (July 1880): 13.

145   *"Vice, my friends"*: Tucker, *Proceedings of the Indignation Meeting*, 44.

145   *"free thought"*: Ibid., 51.

146   *six thousand signatures*: EHH to Rutherford B. Hayes, Dec. 9, 1878, *In Re Application for Pardon of Ezra H. Heywood Filed Nov 25, 1878*.

146   *"People ought to"*: ATH to ED, [1878], F "Angela [Tilton] Heywood to E. M. F. Denton," Denton Family Papers, Joseph A. Labadie Collection.

146   *"if he does not"*: EDS to Friend Hayes, Aug. 6, 1878, *In Re Application for Pardon of Ezra H. Heywood Filed Nov 25, 1878*.

147   *"jerks"*: "Affidavit of Anthony Comstock, Sworn to Nov. 20, 1878."

147   *"My helpless family"*: EHH to Rutherford B. Hayes, Dec. 9, 1878, *In Re Application for Pardon of Ezra H. Heywood*.

147   *ten thousand dollars*: *AR 1877*, 104.

148   *"not that he discussed"*: Charles Richard Williams, ed., *Diary and Letters of Rutherford Birchard Hayes*, vol. III (Columbus: Ohio State Archaeological and Historical Society, 1924), 518.

148   *"The Pres. Pardons"*: *AR 1877*, 104.

148   *Boston . . . Chicago*: *Annual 1879*, 17.

148   *three-hundred-dollar*: Sears, *The Sex Radicals*, 168.

149   *"offensive to the court"*: *United States v. Bennett*, 24 F. 70 (SDNY, 1879).

149   *Around 1879*: Adele Comstock, *1880 U.S. Census, Brooklyn, Kings County, New York* (database online), Ancestry.com.

149   *Chinatown*: Broun and Leech, *Roundsman*, 76.

149   *developmental problems*: Ruth C. Sperry to Ralph Ginzburg, Mar. 11, 1960, B 10, F 7, RGP.

149   *Adele*: Adele Comstock, *1880 U.S. Census*.

9. THE COMSTOCK SYRINGE

150   *"to a broader field"*: "Chase vs. Chase," *Cleveland Leader*, Dec. 16, 1878.

150   *"willful absence"*: "Courts, Record for December 28," *Cleveland Leader*, Dec. 30, 1878.

150   *"terribly bitter"*: "Victimized," *PFP* 3, no. 3 (Oct. 1880): 41.

151   *"had not got done"*: "Excluded from the Mails," *NYTrib*, Apr. 21, 1881.

151   *fifteen new orders*: Samuel H. Preston, "The Inquirer," *PFP* 4, no. 1 (Apr. 1881): 109.

151   *"That is an infamous libel"*: "Comstock Losing his Grip," *Truth*, Apr. 13, 1881.

152 *"a loathsome mortal"*: Samuel H. Preston, "The Pulp of a Little Pungent Public and Private Opinion," *PFP* 4, no. 1 (Apr. 1881): 108.

152 *"We claim this right"*: SBC and Elmina Drake Slenker to T. L. James, quoted in *Monthly Medical Monitor* 1, no. 1 (May 1881): 4.

152 *"backstrokes from Comstock's"*: *Word* 10, no. 2 (June 1881): 2.

152 *"Russian censorship"*: *Truth* quoted in "Miscellaneous," *BI* 51, no. 2 (Apr. 27, 1881): 3.

152 *"gave too much"*: Elmina Drake Slenker, "Elmina's Plea," *TS* 8, no. 18 (Apr. 30, 1881): 277.

153 *"Autocrat of Vaseline"*: "Indignation Meeting at Investigator Hall," *BI* 51, no. 6 (May 25, 1881): 3.

153 *"Here is our"*: SBC, Elmina Drake Slenker, and Samuel H. Preston, "We Would Say," *PFP* 4, no. 2 (June 1881): 31.

153 *"Anthony Comstock has"*: "World-Wide Blessing to Womankind," *PFP* 4, no. 2 (June 1881): 32.

153 *"Comstock's savage effort"*: *Word* 10, no. 3 (July 1881): 3.

154 *"others of like infamous"*: *Annual 1882*, 15. This report was not bylined.

154 *"healthy, middle-aged"*: "Dr. Chase on the Stand All Day," *NYTrib*, June 1, 1893.

154 *"Tommy's letters"*: "He Got There," *Cincinnati Enquirer*, Dec. 7, 1888.

154 *"You have come"*: "An Informal Wedding," *Sun* (New York), Dec. 5, 1888.

155 *"I take thee"*: "Dr. Sara Chase's Romance," *NYH*, Dec. 5, 1888.

155 *"the best character"*: "An Informal Wedding."

155 *"I thought he"*: "Sara's Love Chase," *Minneapolis Tribune*, Aug. 10, 1889.

155 *"If Comstock's mother"*: *Word* 10, no. 3 (July 1881): 3.

156 *"COMSTOCK TRIED"*: *Word* 10, no. 4 (Aug. 1881): 4.

156 *"The Vaginal Syringe"*: Dec. 1881 *Word* quoted in EHH, *Free Speech: Report of Ezra H. Heywood's Defense Before the United States Court in Boston, April 10, 11 and 12, 1883* (Princeton, MA: Co-operative Publishing Co., 1883), 16–17.

156 *"for the cure or prevention"*: NY Criminal Code Ch. 7, § 321 at 126 (1881).

156 *Institute of Heredity*: "The First Public Meeting in New York," *DFHM* 3, no. 5 (Jan. 1882): 1.

157 *"The Corrupters of our Youth"*: "Corrupters of Youth," *NYTrib*, Mar. 1, 1882.

157 *"Don't pollute her"*: EHH, *Free Speech*, iii.

157 *"a notorious offender"*: AR 1882, 232, #107.

158 *"Now, not books merely"*: ATH, "The Woman's View of It—No. 1," 2.

159 *"in which the sexual"*: Benjamin R. Tucker, "On Picket Duty," *Liberty* 2, no. 2 (June 9, 1883): 1.

159 *"If the social relations"*: "Notes," *TS* 10, no. 22 (June 2, 1883): 345.

160 *"died under his treatment"*: EHH, *Free Speech*, 9.

160 *"since Comstockism"*: Ibid., 17.

160   *waited until three*: Ibid., 45.

160   *"turned into"*: "A Foe to his Own Cause," *Liberty* 2, no. 10 (May 12, 1883): 4.

161   *"the real person assailed"*: "Another Raid on Rights of Opinion," *Word* 12, no. 3 (July 1883): 2.

161   *"a mere wife"*: SPA, "The Heywoods," 498.

161   *"male 'obscenity' case"*: ATH, "The Woman's View of It—No. 2," 2.

161   *four times*: EHH, *Free Speech*, 47.

161   *"Our baby Boy"*: "The Struggle for Liberty and Life," *Word* 12, no. 8 (Nov. 1883): 2.

161   *"As I look upon"*: ATH, "Men, Women, and Things," *Word* 12, no. 8 (Dec. 1883): 2.

162   *"Cock is a fowl"*: ATH, "Sex-Nomenclature—Plain English," 3.

162   *"Such graceful terms"*: ATH, "The Ethics of Touch—Sex-Unity," *Word* 18, no. 3 (June 1889): 3.

162   *"Women do not"*: ATH, "Body Housekeeping—Home Thrift," *Word* 20, no. 9 (Mar. 1893): 2–3.

162   *"power to resist rape"*: ATH, "Marriage, the Penis Trust—Free Love," *Word* 18, no. 3 (July 1889): 2.

162   *"I am the wife of defendant"*: *United States v. Ezra H. Heywood*, U.S. Circuit Court, June 21, 1890, 14, NARA at Boston.

162   *"that the motive"*: Ibid., 16.

163   *"Men of Massachusetts!"*: *United States v. Ezra H. Heywood: Extracts from Proceedings in District Court, Boston, July 25, 1890*, 3–4, B 20, F 15, RGP.

163   *"Your Honor"*: Oswald Dawson, *Personal Rights and Sexual Wrongs* (London: Wm. Reeves, 1897), 35.

163   *"made the corridors ring"*: "A Dramatic Scene in Court," *St. Louis Globe-Democrat*, July 25, 1890.

163   *"the he was imprisoned"*: ATH, "Sex-Nomenclature—Plain English," 2.

163   *"I am not ashamed"*: ATH, "The Grace and Use of Sex Life," *Word* 19, no. 2 (June 1890): 3.

164   *"that Mr. Heywood"*: [Pinney], "The Man and the Woman of Princeton."

10. A NEW SECRETARY

166   *"very satisfactorily"*: "Minutes of the Trustees of the University of Pennsylvania, 1882–1892," entry Oct. 3, 1882, University Archives, University of Pennsylvania (hereafter UAUP).

166   *"define the future"*: "All Sorts," *PI*, Oct. 12, 1882.

167   *"all of the facilities"*: "Minutes of the Trustees," entry Oct. 18, 1882.

167   *two other women*: "Local Intelligence," *PI*, Nov. 15, 1882.

167   *"open the doors"*: "The undersigned, believing," n.d., petition in Coeducation Files, UAUP.

167   *"expressing her hearty"*: "Miss Anthony," *PI*, Feb. 20, 1883.

167   *three other times*: "Minutes of the Trustees," entries Jan. 2, 1883, Oct. 2, 1883, June 3, 1884.

168   *August 1, 1857*: Ida C. Craddock, *U.S. Find a Grave Index, 1600s–Current* (database online), Ancestry.com

168   *died in infancy*: Ida Craddock, *Pennsylvania and New Jersey, Church and Town Records, 1669–2013* (database online), Ancestry.com.

168   *six months old*: Joseph L. Craddock died Dec. 31, 1857. *Pennsylvania and New Jersey, Church and Town Records, 1669–2013* (database online), Ancestry.com.

168   *Thomas B. Decker*: Thomas B. Decker, *U.S. City Directories, 1822–1995* (database online), Ancestry.com.

168   *"The old, aching"*: Celanire, "An Old Maid's Reverie," *Potter's American Monthly* 10, no. 75 (Mar. 1878): 216. Thanks to Robert P. Helms for his post "Ida Celanire Craddock & Voltairine de Cleyre: Two Freethinkers of Philadelphia," *Bob Helms' Chin-Wag* (blog), Nov. 18, 2016, https://bobhelmschinwag.wordpress.com/2016/11/18/ida-celanire-craddock-voltairine-de-cleyre-two-freethinkers-of-philadelphia/.

169   *five months*: Lynn Dorwaldt, Special Collections Librarian, Wagner Free Institute of Science, email to author, Feb. 21, 2019.

169   *summer of 1884*: "Vacation Excursion," *Evening Bulletin* (Philadelphia), June 9, 1884.

169   *"With all her intellect"*: ICC, "Story of My Life," 2.

169   *"Miss Ida"*: ICC, "Diary of Psychical Experiences" (hereafter "DPE"), entry Feb. 6, 1900, 23, S 2, B 2, F 3, ICP.

169   *"going dangerously near"*: ICC, "Story of My Life," 2.

170   *"He refrained"*: Ibid., 2–3.

170   *"cut-and-dried bachelor"*: Ibid., 2.

170   *"got me up at the head"*: Ibid., 3.

170   Principles of Psychology: ICC to KW, Dec. 8, 1887, S 1, B 1, F 1, ICP.

170   *"I can say truly"*: Ibid.

171   Open Door: ICC to KW, Mar. 15, 1887, S 1, B 1, F 1, ICP.

171   *"Not only is my horizon"*: ICC to KW, Dec. 8, 1887.

171   *"Telepathy Between the Sexes"*: ICC, *Telepathy Between the Sexes* (Chicago: 1900), S 2, B 5, F 1, ICP.

171   *"hard, unfeminine"*: Ibid., 7.

172   *"As I was saying"*: Ibid., 8.

172   *"Oh, Madam"*: Ibid.

172   *"I have begun"*: ICC to KW, Oct. 1, 1889, S 1, B 1, F 1, ICP.

173   *two hundred fifty*: Sidney Warren, *American Freethought: 1860–1914* (New York: Columbia University Press, 1943), 168–69.

173   *ten thousand people*: Ibid., 170.

173   *"for the bright intellects"*: ICC to KW, Oct. 1, 1889.

173   *teaching at Girard*: Secretary to the President to Theodore Schroeder, Sept. 15, 1913, B 2, F 2, RGP.

173   *"that the secretary"*: ICC, "Story of My Life," 4.

173   *"Do you think"*: Robert C. Adams, "The American Secularists," *Secular Thought*, Nov. 21, 1891, 248, B 20, F 15, RGP.

174   *"How to Make"*: ICC, "How to Make Freethinkers of the Young," *BI* 61, no. 23 (Sept. 9, 1891): 3.

174   *a few dozen*: ICC, "Secretary's Report," *Fifteenth Annual Congress of the American Secular Union* (Philadelphia: Loag Printing House, 1891), 16, 13.

175   *"Free-Lovers"*: ICC, "Story of My Life," 4.

176   *"interior voice"*: Ibid.

176   *"treasure-trove," "Pussy," and "Little womb-man"*: ICC to WTS, Sept. 10, 1901, S 1, B 1, F 1, ICP; "DPE," entry Aug. 26, 1902, 56, S 2, B 2, F 3, ICP.

176   *"Cupid"* . . . L'Amour et Psyche, enfants: ICC to WTS, Sept. 10, 1901.

176   *"unseen spirit lover"*: ICC, "Story of My Life," [7].

176   *November 12, 1892*: ICC, "Memoranda: Indictment in Chicago," B 2, F 2, RGP.

177   *"made love"*: ICC, "Story of My Life," [7].

177   *"Suddenly, as I lay"*: Ibid.

177   *"little pamphlet"*: ICC, *The Danse du Ventre (Dance of the Abdomen) as performed in the Cairo Street Theatre, Midway Plaisance, Chicago: Its Value as an Educator in Marital Duties* ([Philadelphia], 1893), 8, S 2, B 5, F 8, ICP.

178   *"I would say"*: Ibid., 11–12.

178   *"interested in knowing"*: ICC to EBF, Nov. 22, 1893.

179   *"clear-headed"*: "Comstock After the Cairo Dancers," *DFHM* 18, no. 10 (Sept. 1893): 12.

179   *"deranged"*: "Observations," *TS* 20, no. 50 (Dec. 16, 1893): 793.

179   *"in the front rank"*: "The Danse du Ventre," *LLB*, Dec. 22, 1893.

179   *"excited the displeasure"*: "Sex-Morality—the True and the False," *LLB*, Dec. 22, 1893.

179   *"phallic worship"*: ICC to EBF, Nov. 22, 1893.

11. HELPS TO HAPPY WEDLOCK

180   *"Date: Dec. 4, 1893"*: AR 1893, 248, #76, 77, 78.

181   *"a pretty face"*: "Danse du Ventre Stopped," *Sun* (New York), Dec. 3, 1893.

181   *"marvellous control"*: "Danse du Ventre in New York: Where Is Anthony Comstock?," *NYW*, Dec. 3, 1893.

181   *"number of disreputable"*: "Danse du Ventre Stopped."

181   *a headline in the World*: "Danse du Ventre in New York."

182   *"This dance has"*: Ibid.

182   *frightened off*: "The Midway in New York," *NYH*, Dec. 6, 1893.

182   *"immoral conduct"*: "Police and Law Defied," *NYT*, Dec. 5, 1893.

183   *"before ladies and gentlemen"*: "The Midway in New York."

183   *Court of Special Sessions*: Murphy, *Scoundrels in Law*, 269.

183   *"The scar"*: "The Midway Dancers Fined," *BDE*, Dec. 6, 1893.

183   *"Your Honors"*: "The Midway Dancers," *Star-Gazette* (Elmira, NY), Dec. 8, 1893.

184   *"cold unwriggling world"*: Ibid.

184   *"I dare say"*: ICC to EBF, Dec. 20, 1893, S 1, B 1, F 1, ICP.

184   *"It is fair to say"*: "A Very Shocking Time," *NYW*, Feb. 10, 1894.

185   *"perfect Monomaniac"*: Richard B. Westbrook to EBF, Feb. 14, 1894, S 1, B 1, F 1, ICP.

186   *"Mistress Roberts"*: ICC, "Notes, Miscellaneous," 15, S 3, B 6, F 7, ICP.

187   *"nasty"*: ICC, "DPE," entry Dec. 6, 1895, 209, S 2, B 2, F 3, ICP.

187   *"Divine Science"*: Ibid., entry Mar. 2, 1895, 156, S 2, B 2, F 2, ICP.

187   *"Head Master of the occultists"*: Ibid., entry July 2, 1894, 76, S 2, B 2, F 2, ICP.

187   *Iason*: Ibid., entry Apr. 10, 1894, 19, S 2, B 2, F 2, ICP.

187   *"wissenings"*: For example, ibid., entry Apr. 7, 1894, 17, S 2, B 2, F 2, ICP.

187   *"When indications of sex"*: Ibid., entry Dec. 20, 1899, 21, S 2, B 2, F 3, ICP.

187   *"Wednesday night"*: Ibid., entry Oct. 26, 1894, 199, S 2, B 2, F 2, ICP.

187   *"more prolonged"*: Ibid., entry Sept. 12, 1894, 103, S 2, B 2, F 2, ICP.

188   *"going over the brink"*: Ibid., entry May 9, 1894, 45, S 2, B 2, F 2, ICP.

188   *"use the hand"*: ICC, *Advice to a Bridegroom* (Chicago: 1909), 4.

188   *"should be simply saluted"*: ICC, *The Wedding Night* (New York: 1902), 9.

188   *"a failure"*: ICC, "DPE," entry Nov. 6, 1895, 189, S 2, B 2, F 3, ICP.

188   *Onanisme*: Ibid., entry June 2, 1894, 64, S 2, B 2, F 2, ICP.

188   *"My education has been"*: Ibid., entry Oct. 26, 1894, 121, S 2, B 2, F 2, ICP.

189   *"triumphal procession"*: ICC to WTS, July 11, 1895.

189   *"Last Saturday"*: ICC, "DPE," entry Sept. 10, 1895, 186, S 2, B 2, F 3, ICP.

189   *"Lecturer and Correspondent"*: ICC, ed., *Helps to Happy Wedlock No. 1 For Husbands: Consisting of an Anonymous Essay on Male Continence; Part of an Anonymous Essay on Magnetation; and Comments by Ida C. Craddock* (Philadelphia: 1896), title page.

189   *"should learn to suppress"*: Ibid., 12.

189   *"not be burdened"*: Ibid., 15.

190   *"as a convenience"*: Ibid., 14.

190   *November 1896*: ICC, "DPE," entry Dec. 6, 1896, 208, S 2, B 2, F 3, ICP.

190   *"Can I give advice"*: Ibid.

190   *"I don't care tuppence"*: Ibid., 209.

191   *"I have learned to love"*: *Annual 1897*, 28.

191   *"Notwithstanding"*: "New Journalism and Vice," *NYT*, Mar. 3, 1897.

191   *"Blue Bells of Scotland"*: *Annual 1897*, 57.

191   *$5,000*: Broun and Leech, *Roundsman*, 229.

191   *Queen Anne*: "Houses that Tell Summit's History," Summit Historical Society, Summit, New Jersey, [5].

191   *squirrels*: "Interview 13 April 60 over the phone with John S. Beck," B 10, F 4, RGP.

192   *three*: "Chat in March 1957 with Miss Fannie C Moore," B 11, F 1, RGP.

192   *Magna Carta*: "Comstock's Personal Belongings," B 9, F 12, RGP.

192   *"We are going to have"*: "Address of Frances E. Willard, President of the Woman's National Council of the United States at its first triennial meeting, Albaugh's Opera House, Washington, D.C., February 22–25, 1891," 27.

193   *"less hysterical"*: ICC, "DPE," entry Dec. 6, 1895, 209, S 2, B 2, F 3, ICP.

193   *"Little Woman"*: Ibid., 213.

193   *"a dear little box"*: Ibid., 214.

193   *advertisements*: PI, Apr. 15, 1897.

193   *"Scientific Motherhood"*: Business card, B 20, F 16, RGP.

193   *five dollars . . . six dollars*: "Instruction given upon Marriage" card, B 20, F 16, RGP.

194   *"Regeneration"*: ICC, "Regeneration and Rejuvenation of Men and Women Through the Right Use of the Sex Function," title page, S 2, B 4, F 5, ICP. This includes her "Diagnosis for Men."

194   *"Do you usually sleep"*: Ibid., 1.

194   *"love-making"*: ICC, *Advice to a Bridegroom*, 4.

194   *"If the entrance"*: Ibid., 6.

194   *"go straight"*: ICC, *Letter to a Prospective Bride* (Philadelphia: 1897), 17.

195   *"natural law"*: Ibid., 14.

195   *"both direct and delicate"*: "Letter to a Prospective Bride by Ida C. Craddock," *Medical World* 15, no. 10 (Oct. 1897): 440.

195   *November 13, 1897: United States v. Ida Craddock*, August Sessions, 1898, U.S. District Court for the Eastern District of Pennsylvania, National Archives at Philadelphia.

195   *"treated with startling frankness"*: "Why She Resigned," *Evening Bulletin* (Philadelphia), n.d., B 20, F 15, RGP.

196   *"financial, social and legal"*: ICC to My Patrons and Well-Wishers, Dec. 1897, B 2, F 2, RGP.

197   *"Miss Craddock may"*: M. J. Bradley, "Philadelphia," *Bookseller and Newsman* 14, no. 4 (Apr. 1898): 10.

197   *"days were numbered"*: ICC, "Memoranda: Indictment in Chicago," 3.

197   *"Respectfully referred to"*: Envelope from Room 7, #1230 Arch St., Philadelphia, May 7, 1898, RG 28, E 231, B 180, F 422, NARA.

197   *"instructions had come"*: ICC, "Memoranda: Indictment in Chicago," 4.

197   *May 27, 1898*: G. C. Holden to R. W. McAfee, Oct. 16, 1899, RG 28, E 231, B 180, F 422, NARA.

197   *"obscene by mail"*: AR 1898, 64, #29.

197   *"Science is dragged"*: AC, *Traps for the Young*, 158–59.

198   *"that Mecca of Freethought"*: ICC to EBF, June 6, 1898, B 2, F 2, RGP.

198   *"I am hoping"*: Ibid.

199   *"very evident that"*: ICC to KW, Dec. 2, 1898, S 1, B 1, F 1, ICP.

199   *June 10*: ICC to KW, Oct. 8, 1898, B 2, F 2, RGP.

199   *"Had I had the slightest"*: Ibid.

200   *"illicit experience"*: ICC, *Heavenly Bridegrooms: An Unintentional Contribution to the Erotogenetic Interpretation of Religion* (New York: 1918), 3–4.

200   *"Is the literature"*: ICC, "Memoranda: Indictment in Chicago," 6.

200   *"a bigot"*: Ibid., 5.

200 *"I positively would not"*: Ibid., 6.

200 *September 7, 1898*: Owen Copp to Theodore Schroeder, Sept. 20, 1913, S 1, B 1, F 2, ICP.

200 *one hundred dollars*: *United States v. Ida Craddock*, August Sessions, 1898.

201 *"Mrs. Craddock"*: ICC to KW, Dec. 2, 1898.

201 *"I should very likely"*: Ibid.

201 *"become a wanderer"*: Ibid.

12. THE CHURCH OF YOGA

203 *"Mrs. Ida C. Craddock"*: Business card.

203 *"The reason assigned"*: Wallace Moore to M. C. Fosnes, Esq., inspector in charge, Mar. 18, 1899, RG 28, E 231, B 180, F 422, NARA.

203 *three to one*: ICC, "Records of Cases in Marital Reform Work," 1900, 1–41, S 2, B 5, F 12, ICP.

204 *"smiled, as though"*: Ibid., 1.

204 *"planked down"*: Ibid., 17.

204 *"her to unite"*: Ibid., 4.

204 *"When having union"*: ICC, "DPE," entry Sept. 20, 1899, 15, S 2, B 2, F 3, ICP.

205 *"But still my"*: Ibid., entry Dec. 20, 1899, 21, S 2, B 2, F 3, ICP.

205 *"conservation of the male principle"*: ICC, "Right Marital Living," *Chicago Clinic* 7, no. 5 (May 1899): 200.

205 *"the quality of children"*: Ibid.

206 *"preventives to conception"*: ICC, *Right Marital Living* (Chicago: Ida C. Craddock, 1899), 3, 4.

206 *"an act of onanism"*: Ibid., 4.

206 vagina, male organ: Ibid., 26, 27.

206 *"it would be as well"*: Ibid., 41.

206 *"orifice"*: Ibid., 42.

206 *"it is sometimes better"*: Ibid., 43.

207 *"The young woman"*: ICC, "Brief Account of my Indictments," [1902], 4, B 2, F 2, RGP.

207 *"George H. Vorst"*: Ibid., 1.

207 *she mailed a copy*: Ibid., 2.

207 *October 27*: "Report of Indictment, Post Office Department, Office of Post Office Inspector, Chicago, Ill.," Oct. 27, 1899, RG 28, E 231, B 180, F 422, NARA.

207 *"a certain pamphlet"*: *United States v. Ida C. Craddock*, Oct. 31, 1899, U.S. District Court, Northern Division of Illinois, National Archives at Chicago.

208 *"could not do it"*: ICC, "Memoranda: Indictment in Chicago," 1.

208 *"Woman"*: John Farrell, *Clarence Darrow: Attorney for the Damned* (New York: Doubleday, 2011), 104.

208   *five-hundred-dollar bail*: ICC, "Brief Account of my Indictments," 2.

209   *"said it would not matter"*: Ibid., 2.

209   *subpoenaed: United States v. Ida C. Craddock, Oct. 31, 1899.*

209   *"somewhat narrow churchman"*: Ibid., 6.

209   *"I had not yet awakened"*: ICC to HP, Feb. 9, 1902, B 2, F 2, RGP.

210   *December 9, 1899*: "Result of Trial, Chicago, Ill., Dec. 9, 1899," RG 28, E 231, B 180, F 422, NARA.

210   *"Mrs. Dr. Dickinson"*: W. S. Mayer and R. W. McAfee to Colonel J. E. Stuart, Dec. 9, 1899, RG 28, E 231, B 180, F 422, NARA.

210   *"It seemed to me"*: ICC, "DPE," entry Dec. 20, 1899, 21, S 1, B 2, F 3, ICP.

210   *"Church of Yoga"*: "Religious Announcements," *CT*, Dec. 17, 1899, Feb. 25, 1900.

210   *"Man and Woman as They Were"*: *CT*, Dec. 17, 1899.

210   *Otoman Zar-Adusht Hanish*: ICC, "Records of Cases in Marital 23; ICC, address book [1890s], S 3, B 6, F 12, ICP.

210   *"Marriage and Divorce"*: "Sabbath Services," *Inter Ocean* (Chicago), Mar. 4, 1900.

211   *Otto Hanisch*: "Father Exposes Dr. Hanish," *CT*, May 18, 1912.

211   *"Yoga Applied to the Married Life"*: "Sabbath Services," *Inter Ocean* (Chicago), Feb. 4, 1900.

211   *"secure them"*: ICC, "Yoga Applied to the Married Life," 2, B 2, F 2, RGP.

211   *sixteen-page*: ICC to Hugh Pentecost, Feb. 9, 1902.

211   *"an institution"*: "Right Marital Living," LLB, Feb. 17, 1900.

211   *semen to generative fluid*: ICC to HP, Feb. 9, 1902.

212   *"heavy lowland atmosphere"*: ICC to WTS, Sept. 10, 1901.

212   *"and had a satisfying dinner"*: ICC, "Records of Cases in Marital Reform Work," 37.

212   *"reflex action"*: ICC, *The Wedding Night* 7.

212   *"I would add"*: Ibid., 12.

213   *"the embrace"*: Ibid., 13.

213   *"Sometimes the man's organ"*: Ibid., 17.

213   *"from the standpoint"*: "The Wedding Night," LLB, Aug. 11, 1900.

214   *"certain obscene books"*: *United States v. Ida C. Craddock, April 25, 1901,* Arrest Warrant, RG 21, E 77, B 169, F Craddock, NARA.

214   *law in the District of Columbia*: 56th Cong., Sess. II, Ch. 854, Sec. 872, 1901 at 1332.

214   *"to be the pastor"*: "Mrs. Craddock Arrested," *Washington Times*, Apr. 25, 1901.

214   *"people who came prepared"*: ICC, "Brief Account of My Indictments," 5.

214   *"a pre-possessing elderly"*: "Mrs. Craddock in Court," *Washington Times*, Apr. 26, 1901.

214   *three hundred dollars*: ICC, "Brief Account of My Indictments," 7.

215   *"followed by a number"*: "Personal Bonds Accepted," *Evening Star* (Washington, DC), Apr. 26, 1901.

13. COMSTOCK VERSUS CRADDOCK

217 *"Date: Feb. 5, 1902"*: AR 1902, 126, #19.

217 *"Ida C. Craddock, Room 5"*: "In Jail's Shadow Ida Craddock Died," *NYH*, Oct. 18, 1902.

217 *"ringing up the Central"*: ICC, "Record of Cases in Oral Instruction," 2, S 2, B 4, F 8, ICP.

218 *letters to "customers"*: ICC to WTS, Sept. 10, 1901.

218 *"Just as soon"*: ICC to KW, [Aug. 1, 1901], S 1, B 1, F 1, ICP.

218 *"I am now an old offender"*: ICC to WTS, Sept. 10, 1901.

218 *Birth rates were*: Gordon, *Woman's Body, Woman's Right*, 154–55.

219 *45 live births*: Ansley J. Coale and Melvin Zelnik, *New Estimates of Fertility and Population in the United States* (Princeton, NJ: Princeton University Press, 1963), Table 2, 36.

219 *55 births per thousand*: Maurice J. Moore and Martin O'Connell, *Perspectives on American Fertility* (Washington: U.S. Department of Commerce, July 1978), 2–3.

219 *not based on accurate*: Gordon, *Woman's Body, Woman's Right*, 154.

219 *From 1890 to 1910*: Ibid., 203.

220 *"I thought of Anthony"*: ICC, "DPE," 38, entry July 11, 1901, S 2, B 2, F 3, ICP.

220 *$6.96*: ICC to KW, [Aug. 1, 1901].

220 *"What can you give me for a dollar?"*: ICC, "Record of Cases in Oral Instruction," 10.

221 *"I am not here to be touched"*: Ibid.

221 *"Lord! If I could only have castrated"*: Ibid., 11.

221 *E. D. Garnsey*: ICC to HP, Mar. 12, 1902, B 2, F 2, RGP.

222 *Reverend William S. Rainsford*: William Stephen Rainsford, *The Story of a Varied Life: An Autobiography* (New York: Doubleday, Page & Company, 1922), 341. (Rainsford wrote that she came to visit him.)

222 *"I do not feel"*: W. S. Rainsford to ICC, Feb. 13, 1902, quoted in "Ida Craddock's Case," *TS* 29, no. 13 (Mar. 29, 1902): 200.

222 *"You are evidently"*: R. W. Shufeldt to ICC, Jan. 27, 1902, S 1, B 1, F 1, ICP.

222 *"time and time again"*: Annual 1900, 19.

222 *"Frank Lea"*: U.S. Circuit Court v. Ida C. Craddock, indictment, Mar. 12, 1902, National Archives at New York City.

223 *"within the purview"*: Annual 1903, 10.

223 *"But if I should be"*: HP, "One-Ideaed People," *TS* 29, no. 47 (Nov. 22, 1902): 738.

223 *"I personally secured"*: AC to Henrietta Westbrook, Feb. 28, 1902.

224 *"Frankie Streeter"*: Miss Frankie Streeter to ICC, Feb. 3, 1902, quoted in "Comstock and his Methods," *TS* 29, no. 45 (Nov. 8, 1902): 710.

224 *eight and a half years*: "Mrs. Craddock on Her Recent Arrest," *Sun* (New York), Feb. 23, 1902.

224 *"fill your mind"*: ICC to Miss Frankie Streeter, Feb. 4, 1902, quoted in ibid.

224 *"crabbed handwriting"*: ICC to HP, Feb. 9, 1902.

225   *"This is the gentleman"*: "Mrs. Craddock on Her Recent Arrest."

225   *without a search warrant*: AC to T. W. Swift, Mar. 24, 1902, RG 28, E 231, B 180, F 422, NARA.

225   *"opprobrious epithets"*: "Mrs. Craddock on Her Recent Arrest."

225   *"51 books and 536 circulars"*: AC to T. W. Swift, Mar. 24, 1902.

225   *"lecturer of filth"*: AR 1902, 126, #19.

225   *"I would like this"*: AC to T. W. Swift, Feb. 5, 1902, RG 28, E 231, B 180, F 422, NARA.

226   *$2,500*: "Report of Arrest and Preliminary Hearing," Feb. 6, 1902, *United States v. Ida C. Craddock*, RG 28, E 231, B 180, F 422, NARA.

226   *"He should be forced"*: ICC to HP, Feb. 9, 1902.

226   *"She calls herself Pastor"*: "Dr. Rainsford Sent Approval," *Sun* (New York), Feb. 19, 1902.

227   *"quietly and inoffensively"*: EBF, "Comstock Versus Craddock," *LLB*, Feb. 27, 1902.

227   *"I have a horror"*: ICC to HP, Feb. 4, 1902, S 1, B 1, F 1, ICP.

228   *"no decent man or woman"*: AC to Henrietta Westbrook, Feb. 28, 1902.

228   *March 14, 1902*: EBF, "Comstock v. Craddock—Again," *TS* 29, no. 11 (Mar. 15, 1902): 168.

228   *"Is the book indicted"*: "Ida Craddock's Case," *TS* 29, no. 13 (Mar. 29, 1902): 199.

228   *"to her feet"*: Dr. R. W. Shufeldt, "Letters from Gotham—No. 5," *BI*, n.d., fragment, B 2, F 2, RGP.

229   *"The book is not obscene"*: "Ida Craddock's Case," 199.

229   *"high moral character"*: Ibid.

230   *"when put in indiscriminate"*: Ibid.

230   *regarded* The Wedding Night *as "blasphemous"*: EBF, "Convicted of Blasphemy," *TS* 29, no. 15 (Apr. 12, 1902): 230.

230   *"book of the Church of Yoga"*: "Mrs. Craddock Goes to Jail," *Sun* (New York), Mar. 18, 1902.

230   *"I am not ashamed"*: "Mrs. Craddock Goes to Jail."

231   *"This is the most awful"*: Ibid.

231   *suspended sentence*: ICC to HP, Mar. 19, 1902, S 1, B 1, F 1, ICP.

231   *three months*: "Mrs. Craddock Goes to Jail."

231   *"exulted with savage glee"*: EBF, "Convicted of Blasphemy," 231.

14. THE FEMININITY OF THE UNIVERSE

232   *"fault was in the head"*: LD to HP, Mar. 18, 1902, S 1, B 1, F 1, ICP.

232   *"roast Comstock"*: LD to EBF, May 9, 1902, S 1, B 1, F 2, ICP.

233   *"Poor dear girl"*: LD to EBF, Mar. 29, 1902, S 1, B 1, F 1, ICP.

233   *took no action*: "Priestess Ends Her Life to Escape Prison Cell," *Evening Journal* (Philadelphia), Oct. 17, 1902.

233   *"the stuff of"*: WTS to Attorney General Knox, Sept. 24, 1902, B 2, F 2, RGP.

233 *Free Speech League*: "The Craddock Dinner," *TS* 29, no. 26 (June 28, 1902): 409.

233 *"to maintain the right"*: E. C. Walker, letter to the editor, *LLB*, May 15, 1902.

233 *"the anarchists, the agnostics"*: Roger Baldwin quoted in Rabban, "The Free Speech League," 70–71.

234 *"All those whose hearts"*: "The Craddock Dinner."

234 *"Horrors"*: ICC, "Horrors of the Women's Workhouse," *NYW*, July 13, 1902.

234 *Eunice O. Parsons*: ICC, "Record of Cases in Oral Instruction," 22–23, 33.

234 *"I am getting a better grasp"*: ICC, "DPE," 55, entry July 25, 1902, S 2, B 2, F 3, ICP.

235 *"We Liberals"*: ICC to EBF, June 18, 1902, S 1, B 1, F 2, ICP.

235 *"Smutty Tony"*: EC to LD, Nov. 17, 1902, B 2, F 2, RGP.

235 *"The only advice"*: EC to ICC, Sept. 10, 1902, B 2, F 2, RGP.

235 *"more minute"*: U.S. Circuit Court v. Ida C. Craddock, indictment, Mar. 12, 1902.

236 *"The janitress"*: Ibid.

236 *"martyr to Comstockism"*: "Mrs. Craddock Convicted," *Sun* (New York), Oct. 11, 1902.

236 *"indisputably usurping"*: Edwin C. Walker, *Who Is the Enemy; Anthony Comstock or You?* (New York: Edwin C. Walker, 1903), 28.

236 *five years*: ICC, "Brief Account of my Indictments," 4.

236 *"If I don't choose to escape"*: "Escapes Jail by Death," *Wilkes-Barre Times Leader* (Pennsylvania), Oct. 20, 1902.

237 *"illuminating gas poisoning"*: Ida Craddock Death Certificate, Oct. 17, 1902, Municipal Archives, New York, NY.

237 *"Some day you'll be"*: "Ida Craddock's Letter to her Mother," *TS* 29, no. 43 (Oct. 25, 1902): 680.

238 *"Whatever doubts"*: "George Macdonald on the Craddock Case," *LLB*, Dec. 11, 1902.

238 *"could have read"*: "In Jail's Shadow Ida Craddock Died," *NYH*, Oct. 18, 1902.

238 *"to the public"*: "Ida C. Craddock's Last Words," *LLB*, Nov. 13, 1902.

239 *"remanded for sentence"*: AC to E. H. Thorp, Oct. 21, 1902, RG 28, E 231, B 180, F 422, NARA.

239 *Frederic Hinckley*: LD to EBF, Oct. 21, 1902, B 2, F 2, RGP.

239 *twelve hundred*: *Chicago American*, Oct. 27, quoted in "Memorial for Ida C. Craddock," *LLB*, Nov. 6, 1902.

239 *"Let a woman write"*: Juliet H. Severance, letter to the editor, *TS* 29, no. 44 (Nov. 1, 1902): 698.

240 *"Miss Craddock elects"*: "Memorial for Ida C. Craddock."

240 *"a [G]atling gun"*: Flora W. Fox, letter to the editor, *LLB*, Nov. 20, 1902.

241 *"Whatever Mr. Comstock does"*: "Vice Society for Comstock," *Sun* (New York), Nov. 4, 1902.

241   *"inexcusably nasty"*: AC, letter to the editor, *BDE*, Nov. 14, 1902.

241   *"Let him find"*: "Warm Time for Comstock at Philosophical Society," *BDE*, Dec. 8, 1902.

241   *"powerful letter"*: "Comstock in Cold Type," *TS* 29, no. 52 (Dec. 27, 1902): 822.

242   *"If it is right"*: Ibid.

242   *"To all those who"*: *Annual 1903*, 17.

242   *"for years fixed delusions"*: Ibid., 19.

242   *"she was irresistibly impelled"*: Dr. R. W. Shufeldt, "Letters from Gotham—No. 5."

242   *U.S. attorney for the District of Columbia*: "Government Abandons Scores of Prosecutions," *Washington Times*, Sept. 14, 1904.

243   *thrown out*: RG 21 Records of District Courts of the United States, E 74, Docket Vol. 22, NARA.

243   *$4,800 . . . $3,800*: *Annual 1903*, 37; *Annual 1904*, 20.

244   *"During Holiday week"*: *Annual 1904*, 12.

244   *"more quickly excitable"*: Broun and Leech, *Roundsman*, 246.

244   *"The way Comstock"*: "Comstockism Is the Real Enemy," *LLB*, Jan. 21, 1904.

244   *"Great Penis"*: ICC, "DPE," 56, entry Aug. 26, 1902, S 2, B 2, F 3, ICP.

15. WHAT EVERY GIRL SHOULD KNOW

246   *modern anarchism*: "Close Doors to Anarchy," *CT*, Nov. 24, 1902.

246   *"must be something"*: EG, "Free Speech in Chicago," *LLB*, Dec. 11, 1902.

246   *late 1890s*: "Emma Goldman," *LLB*, Oct. 13, 1897.

246   *"coarse and vulgar"*: EG, *Living My Life* (New York: New American Library, 1977), 219.

247   *June 27, 1869*: Emma Goldman, *U.S. Find a Grave Index, 1600s–Current* (database online), Ancestry.com.

247   *"I believe in the marriage"*: Nellie Bly, "Nellie Bly Again," *NYW*, Sept. 17, 1893.

248   *"I would find an outlet"*: EG, *Living My Life*, 61.

248   *"absorption in one human"*: Ibid., 153–54.

248   *"their alarm and worry"*: Ibid., 185.

248   *"I would return home sick"*: Ibid., 186.

248   *October 1897*: "Emma Goldman," *LLB*, Oct. 13, 1897.

249   *"the angel Gabriel"*: Reitman quoted in Alice Wexler, *Emma Goldman: An Intimate Life* (New York: Pantheon Books, 1984), 168.

249   *"womanly, a remarkable orator"*: Agent quoted in Ibid., 168–69.

249   *"Life takes on"*: Margaret Anderson quoted in Ibid., 167.

249   *"remov[ed] despair"*: Hutchins Hapgood, *A Victorian in the Modern World* (New York: Harcourt, Brace and Co., 1939), 170.

249   *closely connected*: Candace Falk, ed., *Emma Goldman: A Documentary History of the American Years*, vol. 3, *Light and Shadows, 1910–1916* (Stanford, CA: Stanford University Press, 2002), 743.

250 *"for viewpoints its members"*: Rabban, "The Free Speech League," 53.

250 *"it was unfit"*: Theodore Roosevelt, "On American Motherhood," Mar. 13, 1905, speech before the National Congress of Mothers.

250 *"Nationality and Religious Creed"*: *Annual 1909*, 16.

251 *"endeavour to attract"*: EG and Max Baginski, "Mother Earth," *ME* 1, no. 1 (Mar. 1906): 4.

251 *"Have they forgotten"*: Ibid., 3.

251 *"her most glorious privilege"*: EG and "The Tragedy of Woman's Emancipation," *ME* 1, no. 1 (Mar. 1906): 15.

252 *"a handsome brute"*: EG, *Living My Life*, 416.

252 *twenty-five thousand*: Ibid., 469.

252 *fifty thousand*: Wexler, *Emma Goldman*, 166.

252 *"blue-eyed Mommy"*: EG, *Living My Life*, 425.

252 *"Hobo"*: EG to BR, Feb. 26, 1914, Ben L. Reitman papers, Special Collections and University Archives, University of Illinois at Chicago (hereafter BLRP).

252 *"baby mine"*: EG to BR, n.d. 1908, BLRP.

252 *promiscuity tore*: EG to BR, July 28, 1911, BLRP.

252 *"Dearest, I wish"*: EG to BR, July 3, 1908, BLRP.

253 *"that the man"*: EG to BR, May 31–June 1, 1909, BLRP.

253 *"that other paternal"*: "Marriage and Love," in EG, *Anarchism and Other Essays* (New York, London: Mother Earth Publishing Association, A. C. Fifield, 1917), 241.

253 *"the social ostracism"*: EG, *Living My Life*, 556.

253 *"'Marriage & Love' is hateful"*: EG to BR, Dec. 18, 1909, BLRP.

253 *"matter of a character"*: *Postal Service Appropriation Act of May 27, 1908*, Ch. 206, 35 Stat. L. 416.

254 *"gives information orally"*: NY Penal Law and Code of Criminal Procedure Art. 106 at 308–11 (1909).

254 *"I did not discuss methods"*: EG, *Living My Life*, 552–53.

254 *three hundred*: "Emma Goldman's Bitter Tirade Against So-called Puritanism," *Buffalo Courier*, May 25, 1909.

254 *"the loud expression"*: "Hypocrisy of Puritanism," in EG, *Anarchism and Other Essays*, 176.

254 *"indiscriminate breeding"*: Ibid., 177.

254 *A few days after*: "Emma Goldman Not Permitted to Talk to Harlemites," *Wasatch (Utah) Wave*, May 28, 1909.

255 *"It is not necessary"*: Leonard D. Abbott, "A Demand for Free Speech," *ME* 4, no. 4 (June 1909): 108.

255 *"respectable"*: EG, "The White Slave Traffic," *ME* 4, no. 11 (Jan. 1910): 346.

255 *"a life of pleasure-seeking"*: *Annual 1913*, 11–12.

256 *Eighty pounds*: Postmaster to W. S. Mayer, Jan. 14, 1910, RG 28, E 36, B 56, F 42550, NARA.

256 *pencil marks*: *ME* 4, no. 11 (Jan. 1910), RG 28, E 36, B 56, F 42550, NARA.

256   *"a history of prostitution"*: EG, "The White Slave Traffic," 346.

256   *not made any complaint*: "Press Agent, Says Comstock," *NYT*, Jan. 27, 1910.

256   *When Berkman called*: "Comstock and Mother Earth," *ME* 4, no. 12 (Feb. 1910): 369–70.

257   *"so-called liberals"*: "Comstock Heckled at Labor Temple," *NYT*, Nov. 2, 1910, 8.

257   *"As a Post Office inspector"*: "Comstock Heckled at Labor Temple."

258   *"I've been in jail"*: Ben Reitman quoted in Candace Falk, *Love, Anarchy, and Emma Goldman: A Biography* (New Brunswick, NJ: Rutgers University Press, 1990), 93–94.

259   *"You'll probably"*: MS, *Margaret Sanger*, 41.

259   *118,000*: Gordon, *Woman's Body, Woman's Right*, 208.

259   *small and lithe*: Ellen Chesler, *Woman of Valor: Margaret Sanger and the Birth Control Movement in America* (New York: Simon & Schuster, 1992), 16.

259   *"Margaret has something"*: MS, *Margaret Sanger*, 76.

259   *"seemed to grant little value"*: Hapgood, *A Victorian in the Modern World*, 170.

260   *"Cross-legged"*: MS, *Margaret Sanger*, 73.

260   *"Short, stocky"*: Ibid., 72.

260   *"groups of from fifty"*: Ibid., 89.

260   *"into a torpid"*: Ibid., 90.

260   *"Tell Jake"*: Ibid., 91.

260   *"was finished with palliatives"*: Ibid., 92.

261   *"caused the death"*: MS, *My Fight for Birth Control* (London: Faber & Faber, 1932), 79.

261   *Abraham Jacobi*: Gordon, *Woman's Body, Woman's Right*, 172–73.

261   *Pro–birth control physicians*: Ibid., 182.

261   *"The Working Girls of the World"*: MS, "What Every Girl Should Know," *New York Call*, Nov. 17, 1912.

262   *"I for one condemn"*: Letter in *New York Call*, Dec. 19, 1912, quoted in Gordon, *Woman's Body, Woman's Right*, 242.

262   *"All over the civilized world"*: MS, "What Every Girl Should Know—Sexual Impulses, Part II," *New York Call*, Dec. 29, 1912.

262   *"unmoved by the Socialist"*: [Anita Block], "Editorial Comment," *New York Call*, Mar. 2, 1913.

263   *"There is no hope"*: MS, "What Every Girl Should Know (The Censored Article)," *New York Call*, Mar. 2, 1913.

263   *"What Every Girl Should Know—NOTHING"*: *New York Call*, Feb. 9, 1913.

263   *officially reprinted*: MS, *Margaret Sanger*, 256.

264   *April 1913*: John S. Sumner, "Half and Half: Somewhat Autobiographical," 60A, B 1 F 6, JSS.

264   *"I had been advised"*: Ibid.

265   *December 1913*: "Anti Vice Society's Work," *NYT*, Dec. 8, 1913.

265   "Sumner took case": AR 1915, 337.

265   "would require sixteen": Trumbull, *Anthony Comstock, Fighter*, 239.

16. WHY AND HOW THE POOR SHOULD NOT HAVE MANY CHILDREN

266   "I'm sure I mean": William Sanger to MS, Dec. 28, 1913, MS-SS.

266   "dedicated to the interests": MS, *Margaret Sanger*, 106.

266   direct action strategy: Gordon, *Woman's Body, Woman's Right*, 222.

267   "Is it not time to defy": MS, "The Prevention of Conception," *Woman Rebel* 1, no. 1 (Mar. 1914): 8.

267   In the postal records: RG 28, E 36, B 56, F 42090, NARA.

267   "To look the whole world": *Woman Rebel*, 1, no. 1 (Mar. 1914): 8.

267   "My dear Margaret": EG to MS, Apr. 9, 1914, MS-LOC.

268   voluntary parenthood: MS, *Margaret Sanger*, 108.

268   Otto Bobsein: Chesler, *Woman of Valor*, 97.

268   May issue included: *Woman Rebel* 1, no. 3 (May 1914): 23, 18.

268   "sells better": EG to MS, May 26, 1914, MS-LOC.

268   "the most degenerating": *Woman Rebel* 1, no. 5 (July 1914).

268   "obscene, lewd, and lascivious": *United States v. Margaret Sanger* (SDNY, 1914), U.S. District Courts Criminal Dockets, RG 21, NARA.

269   "some of the tragic stories": MS, *Margaret Sanger*, 114.

269   "it was never intended": "The Suppressed 'Obscene' Articles," B 5, F 1, RGP.

269   "I expect very little": "A Letter from Margaret Sanger," *ME* 10, no. 11 (Apr. 1915): 77.

269   "very unfair": Ibid., 78.

269   "Exponents of birth-control": "The War's Lesson," *Woman Rebel* 1, no. 6 (Aug. 1914): 48.

269   "cannon fodder": MS, "Woman and War," *Birth Control Review* (June 1917): 5.

270   "I shall always consider": William Sanger to MS, Mar. 12, 1914, MS-SS.

270   "I am essentially": William Sanger to MS, Apr. 2, 1914, MS-SS.

270   "produce the surplus": MS, *Family Limitation* ([New York]: 1914), 1.

271   "a certain Dr. Foote": MS, *Margaret Sanger*, 112.

271   "attempt to nullify": MS to Comrades and Friends, Oct. 28, 1914, MS-LOC.

271   Lorenzo Portet: Chesler, *Woman of Valor*, 108.

271   "my little rebel": quoted in Chesler, *Woman of Valor*, 118.

272   "alert to all": MS to Vincent Brome, Jan. 6, 1954, MS-SS.

272   December 18, 1914: William Sanger to [MS], Jan. 21, 1915, MS-SS.

272   "a grey haired": Ibid.

273   "When I confronted": "William Sanger's Full Statement, Banned by Court, Is Printed Here," *New York Call*, Sept. 11, 1915.

273   "raised the questions": "The Latest Comstock Case—The Arrest of William Sanger" (New York: Free Speech League, n.d.), 2, B 5, F 1, RGP.

273   *"silence the propaganda"*: MS to Comrades, Friends, Feb. 4, 1915, MS-LOC.

274   *1915 to 1919*: Rosanna L. Barnes, "Birth Control in Popular Twentieth-Century Periodicals," *Family Coordinator* 19, no. 2 (Apr. 1970): 160.

274   *"Not more babies"*: "The Age of Birth Control," *New Republic* 4, no. 47 (Sept. 25, 1915): 195.

274   *"a life beyond"*: Ibid., 197.

274   *photo of Comstock*: Mary Alden Hopkins, "Birth Control and Public Morals: An Interview with Anthony Comstock," *Harper's Weekly* 40, no. 3048 (May 22, 1915): 489.

274   *"I was somewhat confused"*: Ibid., 490.

275   Times *printed a story*: "Comstock May Lose Job," *NYT*, June 12, 1915.

275   *"This is not the first"*: "Comstock Charges Plot to Get His Job," *NYT*, June 13, 1915.

275   *Sumner was running*: "Comstock's Rule in Vice Society Near Overthrow," *NYTrib*, June 13, 1915.

276   *"I knew all along"*: "Comstock Keeps his Job," *NYT*, July 8, 1915.

276   *"intending openly"*: EG, *Living My Life*, 553.

276   *"I spoke in the direct"*: Ibid., 554.

277   *"discovered that"*: [EG], "Our Agitation in and about New York," *ME* 10, no. 3 (May 1915): 123.

277   *"not only a burden"*: *Why and How the Poor Should Not Have Many Children*, [1916], title page.

17. I AM GLAD AND PROUD TO BE A CRIMINAL

279   *"Comstock was as active"*: Sumner, "Half and Half," 69.

279   *"subterfuge"*: "Excitement in Purity Congress," *San Francisco Chronicle*, July 19, 1915.

279   *"I consider that question"*: Ibid.

280   *weight and vitality*: Sumner, "Half and Half," 69.

280   *"Your honor, this woman"*: *Masses* 6, no. 12 (Sept. 1915): 19.

281   *"I hope the searchlight"*: "'My Case Not Issue' Says Sanger on Eve of Trial," *New York Call*, Sept. 10, 1915.

281   *a hundred*: Leonard D. Abbott, "The Conviction of William Sanger," *ME*, Oct. 1915, 269.

281   *"I admit that I"*: James Waldo Fawcett, *Jailed for Birth Control: The Trial of William Sanger, Sept. 10, 1915* (New York: The Birth Control Review, 1917), 5.

281   *"self-appointed censor"*: Ibid., 7.

281   *"incurable sexphobia"*: Ibid., 7–8.

281   *had to accompany*: Charles Bamberger, handwritten notes, 12, B 14, F 10, RGP.

281   *"There are too many now"*: Fawcett, *Jailed for Birth Control*, 15.

281   *"I would rather"*: "Anarchists in Wild Defiance Curse Judges in Court," *NYW*, Sept. 10, 1915.

281 *"It was one of life's"*: MS, *Margaret Sanger*, 178.

282 *"Doctor! Doctor!"*: "Chat in March 1957 with Miss Fannie C. Moore."

282 *"lobar pneumonia"*: Anthony Comstock death certificate, B 10, F 7, RGP.

282 *September 3, 1915*: AR 1915, 338–39, #93.

282 *"That Mr. Comstock"*: "Anthony Comstock's Service," *NYT*, Sept. 23, 1915.

283 *"faults were"*: Sumner, "Half and Half," 70.

283 *"While less subtle"*: "Observations and Comments," *ME* 10, no. 8 (Oct. 1915): 260–61.

283 *"Such a condition of mind"*: Annual 1916, 10.

284 *"the provisions of the law"*: Ibid., 8.

284 *"I'm against all war"*: James Reed, *From Private Vice to Public Virtue: The Birth Control Movement and American Society Since 1830* (New York: Basic Books, 1978), 398.

285 *"I really think"*: EG to MS, Dec. 7, 1915, MS-LOC.

285 *"Just kill the movement"*: EG to MS, Dec. 8, 1915, MS-LOC.

286 *"the issue involved"*: MS to My Friends and Comrades, Jan. 5, 1916, MS-LOC.

286 *"from the gutter"*: MS, "Not Guilty!," *ME* 10, no. 11 (Jan. 1916): 365.

286 *"every one followed"*: "T. R. Wrong, Says Anarchist," *NYT*, Jan. 17, 1916.

286 *Mary Ware Dennett*: Chesler, *Woman of Valor*, 130–31.

287 *"the women on the East Side"*: EG, *Living My Life*, 569.

287 *A thousand*: "Emma Goldman Arrested," *NYT*, Feb. 12, 1916.

287 *"searched in the most vulgar"*: EG, "My Arrest and Preliminary Hearing," *ME* 11, no. 1 (Mar. 1916): 426.

287 *"for the right of the masses"*: Ibid., 430.

287 *"fashionable women"*: EG to "Comrade" [W. S. Van Valkenburgh], Feb. 21, 1916, Emma Goldman Archives, International Institute for Social History, Amsterdam.

288 *"If you ever thought"*: Ibid.

288 *"This movement has"*: "Police Note Rally for Birth Control," *New York Press*, Mar. 2, 1916.

288 *"Police and the press"*: "Police Dissect Goldman Speech," *NYTrib*, Mar. 2, 1916.

288 *hundreds*: Leonard D. Abbott, "Reflections on Emma Goldman's Trial," *ME* 11, no. 3 (May 1916): 504.

288 *"it was as if"*: Ibid., 504.

289 *"merely part of a"*: "Emma Goldman Before the Bar," *ME* 11, no. 3 (May 1916): 499.

289 *"to bring to women"*: Ibid., 500.

289 *"one phase in the larger"*: Ibid., 503.

289 *"I'll take the Workhouse"*: Abbott, "Reflections on Emma Goldman's Trial," 504.

289 *A thousand*: The Manager, "Emma Goldman in Jail," *ME* 11, no. 3 (May 1916): 524.

290 *May 20, 1916*: "Birth Control Demonstration on Union Square," *ME* 11, no. 4 (June 1916): 525.

290 *"double standard of laws"*: "Birth Control Talk to Outdoor Throng," *BDE*, May 21, 1916.

290 *handed out*: "Birth Control Demonstration on Union Square," 526.

290 *"Boys and young girls"*: "Big Crowd Fights for Pamphlets on Birth Control," *NYH*, May 21, 1916.

290 *"We are going to break"*: "A Protest of Forty San Francisco Women," *ME* 11, no. 3 (May 1916): 521–22.

290 *Educated and working-class*: Gordon, *Woman's Body, Woman's Right*, 229.

290 *socialist Agnes Inglis*: Ibid., 231.

290 *"would not even mention"*: EG, *Living My Life*, 590–91.

291 *English, Yiddish, and Italian*: MS, *Margaret Sanger*, 215–16.

291 *"Would the women come?"*: Ibid., 216.

292 *"only give the principles"*: Ibid., 215.

292 *almost five hundred*: Ibid., 220.

292 *two dollars*: Ibid., 219.

292 *"received from Mrs."*: Ibid., 220.

292 *"You dirty thing"*: "Mrs. Sanger fights as Police Seize Her in Raid on Clinic," *BDE*, Oct. 26, 1916.

292 *"The mattresses were spotted"*: MS, *Margaret Sanger*, 221.

292 *October 27, 1916*: "Mrs. Sanger Accepts Bail," *NYT*, Oct. 28, 1916.

292 *"Three birth control advocates"*: Ibid.

293 *"the right to copulate"*: People v. Sanger, 122 N.Y. 192 (1918).

293 *"Margaret's coming out party"*: MS, *Margaret Sanger*, 250.

294 *"proved that at least"*: EG, *Living My Life*, 587.

294 *at least twenty*: Gordon, *Woman's Body, Woman's Right*, 231.

295 *"broad enough"*: People v. Sanger, 122 N.Y. 192 (1918).

295 *"Everyone knew that Miss Goldman"*: MS to T. J. Mead, Sept. 27, 1929, MS-LOC.

295 *"not big enough"*: EG to Agnes Inglis, May 10, 1916, Joseph A. Labadie Collection.

295 *"Neither my birth-control"*: EG, *Living My Life*, 553.

18. BREACH IN THE ENEMY'S LINES

298 *sex radicals' playbook*: Sears, *The Sex Radicals*, 274.

303 *"I would lay down my life"*: ICC to EBF, June 6, 1898.

EPILOGUE

305 *1897*: Wight, *Genealogy of the Claflin Family*, 257.

306 *"Capitalist"*: Angela T. Heywood, *1900 U.S. Census, Cambridge, Middlesex, Massachusetts* (database online), Ancestry.com.

306   *election night*: Kenneth Davis, "Ezra Hervey Heywood, Speech for Princeton Historical Society, Tuesday Evening, November 7, 1967," 14, Princeton Historical Society, Princeton, MA.

306   *"I am very well"*: ATH to ED, Apr. 20, 1909, DFP-WHS.

306   *ninety-four*: Daniel Aaron Bradshaw, *U.S., Sons of the American Revolution Membership Applications, 1889–1970* (database online), Ancestry.com.

306   *nine years and eight months*: "Sent to Auburn for Dr. Chase," *NYW*, June 27, 1893.

307   *In June 1900*: AR 1900, 97.

307   *$2,500*: "Aged Woman Physician Arrested," *Newburgh Register* (New York), June 6, 1900.

307   *three examination dates*: AR 1900, 97.

307   *"physician"*: Sarah B. Hookey, *Missouri, Death Certificates, 1910–1963* (database online), Ancestry.com.

307   *"The need of reform"*: SBC, letter to the editor, *LLB*, Feb. 22, 1895.

308   *"I really owe much"*: EG to BR, Dec. 12, 1919, BLRP.

309   *"if 'unfit' refers to races"*: MS to Sidney L. Lasell, Jr., Feb. 13, 1934.

309   *"to reckon with [the organization's] legacy"*: Nikita Stewart, "Planned Parenthood in N.Y. Disavows Margaret Sanger over Eugenics," *NYT*, July 21, 2020.

Bibliography

ARCHIVAL SOURCES

Court Records of Madame Restel[1] 1839–1878, 1839, Schlesinger Library, Radcliffe Institute for Advanced Study, Harvard University (Schlesinger)

Denton Family Papers, Wellesley Historical Society (DFP-WHS)

Ida C. Craddock, RG 28, Records of the Post Office Department, Bureau of the Chief Inspector, Case Files of Investigations, E 231, B 180 and B 154, National Archives and Records Administration, Washington, DC (NARA)

Ida Craddock Papers, Special Collections Research Center, Morris Library, Southern Illinois University Carbondale (ICP)

John Saxton Sumner Papers 1904–1961, Wisconsin Historical Society (JSS)

Margaret Sanger Papers, Microfilm Edition, Library of Congress, Washington, DC (MS-LOC)

Margaret Sanger Papers, Microfilm Edition, Smith College Collections Series (MS-SS)

Ralph Ginzburg Papers 1848–1964, Wisconsin Historical Society (RGP)

Record Group 204, Office of the Pardon Attorney Pardon Case Files 1853–1946, Box 121; National Archives at College Park, College Park, MD (NACP)

Records of the YMCA of the City of New York, Records of the YMCA of Greater New York, YMCA of the USA, Kautz Family YMCA Archives, University of Minnesota (KFYA)

PERIODICALS

Birth Control Review

Boston Investigator (BI)

The Brooklyn Daily Eagle (BDE)

Chicago Tribune (CT)

Dr. Foote's Health Monthly (DFHM)

Lucifer, the Light-Bearer (LLB)

The Masses

Mother Earth (ME)
The New York Call
The New York Herald (NYH)
The New York Times (NYT)
New-York Tribune (NYTrib)
The New York World (NYW)
The Philadelphia Inquirer (PI)
The Physiologist and Family Physician (PFP)
The Sun (New York)
The Truth Seeker (TS)
The Woman Rebel
Woodhull & Claflin's Weekly (WCW)
The Word

BOOKS, PERIODICALS, LAWS, AND DISSERTATIONS

Abbott, Leonard D. "Reflections on Emma Goldman's Trial." *Mother Earth* 11, no. 3 (May 1916): 504–507.

An Act for the Suppression of Trade in and Circulation of obscene Literature and Articles of immoral Use, 42nd Congress, Session III, Ch. 258, Mar. 3, 1873, 598–600.

"The Age of Birth Control." *New Republic* 4, no. 47 (Sept. 25, 1915): 195–97.

Andrews, Stephen Pearl. "The Heywoods, Princeton, Worcester County, and Massachusetts," *TS* 10, no. 32 (Aug. 11, 1883): 498.

"And the Truth shall make you Free." A Speech on the Principles of Social Freedom, delivered in Steinway Hall, Monday, Nov. 20, 1871. New York: Woodhull, Claflin & Co., 1871.

Annual Reports of the New York Society for the Suppression of Vice. New York: Printed for the Society, 1875–1916.

Appelbaum, Stanley. *The Chicago World's Fair of 1893: A Photographic Record.* New York: Dover Publications, 1980.

Baker, Jean H. *Margaret Sanger: A Life of Passion.* New York: Hill and Wang, 2011.

Bates, Anna Louise. *Weeder in the Garden of the Lord: Anthony Comstock's Life and Career.* Lanham, MD: University Press of America, 1995.

"The Beecher-Tilton Scandal Case." *WCW* 5, no. 7 (Nov. 2, 1872): 9–13.

Beisel, Nicola. *Imperiled Innocents: Anthony Comstock and Family Reproduction in Victorian America.* Princeton, NJ: Princeton University Press, 1997.

Bennett, D. M. *An Open Letter to Samuel Colgate.* New York: D. M. Bennett, Liberal Publisher, 1879.

———. *The Champions of the Church: Their Crimes and Persecutions.* New York: D. M. Bennett, Liberal and Scientific Publishing House, 1878.

Blatt, Martin Henry. *Free Love and Anarchism: The Biography of Ezra Heywood.* Urbana: University of Illinois Press, 1989.

Bloom, Sol. *The Autobiography of Sol Bloom.* New York: G. P. Putnam's Sons, 1948.

Bolotin, Norman, and Christine Laing. *The World's Columbian Exposition: The Chicago World's Fair of 1893*. Urbana: University of Illinois Press, 1992.

Bradford, Roderick. *D. M. Bennett: The Truth Seeker*. Amherst, MA: Prometheus Books, 2006.

Braude, Ann. *Radical Spirits: Spiritualism and Women's Rights in Nineteenth-Century America*. 2nd ed. Bloomington: Indiana University Press, 2001.

Brodie, Janet Farrell. *Contraception and Abortion in Nineteenth-Century America*. Ithaca, NY: Cornell University Press, 1994.

Broun, Heywood, and Margaret Leech. *Anthony Comstock: Roundsman of the Lord*. New York: A. & C. Boni, 1927.

Browder, Clifford. *The Wickedest Woman in New York: Madame Restell, the Abortionist*. Hamden, CT: Archon Books, 1988.

Brown, William Adams. *Morris Ketchum Jesup: A Character Sketch*. New York: Charles Scribner's Sons, 1910.

Burns, Ric, and James Sanders. *New York: An Illustrated History*. New York: Alfred A. Knopf, 1999.

Burton, Richard. *Men of Progress: Biographical Sketches and Portraits of Leaders in Business and Professional Life in and of the State of Connecticut*. Boston: New England Magazine, 1898.

Burton, Shirley J. "Obscene, Lewd, and Lascivious: Ida Craddock and the Criminally Obscene Women of Chicago, 1873–1913." *Michigan Historical Review* 19, no. 1 (Spring 1993): 1–16.

Carlson, A. Cheree. *The Crimes of Womanhood: Defining Femininity in a Court of Law*. Urbana: University of Illinois Press, 2009.

Carlton, Donna. *Looking for Little Egypt*. Bloomington, IN: IDD Books, 1994.

Carpenter, Cari M., ed. *Selected Writings of Victoria Woodhull: Suffrage, Free Love, and Eugenics*. Lincoln: University of Nebraska Press, 2010.

Chappell, Vere. *Sexual Outlaw, Erotic Mystic: The Essential Ida Craddock*. San Francisco: WeiserBooks, 2010.

Chase, Sara B., MD. "The Great Evil of Society." *Ohio Medical and Surgical Reporter* 7, no. 1 (Jan. 1873): 37–40.

———. "Responsibility of Sex," in D. M. Bennett, ed., *Truth Seeker Tracts, Upon a Variety of Subjects Vol. III*. New York: Liberal and Scientific Publishing House, 1876.

Chavannes, Albert. *Magnetation, and Its Relation to Health and Character*. Knoxville, TN: 1899.

Chesler, Ellen. *Woman of Valor: Margaret Sanger and the Birth Control Movement in America*. New York: Simon & Schuster, 1992.

Claflin, Tennie C. "My Word on Abortion, and Other Things." *WCW* 3, no. 19 (Sept. 23, 1871): 9.

Clement, Elizabeth Alice. *Love for Sale: Courting, Treating, and Prostitution in New York City, 1900–1945*. Chapel Hill: University of North Carolina Press, 2006.

Cohen, Patricia Cline, Timothy J. Gilfoyle, and Helen Lefkowitz Horowitz. *The Flash Press: Sporting Male Weeklies in 1840s New York*. Chicago: University of Chicago Press, 2008.

Comstock, Anthony. *Frauds Exposed: Or, How the People are Deceived and Robbed, and Youth Corrupted*. New York: J. Howard Brown, 1880.

———. *Traps for the Young*. New York: Funk & Wagnalls, 1883.

———. "The Work of Suppressing Vice: Chapter II." *Golden Rule* 15, no. 17 (Dec. 19, 1889): 188.

———. "The Work of Suppressing Vice: Chapter V." *Golden Rule* 15, no. 21 (Jan. 16, 1890): 251.

———. "The Work of the New York Society for the Prevention of Vice, and its Bearings on the Morals of the Young: An address before the Conference on Child Welfare at Clark University, Worcester, July, 1909." In G. Stanley Hall, *The Pedagogical Seminary: A Quarterly* 16, no. 3 (Sept. 1909): 403–20.

Comstock, John Adams. *A History and Genealogy of the Comstock Family in America*. Los Angeles: Privately printed for the author by Commonwealth Press, 1949.

Craddock, Ida C. *Advice to a Bridegroom*: Its Value as an Educator in Marital Duties: 1909. Microform.

———. *The Danse du Ventre (Dance of the Abdomen) as performed in the Cairo Street Theatre, Midway Plaisance, Chicago*. [Philadelphia]: 1893.

———. *The Danse du Ventre (Dance of the Abdomen)*, 2nd ed., rev. Philadelphia: 1897.

———. "Diary of Psychical Experiences." Unpublished manuscript, 1894–1902.

———. *Heavenly Bridegrooms: An Unintentional Contribution to the Erotogenetic Interpretation of Religion*. New York: n.p., 1918.

———, ed. *Helps to Happy Wedlock No. 1 For Husbands: Consisting of an Anonymous Essay on Male Continence; Part of an Anonymous Essay on Magnetation; and Comments by Ida C. Craddock*. Philadelphia: 1896.

———. *Letter to a Prospective Bride*. Philadelphia: 1897.

———. *Primary Phonography, an Introduction*. Philadelphia: 1882.

———. "Records of Cases in Marital Reform Work," Unpublished manuscript, 1900–1901.

———. "Right Marital Living." *Chicago Clinic* 7, no. 5 (May 1899): 200.

———. *Right Marital Living*. Chicago: Ida C. Craddock, 1899.

———. "The Tale of the Wild Cat: A Child's Game." *Journal of American Folklore* 10, no. 39 (Oct.–Dec. 1897): 322–24.

———. *The Wedding Night*. New York: 1902.

Darewin, G. S. *Synopsis of the Lives of Victoria C. Woodhull (Now Mrs. John Biddulph Martin) and Tennessee Claflin (Now Lady Cook): The First Two Lady Bankers and Reformers of America*. London: J. H. Corthesy, 1891.

Davis, Kenneth. *Ezra Hervey Heywood, Speech for Princeton Historical Society, Tuesday Evening, November 7, 1967*.

Dennett, Mary Ware. *Birth Control Laws: Shall We Keep Them, Change Them, or Abolish Them*. New York: Grafton Press, 1926.

Dennis, Donna. *Licentious Gotham*. Cambridge, MA: Harvard University Press, 2009.

Doggett, L. L. *Life of Robert R. McBurney*. Cleveland: F. M. Barton, 1902.

Donoghue, Terry. *An Event on Mercer Street: A Brief History of the YMCA of the City of New York*. New York: Privately printed, 1952.

Eastman, Max. *Is the Truth Obscene?* New York: Free Speech League, 1915.

Edward Bond Foote: Biographical Notes and Appreciatives. New York: Free Speech League, 1913.

"Emma Goldman Before the Bar," *Mother Earth* 11, no. 3 (May 1916): 496–503.

Falk, Candace, ed. *Emma Goldman: A Documentary History of the American Years*. Vol. 1, *Made for America, 1890–1901*. Berkeley: University of California Press, 2003.

———, ed. *Emma Goldman: A Documentary History of the American Years*. Vol. 2, *Making Speech Free, 1902–1909*. Berkeley: University of California Press, 2004.

———, ed. *Emma Goldman: A Documentary History of the American Years*. Vol. 3, *Light and Shadows, 1910–1916*. Stanford, CA: Stanford University Press, 2002.

Falk, Candace Serena. *Love, Anarchy, and Emma Goldman: A Biography*. New Brunswick, NJ: Rutgers University Press, 1990.

Fawcett, James Waldo. *Jailed for Birth Control: The Trial of William Sanger, Sept. 10, 1915*. New York: The Birth Control Review, 1917.

Foote, E. B. *A Fable of the Spider and the Bees, Verified by Facts and Press and Pulpit Comments Which Should Command the Serious Attention of Every American Citizen*. New York: National Defense Association, 1881.

Foote, E. B., Jr. "Convicted of Blasphemy," *TS* 29, no. 15 (Apr. 12, 1902): 230–31.

Flynn, Tom, ed., *The New Encyclopedia of Unbelief*. Amherst, NY: Prometheus Books, 2007.

Frisken, Amanda. *Victoria Woodhull's Sexual Revolution: Political Theater and the Popular Press in Nineteenth-Century America*. Philadelphia: University of Pennsylvania Press, 2004.

Gabriel, Mary. *Notorious Victoria: The Life of Victoria Woodhull, Uncensored*. Chapel Hill, NC: Algonquin Books of Chapel Hill, 1998.

Gilfoyle, Timothy J. *City of Eros: New York City, Prostitution, and the Commercialization of Sex, 1790–1920*. New York: W. W. Norton, 1992.

Goldman, Emma. *Anarchism and Other Essays*. New York: Mother Earth Publishing Association, A. C. Fifield, 1917.

———. *Living My Life*. New York: New American Library, 1977.

———. "My Arrest and Preliminary Hearing," *Mother Earth* 11, no. 1 (Mar. 1916): 426–30.

———. "The White Slave Traffic," *Mother Earth* 4, no. 11 (Jan. 1910): 344–51.

———, and Max Baginski. "Mother Earth," *Mother Earth* 1, no. 1 (Mar. 1906): 1–4.

Goldsmith, Barbara. *Other Powers: The Age of Suffrage, Spiritualism, and the Scandalous Victoria Woodhull.* New York: Alfred A. Knopf, 1998.

Gordon, Linda. *The Moral Property of Women: A History of Birth Control Politics in America.* Urbana: University of Illinois Press, 2002.

———. *Woman's Body, Woman's Right: A Social History of Birth Control in America.* New York: Penguin Books, 1977.

Gornick, Vivian. *Emma Goldman: Revolution as a Way of Life.* New Haven, CT: Yale University Press, 2011.

Heywood, Angela T. "The Ethics of Sexuality." *The Word* 9, no. 12 (Apr. 1881): 3.

———. "The Sex-Education of Children." *The Word* 13, no. 1 (May 1884): 2.

———. "Sex-Nomenclature—Plain English." *The Word* 15, no. 6 (Apr. 1887): 2–3.

———. "The Woman's View of It—No. 1," *The Word* 11, no. 9 (Jan. 1883): 2.

———. "The Woman's View of It—No. 2," *The Word* 11, no. 10 (Feb. 1883): 2.

———. "The Woman's View of It—No. 5," *The Word* 12, no. 1 (May 1883): 2.

Heywood, Ezra H. *Cupid's Yokes: or The Binding Forces of Conjugal Life.* Princeton, MA: Co-operative Publishing Co., 1877.

———. "Debt—A Lesson in Equity." *The Word* 16, no. 8 (March 1888): 2.

———. "Free Speech and the Right of Association—Their Latest Denial." *TS* 5, no. 19 (May 11, 1878): 299.

———. *Free Speech: Report of Ezra H. Heywood's Defense Before the United States Court in Boston, April 10, 11 and 12, 1883.* Princeton, MA: Co-operative Publishing Co., 1883.

———. "The Impolicy of Repression." *Index* 8, no. 414 (Nov. 29, 1877): 573.

———. *Uncivil Liberty: An Essay to Show the Injustice and Impolicy of Ruling Woman Without her Consent.* Princeton, MA: Co-operative Publishing Company, 1872.

Hopkins, Mary Alden. "Birth Control and Public Morals: An Interview with Anthony Comstock." *Harper's Weekly* 40, no. 3048 (May 22, 1915): 489–90.

Horowitz, Helen Lefkowitz. "Victoria Woodhull, Anthony Comstock, and Conflict over Sex in the United States in the 1870s." *Journal of American History* 87, no. 2 (Sept. 2000): 403–34.

———. *Rereading Sex: Battles over Sexual Knowledge and Suppression in Nineteenth-Century America.* New York: Alfred A. Knopf, 2002.

Hovey, Elizabeth Bainum. *Stamping Out Smut: The Enforcement of Obscenity Laws, 1872–1915.* PhD diss. New York: Columbia University, 1998.

Howe, William F. *In Danger; or, Life in New York.* Chicago: J. S. Ogilvie & Company, 1888.

Katz, Esther. *The Selected Papers of Margaret Sanger.* Vol. 1, *The Woman Rebel 1900–1928.* Urbana: University of Illinois Press, 2003.

Keller, Alan. *Scandalous Lady: The Life and Times of Madame Lohman, New York's Most Notorious Abortionist.* New York: Atheneum, 1981.

King, Mary Louise. *Portrait of New Canaan: The History of a Connecticut Town.* Chester, PA: John Spencer, 1981.

Kneeland, George J. *Commercialized Prostitution in New York City.* New York: Century Co., 1913.

Landmarks of New Canaan. New Canaan, CT: New Canaan Historical Society, 1951.

Laws of the State of New York, 91st Session (1868), Ch. 430 at 856–58.

Laws of the State of New York, 95th Session (1872), Ch. 747 at 1795–96.

Laws of the State of New York, 96th Session (1873), Ch. 527 at 828.

Leach, William. *True Love and Perfect Union: The Feminist Reform of Sex and Society.* Middletown, CT: Wesleyan University Press, 1989.

Macdonald, George E. *Fifty Years of Freethought* [Vols. I & II]. New York: Arno Press and The New York Times, 1972.

MacPherson, Myra. *The Scarlet Sisters: Sex, Suffrage, and Scandal in the Gilded Age.* New York: Twelve, 2014.

Mauriceau, A. M. *The Married Woman's Private Medical Companion.* New York: 1852.

"A Memorandum Respecting New-York As a Field for Moral and Christian Effort Among Young Men; Its Present Neglected Condition; and the Fitness of the New-York Young Men's Christian Association as a Principal Agency for Its Due Cultivation." New York: The Association, 1866.

McCabe, James D. *New York by Sunlight and Gaslight.* Philadelphia: Hubbard Brothers, 1881.

McElroy, Wendy. *Individualist Feminism of the Nineteenth Century: Collected Writings and Biographical Profiles.* Jefferson, NC: McFarland, 2001.

Mohr, James C. *Abortion in America.* New York: Oxford University Press, 1978.

Morse, Verranus. *The Work of the Young Men's Christian Association: What It Is, and How to Do It,* 2nd ed. New York: The Association, 1865.

Murphy, Cait. *Scoundrels in Law: The Trials of Howe & Hummel, Lawyers to the Gangsters, Cops, Starlets, and Rakes Who Made the Gilded Age.* New York: Smithsonian Books, 2010.

"The New Office of Literary Censor." *WCW* 5, no. 11 (Feb. 15, 1873): 9.

New York Society for the Suppression of Vice records (microfilm). New York: New York Society for the Suppression of Vice, 1871–1953.

New York Supreme Court, The People of the State of New York Against Sara B. Chase. New York: C. G. Burgoyne, 1894.

Nichols, Thomas L. *The Lady in Black: A Story of New York Life, Morals, and Manners.* New York: 1844.

Noyes, John Humphrey. *Male Continence*. Oneida, NY: Oneida Community, 1872.

"The N.Y. Physiological Society." *PFP* 1, nos. 3 and 4 (June and July 1878): 42–43.

"Official Report of the Equal Rights Convention, Held in New York City, on the Ninth, Tenth, and Eleventh of May, 1872." *WCW* 5, no. 2 (May 25, 1872): 3–9.

Passet, Joanne E. *Sex Radicals and the Quest for Women's Equality*. Urbana: University of Illinois Press, 2003.

People v. Sanger, 122 N.Y. 192 (1918).

"The Philosophy of Modern Hypocrisy—Mr. L. C. Challis the Illustration." *WCW* 5, no. 7 (Nov. 2, 1872): 13–14.

[Pinney, Lucian V.] "The Man and the Woman of Princeton." *Word* 19, no. 2 (June 1890): 1.

Pivar, David J. *Purity Crusade: Sexual Morality and Social Control, 1868–1900*. Westport, CT: Greenwood Press, [1973].

"Proceedings of the Tenth Annual Convention of the American Association of Spiritualists." *WCW* 6, no. 20 (Oct. 18, 1873): 2–7, 12–15.

"The Progress of the Revolution." *WCW* 5, no. 8 (Dec. 28, 1872): 9–12.

Putnam, Samuel P. *400 Years of Freethought*. New York: Truth Seeker Company, 1894.

The Queen v. Hicklin, L.R. 3 Q.B. 360 (1868).

Rabban, David M. *Free Speech in Its Forgotten Years*. Cambridge: Cambridge University Press, 1997.

———. "The Free Speech League, the ACLU, and Changing Conceptions of Free Speech in American History." *Stanford Law Review* 45, no. 1 (Nov. 1992): 47–114.

Reed, James. *From Private Vice to Public Virtue: The Birth Control Movement and American Society Since 1830*. New York: Basic Books, 1978.

Reed, Miriam. *Margaret Sanger: Her Life in Her Words*. Fort Lee, NJ: Barricade Books, 2003.

Rowbotham, Sheila. *Dreamers of a New Day: Women Who Invented the Twentieth Century*. London: Verso, 2010.

———. *Rebel Crossings: New Women, Free Lovers, and Radicals in Britain and America*. London: Verso, 2016.

Sachs, Emanie. *"The Terrible Siren": Victoria Woodhull (1838–1927)*. New York: Harper Brothers, 1928.

Sanger, Margaret H. *Family Limitation*. [New York]: [1914].

———. *Margaret Sanger: An Autobiography*. New York: W. W. Norton, 1938.

———. *My Fight for Birth Control*. London: Faber & Faber Limited, 1932.

Sanger, William W. *History of Prostitution: Its Extent, Causes, and Effects Throughout the World*. New York: Harper & Brothers, 1858.

Sante, Luc. *Low Life: Lures and Snares of Old New York*. New York: Farrar, Straus and Giroux, 2003.

"The Scare-Crows of Sexual Slavery." *WCW* 6, no. 17 (Sept. 27, 1873): 3–7, 14.

Schmidt, Leigh Eric. *Heaven's Bride: The Unprintable Life of Ida C. Craddock, American Mystic, Scholar, Sexologist, Martyr and Madwoman.* New York: Basic Books, 2010.

———. *Village Atheists: How America's Unbelievers Made Their Way in a Godly Nation.* Princeton, NJ: Princeton University Press, 2016.

Sears, Hal D. *The Sex Radicals: Free Love in High Victorian America.* Lawrence: Regents Press of Kansas, 1977.

Seldes, Gilbert. *The Stammering Century.* New York: New York Review of Books, 2012 (1st ed. 1928).

Silberman, Marsha. "The Perfect Storm: Late Nineteenth-Century Chicago Sex Radicals: Moses Harman, Ida Craddock, Alice Stockham and the Comstock Obscenity Laws." *Journal of the Illinois State Historical Society* 102, nos. 3 and 4 (Fall and Winter 2009): 324–67.

"Sketch of Life of Anthony Comstock taken down stenographically, from his own words, on Friday evening, December 17, 1886, at the Massasoit House, Springfield, Massachusetts."

Smith-Rosenberg, Carroll. *Disorderly Conduct: Visions of Gender in Victorian America.* New York: Alfred A. Knopf, 1985.

Stern, Madeleine B. *The Pantarch: A Biography of Stephen Pearl Andrews.* Austin: University of Texas Press, 1968.

———, ed. *The Victoria Woodhull Reader.* Weston, MA: M & S Press, 1974.

Stiles, T. J. *The First Tycoon: The Epic Life of Cornelius Vanderbilt.* New York: Alfred A. Knopf, 2009.

Stockham, Alice B. *Karezza: Ethics of Marriage.* Chicago: Alice B. Stockham & Co., 1896.

———. *Tokology: A Book for Every Woman.* Chicago: Sanitary Publishing Co., 1885.

Stoehr, Taylor. *Free Love in America: A Documentary History.* New York: AMS Press, 1979.

Storer, Horatio Robinson. *Why Not? A Book for Every Woman.* Boston: Lee and Shepherd, 1866.

Tilton, Theodore. *Biography of Victoria C. Woodhull.* New York: Golden Age, 1871.

Tone, Andrea. "Black Market Birth Control: Contraceptive Entrepreneurship and Criminality in the Gilded Age." *Journal of American History* 87, no. 2 (Sept. 2000): 435–59.

———, ed. *Controlling Reproduction: An American History.* Wilmington, DE: SR Books, 1997.

———. *Devices & Desires: A History of Contraceptives in America.* New York: Hill and Wang, 2001.

Trial of Madame Restell, Alias Ann Lohman, for Abortion and Causing the Death of Mrs. Purdy; Being a Full Account of All the Proceedings on the Trial, Together with the Suppressed Evidence and Editorial Remarks. New York: 1841.

Trumbull, Charles Gallaudet. *Anthony Comstock, Fighter.* New York: Fleming H. Revell Company, 1913.

Tucker, Benjamin R. *Proceedings of the Indignation Meeting Held in Faneuil Hall, Thursday Evening August 1, 1878, to Protest Against the Injury Done to the Freedom of the Press by the Conviction and Imprisonment of Ezra H. Heywood.* Boston: Benj. R. Tucker, 1878.

Underhill, Lois Beachy. *The Woman Who Ran for President.* Bridgehampton, NY: Bridge Works Publishing Company, 1995.

United States v. Bennett. 24 F. 70 (SDNY, 1879).

United States v. Ezra Heywood. Circuit Court Federal Records, vol. 78, 1877–1878. U.S. District Court of Massachusetts. National Archives at Boston.

United States v. Ezra Heywood. U.S. Circuit Court. Massachusetts Case Papers. May Term 1890. Criminal.

United States v. Ezra Heywood. U.S. District Court of Massachusetts, March Term, 1883.

United States v. Ida C. Craddock. August Sessions, 1898, U.S. District Court for the Eastern District of Pennsylvania. National Archives at Philadelphia.

United States v. Ida C. Craddock. (Oct. 31, 1899). U.S. District Court, Northern Division of Illinois. National Archives at Chicago.

United States v. Margaret Sanger. (SDNY, 1914). U.S. District Courts Criminal Dockets.

U.S. Circuit Court v. Ida C. Craddock. Indictment, March 12, 1902.

Victoria C. Woodhull, Tennie C. Claflin, and James Blood Indictments. Circuit Court of the US of A for the SDNY, Second Circuit, third Monday of Oct. 1872–Nov. 4, 1872, Circuit Court Criminal Docket 3:3–4 (1872) and Circuit Court Case F 3:3 (1872).

"Victoria C. Woodhull's Address." *WCW* 5, no. 9 (Jan. 25, 1873): 3–7, 14–15.

Walker, E. C. *Who Is the Enemy: Anthony Comstock or You?* New York: Edwin C. Walker, 1903.

Warren, Sidney. *American Freethought: 1860–1914.* New York: Columbia University Press, 1943.

West, William Lemore. "'The Moses Harman Story." *Kansas History: A Journal of the Central Plains* 37, no. 1 (Spring 1971): 41–63.

Wexler, Alice. *Emma Goldman: An Intimate Life.* New York: Pantheon Books, 1984.

Why and How the Poor Should Not Have Many Children. [1916].

Wight, Charles Henry. *Genealogy of the Claflin Family.* New York: Press of William Green, 1903.

Williams, Charles Richard, ed. *Diary and Letters of Rutherford Birchard Hayes.* Vol. III. Columbus: Ohio State Archaeological and Historical Society, 1924.

Wilson, Serena, and Alan Wilson. *The Legacy of Little Egypt: A History of the Belly Dance in America.* Vol. 1, *1893–1908.* New York: Serena Studios, 1994.

Wood, Janice. "Prescription for a Periodical: Medicine, Sex, and Obscenity in the Nineteenth Century, As Told in 'Dr. Foote's Health Monthly.'" *American Periodicals* 18, no. 1 (2008): 26–44.

Woodhull, Victoria C. "Tried as by Fire; or, The True and the False Socially." New York: Woodhull & Claflin, 1874.

Woodhull, Victoria Claflin, and Tennessee C. Claflin. *The Human Body the Temple of God.* London: 1890.

Acknowledgments

The Man Who Hated Women has been a five-year journey, and for help with its completion I am indebted to Wellspring House, Art Omi, Headlands Center for the Arts, the Studios at MASS MoCA, the Allen Room at the New York Public Library Stephen A. Schwarzman Building, and the Brooklyn Writers Space. Special thanks to the Whiting Foundation for its regrant program.

Invaluable assistance was provided by Aaron Michael Lisec at the Ida Craddock Papers, Southern Illinois University Carbondale; Simone Munson at the Wisconsin Historical Society; Melanie Locay and Paul Friedman, New York Public Library; and Jonathan Deiss, an independent researcher with a Craddock and Comstock fixation.

The following resources and individuals helped me to dig deep into my subjects' lives.

Anthony Comstock: Leah King and Kate Mollan, NARA; Michael Murphy, New Canaan Museum and Historical Society; New Canaan Town Hall; Louise Merriam and Ryan Bean, YMCA Historical Library and Kautz Family YMCA records.

Victoria Woodhull and Tennessee Claflin: Tal Nadan, the Brooke Russell Astor Reading Room for Rare Books and Manuscripts, New York Public Library.

Ann Lohman: Sarah Hutcheon, the Schlesinger Library, Radcliffe Institute for Advanced Study, Harvard University.

Dr. Sara B. Chase: Laurie Lounsberry McFadden, Alfred University; Christina E. Barber, Amherst College; Jennifer K. Nieves, Dittrick Medical History Center, Case Western Reserve University; Ann K. Sindelar, Cleveland

History Center of the Western Reserve Historical Society; Kirsten Wise, Cayuga Museum of History and Art; the New York State Library; Jack Eckert, Francis A. Countway Library of Medicine, Harvard University; National Library of Medicine; and Leigh Eric Schmidt, for his portion on Chase and Elmina Drake Slenker in *Village Atheists: How America's Unbelievers Made Their Way in a Godly Nation.*

Angela T. Heywood: Epsom Historical Society; Nancy Orlando, Princeton Historical Society; Sarah Rogers, the Dobkin Family Collection at Glenn Horowitz Bookseller, Inc.; Jennifer Betts, John Hay Library, Brown University; Julie Herrada, Joseph A. Labadie Collection, Special Collections Library, University of Michigan; Kathleen Fahey, Wellesley Historical Society; Joan Gearin, NARA at Boston; and Marty Blatt, author of *Free Love and Anarchism.*

Ida C. Craddock: Lynn Dorwaldt, Wagner Free Institute of Science; Robert P. Helms, Deadanarchists.org; University Archives, University of Pennsylvania; Trina Yeckley and Carey Stumm, National Archives at New York City; Gail E. Farr, National Archives at Philadelphia; National Archives at Chicago; Ken Cobb, New York City Municipal Archives; Rare Book and Special Collections Division Reading Room, Library of Congress.

Emma Goldman: The Emma Goldman Papers Project, University of California, Berkeley.

Margaret Sanger: Esther Katz, the Margaret Sanger Papers Project, New York University.

Thanks to Arlene Shaner, New York Academy of Medicine; the International Association for the Preservation of Spiritualist and Occult Periodicals; Interlibrary Services at NYPL; and Manhattan Research Library Initiative for help in many areas. Thanks to Catherine Texier, E. M. Wolfman bookstore, Headlands Show & Tell, and Art Omi for performance venues; to my cohorts at Art Omi: Writers, Headlands, and Studios at MASS MoCA for encouragement and camaraderie; and to Ruth Franklin, Keith Gessen, and Edie Meidav, Candace Falk, Abbott Kahler, Matthew Goodman, Joshuah Bearman, Josh Davis, Will Blythe, and Mike Lenore. For shepherding the work, thanks to Richard Abate, James Gregorio, Colin Dickerman, and Julia Ringo. Deep gratitude and everlasting love to Josh Sohn, Peter Sohn, Elaine Sohn, and most of all, D. M.

Index

Page numbers in *italics* refer to illustrations.

A NOTE ABOUT THE AUTHOR

Amy Sohn is the author of five novels, including *Prospect Park West* and *Motherland*. A former columnist at *New York* magazine, she has also written for *Harper's Bazaar*, *Elle*, *The Nation*, and *The New York Times*. She has been a writing resident at Headlands Center for the Arts, Art Omi, and the Studios at MASS MoCA. A native New Yorker, she lives in Brooklyn with her daughter.